ELIZABETH ROBINS

STAGING A LIFE

ELIZABETH ROBINS

ROBINS

STAGING A LIFE

ANGELA V. JOHN

TEMPUS

ABOUT THE AUTHOR

Angela V. John is a historian and biographer. She was, for many years, Professor of History at the University of Greenwich and now lives in Pembrokeshire. Her other books include a biography (with Revel Guest) of the translator, businesswoman and collector, Lady Charlotte Guest and a life of the war correspondent Henry W. Nevinson. She is currently working on a biography of Nevinson's second wife, the writer and suffragette Evelyn Sharp.

Cover Illustration: Elizabeth Robins as Britain's first Hilda Wangel in *The Master Builder* (1893) (The Fales Library, New York University)

First published 1995.
This edition first published 2007.

Tempus Publishing Limited
The Mill, Brimscombe Port,
Stroud, Gloucestershire, GL5 2QG
www.tempus-publishing.com

© Angela V. John, 1995, 2007

The right of Angela V. John to be identified as the Author
of this work has been asserted in accordance with the
Copyrights, Designs and Patents Act 1988.

British Library Cataloguing in Publication Data.
A catalogue record for this book is available from the British Library.

ISBN 978 07524 4028 6

Typesetting and origination by Tempus Publishing Limited
Printed and bound in Great Britain

813.4 JOH

CONTENTS

Part V From E.R. to Anonymous

For she had a great variety of selves to call upon, far more than we have been able to find room for, since a biography is considered complete if it merely accounts for six or seven selves, whereas a person may well have as many thousand.

(From Virginia Woolf, *Orlando, A Biography*, London, Hogarth Press, 1928)

To posterity the biography is indeed the life.

(Elizabeth Robins: *Ancilla's Share*, London, Hutchinson, 1924)

FOR LLOYD
who had the idea …

ILLUSTRATIONS

Plates

Frontispiece: Elizabeth Robins as Britain's first Hilda Wangel in *The Master Builder* (1893)

FIGURES

ACKNOWLEDGEMENTS

This book was largely conceived, researched and written in south-east London, New York City and west Wales. I owe a great debt to friends and colleagues and students who helped sustain me through discussing ideas, whether in the University of Greenwich, the Violet Caffè, Washington Square or in the less frenetic atmosphere of Upper St Mary Street, Newport, Pembs. I must, however, single out one person without whom my inchoate plans could not have been transformed into book form: Mabel Smith, trustee of Backsettown. I thank her for her faith in me, for her generosity in sharing her knowledge of Elizabeth and Octavia and for becoming a firm friend.

My fond memories of my sabbatical and summer vacations in New York are largely shaped by the reception I received at the Fales Library in the Elmer Holmes Bobst Library of New York University where the Elizabeth Robins Papers are housed. Frank Walker who was the librarian could not have been more supportive. I thank him and Sherlyn Abdoo, Alan Mark and, most recently, Maxime La Fantasie for their generous assistance. I am also immensely grateful to the Pioneer and Historical Society of Muskingum County, Ohio and to Gary Felumlee and Wendell Litt in particular. Amongst the many helpful archivists and librarians I must mention Lesley Gordon in Special Collections, the Robinson Library, University of Newcastle upon Tyne. Her knowledge of the Gertrude Bell and C.P. Trevelyan Papers has aided me considerably. Thanks also to the staff at the Harry Ransom Humanities Research Center at the University of Texas at Austin for their help and to the librarians at the Berg Collection, New York Public Library where I spent many sweltering Saturdays. I am also grateful to staff at the following: Boston Public Library; BBC Written Archives, Caversham; British Library (Reading Room, Manuscripts, Colindale and India Office Library); Churchill Archives Centre, University of Cambridge; University of Greenwich Library; The Fawcett Library, London Guildhall University; the Institute of Historical Research, University of London; Museet Lysøen, Norway; Museum of London; Department of Special Collections, University of Florida Libraries, Gainesville; Manchester Central Library, Local Studies Unit; National Council of Women, National Library of Wales; Newcastle Public Library (Reference Department); Manuscripts Section, University of Sussex Library; Tamiment Institute Library, New York University; Theatre Museum, Covent Garden; Special Collections UCLA Library and Woolwich Public Library (Reference Department).

I must record my especial gratitude to: Lisa von Borowsky for her memories and an unforgettable day at Chinsegut; Ted Dreier for his valuable recollections; Peter Whitebrook, author of a fine biography of William Archer, for his illuminating conversations and correspondence; Joanne Gates, author of a forthcoming biography of Elizabeth, who generously shared her knowledge with me; Jane Marcus who began researching the subject before I even knew who Elizabeth Robins was and gave me a much appreciated welcome in Texas; Neil Salzman, author of the authoritative biography of Raymond Robins who enlivened brunch with his ideas; Liz Staff, intrepid travelling companion in Florida; Jane Lewis for the Backsettown experience; Sue Thomas for her bibliographical expertise; Margrethe Aaby of the Press Office, Ibsen Festival 1992, Oslo for her help; Kali Israel for stimulating discussions about writing biography and Kirsten Wang for sharing her understanding of Florence Bell. Thanks also to May Morey, Lady Plowden, Patricia Jennings, Susannah Richmond, Olea Karland, Geoffrey Trevelyan and Mrs Vester for their recollections.

The other individuals who have helped me are too numerous to cite here but the following must be mentioned: Diane Atkinson,

Ron Ayres, Jo Baylen, Joanne Cayford, Elizabeth Crawford, Elin Diamond, Joy Dixon, David Doughan, Iris Dove, Imogen Forster, Carmen Russell Hurff, Philippa Levine, Gail Malmgreen, Bentley Mathias, Eddie Money, Kerry Powell, Peter Searby, Harold Smith, Marcus Staff, Anne Summers, Claire Tylee, Linda Walker, Judith Zinsser.

I am grateful to the following for permission to reproduce material: The Henry W. and Albert A. Berg Collection, The New York Public Library, Astor, Lenox and Tilden Foundations; The British Library; the Master and Fellows of Churchill College, Cambridge; The Fales Library, New York University; The Fawcett Library, London Guildhall University; Department of Special Collections University of Florida Libraries, Gainesville; Alexander R. James for the Estate of Henry James; Manchester Central Library, Local Studies Unit; Middlesbrough Public Library; Museet Lysøen, Norway; Richard Pankhurst; Lady Plowden; Special Collections, The Robinson Library, University of Newcastle upon Tyne; Mabel Smith for the Backsettown Trust; The Society of Authors as the literary representative of the Estate of John Masefield and of the Bernard Shaw Estate for quotations from the works of Bernard Shaw; Manuscripts Section, University of Sussex Library; The Trevelyan Family Trustees; A.P. Watt on behalf of the Literary Executors of the Estate of H.G. Wells. Every effort has been made to trace copyright holders.

Thanks also to the individuals and institutions where I tried out my ideas in lectures, seminars and conferences: the University of Greenwich, the Universities of Birmingham, East Anglia and Wolverhampton, the Women's History Network, Friends of the Fawcett Library, Museum of London, Swedish Council for Research in the Humanities, Pioneer and Historical Society of Muskingum County, Ohio and Ohio State University.

My research was facilitated by grants from the Twenty Seven Foundation and the Nuffield Foundation to which I am extremely grateful. I much appreciate the support I have received from the University of Greenwich. I was delighted to have Claire L'Enfant as my editor at Routledge and I thank her, Sue Bilton, Jenny Overton, Heather McCallum, Catherine Turnbull, and also Cecilia Cancellaro in New York, for their support. Finally, a big thank you to those who read and commented on all or parts of the manuscript, Paul Stigant, Lloyd Trott and Mabel Smith. I am especially grateful to Norma Clarke for her wise comments.

Angela V. John,
December 1993

INTRODUCTION

One fine November afternoon in 1960, about forty people gathered in the garden of Backsettown, a pretty, fifteenth-century house
in the Sussex village of Henfield. They had come to witness the
unveiling of a blue plaque which declared that 'Elizabeth Robins
1862–1952 Actress-Writer lived here'.[1] The ceremony was performed
by Dame Sybil Thorndike who talked of that 'selfless, bright-eyed
actress who was a pioneer of Ibsen in this country, a fine novelist, a
good playwright, a powerful supporter of women's suffrage, a soci-
ologist, a humanitarian generally'. The distinguished group included
the eighty-nine-year-old Lord Pethick-Lawrence, Labour politician
and erstwhile advocate of women's suffrage. He recalled first meeting
Elizabeth Robins more than half a century earlier when she explained
to him the nice distinction between suffragist and suffragette.

In 1993 Elizabeth Robins appeared in a 'Missing Persons' supplement to the *Dictionary of National Biography*, that other British
measure of the successful public life.[2] Yet she has not, on the whole,
been well remembered and at the time of her death in Brighton in
1952, aged eighty-nine, she was fast becoming forgotten. Nationality
and fashion can help explain her oblivion and subsequent resur-
gence. Kentucky-born and always retaining her American nationality,
Elizabeth actually spent over two-thirds of her long life in England.
Although her family was American and she had begun her acting
career in the United States, set some of her novels there, returned
many times, part-owned a home in Florida and helped promote

international feminist connections (her sister-in-law was president of the American Women's Trade Union League), in American eyes Elizabeth became primarily identified with Britain. Her American background gave her perspectives and even freedoms denied to her British counterparts. Yet it also meant that she could not be claimed as a British actress or writer.

She became renowned for her acting in Ibsen's plays yet chose to retire from the stage at the age of forty, soon after the turn of the century. It is not therefore surprising that, although known to students of drama, she has not become a household name. The revival of feminism in recent years has, however, rescued her in the form of Elizabeth Robins, suffrage novelist. Although her obituary in *The Times* dismissed her 1907 novel *The Convert* as 'frankly propagandist',[3] it was republished in both Britain and the States in the 1980s and is now viewed as a significant contribution to the literature of women's suffrage whilst her play *Votes For Women!* (on which the novel was based) is acknowledged as inaugurating suffrage drama. Over the past decade the Backsettown Trust has received over two dozen requests to publish or perform her work, ranging from reprinting a short story to stage performances of her suffrage play and a musical based on *The Convert*.[4] The programmes of recent British productions of Ibsen's *Hedda Gabler* and *The Master Builder* have devoted print and photographs to Elizabeth who was the first to play Hedda in English and introduced Britain to Hilda in *The Master Builder*. She has been the subject of several American doctoral theses by literary and drama scholars, one of which has been published in book form.[5] A bibliographical survey has been made of her voluminous publications.[6] She wrote fourteen novels, two volumes of short stories, two memoirs (one about her brother), a children's recipe book-cum-adventure story, several booklets, two hefty works on feminism, a volume of correspondence with Henry James and many newspaper and journal articles. Two of her novels were turned into films. There is also a vast amount of unpublished work.

What other traces remain of Elizabeth Robins? How was she seen by those who knew her? And how do we—and should we—attempt to square the competing representations of her? There is the spirited young girl living with her beloved grandmother in Zanesville, Ohio in the 1870s. Her schoolfriend Nellie Buckingham declared that

Bessie Robins was full of pranks and once put a Sunday School book down the privy.[7] Bessie became an actress. The Bessie in Boston became transmogrified into Lisa in London, scarred by a personal tragedy which brought with it 'self reproach which I have carried through the whole of life'. She made her home in London from 1888. Through her close friend Florence Bell (Lady Bell), we can glimpse her in high-heels, pink velvet jacket and white boa and gain some impression of her mercurial vitality and determination. Florence once wrote, 'The passage of Elizabeth Robins through the world, a flaming torch in her hand may well bewilder those whose path in life is the beaten track'.[8] A journalist presented another version of the late Victorian actress:

> The glow from a pink lamp fell on her loose, clinging white cashmere dressing gown with its edging of dark fur, and flushed her face … dreaming eyes, well marked deliberately arched eyebrows, broad forehead, masses of brown hair.[9]

She was especially proud of that long, chestnut hair but time and again it was her eyes which would command attention. In a BBC broadcast profiling Elizabeth just after her death, Sybil Thorndike declared:

> I will never forget the effect of her eyes. I think, except for Duse, I have never seen such eyes. There did actually seem to be a light behind them that could pierce through outward and visible things and see the invisible.[10]

One of Florence Bell's grandchildren has recalled meeting Lisa at the railway station where her eyes could be seen 'blazing down the platform'.[11]

In contrast Max Beerbohm found the actress of the 1890s a formidable prospect. He attended a luncheon held by the editor of *The Yellow Book* at which Aubrey Beardsley and Elizabeth were present:

> Altogether a rather pleasing meal—save for the Robins … Conceive! Straight pencilled eyebrows, a mouth that has seen the stress of life … She is fearfully Ibsenish and talks of souls that are

involved in a nerve turmoil and are seeking a common platform.
This is *literally* what she said. Her very words. I kept peeping under
the table to see if she really wore a skirt.[12]

At the same time as acting, Elizabeth was writing fiction which she
initially published under the pseudonym of C. E. Raimond. She
decided to assume her own name at the end of the century after press
revelation of her identity. She withdrew from the stage at about the
same time. This move and the dropped pseudonym may be linked to
a new search for identity and identification through a confrontation
with her brother Raymond with whom she had retained a romanticised symbiotic relationship forged from their fractured childhood.
In 1900 Elizabeth and Raymond met in the suitably dramatic setting
of Alaska. He had travelled there in search of gold but instead found
God. From her Alaska encounter came the novel for which Elizabeth
was most acclaimed in her lifetime and for which she was compared
to Defoe, *The Magnetic North*.

During the Edwardian period Elizabeth became a committed
suffragette, a public persona who nonetheless shunned personal
publicity whilst she sought it for the cause. Understanding that she
needed to tackle the prevailing conceptions of gender now focused
on the struggle for the vote, she took on the establishment both from
without and from within, becoming an apologist for militancy in the
daily press. She sat on the committee of Mrs Pankhurst's Women's
Social and Political Union (WSPU) but, whenever possible, retreated
to her newly acquired Sussex home. The image she presented to local
people was a far cry from Max Beerbohm's 'New Woman' and those
who lampooned the suffragettes. May Morey who also attended
the unveiling of the plaque was the daughter of Henfield's bicycle
manufacturer whose shop was in the High Street. Elizabeth was a
frequent caller and little May Powell, as she was then, adored the
Miss Robins who made clothes for her doll. She recalls her as a kind
of benevolent aunt, much respected in the village.[13] Nevertheless
Elizabeth's personal life remained secretive, her friends unaware of
her love affair in the 1890s with the Ibsen translator William Archer
or her more recent intimate friendship with John Masefield.

Paul Fussell has observed that during the First World War period
British society was especially rich in its appreciation of literature.

To the faith in classical and English literature was added the appeal generated by popular education and self-improvement, aristocratic meeting democratic forces and establishing 'an atmosphere of public respect for literature unique in modern times'.[14] Bolstered by a larger literate public than previously but escaping serious challenge by the screen, the written medium still managed to be the message. For Elizabeth, who could also draw on an American readership and particularly appealed to women readers, the years after 1905 saw her at the height of her success as a novelist. In 1907, after the publicity of her suffrage play on the London stage, she received the extremely handsome advance of £1,000 for *The Convert* (someone with an annual income of £1,000 in 1907 would need to earn over £160,000 today). Even the newly famous Arnold Bennett could only command advances of £300–400 from the same publisher.

During these years Elizabeth met Octavia Wilberforce who was to be her companion for the rest of her life. As part of a literary intelligentsia with an exotic past, outspoken and boasting an international reputation, she became quite literally a woman of letters whose correspondence to newspaper editors, almost invariably concerning some aspect of women's rights, appeared regularly in the press.

Her later fiction lacked the force and originality of works such as *The Open Question* (1898) and *The Convert* (1907), though both *Camilla* (1918) and *Time Is Whispering* (1923) are novels with powerful messages for women. Critics of her work did, however, detect a penchant for sensationalism prompted by lucrative opportunities for serialising stories in magazines whilst her non-fiction invited the very different charge of shrillness. Elizabeth's indictment of sex-antagonism entitled *Ancilla's Share* and published anonymously in 1924 was a polemical work of non-fiction which alienated support amongst those who liked to believe that the gaining of the vote was synonymous with women's equality. Illness, war and the dislocation caused by changing continents (she spent the Second World War in America) made her last years troubled ones. Leonard Woolf who was also present at Backsettown in November 1960, published some of her later works. He and Virginia had known Elizabeth socially and he became a member of the Backsettown Trust which administered the convalescent home for women which Elizabeth and Octavia created in 1927. Leonard Woolf remembered both her mesmeric appeal and tenaciousness. Like others, he acknowledged that she possessed 'in a very high degree, that inexplicable and indefinable quality, personal charm'.[15]

Such was her time-span and the changes she witnessed that the neat historical labels of periodisation seem inadequate. How can a woman raised in the shadow of the American Civil War, later surviving two world wars, be labelled? As a young girl her main mode of transportation was an open carriage. When old, the seasoned transatlantic traveller took to flying many thousands of miles. She was both pre- and post-Freud. She confounded expectations about women of her time(s), challenging her class and gender by being the first woman in her genteel family to earn her own living, being widowed young but having no children and not remarrying, living into her ninetieth year and straddling two continents. She crossed the Atlantic over thirty times.

How did she see herself? Her passports provide a succinct visual picture. She described her face as oval, her chin square and her height 5 feet 6 inches (1.67 m), though this would not remain so, curvature of the spine losing her 3 inches (76 mm) in height; and in her seventies her weight was reduced to under 7 stone (44.4 kg). Despite adulation of 'Lisa of the blue eyes', she submitted that her eyes were grey. And how did she want, or rather seek, to be remembered? She told Leonard Woolf, 'If there has been a governing passion in my life, it has been for liberty.' Yet, as we shall see, she always recognised the power of withholding truth, aware of her own role in shaping latterday images of her. In her unpublished memoir 'Whither & How?' she wrote, 'all that I go to find is my lost self', qualifying this with, 'or, to be as honest as possible—I go to find such fragments as I shall be willing to declare'. She delighted in her very elusiveness and actually called one novel *Come and Find Me*.

All biographies are necessarily historical though some are less historically sensitive than others. In some biographies the 'times' are presented as a rather dull backcloth to the life of the individual which becomes elevated out of all proportion. My intention is not to reduce my subject. She must remain under the spotlight of investigation but as a historian I also seek to integrate Elizabeth into her surroundings, to explore something of the circumstances and tensions which she might have faced at a particular historical moment.

The assumptions and complacency of biography writing have recently been subjected to critical scrutiny.[16] On both sides of the Atlantic feminist biographers such as Nina Auerbach, Carolyn Steedman and Rachel Brownstein have experimented with the form.[17] Concern has been expressed about, for example, the authorial voice and the proprietorial biographer as active agent. Barthesian claims that biography is disguised fiction have been examined and emphasis placed on seeing the life-story as a kaleidoscope of images, reconstructing through *bricolage* or the process of building up an image in parts in place of a unitary whole and sequential cradle-to-grave narrative. Postmoderist insistence on 'the impossibility of knowing and writing outside of representation',[18] guides us back to the text and refuses neat, definitive accounts of a transcendent self. It also raises questions about the multiplicity of sources/texts the historian encounters which preclude 'close reading' along the lines of literary critics. Justifiably, historians also express some concern about the denial of agency, about the unwritten prior shaping and censorship of texts, about sufficient recognition of the past as continually in process and respect for historical particularity and temporality. And what of the danger of so reducing an individual to a cultural construct that we lose sight of the very humanity which is what tends to attract a reader to a biographical subject in the first place?

Nevertheless, such approaches have alerted historians to the fallacy of believing that we can extract the 'real' Elizabeth from the many layers, self-constructions and constructions by others which have composed how we 'read' her. We are also encouraged to question how a biographer selects and adumbrates a chosen individual, revealing something of her or his own preoccupations.

Quite apart from her fiction, Elizabeth has left us several written versions of her life-story. From the age of thirteen she kept a diary. Although her entries for most of the 1890s no longer exist (though we do have her tiny, cryptic notebooks for this period), her diary spans more than seventy years and became a regular part of her life with entries right up to the year she died. Up until virtually the end it is a reflective and detailed source (the account of the Alaska trip alone covers over 300 pages). It was used as an *aide-mémoire* and exercise in revising her conceptions of self and of others. It is also carefully and knowingly shaped, demanding attention as a text in the same way as her acknowledged literary work. In the diary Elizabeth practised her style and ordered her thoughts. It became a major source for her fiction and memoirs, 'a storehouse of ideas or sensations'. Therefore as an adult she was conscious of its potential use. She also kept one eye on a possible reader. She wrote (in 1891):

> I will try to write the real happenings within and without—excusing myself to myself for lack of complete frankness by calling my silences self-reverence, a dignified reserve, a 19th century—shrinking from the nude. And yet since I take the trouble (and v'y great trouble it is) for my own future guidance let me have as little dark as I can with decency reveal. As I write I feel sure I'll forget 'decency' and all self-consciousness in its narrow sense as soon as I am interested in what I'm putting down.

Can the biographer so determine the points at which calculation gives way to outpourings? It may be possible to discern such shifts, aided, for example, by subtle changes in language and style, but even though we might divine some of her less crafted comments in the course of such a vast document, we shall never really 'know' Elizabeth. She re-read her diaries, excising, burning and commenting on entries. Yet intention was not always matched by implementation. For example, what might have become an arcadian existence with her brother in Florida, turned out very differently and although Elizabeth intended burning the less happy aspects of one of these visits, she never actually did so.

Her diary remains both rich and problematic as a source. The correspondence between Elizabeth and John Masefield reveals an aspect of her which could never have been discerned from her diaries for the same period.[19] She once boasted that she told 'not a hundredth & I tell that little to *remind* myself of what I do not tell'. She freely admitted that she was 'born romancing', that 'There is something in people like me, secret; something that shuns the comprehension of others'. In this she was less exceptional than she liked to think but she was perhaps more frank than many in acknowledging her trait.

Even though the diary may be far from raw material, to judge diarists from what they reveal in such private writing is open to question. In the final chapter there is some consideration of Elizabeth's views

on race and ethnicity. Her combination of somewhat progressive
views and reactionary fictional stereotypes was not a straightforward
matter of enlightenment over time. Yet to criticise Elizabeth from
views expressed in her diary raises very different issues from holding
her responsible for her published accounts not least because others
may have held far more questionable views than she but never been
taken to task since they did not commit their thoughts to paper or
if they did, ensured that others would not read them.

Used alongside other sources, the diary can be of great value to
the historian through its very fashioning, subjectivity and self-cen-
sorship, helping to explain how an individual uses such a form to
construct another persona. It may also be revelatory in the way that
the diarist negotiates ambivalences and confronts inconsistencies and
tensions (particularly in an era when much could not be articulated
in public) and may help expose over time and at the same time,
competing discourses.

Elizabeth's diary forms the basis of *Both Sides of the Curtain*, the
memoir on which knowledge of her has, to date, largely been based.
It is a highly misleading source. Written during the 1930s when
she was in her seventies, it is a partial (in both senses of the word)
account of a thin slice of her life, the two years after her arrival in
England in the autumn of 1888, with a few backward glances. Her
original plan had been to cover a dozen years on the London stage
and she did write an unpublished sequel, 'Whither & How?', about
her more illustrious career from 1891.

In *Both Sides* she appears to be writing her own story but actually
makes the English theatre the star of the book, sublimating the self
so effectively that she becomes conspicuous by her very absence, a
process all the more remarkable since the acting profession has not
been renowned for its modesty. There are many people mentioned
'like figures in a stage crowd' (her words)[20] but a few individuals
stand out. Ironically, they are the very people she had railed against
in her diary, notably George Bernard Shaw (whose correspondence
with Elizabeth forms a Preface) and the actor-manager Herbert
Beerbohm Tree. The latter is transformed into a leading man.

It is a curious memoir from a woman who had led a long and
eventful life. It focuses on one of her least successful periods. Although
more women were now writing autobiographies, the model remained

that of the male achiever. Perhaps this partly explains the book's tone and emphasis. Jill Conway's study of accomplished American women of the Progressive Era born between 1855 and 1865 (the decade in which Elizabeth was born), emphasises the narrative flatness of their autobiographies.[21] 'When the early women suffragists wrote their memoirs they were overwhelmingly concerned with the movement's achievements, occluding their personal lives.[22] Elizabeth's frustration and anger at the blocking of women's opportunities on the late nineteenth-century stage, so evident in her diary, would have receded by the 1930s and having once been articulated, was not repeated. She was now more ready to make peace with characters like Shaw particularly since few of their generation were left. The book can be seen as a commentary on how she chose to remember the past rather than how she lived it, an adjustment of the record. Possibly Elizabeth elevated the importance of men such as Tree and Oscar Wilde in order to deflect attention from the man who, slightly later, became her 'Significant Other', the married William Archer (who does feature in 'Whither & How?').

The book's title hints at a camouflaging, a hiding behind a curtain as much as a revelation, reminding us that only at the end is the actress expected to reveal herself to the audience. Maybe Elizabeth was strategically positioning herself in this memoir. As an elderly woman, far removed from the young actress of the late 1880s who composed her diary when she was centre stage in her own produc-tion, she could now retrospectively savour her early years in London when she was poised for success. This time contrasted neatly with her imminent stardom, indicating the heroine waiting in the wings. By becoming an actress-manageress herself; Elizabeth would show her independence of the actor-managers and hangers-on of the thea-tre who thought they knew best and actually hindered rather than helped her success. Even her use of Shaw's letters is double-edged since her Preface closes with her having the final word, claiming, as she had done in the past, that Shaw did not really understand her.

Both Sides provided a neat contrast to the conventional autobiog-raphies which dwelt on the successful moments not the interstices. Known as a writer whose non-fiction was controversial, Elizabeth did not want to provide an anodyne account of life on the stage. Moreover, some of her earlier writing such as the novel *The Open*

Question and the pamphlet *Ibsen & the Actress* had already revealed aspects of her life, the latter dealing with her Ibsen performances. The problem, as Jane Marcus has discerned,[23] is that Elizabeth tried to be 'too clever by half'. She may have assumed the ancillary role (evident in titles such as *Raymond and I* and *Ancilla's Share*) but her modesty may well have been a veneer which did not always pay off. Several publishers turned down *Both Sides*, finding it too esoteric, detailed yet not sufficiently alert to informing the reader. In August 1940 Elizabeth protested to the American publisher Putnam's:

> the kind of writer I am has a view and a purpose which are insepar-
> able from her work. It is, briefly, to represent a phase of life, not to
> hop, skip, & jump over the years picking out the exceptional inci-
> dents which other people might reflect on as you are recording.

Both Sides was published in 1940 but in wartime Britain it did not receive much attention.

However calculated her self-effacement, it is significant that Elizabeth's book was about the London stage. Her move to London represented a rebirth after personal tragedy in America. Although she made her name in European drama, Elizabeth did not, however, became a legend like Rachel the French tragedienne, remembered in the history of European theatre as 'the first great international dramatic star', or like Sarah Bernhardt or Eleonora Duse whose funeral in New York produced a crowd of 3,000 outside the church (tickets were issued).[24] Neither did she attain the status of a Mrs Siddons or Ellen Terry. Indeed Elizabeth Robins's name was largely associated with the non-commercial theatre and the shock of the new.

She was indubitably shaped by her years on the stage. Acting before modern sound[25] or visual techniques, the Victorian actress's work seems especially ephemeral to us today. Yet precisely because of the lack of such alternative means of entertainment, live performance was valued. It was Elizabeth's role as Hedda Gabler which caused the greatest stir. As the *Sunday Times* put it, here was 'one of the most notable events in the history of the modern stage … it marks an epoch and clinches an influence'.[26] And whether critics loved or hated Ibsen, they certainly took notice of him and those who played his characters. Elizabeth may have left the stage prematurely but the stage was not allowed to leave her. Mrs Pankhurst was attracted to the idea of Elizabeth Robins as a leading suffragette precisely because she had been an actress.

Although, as we shall see, Elizabeth disliked theatricality in others and stage-managed, produced and performed many different jobs connected with the stage, including establishing a radical new theatrical company, it is as an actress and especially as an interpreter of Ibsen on the stage (despite having a much wider repertoire) that she is remembered in the theatrical world. She became framed by her Hedda role and typecast as the Ibsenite 'New Woman'. When the poet Richard Le Gallienne met Ibsen in Norway in the 1890s he said the great dramatist put one question to him: 'Did I know Miss Robins?'[27] When Elizabeth died, one of her obituaries was headed 'The last of the Ibsenites'.[28]

Elizabeth's two careers, acting and writing, required acute observation. Her travels and her connections gave her rich material. Her address books read like *Who Was Who*. She dined with society figures, with leading names in the artistic and political world and international thinkers, radicals and feminists over a period of about sixty years. She learned to watch closely and she took care to compartmentalise her activities. Her catholic range of friends and interests, not always gelling well with each other, laid her open to charges of being double-faced. Her intense concern about whatever subject was currently absorbing her, invited charges of self-centredness and a suspicion that she wilfully used people for her own advantage. There was an element of truth in this. From an early age Elizabeth had had to learn to fend for herself and she understood that her determination played no small part in her success. Nevertheless, there were those, usually successful men, who were slightly unnerved by her. She disturbed their expectations and stereotypes: why did she insist to actor-managers that she knew best when they were the ones who could help her? Why did such a beautiful woman become a suffragette? From theatrical figures like Charles Wyndham to literary names such as Leonard Woolf she was something of an enigma, refusing to be typecast and inviting simultaneously both their admiration and their desire that she were less 'vampiric'.

She seems to have been highly sensitive about how people perceived her and concerned that they should not come too close.

She was well practised in the art of dissimulation and acknowledged that 'Most if not all of us, are occasionally engaged, consciously or unconsciously in making ourselves out better or worse than we really are'. In the spring of 1895, ill and conscious of mortality, she penned a brief record 'for the enlightenment of the people who care for me', admitting that 'any account of the way I have spent my life must be more misleading than true' and acknowledging her

> constitutional unwillingness to letting people know what seems to myself to be the real 'me'. I am afraid I have moods when I delight to darken counsel on this subject. If I see any one trying to ferret me out, my greatest delight is to baffle & elude my pursuer & leave him contentedly following a false scent … I have partly deliberately & partly unconsciously 'cooked my accounts'.

Yet the 'cooking' of her accounts matters less than the need she felt to do this. This biography will explore such issues through her and others' words. There are plenty of these. In the Elizabeth Robins Papers in the Fales Library of New York University there exist nearly a hundred linear feet of her material. The Finding Aid alone exceeds a hundred pages. Numerous other sources by and about her exist elsewhere in America and Britain.

Appreciating the significance of naming, I have divided the book into five sections, each with a name by which Elizabeth was known: Bessie, Lisa, C.E. Raimond, Elizabeth Robins and the term latterly used by friends, E.R. They correspond to different stages in her life but clearly there is overlap: to childhood friends and family she was always Bessie just as she is still Lisa to the Bell descendants. These divisions however, permit both a broadly linear structure and the opportunity for examination of her major concerns and interests in a thematic form which places them in a historical context and does not isolate the individual from wider societal change.

Bearing in mind the fact that I am a woman historian writing in the late twentieth century and thereby privileged to enjoy the perspective which only time and distance from the subject can provide, yet also inevitably bound by my own period, I have placed emphasis on how I see Elizabeth Robins having *staged* her life. Part I focuses on her in America, considering her early influences and how she created a career on the stage. The second part shifts to London, her years in the British theatre and the friendships she made during this time. There follows an examination of Elizabeth as a writer of fiction and journalism in the 1890s and 1900s and of the significance of her Alaskan trip. Part IV evaluates her contribution to the women's suffrage movement, discussing not only her fiction but also her lesser-known writings on militancy and her shifting commitments. In addition it considers her exposition of the white slave trade and the origins of this work through her connections with John Masefield. The final part discusses her deep friendship with Dr Octavia Wilberforce and their efforts to improve women's health. It considers Elizabeth's feminism during and after the First World War, her opposition to militarism and her contribution to *Time and Tide*. We see her return to America, her concern about race, difficulties with Raymond and final troubled years. Each chapter is named after one of her works.

Elizabeth may have gained a plaque and she is now be celebrated at her childhood home in Ohio but we cannot unveil the quintessential self, what she called 'the real "me"'.[29] Yet we can examine through her words and those of her contemporaries how multiple, shifting identities were constructed by her and for her at particular times and in different places. Through this individual and biographical history, perhaps we can also begin to understand somewhat better some of the demands and concerns of, for example, the theatre, literature and the women's movement in the second half of the nineteenth and first half of the twentieth centuries.

PART I

BESSIE ROBINS

1

WHITHER & HOW?

On 6 August 1862 during the American Civil War and in the middle of a wild storm, Elizabeth Robins was born. Her parents, Hannah Maria Robins (née Crow) and Charles Ephraim Robins, were first cousins living on East Walnut Street, Louisville, Kentucky.[1] Elizabeth, known as Bessie, was their first child though Charles had a son from a previous marriage. In later years Elizabeth would refer proudly to her Kentuckian heritage though she actually spent little time living there.

The family moved to St Louis for some months when she was under a year and although they returned to Louisville briefly, they went east before she was three. Her father, fascinated by science and the social sciences, tried to convince himself that he was a business-man. He worked in insurance (his own father had been a pioneer in the development of life and fire insurance) and as a bank cashier. His bank somehow survived the panic of 1857 but a few years later a recently formed banking partnership (Hughes and Robins) col-lapsed. So before the end of the Civil War the family moved to New York in search of better times. Charles was employed by the Home Insurance Company on Broadway and they lived on the south shore of Staten Island, just outside Eltingville. Here he cultivated the soil and conducted chemistry experiments in the barn. He spent much of his time planning for the future though few of his dreams were realised. Foundations were laid for a big house but typically it never got built, the family residing instead in the lodge on their Bayside land.

There is not much evidence about Hannah in this period. Refined, of gentry stock and musical—Elizabeth later recalled her singing haunting airs and one particular aria from *Il Trovatore*—she was in her mid-twenties when she moved to Staten Island. For much of the next decade she was pregnant. A son, Edward, born in Louisville two years after Elizabeth, did not survive. Hannah then had five more children in the next eight years. Eunice, known as Una, was Elizabeth's only surviving sister since baby Amy also died in infancy. The eldest boy was Saxton, seven years younger than Elizabeth. In 1872, the year that Vernon was born, Charles was devastated by the death of Eugene, his adolescent son from his first marriage. Eugene had studied at a military academy. It was, however, the birth of the youngest and ultimately most successful son in the following year which ironically presaged the greatest tragedy for the Robins family. Raymond's birth resulted in severe post-natal depression for Hannah and thereafter a perilous mental state. There was also financial disaster: her fortune was lost on Wall Street. The marriage floundered.

The young Elizabeth's life now changed dramatically. In August 1872 the family moved to her paternal grandmother's home in far-off Zanesville, Ohio. Her beloved papa left for a metallurgy course in St Louis then headed west for a mining life in Colorado. Her ailing mother was soon placed under the watchful eye of her brother-in-law Dr James Morrison Bodine, Dean of the Faculty of Medicine at the University of Louisville. Saxton joined his mother in Louisville. Vernon and the baby of the family, Raymond, who was always Elizabeth's favourite, remained with their sisters in Ohio for the time being though eventually the boys also left for Kentucky.

Not surprisingly given the upheavals of her childhood, at the age of ten Elizabeth saw herself as already 'disagreeably old in observation and experience'. Yet her new life actually gave her a stability she had long been denied. This was largely because of her remarkable grandmother, Jane Hussey Robins, who now became the central figure in her life. Long widowed and in her seventies she appeared undaunted at the prospect of once more raising a young family. She earned Elizabeth's lifelong respect and love. Elizabeth dedicated her most personal novel *The Open Question* (1898) to this 'most stern and upright judge', her grandma.[2] Elizabeth's notes for this book show that it was written 'just for her and me', a tribute to the woman who had been her guide and mentor. Its most memorable character is Mrs Gano, a thinly disguised grandma. In fact Elizabeth's grandfather had founded a Baptist theological seminary in Cincinnati and one of his co-founders was an Aaron Gano. Elizabeth would comb her family history for names and incidents for her stories. She found particular delight in an aunt, Sarah Elizabeth Robins (Aunt Sallie) who not only possessed her name but also wrote drama and poetry, was inspired by seeing the French tragedienne Rachel, knew Edgar Allan Poe and published stories. It was, however Grandma who was, in Elizabeth's words, her 'touchstone', always far closer to her than her own mother.

Tall, with a commanding presence, she was a deeply religious and principled woman with a keen sense of loyalty, strict yet fair. At the same time she was acquainted with modern literature. In 1882 she was reading *The Portrait of a Lady* by Henry James, later to become one of her granddaughter's close friends. She explained in a letter to Elizabeth that James seemed to be ignorant of woman's nature, 'its complex machinery, its hidden springs of motive and passion— its actual working and latent possibilities'. In contrast, George Eliot, Charlotte Bronte and George Sand wrote differently, understanding their own sex 'and by strokes of genius, have succeeded in portraying womankind'. The *Zanesville Signal* felt the portrayal of Mrs Gano in *The Open Question* to be a little harsh[3] but Elizabeth was concerned to represent her in this story as a child might perceive her.

The novel also dwelt lovingly on Elizabeth's Ohio home, the Old Stone House. Her grandmother had moved there from Cincinnati in 1858. Charles Robins who was then working as a cashier at the Franklin bank of Zanesville also lived there with his mother and, until she left him, his first wife, Sarah.

The Old Stone House on Jefferson Street in the township of Putnam had its own distinguished history.[4] In the year that Elizabeth settled there Putnam became part of Zanesville though this old township on the bank of the Muskingum river retained a sense of separate identity since it had originally been founded by New Englanders. Unlike the other local houses Elizabeth's home was built of stone. This well-proportioned, Federal-style building had been erected in 1809 in the hope of its becoming the permanent legislative seat for the new state of Ohio. Although Zanesville on the other side of the river enjoyed this honour between 1810 and 1812, Columbus became the state capital thereafter. The Stone Academy, as Elizabeth's home was originally called, housed a grammar school between 1811 and 1826. The women of Zanesville and Putnam Charitable Society also met there as did, for a time, the United Presbyterians. Elizabeth's school, the Putnam Seminary for Young Ladies, originated there but soon moved to a handsome building on nearby Woodlawn Avenue. The Old Stone House's secret passage leading from the cellar to the river may have been part of the 'underground railroad' network for runaway slaves and the house hosted one of the first conventions of ante-bellum Abolitionists.

Such a home helped instil in Elizabeth a love of history. This later found expression in her wanderings round London, her perusal of books on the history of Sussex and a loving account, written in England, of one of the books kept in the Old Stone House library, *The British Merlin*, a detailed almanack for the year 1773.

Yet the young Bessie Robins was far from being an introverted bookworm. Within a few months of arriving in Putnam she was part of a group of nine who called themselves The Busy Bees, held their own fair and wrote a song about the wares they sold.[5] After a week in the Putnam Seminary (granted collegiate status in 1836), Elizabeth was writing to her mother explaining that she was studying geography, arithmetic, reading and spelling and liking school very much. Certainly her spelling had improved since an earlier letter (probably dating from about 1870) in which she had described a visit to the zoo in 'scentrail' Park, Manhattan and signed herself 'Your affectionate dater'. Elizabeth remained at the Put. Fem. Sem. as it was known, for nearly seven years though by the age of sixteen her appreciation of school was less dutiful. Fresh from George Eliot's *Middlemarch*, she wrote that the start of term and 'continual chemistry, geometry etc etc is enough to cloud the sunniest temper'. Her father had already warned against time-wasting novels. He was anxious that she regained her position as the school's best scholar. To his dismay she found science a tribulation though reading and writing provided welcome scope for her fervent imagination.

One of her compositions about a lawyer's wife declares her occupation 'far more necessary than that of a lawyer'. Where would the latter be without his wife's cooking? His very words depended on her.

The title of another story about the fortunes of a button includes the word 'Herstory' now incorporated into feminist vocabulary. It can, however, be questioned whether the twelve-year-old writer was actually 'conscious of its feminist content' as has recently been claimed even though Elizabeth chose her words carefully.[6] Two years later, influenced by the presence of her grandmother, disillusioned by the absence of her mother and infrequent appearances of her father, she declared that if women did their duty better there would be fewer worthless men. On leaving school she studied at home, her father's influence evident in her diet of reading which included the *Boston Journal of Chemistry* and the *Engineering and Mining Journal* (for which Charles was briefly a sub-editor).

The teenage Elizabeth was now dreaming of a life far away. In later years the *Zanesville Signal* (with the benefit of hindsight) recalled her as 'excessively, almost immodestly, ambitious'.[7] Since 1876 she had kept a diary. Early entries such as 'Going to begin to be good tomorrow' suggest her rebellious spirit. Her schoolfriends Kate Potwin and Emma and Julia Blandy feature prominently in her diary as do the boys they know. With these friends—characteristically Elizabeth was still corresponding with Emma in the 1920s—Elizabeth developed a love of the stage. She was prominent in school recitals. Her rendition of part of the closet scene in *Hamlet* at the age of fifteen prompted the local newspaper to comment on the 'fire and effect' usually attributed to 'the sterner sex' and after another recital to speculate whether she might have a future as a reader. The future actress later commented that Mama had once been considered the finest reader in the Shakespeare Club. Elizabeth and four Blandy girls were members of an Amateur Dramatics Club and performed a two-act comedietta *Which of the Two?* which she stage-managed. She also played the flirt Arabella in a short comedietta set in England entitled *Who's to Win Him?* This was a substitute role in the newly opened Schultz Opera House in Zanesville. Schultz lived in a mansion opposite Elizabeth's home.

The first professional play she saw was at Macaulay's Theatre, Louisville where, aged fourteen, she watched Edwin Adams as Macbeth. Her early adulation of Mary Anderson was partly because the actress shared her birthplace and it was after seeing her that she wrote a 'wild letter' to her father about going on the stage. He was shocked. Acting in school and family theatricals was one thing: going on the stage professionally was quite another and anathema to a family which saw itself as part of the gentry despite its impoverished position. Other young women from more modest backgrounds faced opposition on choosing the stage for a living. Clara Morris's mother, a housekeeper and seamstress, was 'stricken with horror'.[8]

The position of the American actress seems to have improved slightly from the 1860s. Elizabeth's grandmother certainly felt that there was less superstition and bigotry surrounding the theatre than there had been earlier. Nevertheless, the legacy of New England Puritanism remained strong as did any threat to the deification of the home. Constantly in the public eye and deliberately shunning anonymity, the actress enjoyed almost unparalleled freedom in a profession which anybody could enter and where it was still possible to succeed without formal qualifications. Elizabeth's father criticised the way the press appropriated and exaggerated the personal lives of actresses. Associations with immorality lingered on. The term 'public woman' was used interchangeably for performer and prostitute.[9]

Those outside the theatre were also often wary of people whose livelihood depended on perfecting the skills of deception. In *Both Sides of the Curtain*, Elizabeth tells of her father's encounter in the mid-1880s with his actress daughter.[10] On tour with James O'Neill (father of the playwright Eugene) in *The Count of Monte Cristo*, she played his lover Mercedes in her home town. To her profound humiliation, 'Before all the world' her father walked out of the Zanesville Opera House in the middle of the second act. His objection was to her *assumption* of distress, 'all *that* in a world of real suffering—of disaster' and he refused to watch any more of what he disparagingly called 'play-acting life'. And Grandma was mortified to think that Elizabeth was playing an outcast (Martha in *Little Emily*) before the Boston public. She also objected to her playing King Lear's daughter Goneril: 'How can you successfully assume such a character as the undutiful, unnatural daughter of the poor distraught king?' Hannah's letters urged her daughter to play modest and appropriate roles: 'Don't accept any role that a lady or pure girl would be ashamed to own, I could almost rather see you *dead* than personating vile women.' Ironically, years later a distinguished playwright who rather specialised in writing about 'women with a past' told Elizabeth: 'I see your line is sympathetic outcasts.'

Before Elizabeth reached the stage, her father made one serious effort to deflect her attention. In the spring of 1880 she boldly sought out the great actor Lawrence Barrett when he came to Zanesville and asked him if a young girl could become a fine actress without dramatic training. He denied that training could ever make a great actress. It was necessary to start at the bottom and by careful observation and practice work up to the top. She wrote to tell her father that as soon as Grandma no longer needed her she must carry out her plan to act. Aware that she might run away rather than be consigned to a life at home with her uninspiring sister, Charles now dangled before his daughter the prospect of a summer in a camp at the highest gold-mines in the world up in the Rocky Mountains of Colorado. He had once more changed jobs and was now employed by the Little Annie Mining Company as the financial agent at the Summit camp, Rio Grande, 11,300 feet (3,444 m) above sea level. It was a somewhat extreme move taking an adolescent daughter to live in a mountain mining camp but so, in her father's view, was a future on the stage.

Early in June 1880 the *Juan Prospector* reported the arrival of 'Professor Robins and his accomplished daughter Miss Bessie' (Charles had taken a metallurgy course at the University of St Louis so was known to the miners as the Professor or the Doctor). During the ensuing months Elizabeth and her father were at their closest. Here he could expound his scientific and political theories, show his daughter the mines and mills, teach her to assay and operate the weather signal service, and generally shape her reading and thinking. For a father who maintained that 'The only knowledge worth having is knowledge of nature' she was in the right place. She enjoyed freedoms unheard of at home, travelling like Isabella Bird before her in a Mountain Costume complete with alpine stock (long before she created the role of Hilda Wangel). On 4 July the future actress read out the Declaration of Independence above the timberline to an appreciative audience. She went snow-shoeing (skiing), climbing and riding, collected wild flowers and specimens of ore for her cabinet. On her eighteenth birthday she made an assay of the San Juan tailings, her father presented her with $1,000 of Little Annie stock and the men made her a gold ring.

There are several sources for the fourteen-week adventure in a mountain camp including Elizabeth's own diary and the letters she wrote to her grandmother. In the late 1920s she reworked much of this material into a sprawling story of over 600 pages, initially called 'Kenyon and His Daughter'; she later changed the title to 'Rocky Mountain Journal'. It seeks to present these months from the viewpoint of her father. In addition to name changes, Grandma is conspicuous by her absence 'which I regret to the deep of me'. This was a deliberate decision to avoid too much similarity to *The Open Question* though in fact 'Rocky Mountain Journal' never found anyone prepared to publish it. Elizabeth probed the apparent innocence of the original diaries and letters. The 'yellow-haired' unkempt girl had given way to an attractive and tanned young woman with long, chestnut hair. She had come to a camp full of miners who saw little of women. In the story she portrays the anxiety she presumes her father felt about her and his bewilderment at her mixture of precocity and naïveté. There is a suggestion, probably enhanced by the gap in time and the author's later feminism, of the young woman in control of herself and deliberately choosing not to 'tell all', the woman's use of silence to which she would refer so frequently in her writing. Her father is so disturbed when he finds a miner kissing her and his daughter never alluding to it, that in this fictional account he reverts to urging a suitable marriage as the solution.

The story underscores the hopelessness of her father's own marriages and here and in another story, 'The Pleiades', there is a suggestion of his involvement with other women. Some of this—for example, his wife bolting the door against him and making him homeless for five years—may simply have been for dramatic effect but it is interesting to see that the feminist Elizabeth Robins reserves the sympathy for him, presenting her (fictional) mother as unsympathetic, shallow and stiff. The heroine, named Theo (not Thea) is the daughter who replaces the son who has died, or at least seeks to fulfil this impossible task. Above all, this story is Elizabeth's attempt to come to terms with her father.

Despite the blows life dealt him, Charles Robins liked to impress his own experiences upon his children's minds. He reminded them how he had studied as a young man but earned his living since he was eighteen (his father had died when he was twelve).

Elizabeth was told that she was descended from intellectuals on both sides of the family and, as the eldest, could not fail to mould the boys' tastes (Una always seems to have been left out of such considerations). Charles had been influenced by the communitarian experiments of the Welshman Robert Owen and the French utopian socialist Charles Fourier. He was attracted by Auguste Comte's positivism and by Herbert Spencer. Perhaps the two greatest influences were the American Henry George, author of *Poverty and Progress*, and the British evolutionist Charles Darwin. As Elizabeth observed, science became his religion. In one of his many long letters he told her that 'The change wrought by Darwin is incomparable and universal. It will bury Theological agnosticism in the same grave with teleology—for it not only shows a way by which the Cosmos *might* have come to the point where we see it without God—but its demonstrations definitely excluded Him from all that we see of Nature.'

Yet although she does not appear to have openly challenged him, Elizabeth was painfully aware that, however laudable his beliefs, her father's own career pattern was hardly one to be emulated. His idealism and refusal to compromise made business life difficult for him yet he continually deluded himself with plans for improving society and the family's finances in his next scheme. By the end of 1880 he had been ousted from his Colorado job. He then joined a Gas Light Company and before long was company secretary in his half-brother Burnet's Alba Light Company in Cincinnati. Although he helped revolutionise domestic lighting and amongst his several hundred patents was his invention of the garden sprinkler, Burnet was another extremely clever individual yet incompetent businessman (he eventually died in a charity hospital). Within a couple of years the Alba Company was in serious financial trouble and Charles was dreaming of bee-keeping, wondering whether his sons and, even more fancifully, Elizabeth, far away on the stage, would join him in this venture. In his early fifties he began pursuing the Florida dream, seeking a return to nature, putting his faith in the cultivation of land and developing the physical strength, of his sons, seeking survival through fitness.

When it came to women's opportunities, Charles was divided. On the one hand he had some traditional reservations about women studying. Influenced by Spencer he argued that 'it is in opposition to female genius which is of the intuitive sort. Study is the *man's* business.'

Yet, on the other hand, he could also appreciate the writings of feminists like Frances Power Cobbe. Moreover his own failures, distrust of marriage and of idleness, recognition of Elizabeth's capabilities and ambitions, and opposition to acting combined to suggest a progressive path via a profession with far fewer women than the theatre. He wanted his daughter to study medicine. In the autumn of 1880, more from filial duty than desire, Elizabeth contacted a number of universities and colleges including the New England Female Medical College in Boston (the first women's medical college in the United States) and the Female Medical College of Pennsylvania. A draft of her letter to Cornell suggests her frame of mind. The entrance requirements included algebra. Elizabeth baldly stated that she was not likely to pass mathematics and 'do not intend to spend my time in learning that which does not interest me … I wish to ascertain whether Cornell University is really an institution where anybody can find instruction in any study.' She did not send this copy because of 'several mistakes'. There is no overt acknowledgement that the entire tone of her letter was a mistake!

Elizabeth was, however, aware that her father could not afford the tuition fees and books for her medical training. In later life she would deliberately describe the stage as the nearest approach to the ideal university. When suggesting titles to her publisher for her account of twelve years on the British stage, she wrote: 'It might be called Going to School or Both Sides of the Curtain or The Education of Elizabeth Robins (education of a woman in the Life School).'

Elizabeth chose careers in the very areas her father most despised, acting and novel-writing. He boasted that he had not read over a dozen novels since he was twenty-five but the subjects he revered, science, social science and the outdoor life, had little appeal for her. Yet she admired and emulated his thirst for knowledge though her cultural interests (divested of religious connotations) were more akin to her grandmother's than her father's. Most of all, she sought to make her own mark. In her, as in her countrywoman Louisa May Alcott, the presence of an intellectual father who sought refuge from failure in ideas and idealism helped produce a daughter who challenged prescribed gender roles, was wary of marriage, and possessed what Alcott called 'stage fever' and a commitment to writing for self (via the diary) and for a living. Both also supported women's rights.[11]

Returning from Colorado in the autumn of 1880 was deflating. Life seemed destined once more to centre on Zanesville. Fortunately Elizabeth's father let her accompany him on a business trip to New York in December. She stayed with him in Jersey City and on Staten Island with old neighbours, the Hedleys. At a *conversazione* Elizabeth declared that man was the product of his environment and heredity. At the same time she showed that her father and background had not entirely dominated her: the highlight of her trip was visiting the theatre. At New York's most elegant theatre, the New Park, she saw Lawrence Barrett. She was 'spellbound' by a visit to the Union Square Theatre to see *Daniel Rochat*. 'This', she wrote in her diary, 'is *living.*' She dabbled in spiritualism, attended a seance and fiercely denied the claim that she would marry. For a dollar she had two hours with a clairvoyant, savouring the prediction that she would do her duty by her family 'but such a life will never satisfy you, you will be like a caged bird, you are not domestic you were never born for a quiet existence you will live a public life and make for yourself a name'.

In the New Year she returned home via Baltimore (her grandmother's birthplace) and Washington. Like many other young American women, Elizabeth now found herself in the unwelcome position of housekeeper, her father providing $50 monthly. She recorded the family's praise for her buckwheat cakes, the whist parties she attended and the lessons she gave to Vernon and Raymond. There were occasional letters from Mr Fell, an English mining engineer she had met in Colorado, but with the highlight of a week being a trip to the Athenaeum for books with Raymond or driving Grandma in the phaeton, this was far from 'living'. Due to the family's straitened circumstances they were soon without a servant and housekeeping burdens increased. Later in England, Elizabeth described how she was 'chaffing against home's restraints and petulant for freedom & a glimpse of a larger horizon—a dreaming girl full of romance and checked ambitions—a determined stout-hearted young woman of 18'.

It was a time that she and Raymond would later romanticise. He would recall sister Bessie swinging in the hammock and their pledging their faith to each other but in reality after eight months Elizabeth had had more than enough of domestic life. In the state of Ohio eighteen was the age of majority and Elizabeth was now prepared to risk a future seeking work on the stage. Grandma gave her Aunt Sallie's copy of Shakespeare's plays and a prayer book and on 24 August 1881, a few weeks after her nineteenth birthday, she left Zanesville for New York. Considering she knew no actresses and few people there and had no independent means of support, it was an extremely brave or foolhardy move. On the journey she read the autobiography of Anna Cora Mowatt and was impressed by her versatility and success. When first published in mid-century this book had sold 20,000 copies within a year. It told how the actress had eloped when fifteen with a twenty-eight-year-old businessman turning to the stage when he lost his eyesight and money and she was twenty-six. For a decade she was a leading actress in New York and abroad, then married a wealthy Virginian, leaving behind the stage but not southern prejudice against her former profession.

Charles Robins remained opposed to the stage. In 1884 he wrote, somewhat prematurely: 'I have no sympathy with the stage or with stage life; and feel that your capabilities and training have made possible for you a larger and stronger career than ever they may win before the footlights.' Yet, despite his persistent antipathy, Elizabeth does appear retrospectively to have magnified some of the family opposition. She continued to return home whenever possible. Charles Robins remained in close contact with his daughter and they wrote to each other frequently. As we have seen, *Both Sides of the Curtain* concentrates on one tale about her father seeing her act. Significantly, Elizabeth's diary does not tell this story. She does refer to performing on tour at Zanesville merely adding that there was a full house and that her father and the boys came backstage after the performance. She may have destroyed the original account since she was adept at 'doctoring' her diary but her father's initials next to a list of performances she had given in 1882 suggests that he actually saw her act more than once and attended a performance in Indianapolis that year. In December of that year she played the minor role of Miss Holdfast in *The American King* in Louisville (having persuaded O'Neill not to take a booking in Zanesville). Her father escorted her to the theatre and dined with her over the next few days. Her Uncle Morrie (Dr Bodine) to whom the entire family tended to defer, compared her to Mary Anderson. He wrote to Elizabeth after seeing her act, declaring: 'Your art when raised to its highest standard does, indeed, represent a many-sided culture … I am happy in the belief that you have given signs of promise that justify the highest hopes. My heart is full of yearning for your success.'

Elizabeth's mother appears to have been proud of her daughter yet worried about the effects of a stage career on a woman's health. She lent her money from her private trust fund until an extremely wealthy distant relative, the banker Lloyd Tevis, came to the rescue. Tevis had gone west from Kentucky in that year of gold 1849 and had eventually become President of Wells, Fargo and Company.

Grandma acknowledged that Hannah's father had seen the theatre as 'the high road to perdition' but once again demonstrated her own farsightedness. Her letters to her hopeful Bessie are full of loving encouragement: 'Yes, fly high! reach for the moon and you may catch a star has been wisely said.' Admittedly she did not divulge her grand-daughter's doings to the good folk of Putnam. In fact, in a reversal of the usual situation she did not even inform Elizabeth's devout sister but she did understand determination. If people began talking she would say to them 'that the profession was your own decided choice and that I helped you all I could, and would not hinder by word or deed'. It was she who informed Elizabeth of relevant books such as a biography of the Booths. For her nineteenth birthday she had given her the money to buy a biography of Charlotte Cushman, who was from a privileged background (her nephew married a distant relative of Elizabeth's). Cushman survived her father's business failure and became both a great actress and a shrewd businesswoman.[12] Grandma, whose letters betray a certain melodrama of their own, also knew the kind of language that would appeal to Elizabeth, writing just after her birthday that it was seventy-seven years 'since I was ushered into being to perform my part on the Stage in the Drama of Life'.

So, this is not a 'do not darken my door again' tale. Perhaps she chose to play down the support she actually received in order to deflect attention from the real tragedy of her early life, her mother's problems. In her memoirs, written long after the nineteenth century and in another continent, she presented a conventional yet satisfy-ingly dramatic story of the young lady whose papa disapproved of the stage. This helped preserve her family's sense of class and propriety, enhanced her own independence and contributed to that creation of a self which was so important to Elizabeth Robins.

At first Elizabeth remained on familiar territory, staying on Staten Island with Mrs Andariesi, a kind widow interested in spiritualism. She travelled by ferry to the theatre district of Manhattan, doing the rounds of dramatic agencies and theatres, finding that managers had the knack of being out just as she arrived. Twelve acting lessons cost $40 (borrowed from her mother) and from her somewhat old-fashioned teacher she graduated to elocution lessons with Mrs Boucicault, 'mistress of the natural school'. Elizabeth also took the first step in her construction of a new persona, naming herself Clare Raimond.

Eager to be closer to the theatres, in October she joined Mrs Andariesi's daughter Annie and her husband Alfred Parmele who had decided to rent rooms in a lower Manhattan lodging house for the winter. Their attic room which she shared with the Parmeles' daughter cost her $8 weekly including meals. They soon moved to a cheaper place on West 24th Street. Here Elizabeth paid $4, providing her own frugal meals. Breakfast was usually oatmeal and cream for 20 cents and buns and soup became her staple diet, food being sacrificed for cheap matinées. By moving into a converted hallway she saved another dollar. In a later unpublished fictionalised account of this period called 'Theodora or The Pilgrimage' (which seems to have been closely modelled on actual experience), Elizabeth describes obtaining cheap tickets for matinées from music stores in return for putting up posters advertising plays. Not surprisingly, there is no mention of such activity in letters to Grandma. This tale also has the heroine attend Lucretia Mott's Commemoration Service and a women's suffrage convention addressed by Susan B. Anthony. There is no mention of interest in women's rights in Elizabeth's writing at the time, though she does mention Mrs Parmele attending a suffrage convention in 1885, and the inclusion of feminist interest in the story is probably explained by the date at which it was written, 1910.

Elizabeth found New York exhilarating though part of the thrill evaporated rapidly when you had to walk everywhere and count every cent: 'It is such a struggle to live in this splendid city, one has to pay so *much* in gold or brain or brawn for the poor privilege of breathing.' She did, however, compensate for her relative deprivation by seeing Edwin Booth act. His Iago was 'a perfect piece of unrestrained art', free from obvious effort and effect and Elizabeth would try hereafter to emulate such an approach. Any social connections which led to theatrical contacts were eagerly exploited but the all-important breakthrough came not via friends who knew people on the stage but through her own digs. James O'Neill was boarding in the same house. The charismatic Irish actor, known as the 'black-moustached Adonis', was then in his mid-thirties.[13] He recognised Elizabeth as a suitable companion for Ella his convent-educated wife who had never felt at home with theatrical folk. He spoke on Elizabeth's behalf at Booth's theatre where he was currently performing, describing her as 'finely educated with a powerful voice'.

This led to a 'little engagement'. At first a place in the ballet looked like the only opening. This was the entry point (and exit) for many aspiring actresses though after encountering one of the ballet 'girls' whose every other phrase was 'My God!', Elizabeth was relieved to be spared this fate. It was probably the first time she had been set alongside women of another class and treated in the same way as them. She was soon acknowledging in her diary the fact that many actresses thought her ill-tempered. She chose to attribute this to being reserved and less tactile and familiar with men than they. She was clearly further distinguished from them by having the Parmeles' maid accompany her at night.

Thanks to O'Neill, 'my first useful dramatic friend', and Kate Claxton his leading lady, Elizabeth now had a small speaking part as a nun. It was three lines according to her diary but reduced to one in her memoirs. The play was *The Two Orphans* set in pre-revolutionary France. She was also one of a number of speechless guests at the Capulet ball and a white-robed mourner at Juliet's grave. Juliet was none other than Mary Anderson. Elizabeth's first Christmas in New York was spent rehearsing and her debut came on Boxing Day 1881. Within weeks she was on tour with *The Two Orphans*. In her autobiography she describes this opportunity as 'an incredible fluke' but at the time her youthful self-assurance and innocent determination—'I am simply burning up with restless eager ambition'—seem to have convinced her that it was the least she deserved. Not for nothing is the 1910 story also called 'A Study in Egoism'.

Before long there was a slight rise in salary and the name Clare Raimond, not always printed correctly, appeared on the bill. Elizabeth was earning $25 weekly when performing over the next few years. Such high wages formed part of the attraction of the stage for women, especially since actresses were in the rare position of being able to earn the same money as men. Nevertheless, expenses were high. Actresses had to provide their own costumes (a new peasant dress cost her $13) and had to pay hairdressers. Some of Mrs Robins's clothes were converted, and relatives on tour in St Louis (the Crows) came to Elizabeth's rescue, supplying some stage clothes. On arriving at St Louis the cast had divided into those who could afford decent accommodation and the rest. Elizabeth was consigned to what she described, in characteristically hyperbolic language, as 'the worst hotel in the United States'. She was luckier than most. Her relatives whisked her away to their elegant home as did relations in Chicago.

Eugene O'Neill's play *Long Day's Journey into Night*, based on his family, has Mary (his mother Ella) repeatedly complain about the second-rate hotels she had to endure whilst accompanying her husband on tour.[14] She also detested the continual travelling. Elizabeth found the long railroad journeys, often made in heat and dirt, debilitating especially since tours enabled only a few hours' snatched sleep between studying and rehearsing with no concession for occupational hazards such as sore throats. In 1909 she gave a lecture at St James's Hall, London entitled 'Shall Women Work?'. In it she drew attention to the physically demanding work of women and their staying power, mentioning in addition to jobs such as cooking, being an agricultural labourer and a pit lassie, the arduous work of the actress. As she recalled, women in America played long exhausting parts nightly, 'ten months at a stretch, throughout a lifetime', and

> in addition to the strain of such journeys as no actress makes in England, the custom was, not only to play on Sunday (as well as other days), but to play twice, making ten performances a week. Even in many first-class companies there was not always an understudy for the leading lady. She was expected never to be ill—never to fail her manager. She did not fail him. I never knew a theatre closed on her account unless, being a star, she could consult her own mere convenience.[15]

In October and November 1882 Elizabeth travelled around the southern states yet had little opportunity to see much of the many towns she visited. Most of the time she was too busy being the spinster Miss Holdfast in *An American King* or the coquette in Dion Boucicault's *Led Astray*, or playing several parts in *A Celebrated Case*, an adaptation of a French thriller. O'Neill wanted her to understudy many different parts and thus gain experience. She was, however, already impatient of 'wretched' small character parts. The company was now under O'Neill's direct control since he had fired his inefficient manager after a period of uncertainty when the actors had not received their salaries and closure had seemed imminent.

Elizabeth's letters and diaries are adamant about her commitment: 'you might as well try to turn back Niagara as me from my purpose'.[16] Sometimes she needed to convince herself, quite apart from her family, that such demanding work was worth the effort. During the summer break she visited Zanesville, talked 'sociology, theology & hygiene' with Papa then visited her mother and brothers in Louisville. It was less easy returning to 'A grey, rainy morning alone in a New York boarding house' though her grandmother still bombarded her with encouragement and advice. She was warned that 'A young girl cannot be too careful in a great city' and to watch that she did not trifle with the attentions of young men.

From the outset Elizabeth was indignant at the way men treated actresses. 'Never did a girl live a more unostentatious unobtrusive pure life' she protested. But this was not how women in her profession were perceived. The term 'parasexual' has recently been coined to denote the 'come hither but' element commonly implied in barmaid's work.[17] The actress was also seen as titillating, particularly at a time when a public demonstration of emotions between the sexes was not considered correct yet acting styles encouraged exaggerated emotional (though not explicit) expression on stage. Just as the barmaid is physically separated from her customers in her workplace by the barrier of the bar, so too is the actress subject to the direct gaze yet divided from the audience on stage. An actress creates a world of make-believe whilst the admirer watches. Her very inaccessibility can add to the fantasy and be conveniently seen as temporary, the presumption being that she is available once the performance is over.

Elizabeth was disconcerted to find that men believed they were free to flirt with her. Strangers sent her roses, followed her in the street and pursued her from theatre to theatre. Actors sought to entice her with promises of oyster dinners and tried to accompany her to and into her digs. Such accommodation offered little space for respectable entertaining. Young women also had to be wary of advances from fellow lodgers, quite apart from other dangers—one of Elizabeth's landlords in New York threatened a woman with a pistol. In her story 'Theodora' a young man with shifty eyes knocks on her bedroom door and tries to stop her shutting him out. The middle-aged feminist Elizabeth writes how her security has been punctured, 'not only in her little eyrie but in the great spaces of the world … a new ugliness had touched her'. At the time her diary records her telling one persistent male 'fan': 'Do you think because I am an actress you can get acquainted with me in this irregular fashion? No indeed I assure you.' Ella O'Neill kept a watchful eye and was concerned when a young actor from Columbus, Ohio joined the cast and appeared to monopolise her attention. Elizabeth, however, was soon writing to her grandmother, assuring her that this Mr George Backus was not her type. Many men she simply and literally wrote off as 'idiots'.

Early in 1883 O'Neill's Dramatic Company disbanded. He was about to embark on *The Corsican Brothers* followed by his most famous leading role in *The Count of Monte Cristo*, a part he would play 4,000 times. Annoyed at the fact that he had not personally invited her to join him and unprepared to play the part of 'a fast woman' in *The Corsican Brothers*, Elizabeth now went her own way. She joined H.M. Pitt's company and in February 1883 in a gesture signalling her independence and new step in her career, she reverted to her own name, Bessie Robins. Her family persuaded her that Elizabeth was more dignified than Bessie. Her father, now resigned to his daughter's career, added that it was 'better for life & action, better for biography and history'. In June she therefore made a final change in her stage name, announcing herself as Miss Elizabeth Robins.

She had spent the first half of the year with her new company, mainly acting in James Albery's sentimental plays, *Two Roses and Forgiven*. A picture of her as Rose in *Forgiven* became a cigarette card, showing her with frills and flowers and a bonnet placed at a jaunty angle.[18] The *Dramatic Times* of 12 June repeated the tone of other notices, commenting that she was 'attractive in appearance, remarkably intelligent and does her work with an artistic discrimination and a natural force that promise much for the future'. Actresses' physical attributes were only too often commented upon: it was less usual for notices to remark on their intelligence.[19]

Her actor-manager Pitt was facing severe financial problems but was helped by Elizabeth's benefactor relative, Lloyd Tevis. Her mother's cousin had materialised as her *deus ex machina* just when Elizabeth most needed help. He had offered to be her 'good genie & good friend', paid for language classes and supplied advice and money. Thanks to Tevis Elizabeth now received acting lessons from Mrs Pitt. Her role in *Forgiven* was part of a bargain whereby Tevis loaned Pitt money. This was not, however, ultimately sufficient to save the company. By mid-1883 the actors, on tour in Boston, were not being paid their salaries and they (including Elizabeth) held an 'indignation meeting' with their employer in the foyer of the Park Theatre then went on strike. Elizabeth's diary became more melodramatic than ever: 'Life seems shadowy unreal and phantasmagorical.' The manager of the Boston Museum Company saw the opportunity to poach some players and signalled his interest in Elizabeth, suggesting she might work for him for a season in leading juvenile roles. Once more Lloyd Tevis came to the rescue, negotiated with Mr Field and secured a three-year agreement on better terms than she could have arranged. Her salary would rise annually from $25 weekly in the first year to $50 by the third year.[20]

With her future suddenly looking relatively secure, Elizabeth went home to Zanesville. With his sights now set on Florida, her father had bought her 32 acres (14.8 hectares) of land there which he intended to cultivate. After attending a party, Elizabeth noted with delight her successful creation of an image in the space of two years: 'people acted as if I were some rare new species.' On 25 August 1883 the twenty-one-year-old actress arrived at her new theatrical home, the famous Boston Museum Company.

2

THE OPEN QUESTION

It may seem highly appropriate that Elizabeth, who became a passionate supporter of women's rights, should have moved to the New England 'City of Reform'. Two years earlier Boston had hosted the National Woman Suffrage Association Convention. Female suffrage had become the topic of the day. Yet there is little reflection of this in Elizabeth's diary and, with the exception of her novel *The Open Question*, Boston does not feature in her fiction. For the Miss Robins of 1883 it was acting which absorbed her energy and although increasingly she found competing claims on her time, at this point they were not ones related to suffrage or other organised politics.

The Boston Museum was a stock company established in the 1840s. Its imposing premises, Italianate in design, were in Tremont Street. Although past its greatest decade and most formal period, as Elizabeth explained many years later, the 'Boston old order there had not quite been superseded'.[1] Under its manager R.M. Field it boasted a varied programme which encompassed both Shakespeare and melodrama. Entertainments began with a short curtain-raiser, followed by a lengthy play, and ended with 'a farce to send them all home happy'. A newcomer would be expected to act in at least two of the three pieces, frequently undergoing a miraculous and speedy transition from a schoolgirl to an old woman, and there were numerous parts to be understudied. In 1928 Elizabeth claimed that she played nearly 300 parts in her two years at Boston.[2] This may have been an exaggeration. In 1898 she was claiming over 200. She played several characters in some plays. She probably also included parts in which she understudied as well as roles in small pieces and benefits. Certainly she served a valuable apprenticeship with a reputable company.

Elizabeth began rehearsing early in September. She made her debut playing Adrienne in *A Celebrated Case*. Familiar with this play (she had previously acted as Adrienne's mother), she was both flattered to be playing the heroine and 'half benumbed with anxiety'. The sophisticated Boston theatregoer was very different from the typical audience in the remote towns Elizabeth had visited on tour only to leave again the day after the performance. She had three weeks to conjure up appropriate costumes. Once more Lloyd Tevis came to the rescue though she tried sewing herself to save money. She read aloud to strengthen her voice and practised fainting ''til I'm black & blue' in her lodgings at Somerset Street in the Beacon Hill district, close to the theatre. Soon after the opening—and a sense of disappointment in her performance—she moved round the corner to non-theatrical digs at 16, Ashburton Place, recommended by cousins. In the mid-1860s the young Henry James had lived at number 13, observing the Bostonian scene before moving across the river to Cambridge. In *The Open Question* the hero's family live at Elizabeth's Boston address.

Perhaps influenced by the intellectual milieu of the city, Elizabeth now combined learning parts in the daytime with reading ten pages of French daily then turned to studying German grammar and Greek history in 'homeopathic doses'. Just twenty-one, the young actress was impatient. Her diary reflects both her dramatic roles and the novels she was reading such as *Wuthering Heights*. 'Alone! Waiting! For What! Destiny. I wonder if it awaits me at the Museum' she declared—more prophetically than she realised. Within a few weeks she had been cast for the next play *In the Ranks* and was doing a brief tour in Providence, Rhode Island with a 'popular novelty' called *Warranted*. Quite a lot of her time would be spent on tour, mainly in New England and Canada.

Elizabeth's diary mentions her 'very pleasant' fellow actors, including a George Parks whom she soon admits to rather liking. Never short of admirers, she now registers annoyance with the continued attention of the actor George Backus. By early November she seems to have settled well into her Boston life, Parks is mentioned daily and is becoming bolder. He talks to her about the influence of romance on the artist's life: 'He takes me into rather deep water & I am a little non-plussed at his unconventionality.'

George Parks was five years older than Elizabeth. Born in east Boston he had attended (but not graduated from) the Boston Public Latin School. His father was an unsuccessful hotelier who died young. For a time George was a clerk for his father at the Maverick House hotel then became a salesman in a dry goods store. According to newspaper reports he also spent several summers as a purser on a steamship.[3] He had to support his mother and two sisters in Medford, Massachusetts. Interested in amateur dramatics, like Elizabeth, he made the transition to professional acting without formal training. He began at the Boston Theatre Company then moved to the Museum. Tall, fair-haired and known as 'Handsome George', he was often cast as the villain. Elizabeth acted with him in a number of plays.

On 19 November he asked, 'with apparent hesitancy', if he might call on her in the public rooms at her lodgings. He wooed her with flowers, bought her lubricant to soothe her sore throats and used discussion of theatrical roles as a means of getting to know her better. In the diary Mr Parks became George Parks and eventually G. Yet, from the start, Elizabeth was wary: 'I try to avert the inevitable.' They walked on Boston Common but she felt this should be 'the last chapter of that Romance. Finis.' When she told him she had written a letter to this effect he admitted how much he loved her. Her sudden shifts of mood are hardly unusual for somebody of her age and temperament, attracted by a dashing young actor. Yet Elizabeth's life, or at least what we can tell of her perception of her fortunes, seems to have been invested with a remarkably strong dose of drama, dramatic irony and tragedy. Neither can her hesitancy be entirely attributed to conflicts between propriety and attraction or even to her clear ambition to achieve which she recognised would be compromised by a permanent attachment. As she studied *Macbeth* and flirted with George, so an alarming letter arrived from home about her mother's health. Never far from her mind were forebodings about her family, herself and heredity.

In March her father had alluded to his estranged wife being 'in a state of frenzy', imagining Elizabeth to be romantically involved with Lloyd Tevis: 'The wild, distracted tone of these letters, are a reproduction of the state of mind which she cherished in regard to myself; and which I found insupportable years ago.' In her own letters to Elizabeth, Hannah Robins sounds, more than anything else, world-weary: 'I am now a worn and used up broken down prematurely old woman.' She kept reiterating her wish for death. She was in her late forties. She was apparently hearing voices which terrified her. Dr Bodine, her brother-in-law, felt helpless: 'The weapon of reason turns back when directed towards a pathological state like that presented by her—absurdity and improbability become obsolete terms.' Young Raymond had already been the victim of fits and Bodine feared that, as the offspring of first cousins (and marriage between first cousins was not legal in some states) and an unstable mother, he was in danger of 'mental alienation'. As Hannah put it, 'We know there is a fatal infirmity in the Robins family and much eccentricity among the Husseys.' On 7 December when Elizabeth might have been concentrating on a career and a romance, her correspondence was concerned with the incompatibility of the two. Her father and grandmother emphasised words like 'disordered', 'distracted', 'distress' when describing Hannah's condition. Grandma feared that a crisis was approaching, warning 'Ah! this thing of heredity—Do not, I beseech you, my darling child, rush into matrimony which may plunge you into a sea of difficulties where you may sink to rise no more! Never mind sentiment, feeling, preference, and all that, do not commit yourself.' Elizabeth had written to her in confidence about George. Her response was that 'The consequences of marriage are too serious to be ignored'. Elizabeth should extricate herself. Long before she had heard of Ibsen, Elizabeth and her family were tormented by fears of hereditary mental instability brought about by intermarriage. At this time there was only limited understanding of mental illness and of effective birth control methods. Moreover her father's fascination with social Darwinism, which linked evolution and social progress, resulted in a stark warning to his daughter. Although the most promising and stable member of the family, there was concern about her becoming a mother. In her later autobiography, Elizabeth conceded that there had been more than one warning, especially through the women of her family.[4]

She wrote her grandmother a seventeen-page letter, outlining how she had already told George her intention never to marry and asked him to leave her alone. His refusal to accept the situation prompted a telegram from her father, peremptorily demanding that she 'break from the Parks entanglement'. Elizabeth watched the famous on- and off-stage lovers, Irving and Terry, in *The Merchant of Venice* and her own life lurched from snatched words with George behind the scenes to walking with him, then reproaching herself for not being more dignified. Whilst the feminine ideal remained marriage and motherhood, Elizabeth received contrary advice from her elders. Grandma narrated tales of misery and separation—'almost the common lot of actresses'—which would follow a short period of 'fancied happiness' whilst her father stressed how marriage 'claims, involves, subordinates, the destiny of the individual to the destiny of the race'. He lamented that Mr Parks occupied too much of Elizabeth's thoughts and feelings, expending much time and ink himself in the process.

In the New Year Annie Parmele visited from Staten Island acting as a chaperone whilst Elizabeth toured. George, however, was still asking if he might '"carry my satchell" and do all that implies'. Determined to allow 'no evanescent influence to turn me from my purpose' Elizabeth concentrated on her acting in a bid to '*crowd out* all commoner interests … oh Bessie Robins open yr [*sic*] eyes; time for dreaming is gone by'. The titles of some of her plays are somewhat ironic given the circumstances: *Led Astray*, *Broken Hearts*, *Marble Heart*. The diary entries became more and more emphatic: 'I crave *pronounced success* applause—enthusiasm' and 'I was born in the superlative degree no half-way measures can ever satisfy me'. Her career must be her future. 'This dark thread of Tragedy that has run through our daily lives & final fate of many of our house I will cut out of my personal experience & transfer to a profession where it will turn to gold.'

In letter after letter, Grandma appealed to this side of Elizabeth. In words which sound remarkably modern and perspicacious, the old lady wrote: 'I see how it is my dear child, he, the actor, does not wish his wife to be an actress. His jealous temperament would not bear it.' She begged her not to leave the stage to please him. It would ruin both of their lives. Essential was

> freedom of thought, liberty or action, [you] must work out your own life in your own way ... At home he is the Great Mogul—after marriage he will be the Grand Turk—his sultana must not be gazed upon by other eyes than his own—her liberty will be restricted. <u>Be you sure of this</u>.

Mr Parks was pronounced 'a veritable Turk' in his ideas about women. She stressed that her granddaughter must liberalise him since he surely could not convert her to his 'prejudicial and narrow, unconventional obsolete opinions'. Elizabeth, who must at times have been regretting that she had taken her grandmother so much into her confidence, was trying to fortify herself 'against capture, or defeat in my long purpose'. Her language suggests something of her belief that she was 'never made to blindly follow one man's bidding or live content in one man's smile'. Yet she had also experienced loneliness and it was difficult to reconcile her love of freedom and 'intoxicating sense of the boundless possibilities' of youth with her 'longing for sympathy and love'.

When the season ended Elizabeth visited Zanesville, shocked to find that her grandmother, so strong in words, was so thin and weak in person. She read Emerson's essay on self-reliance whilst her father reiterated the old fatalistic tale: 'A horrible nightmare or more truly an apparent Curse seems to have settled on this hapless race from a dim unspeakable past.' She missed George. She visited her mother briefly and soon after returning to Boston read a book on matrimony.

On her father's insistence she had engaged a maid who now accompanied her home from the theatre at night. George, however, was as obdurate as the Robins family. In mid-October he began threatening to leave the company. By December Elizabeth was meeting his demands for a marriage licence with her father's arguments. George's chilling response was that without her 'at the end of 6 mos [*sic*] I shall not be living'. She made a 'half hesitating plea for freedom' at the start of 1885 but his desperation was such that 'the result is only to hasten the dénouement ... this tide is surging nearer & nearer', hardly the words of a young woman longing to be married. Neither was the setting for their secret wedding ceremony—Salem, famous for its seventeeth-century witch trials—a conventional one. Here was enacted on 12 January 1885 'A strange little drama'. Elizabeth's friend from her lodgings, Nina Cutter, was witness at the Grace Episcopal church. Elizabeth spent her wedding night alone on tour. The press and company soon found out, though Elizabeth, unlike George, had initially not wanted to let 'the affair become public'. Her family had not been consulted and learned the news through Zanesville gossip. Indeed, Elizabeth had written to her grandmother on the day of the wedding, casually mentioning that she was leaving for Salem as though it were merely one more theatrical venue. Her name was misspelt on her marriage certificate.

Their honeymoon was at the Sturtevant Hotel in Manhattan in mid-January. George was now rehearsing for *Othello*. Elizabeth was keen to show off her husband to her Staten Island friends: 'G. wants me to give up our engagements but I persevere.' He was wondering about leaving the stage and re-entering the hotel trade but in late February the Boston Museum manager wrote to release Elizabeth from her contract with the company. To his surprise she confronted him in person. He spoke 'candidly but without the least cordiality of my marriage', telling her what he would have done for her had she not married. Elizabeth, who always retained her own stage name, begged Mr Field to 'think of Mr P. and myself as *two* & not to allow consideration of me to sway his intentions regarding Mr P'. On 1 June she bade farewell to the company.

During his summer break George joined Elizabeth in Zanesville. Forced to recognise the inevitable, her grandmother had become progressively less hostile towards the new member of the family in her letters, stressing instead his obvious devotion, thereby easing the tension when they finally met. There were anyway now more imme-diate troubles. In May Elizabeth's mother had entered an asylum (as would later one of her aunts). Unknown to George, Elizabeth and her father visited the Oxford Retreat, Ohio. She observed: 'There was never one who has suffered a sadder more tragic fate.'

For the modern reader, so removed in time, with modern approaches to mental health and means of controlling illness through medication, and with the evidence of Hannah's depressed but not

unreasonable letters to her daughter, it is only too easy to disap-
prove of her incarceration. All descriptions of Hannah's 'delusions' are
secondhand, emanating from other letters about her. Although, not
surprisingly, rather morbid, the letters that we can read do not immediately suggest somebody who would necessarily be best served by
being permanently placed in an asylum. Yet, as for so many others,
the removal of immediate family support—Charles leaving for
Florida and his own mother fast failing—hastened Hannah's commitment to what she perceived as 'a living grave'. With such a move
came the likelihood that once dependent on such an institution, it
would become less and less possible to adjust properly again to living
outside it.

Before the end of the year Hannah had been removed to the Oak
Lawn Asylum in Illinois. Elizabeth visited and said: 'The picture will
haunt me to my grave.' Dr Andrew MacFarland pronounced Hannah
physically fit but haunted by voices and fears that her children were
in danger of being murdered. Memory of such visits placed Elizabeth
under enormous strain: 'I wonder sometimes I am able to play my
part & keep up courage before the world … would I could take *all*
the pain & set her spirit free.' Many years later Octavia Wilberforce
(whose first job as a qualified doctor was at an English mental hospital) wrote of Elizabeth's horror of such institutions.[5] At first Elizabeth
had clung on to the hope that her mother's incarceration was temporary. The situation was exacerbated by the increased physical distance
between mother and daughter. When she earned her first fee (£2 2s)
on the English stage, Elizabeth dedicated it to that

> home fund that must grow & ever increase, with God's help & my
> devoted endeavor, my self-consecration to the chief of all hopes &
> aims—A home for my mother where my love & care can nurse
> her back to health & surround her days with peace.

It was her personal tragedy that she could not achieve this.

There were times when the family considered removing Hannah
(prompted by circumstances such as the unfortunate suicide of Dr
MacFarland) but they came to nothing. Dr Bodine, both a relative
and a revered professional, tended to have the final word. His wife
persuaded him to try having her home in 1898 but her schizophrenia

caused severe problems and after three weeks she was taken back; 'She was constantly hearing the most awful allegations against her character & there was a Court being held above her head' with her loved ones testifying against her. Elizabeth visited several times in the 1890s, shrinking, as she told her brother Vernon, from thinking what life must be like to

> a sensitive delicately nurtured gentlewoman in one of those great cities of the sick where the air is full of the vague suggestion of madness … I feel that if I'd been 10 years in such a hell I would be as mad as the maddest. I grow sick that my mother has suffered this long martyrdom all these years & years. *If* I were a free agent—if I were an independent woman with a sure & steady income I do not think I could live on without trying the experiment of quiet home life for this old disease.

Elizabeth believed the aural delusions to be harmless and not dissimilar to the spiritualist's belief in communing with the dead. There was something especially tragic in Hannah's constant plea to come home since she had not had her own family home since her children were very small and the daughter who felt so keenly the burden of guilt and helplessness about her mother so far away had been largely brought up by her grandmother. Hannah's last few years were less traumatic being spent in a church home in Louisville. Not until 1901 did she die.

As though there had not been enough family upheaval, a further blow was struck in September 1885. Desperate for work, Elizabeth had returned to O'Neill's Company for $40 a week. As the curtain fell at the end of a New York performance, she learned that her seventy-eight-year-old grandmother had died. She immediately travelled by train to Zanesville and attended the funeral. George, who had been on tour, saw her briefly before they returned to their respective companies. Elizabeth arrived back in Pittsburgh just in time for the first act of yet another performance as Mercedes in *The Count of Monte Cristo*. She was increasingly bored with the repetition of this role, grief-stricken by her loss and resentful at having to spend the majority of her time away from her husband. Some venues left a lot to be desired: in Austin she slept with a revolver under her bed as stories abounded of mysterious murders. Many arrangements were makeshift: in another Texan town the dressing room was a dentist's study. At one theatre her costume was ruined when a boiler burst in the dressing room.

Elizabeth's health began to suffer from a daily routine of studying by day and performing in the evenings, interspersed with long, often uncomfortable hours of travel. When they visited Boston (which must have underscored her sense of having made a retrograde career move), Elizabeth wrote: 'I've never felt so hopeless so unutterably wretched. Discouraged in present work & a shuddering fear of the future.' Now she was without Grandma's epistolary encouragement, deeply concerned about her mother and 'Penniless, friendless' with no prospect of help from George who was also very depressed. In mid-March came the first suggestion (in her diary) of the idea of going to England professionally. When the couple met in May at the end of the tour, discussion of finances only resulted in a scene '& a terrible "facing of the end" … *poor poor* G. what's to be done'.

They spent the summer in Medford with George's relatives, then he returned to New York for an engagement at Madison Square Gardens. Tension resurfaced when Elizabeth discovered that she could have been his leading lady there had he wished it: 'It's no wonder wiser women than I have not looked to husbands for aid in advancement.' Reluctantly returning to rehearsals for a new season with O'Neill, Elizabeth wrote in September (in words more suggestive of George than of her old positive self), 'If this state of things continue long I should feel justified in cutting short the wretched farce.' George was feeling the strain of separation so keenly that he wrote: 'You must come to me in 2 wks [*sic*] or I'll be a maniac.' Elizabeth sent in her resignation to O'Neill and joined George in Providence, only to face a further disaster. With George feverish and facing debts on furniture and herself with pleurisy, she learned that her younger sister Una had died.

When Una had lived in Zanesville she had appeared to lack the spirit and imagination so evident in her older sister. Her correspondence with Elizabeth said little since she admitted the 'sheer lack of anything to say'. Living with an elderly woman who had a deep-seated faith, Una had become increasingly devout and withdrawn (Emmie, who is the character based on Una in *The Open Question*, becomes a nun). The move to Florida was disastrous for her. It may have proved a valuable testing ground for Charles Robins who always had one eye on the 'constitutional defects which degenerate persons transmit to their offspring' and sought to improve the family stock through the cultivation of physical strength, and manliness in his sons. But this undeveloped, swampy southern state did not prove to be attractive to the twenty-year-old woman from a very settled community.

On first moving south Una stayed with another family (the Englishes) until the completion of the new Robins enterprise, a home called Nama built on a coral reef near Fort Myers in Lee County. Una was to be the Robinses' housekeeper, caring for her father and brothers. According to her father she deluded herself into thinking she might marry Jim English, was foolishly extravagant and erroneously believed that sister Bessie could supply an endless stream of clothes and money. Charles Robins's letters to Elizabeth are remarkable for the rancour he openly expresses towards this younger daughter. There is clear resentment of Una's dislike of this new life and her lack of survival becomes almost inevitable. Like her mother, she has, in his eyes, made herself a hopeless case beyond redemption. Charles fears that she will do '*some* crazy & wicked thing. There lurks a devil behind those Madonna-like eyes, charged with destructive possibilities.' She is a 'brainless & a disloyal daughter & sister, & an incredible slattern'. Una was obviously neglecting her domestic duties and was 'forever scribbling' (something that, in earlier days, Charles might have applauded). In his view 'U. will never make anything but trouble for everybody who has anything to do with her'. There is no mention of the difficulties of adjustment for this sheltered young woman whose life had been abruptly upturned when she had to join an all-male household relishing the pioneering life.

Although Charles's letters to Elizabeth do not specifically name Una's illness, she had probably contracted malaria which was widespread in this swampy area. She deteriorated rapidly and Charles was soon looking for 'some retreat whither she must be carried for safety'. By November she was in Palatka in north-east Florida being examined by a physician experienced in working with the insane. She lapsed into a comatose state and died.

At Christmas Elizabeth travelled to Florida, breaking her long journey by seeing Una's grave *en route*. A second wedding anniversary was spent without her husband. For a few weeks Elizabeth played a domestic role, making biscuits, puddings, even squirrel stew. She and her brothers made a boat trip along the Caloosahatchee river, fishing and camping. On the long journey back to Manhattan, Elizabeth was ill. A doctor diagnosed malaria as well as nervous depression.

George was faring no better. He had been ill in Cleveland and forced to give up his part, thus adding to his financial distress. Elizabeth now returned to Staten Island, temporarily cheered by meeting the actress-manageress Genevieve Ward and seeing on stage Sarah Bernhardt ('memorable') and Lily Langtry ('lovely woman abominable actress'). In the next decade *The Welsh Review* would make a comparison: Mrs Langtry was a 'beauty' but 'Miss Robins is an actress'. When George went to Medford she began negotiating with Barrett and Booth to join their touring company. She travelled to Hartford, Connecticut and talked her way into a successful inter-view with Barrett. But a letter from George prompted her to write in her diary, 'Crisis approaches'. Just under a month later, on 13 June, her husband's body was found in Boston Harbor.

It is impossible to piece together exactly what happened and why during this last month. As in a piece of fiction where heightened gaiety suddenly and fatally turns sour, so Elizabeth's diary records her going to the fair on Staten Island then stops abruptly. Six pages have been torn out, between the end of May and 12 June, marking a period of waiting for news after George's disappearance though the words 'usual shuddering dream' are decipherable. During this time she received a suicide note written on 31 May and deliberately planned to reach her when it was too late. Some of the letter is missing but enough survives to suggest something of the horror and guilt the twenty-four-year-old now had to endure. In his letter George had baldly stated: 'Your love for me is dead.' He had found the last four weeks 'a fearful strain'. His hope that Elizabeth would find some means of getting money and joining him had been dashed. Ironically, papers authorising the mortgaging of Elizabeth's interest on the Stone House arrived too late from her father in Florida to be of any help. Only too aware of his wife's ambitions and his own disillusionment with the theatre, George had also written, 'I will not stand in your light any longer.' He would take his own life that night at midnight. The actor about to make his quietus ended:

> Think the best you can of me. I die loving you if possible more than ever—I die to save you pain and sorrow in the future—may your lines be cast in pleasanter places than in the past four years.
> Good-bye   good-bye
> good-bye
> 　　Yours in death
> 　　George

In what the press dubbed the most consummate acting of his life, he had left his apartment at the Tremont House and chatted casually to George Backus before making his way to a West End bridge from which he had leapt into the Charles river. His disappearance was widely reported by newspapers as was the fact that he had written letters to both his wife and mother. When his decomposed body was discovered by a police patrol boat he became front page news with headlines such as 'The Absorbing Mystery at last Solved'. He had weighed himself down with a suit of theatrical armour attached to a leather belt round his waist. The Boston and Medford papers speculated about the cause, referring to financial problems.[6] It was hinted that his worry over 'Bills, bills, bills; nothing but bills, & here's an end of it' was exacerbated by his having a wife who enjoyed good living. Death by drowning was usually portrayed as the fate of the fallen woman not of the disappointed man. This same wife had been obliged to retire because her health had failed! Elizabeth is virtually unrecognisable in such accounts though it is true that the couple had, in the Boston days, enjoyed oyster dinners at the Parker House and other smart hotels. Suggestions of gambling or drinking were hastily refuted by fellow actors keen to protect their profession. The previous summer George's mother had admitted to Elizabeth her concern about his drinking and his correspondence to his wife had included references to his own recognition of the need to cut down his consumption. The press also mentioned that he had been engaged to an actress Mary Beebe in 1880 and badly affected when she married another man. George had told Elizabeth about this relationship soon after they met but it does not seem to have been of significance at this later date.

A picture was painted of a cheerful, outgoing character which does not square with descriptions in Elizabeth's diary suggesting a much less secure personality, somewhat histrionic and with a capacity for deep depression. In her diary she commented how he would growl, 'I hate people.' Years later in 1912, addressing his spirit, she emphasised how his letters (mostly now destroyed) were full of 'a passionate wish to turn your back on art & on ambition & bury yourself in some place where [there] was greenness & running water & no people'. The irony was that he attracted people yet felt he had no need of them. The one person he did want to be with was neither used to nor able to become as dependent on him as he wished and indeed the role was reversed. In one letter he had written: 'You know how prone I am to look upon the dark side of affairs knowing what a "death in life" it would be to me if you were not with me next season.'

In her most autobiographical and sombre novel, *The Open Question*, which has people, places and philosophies closely modelled on those of her own family, it is said of the hero, Ethan, 'I never knew a fellow so much at ease in the world, who seemed so anxious to be rid of people.'[7] Ethan was a young man from Boston whose recognition of the tragedy of life 'seemed out of all proportion to his possible experience'. The novel is subtitled 'A Tale of Two Temperaments'. Elizabeth's grandmother had described her as an optimist 'always inclined to look on the bright side of life—A Happy temperament'.

George's ideal seems to have been the businessman who could settle down 'with my darling little wife never to leave her again'. As Elizabeth's grandmother had predicted, the idea of uninterrupted domesticity was, however, a far cry from Elizabeth Robins's plans even though in some circles she had become known as Mrs Parks. On a number of occasions the couple had disagreed about woman's ability and from the start George had displayed 'morbid jealousy' and a 'capacity for being bluer than indigo'. He admitted that when separated from Elizabeth he never ceased to think of her with anything but anxious fears. It is conceivable that he thought she was seeing somebody else though neither Elizabeth's diary nor his note suggest this. Elizabeth's other troubles and her care and concern for George make this possibility unlikely though suspicion alone would have been enough to make the situation intolerable for George.

Although his note, Elizabeth's diary and newspaper reports together suggest that financial difficulties precipitated a final dramatic act of desperation by a man who was profoundly pessimistic and lacking in self-confidence (a far cry from the dashing image of the stage actor), it is possible that there were further strains on his personal life which could not be openly articulated in writing. Elizabeth might have become pregnant and had a miscarriage or an abortion. Alternatively she might have had a serious disagreement with George over their having a child. Her relishing of the secretive and later careful camouflaging of expressions of her most personal feelings lest she make herself too transparent and discernible, make it impossible to know for sure.

Many years later she asked herself whether George went away 'because of "people" or because I couldn't tell the truth—shrank from bearing the child'. Given her family's dire warnings and her mother's experience of childbirth, it is possible that she became pregnant but was unable to accept the burden of responsibility involved in becoming a mother. It can surely be no coincidence that not one of the surviving Robins offspring became a parent. Soon after George's death Elizabeth talked to her New York friend Mrs Longstreet, a doctor's wife, about pre-natal recollections and presentiments. She wrote in her diary, 'She thinks I *wish* to disbelieve—how little she knows.' In her later years in Sussex she apparently once described to Marjorie Hubert (who had no children of her own but was a doctor), the physical sensation of carrying a child.[8] Yet this could have been the novelist and actress wanting to understand and wanting to convince. In an interview for the *Book News Monthly* before the First World War Elizabeth apparently told the journalist, 'I have no child of my own alive.' Perhaps she was pregnant at the beginning of 1886 or during the autumn or even at the time of George's disappearance. In one of his surviving letters from the autumn of 1886 he refers to 'my little ones'. And in 1951 the elderly Raymond wrote a somewhat confused letter to Elizabeth (drawing on earlier information about Parks from brothers Saxton and Vernon). Raymond told Elizabeth that Parks, knowing he had lost 'you and his child forever', had preferred death to life without her.

The Open Question (which draws on material in her diaries and letters) is concerned with the right to bear children—within families exhibiting a tendency towards inherited disease, in this case, consumption. The two main characters, first cousins, are seen as victims of intermarriage over generations: 'You each have in you the concentrated essence of a single family's strain.' They exhibit the opposing temperaments of the optimist and pessimist though the heroine Val who as an exuberant girl and young woman has much in common with Elizabeth, increasingly empathises with the very different outlook of Ethan who becomes her husband.

In the mid-1890s Elizabeth made some notes for the book. Here she outlined how her handsome, clever couple would marry and 'take care'. At worst they would have a perfect year. They might even have a lifetime without the one ill they most dreaded. They would make a suicide pact and 'If caught' they would die together before new life was born into the world. Thus nobody would ultimately 'pay'. Elizabeth's tone may have been euphemistic, reflecting a time before the broadening of moral values liberated language, but she nevertheless makes the situation clear. Should personal happiness be sacrificed to duty to the race and does not fear of the latter make the former and, therefore, real choice impossible? In the novel the ending is both tragic and triumphant. In a scene reminiscent of Wagner (Elizabeth visited Bayreuth the year before the book was published) and not wholly unlike the ending of Ibsen's *Rosmersholm*, the couple sail out to sea *together* and face their fate, with Val steering for the sunset to bring them out at the Golden Gate.

The Open Question fuses social Darwinist concerns with a vindication of the right to take one's life in particular circumstances. It can be viewed both as a *fin-de-siècle* retrospective rationalisation of Elizabeth's husband's desperate act and as evidence of her personal concern about consanguinity, reproduction and destiny.[9] Published in 1898 it drew on both personal and public contemporary material at a time of considerable interest in the rates of and reasons for taking one's life. Durkheim's *Du Suicide* had appeared the previous year and Elizabeth had previously heard Felix Adler lecture in New York on the philosophy of suicide. She had read Schopenhauer who believed those who took their lives to be misguided but did appreciate the moral justification for suicide, distinguishing between life and its conditions—the suicide actually willed life but could not tolerate it in its present form. Much closer to home, her friend William Archer defended (in print) suicide as a rational act though he disapproved of Ibsen trivialising Hedda Gabler's action.

The first edition of Elizabeth's book was published under the pseudonym of C.E. Raimond but when the *Daily Chronicle* announced on 10 December 1898 that its author had acted in Ibsen's plays, Elizabeth's identity was revealed. To her intense annoyance critics on both sides of the Atlantic now argued that the subject was prompted by Ibsen. For example, the *Westminster Gazette* referred to her 'deep preposessions, chiefly from Ibsen on the subject of heredity'. Clearly Ibsen's influence should not be minimised but neither should it be exaggerated. After initial revulsion over *Ghosts*, Elizabeth became interested in playing the character of Mrs Alving after hearing about the success of the Paris production. Due to a number of factors, not least her problems with actor–managers, she never did act in the play. She wrote in her diary in 1890: 'It is the kind of thing that fascinates me … it reads like fate, & destiny is the most engrossing of all studies.' This and *The Open Question* use bohemian Parisian life as a symbol for decadent and degenerative influences. Paris was also seen by contemporaries as the city most closely associated with suicide. Michael Meyer has pointed out that the real concern of the play is with 'the devitalising effects of inherited convention' rather than syphilis.[10] So too the questions raised by Elizabeth's book range far beyond consideration of the frightening effects of tuberculosis in the family and demonstrate our ultimate inability to lay the ghosts of the past and free ourselves entirely from ideas and beliefs we have inherited.

Critics who felt Elizabeth's subject to be derivative were also making connections with *Hedda Gabler* since in England her name had become indelibly linked with acting in that play. Her book showed how, despite Judge Brack's final line (previously anticipated by Krogstad in *A Doll's House*), people *can* 'do such things'. In a lecture on Ibsen in 1928 Elizabeth drew attention to the dramatist's perspicacity, his understanding 'that a good many women have found it possible to get through life by help of the knowledge that they have the power to end it rather than accept certain slaveries'.[11] She viewed Hedda's 'power of escape' as a governing factor in her outlook. In *The Open Question* the question is posed: 'How shall any of us justify the desperate clinging to life for the mere sake of living?'[12]

For Ethan, from the day that he realised 'that life was voluntary, it became sweet'.[13] The courage to live is to be found by first assuring ourselves of the courage to die. One theatre historian has suggested that Elizabeth's posture as Hedda taking her life demonstrates the character's triumph.[14] Time and again Elizabeth would speak of Hedda's courage. Her admirers and detractors could never know how important it had become to her to validate the act of suicide and come to terms with her own relationship to life and death and the way that suicide as a possible choice and solution helped to keep her going. When faced with worries about her personal life Elizabeth would write: 'I am *free* I can come and go I even have the right to die and no man is my master.' Neither could the public appreciate that she had been grappling with such issues before she acted in Ibsen's plays. Moreover Elizabeth was critical of those who interpreted her message as 'an indication of the duty of suicide'. As she pointed out to W.T. Stead, pulsing through the book was also an emphasis on life.[15]

Independently of Ibsen, a number of other literary influences helped shape this novel, both conscious and less conscious, recent and more remote, and reviled and revered for the modern reader. They range from George Eliot to Nietzsche and the English eugenicists. Soon after George's death Elizabeth read *Aurora Leigh*, the long prose poem by Elizabeth Barrett Browning. In *The Open Question* Val's aunt Valeria (first names are also passed on between generations) reads this poem about the two cousins who eventually marry. Romney was always 'looking for the worms, I for the gods' explains Aurora whose strength and intellectual power grow as the story develops and Romney is physically weakened.[16]

The books mentioned in this novel have been carefully chosen: towards the end Val reads *La Dame aux Camélias* with its fated consumptive heroine. In her production of *Hedda Gabler* Elizabeth had the eponymous 'heroine' read a French novel. Elizabeth had read in 1890 the journal of Marie Bashkirtseff which revealed the 'drama of a woman's soul'. The author was denounced by some as the 'very antithesis of a true woman', and Shaw would refer to a third or Bashkirtseff sex.[17] This frank account of a young Ukrainian woman experiencing love and art in Paris (like Val she originally wanted to be a singer) was especially poignant since Marie died aged twenty-four from consumption diagnosed when she was sixteen. The journal, like Elizabeth's own, confronts the conflicts facing ambitious women and Elizabeth was astounded how 'being so radically different we should yet be so alike in many things'. Something of its spirit is injected into the character of Val. The story and ideas of *The Open Question* are, however, most clearly informed by the tragedy of 1887, something of which her critics were unaware. Shaw wrote to warn her: 'Beware, beware, beware, beware, BEWARE. All this undertakers' philosophy that you call "The Open Question" is nothing but fright. What has frightened you?'

After George's body was found, Elizabeth veered between 'a sort of twilight of semi-consciousness' and a 'dry-eyed agony'. He was buried in an unmarked family plot with her little sister and brother, Amy and Edward, at St Andrew's Church, Richmond on Staten Island. George's brother-in-law Dr Eaton who had married Emily Parks denied Elizabeth her wish to have her husband's papers and books. George's family appear to have blamed her for the tragedy and connections between them now ceased (though some years later Elizabeth did receive a letter begging for financial help).

From now on she would remember anniversaries with great tenderness. George had become 'the one Matchless Man'. She read and reread her husband's letters and wrote in her diary that few women had been so loved, adding: 'I must prove that love is *deathless* & that union in *spirit* is true marriage.' She excised the pain as far as possible, recalling happy hours burning joss sticks together, his presents of violets and lilies, and nearly nine years after his death she wrote: 'he walks my world with smiling face—the sun still shines in his eyes.' She had thus rewritten her script to accommodate her need to develop her own present and future and the desperately unhappy man had been transformed into a gentler memory. When Elizabeth finally took possession of her own home, she consecrated it by burning and burying his letters (though not his final anguished note) under the fir tree where she had planted white violets.

Long before this she had to learn to face again her career. On her twenty-fifth birthday she began studying *Macbeth* for her new position with Barrett and Booth, America's most celebrated Shakespearean actors. She had previously acted with Booth in Boston (for example as Jessica, in *The Merchant of Venice*) and now joined their ocean-to-ocean tour. Rehearsals began in Buffalo early in September 1887. There followed one 'night stand' after another. This tour marked a turning point in Elizabeth's life. It was her last American tour. During this time she wrote her first fiction with an eye to publication. It gave her material for her first published article, 'Across America with Junius Brutus Booth' (the 'VIP' pullman car or carriage named in honour of Edwin Booth's father). Elizabeth's account of this winter and spring touring appeared in *The Universal Review* in July 1890 under her own name.[18] She was paid £7 for her seventeen pages of text and photographs, opening her article with a seventeen-line sentence which captured something of this breathless railroad chase around America. It described places rather than plays, reading like an itinerary of the American south. It also told how the great actors regaled the chosen few with stories of the stage in their luxury carriage. Both men were past the height of their success. Booth had suffered for years as the brother of Abraham Lincoln's assassin. He had made his professional debut in 1849 at the Boston Museum, where Barrett was also to work.

Some parts of the tour were tougher than others. Elizabeth had to face Boston in December: 'G. seems all about the place' she wrote. Yet although there are numerous references to him in her diary, much of the time she was absorbed in packing and unpacking her trunk, performing, savouring the south and experiencing a luxury of travel she had never known with O'Neill. She gave 258 performances in seventy-two venues and could now boast that she had been to the capital of every state and to every sizeable town in the Union. She travelled 30,000 miles (48,000 km) from Canada to the Gulf of Mexico and from the Atlantic seaboard to the Pacific. Her final performance was in *The Merchant of Venice* in San Francisco. Afterwards she visited her cousin Lloyd Tevis and stayed with her old Boston friends, the Cutters, in Oakland. She decided 'to go it blind' and return east by ship via Panama. She arrived back in New York at the beginning of May 1888.

In an attempt to get her away, Elizabeth's friend Mrs Bull proposed that she accompany her to Norway. Sara Bull was the American widow of the noted Norwegian violinist and nationalist Ole Bull, who had died in 1880. He had been Norway's foremost exponent of Romanticism but had also toured all over Europe for many years and founded and seen flounder an experimental socialist community in Pennsylvania called Oleana. Sara had been his second wife, forty years younger than her husband, the daughter of a wealthy Wisconsin senator (and sister-in-law to Longfellow's daughter). She too was musical and had accompanied Ole on the piano. In the 1880s she held musical At Homes at her Cambridge, Massachusetts house, Elmwood (formerly James Lowell's home). Lawrence Barrett was one of many personalities who attended. Elizabeth knew Sara by 1886 and may well have first met her through her New York friends such as Mrs Longstreet. They shared with Sara an interest in spiritualism. Sara was also interested in writing and had written about her late husband.

In order to help preserve her teenage daughter's memory of Norway, summers were spent on the 175 acre (31.5 hectare) island of Lysøen (meaning 'Island of Light'), about 18½ miles (30 km) south of Bergen, purchased by Bull in 1872. In return for helping direct Olea's reading Elizabeth would receive $300 expenses along with bracing air, fjords and 'a feeling that you are out of the world'. As an added incentive, Sara mentioned that they would travel via England and a friend in London could help Elizabeth with her profession.

On 30 June Elizabeth, Sara, Olea and a college friend Hetta Hervey sailed from east Boston on the SS *Cephalonia*. On board they got to know a Mrs Meteyard, steeped in Dante and writing a book about medieval glass. Not being in time for the weekly boat from Hull Elizabeth travelled from Liverpool to London where she spent a week visiting galleries and seeing plays with Mrs Meteyard and her son Tom. She then rejoined her travelling companions for Norway and they caught the steamer to Bergen. Edvard Bull (Ole's brother) met them with his 'quiet old wife' a former actress and together they sailed down the fjords to Lysøen. In her youth the latter had helped create some of the original Ibsenite roles at the Norwegian Theatre in Bergen founded by Ole Bull. Ibsen had worked there for six years as a stage instructor and dramatic author and put on his early plays.

Elizabeth thus got to know a tiny Norwegian island before she became familiar with Ibsen's plays. He once wrote: 'Anyone who wishes to understand me fully must know Norway.'[19] Lysøen was also the site of her first acquaintance of any length with Europe (though she never returned to the island or country in later years). The journey to the island was magical, 'like a dream floating into fairy harbors & seeing shores that fade with day': The villa was (and is) a wonderful piece of fantasy. With its onion dome and elaborate trelliswork it is known locally as the '*lille* Alhambra'. Yet it is built and carved entirely out of Norwegian pine. Its centrepiece is its elaborate music hall replete with Bull's European treasures. Here Elizabeth found two pianos, an organ and Olea's guitars. She began reading Norwegian history and studying the language and literature, buying Björnson's *Stöv*. She helped Olea in her studies though her chief legacy may well have been imparting a love of acting since soon after this Olea became an avid amateur actress.[20] Elizabeth also walked in the woods, following carefully laid paths, and made an excursion to the Hardanger fjord. Like her predecessor Mary Wollstonecraft she carefully noted the customs of the Norwegian countryside.

Now she could write: 'I am perhaps coming out of "the valley" but "the shadow" is still heavy over me.' Leaving Norway at the beginning of September was difficult, though kindly 'Uncle Edvard' gave her one of his paintings of the Lysøen woods as a memento. On 3 September 1888 Elizabeth Robins arrived back in London. Soon, somewhat unexpectedly, began the most illustrious stage of her career.

PART II

LISA OF THE BLUE EYES

3

IBSEN & THE ACTRESS

London was not awaiting the American actress. Elizabeth, who had worked so hard in the United States and had starred with Barrett and Booth, was an unknown in Britain. She was anyway in transit. During her first week in the country she had been offered a part in Daly's forthcoming New York production and had accepted by post from Norway. So her return to England was supposed to be for a few days *en route* home until her boat sailed. In practice it lasted for the rest of her long life.

The impetus to stay had been partly provided by that first week in the capital before the Norwegian trip. Renting a room for 3*s* 6*d* (17½p) a day in the London house of a Boston poet and socialite, Mrs Louise Chandler Moulton (a friend of Mrs Bull's), Elizabeth had been propelled into a succession of At Homes. At Lady Seton's she encountered a tall, somewhat fleshy figure, 'the man who, all unconsciously, was to give me England for my home'. He was Oscar Wilde, then at the height of his success. More valued than his wit was his encouragement: 'I could do nothing for him; he could & did do everything in his power for me' was her somewhat overgenerous retrospective comment on Wilde's contribution to her early years in London. Through Wilde, Elizabeth did gain an agent (Harrington Baily) and a solicitor who became a friend (Sir George Lewis). Once Wilde realised that she was not just one more wealthy American who could stage her own matinée, he guided her movements and proffered advice. Yet he did not really devote much energy to her

career and indeed his casual dismissal of some of her plans was not
necessarily for the best.[1]

Their paths crossed on a number of occasions. Wilde had met
one of her Crow relations in America. Elizabeth would later write
a play about the Renaissance sculptor and goldsmith Benvenuto
Cellini. Wilde had lectured in the early 1880s in Leadville, Colorado
on the aesthetics of Cellini. The young Elizabeth had stayed at a
mining camp in Colorado and her brother Raymond later worked
in the silver mines at Leadville. Wilde's cousin Mrs Cashel Hoey
generously lent Elizabeth money when her finances were low and
Wilde helped raise subscriptions for Elizabeth's Ibsen productions,
describing her as a 'brilliant & subtle' artist though they met only
infrequently in the 1890s. After his trial Elizabeth wrote an (unpublished)
appreciation of him.[2]

Back in September 1888 Wilde had introduced her to Herbert
Beerbohm Tree, actor-manager at the Haymarket. Tree's riveting
performance in *Captain Swift* and encouraging noises about the possibility of parts, persuaded Elizabeth to postpone her passage home
and eventually abandon it altogether.

She had joined the Meteyards in lodgings at 10, Duchess Street,
Portland Place. Together they saw the sights. The Meteyards' artistic
leanings resulted in her meeting Holman Hunt and visiting Dulwich
Picture Gallery. Not surprisingly, she was impressed by Sir Joshua
Reynolds's immense portrait there of 'Mrs Siddons as the Tragic
Muse' (taken from Isaiah's pose in the Sistine Chapel ceiling). She
explored what she could find and imagine from Chaucer's and
Shakespeare's London, became only too familiar with London fogs
and spent most of her time innocently hoping that Tree's promises
would materialise into parts.

Sedulously cultivating connections though she was, there were
nevertheless moments when the situation seemed hopeless and she
would begin repacking her trunk. One such occasion came after her
first meeting with her agent, 'I depart feeling there is no place for me
in this London world & almost doubt if I'm needed *anywhere*', but
an encouraging word from Tree, that master of prevarication, revived
her spirits. Initially Elizabeth believed British dramatists and actor-
managers to be more approachable than their American counterparts
but experience of the system in London soon made her criticise

the predomination of pecuniary interests and deplore the actor-managers' tendency to select only those plays which gave themselves the best parts, denying talented actresses openings based on ability. She became their *bête noire*, known for her determination to secure flexible contracts: 'the better actor-managers find my point of view & my active policy antagonistic—the ineffective ones I loathe having converse with.' When elderly she wrote: 'What was wanted of the women of the stage was, first and mainly, what was wanted of women outside—a knack of pleasing.'[3] Yet her diary of the late 1880s shows her only too well aware then of the constraints under which women laboured. In an early unpublished novel, 'The Coming Woman', she wrote, 'The world of to-day would forget what autocracy was but for the Czar, the censor of plays and the actor-manager; but the greatest of these is the actor-manager.' Her initial reverence for Irving was soon dispelled when he calmly told her: 'Women have an easy road to travel on the stage. They have but to *appear* and their sweet feminine charm wins the battle.'

There had been a number of improvements in the English stage in recent years. For example, the old composite programmes now tended to be replaced by one play, the interiors of many theatres had been modernised and audiences were less rowdy. Yet, as in America, performers still faced many hurdles.[4] For a start there were too many after too few jobs: there was a 44 per cent increase in the number of actresses between 1851 and 1871. The debut Elizabeth so desperately needed came about not through an actor-manager but via the women in the profession. It was her countrywoman Eleanor Calhoun (also helped by Lloyd Tevis in the past) who suggested that Elizabeth contact Mrs Beringer who was casting her new play *Tares*. This entailed a day-trip to Bath. Being a hopeless early riser Elizabeth was soon wishing that 'Bath & Beringer were at the bottom of the sea'. But Mrs Beringer and Mrs Kendal engaged her for the 'sugar-coated' *Little Lord Fauntleroy*. (See Appendix 1 for details of Elizabeth's British stage appearances.) She played the widowed Mrs Errol on Saturday afternoons when she replaced Mary Rorke for £2 10s. (£2.50) a week. The night before beginning she 'slept little, quivering with excitement' and 'I pray for help as I never did before'.

Never was a debut 'so unmarked by any public sign' commented Elizabeth on her first appearance at the Opéra Comique in the

Strand on 17 January 1889. The only notice erroneously called her
Miss Rivers. It must have been especially chastening for such an
experienced actress even though her stage experience had been
gained thousands of miles away. It was belatedly explained that she
should have alerted the critics herself. This was done and the *Era*
rewarded her with a few lines: 'She possesses a sweet individualism, a
refinement of manner, and a delicacy of style.'[5] The weekly performance lasted only until early April when the drooping fortunes of the
play led to the better-known Marion Terry (sister of Ellen) replacing
Elizabeth at only one week's notice.

Before this she had appeared in a semi-private matinée at St
George's Hall on 20 October 1888 in William Poel's comedietta
Cheiromancy which he dismissed as a 'shallow little part in the shallow
little play'. Although Tom Robertson's dramas briefly challenged the
staple diet of predictable farces and melodrama, realism was sadly
lacking on the British stage.

Elizabeth had also acted in a Frank Benson production of *The
Merchant of Venice* in Exeter, playing Portia. This was her only
Shakespearean role on the English stage (though she did briefly
replace Genevieve Ward in *Coriolanus* in Scotland in 1899) and it
was well away from London where Ellen Terry reigned supreme as
the Shakespearean heroine.

She visited the legendary Miss Terry, ostensibly to interview her
for an American magazine but left both charmed and convinced that
the tables had been turned and that Ellen Terry now knew much
more about Elizabeth Robins than vice versa. The article never saw
the light of day. The occasion is, however, recorded in *Both Sides of
the Curtain*.[6] There is a virtually identical account in the 1890 diary,
an example of the way in which Elizabeth was increasingly and
consciously fashioning her diary-writing with an eye on journalism
and novels as the precariousness of depending solely on the stage for
an income became more apparent. Walking to Charing Cross to save
twopence, she wrote: 'Ah will the time ever come when I need not
count the *pennies* so closely?' It was not just the expense of living in
London without a guaranteed regular wage. There was also the need
to send money to her increasingly impecunious relatives.

Fortunately the dramatist Pinero had seen Elizabeth as Mrs Errol
and after she wrote to him, he secured her an understudy role in his

play *The Profligate*, the opening production for the splendid brand-new Garrick Theatre. A somewhat melodramatic but serious study of the effects of seduction, the cast included Johnston Forbes-Robertson, Lewis Waller, Kate Rorke and 'brilliant and most short-tempered of stage-managers', John Hare. Elizabeth understudied two actresses but never got to play the better part of the seduced woman since Olga Nethersole had an infuriating habit of falling ill but recovering just in time for the performance. Elizabeth felt the understudy's job to be 'the most thankless of all'. She was not always alerted to last-minute script changes and might continue studying lines that had been abandoned. Equally frustrating were drawing-room performances. After doing one for the Bass brewery family she wrote: 'I have a sensation that this dressing up & affecting passion for the amusement of a lot of stupid people is unworthy.'

The six-month stint at the Garrick was followed by another unrewarding position understudying Mrs Tree (Maud Holt) and Julia Neilson at the Haymarket in *A Man's Shadow*. In the meantime Elizabeth supplemented her income by fitting in other parts (something actor-managers never liked). The American Genevieve Ward, the first woman to be rewarded in Britain for her services to the stage—she became a DBE in 1921—was a good ally. She urged Elizabeth to take Bovril to build up her strength and secured her the part of Alice in a few matinées, reviving her own acclaimed *Forget-Me-Not*. Elizabeth fared slightly better in another production (for three afternoons in November) when she played the somnambulist lead in Dr Dabbs's *Her Own Witness* at the Criterion. During the first half of 1890 she was engaged at the Royal Avenue Theatre managed by George Alexander. She understudied Fanny Brough and had a small part in Hamilton Aidé's *Dr Bill* (adapted from a French farce). Elizabeth and Alexander parted in acrimony. He filed a legal complaint against her and threatened never to have her in his theatre again. Her lack of total dedication to his production alone, her continued friendship with his rival Tree and Alexander's belief that he could tell her exactly what to do had proved to be a recipe for disaster. Yet she did work with him once more—in one of her final stage roles. But by then Elizabeth Robins was famous.

In 1890 Elizabeth had found a lot to complain about: understudying, drawing-room performances and second-rate plays all seemed to suggest that her career was going backwards rather than forwards. Yet she could not have predicted that in a few months she would become one of the leading serious actresses in England, involved in acting and producing the work of a playwright who would eventually be revered as one of the greatest writers in the history of the European stage. This playwright, Henrik Ibsen, hailed from Norway, little-known to most outside Scandinavia yet the one European country in which Elizabeth had spent some time before settling in England. Ibsen's plays gave her the chance to show her acting talent and to help further the cause of serious European drama on the British stage. Her transition from an unknown into a 'star' was largely made possible by the fact that, although new to the English stage, she was of course far from a stranger to stagecraft. Her years of experience in America at last told in her favour. She was also fortunate in her timing, being in England when decent translations of Ibsen became available and his plays began to be staged.

William Archer's Ibsen translation, *Quicksands or The Pillars of Society*, had been produced as early as 1880. It had not created a stir but in 1889 the production of *A Doll's House* did just that. Five years earlier London had seen *Breaking A Butterfly*, very loosely based on Ibsen's play and in 1886 *A Doll's House* received a private reading. But it was the pioneering Charrington production of 1889 with Janet Achurch as Nora that marked the first unadapted production in Britain and a seminal experience for Elizabeth and the stage. As George Bernard Shaw put it, 'In 1889 the London stage had come into shattering collision with the Norwegian giant, Ibsen.'[7]

It was on 18 June that Elizabeth saw the play, accompanied by a young Philadelphian actress, Marion Lea, whom it also inspired. Elizabeth's diary did not elaborate on the production's merits, merely calling it a 'Remarkable play'. In later years, with the benefit of hindsight she would recall how the radical message, style and technique made it 'less like a play than like a personal meeting—with people and issues that seized us and held us, and wouldn't let us go'.[8] The seasoned actress viewed this production with its little-known cast and simple set as 'not only the most thrilling, it was the most satisfyingly *done* modern play I had ever seen'.[9]

A Doll's House also marked an important step in the representation of women by dramatists. Despite the emphasis by Ibsen himself and others since, that the theme of the play (written in 1879) is how the individual strives for personal understanding rather than a treatise on women's rights, the timing of the English production turned it into something more. It coincided with an upsurge of interest in the subject and an enhanced awareness of the need to declare oneself for or against women's rights. In the same year an influential anti-suffrage petition was published in the journal *The Nineteenth Century*. The early 1880s had seen further reform in married women's property rights and Ibsen's focus on the institution of marriage was especially pertinent. In 1888 over 27,000 people responded to the *Daily Telegraph* on the issue of 'Is Marriage A Failure?', prompted by the novelist Mona Caird's article in the *Westminster Review* which had argued that marriage depended on the economic subordination of the wife and restricted the freedom of both sexes.[10] Meanwhile between 1885 and 1889 the progressive Men and Women's Club in London debated issues such as free sexual unions and discussed Ibsen's work.[11] Since women like Elizabeth were only too used to playing melodramatic roles, the creation of believable, modern, intelligent women on stage who were not simplified stereotypes was in itself a breakthrough. As Elizabeth put it, 'we owe it to Ibsen that the world was effectually familiarised with the fact that woman's soul no less than her brother's is the battleground of good and evil'.[12]

The ending of the play has become a kind of shorthand for a turning point in attitudes. A late twentieth-century BBC television series and book on the history of the women's movement is entitled *Out of the Doll's House*.[13] Yet Nora's slamming—rather than merely shutting—of the door did not, as Shaw and others liked to think, mean the total abandonment of older Victorian values on the stage or elsewhere. Not only has it been argued that Nora still harboured romantic illusions on leaving but, more significantly, women met severe resistance to constitutional claims in the 1890s. Although many of the so-called 'New Woman' plays by British male dramatists centred around struggles for sexual freedom, as Julie Holledge suggests, they tended to present woman's greatest tragedy as growing old and unattractive to men.[14] It is perhaps significant that the German productions of *A Doll's House* in which the ending was changed and Nora forced back into the home, have been presumed to be synonymous with a happy ending whereas Ibsen's original published ending has been viewed through the eyes of the male critics and prism of familial consequences as a tragedy.

On 27 January 1891, Elizabeth acted in a matinée of *A Doll's House*. It was not, however, her first Ibsen part. In July 1889, just over a month after seeing this play, she had taken part in a benefit performance of *The Pillars of Society*, Ibsen's study of hypocritical respectability and questionable community loyalty. Elizabeth was Martha Bernick. A relatively small part (in a large cast of nineteen which included Genevieve Ward as the Americanised Lona Hessel), it nevertheless enabled her to show how a woman might appear long-suffering but possess a depth of imagination and awareness of the narrowness of convention which few suspected. The play also hinted at how women might ultimately help each other in much more positive ways than via the sewing circle. The extent to which this production (on 17 July at the Opéra Comique) was *not* perceived as path-breaking is indicated by the fact that the same programme included Mrs Kendall's 'full-bodied recitation' of G.R. Sims's 'Ostler Joe' and Antoinette Sterling's rendition of a ballad. But the critic William Archer had noted that 'the unaffected charm of Miss Robins's performance was quite memorable'.[15]

The London matinée revival of *A Doll's House* was organised by Marie Fraser who had played Nora in the provinces. Marion Lea's wish came true and she was Nora with Elizabeth as the widowed Mrs Linden, a woman who, like Elizabeth herself, had dutifully cared for her mother and brothers and was now on her own. Christine Linden had been too self-sacrificing for her own good but was capable of change and could teach Nora something. The influential critic Clement Scott deplored the atmosphere of the play—'it is all self, self, self!'—but now and later, was prepared to praise Elizabeth's acting. In her scene with Krogstad he felt that she

> touched the keynote of genius. It was that acting—so rare!—that appeals so strongly to the sensibility that the actress has her audi- ence at her mercy. It was worth sitting out hours of Ibsen to get a natural touch like that.[16]

Here was recognition of a different order from that of her English debut.

By this time Antoine of the Théâtre Libre, famed for its new naturalistic acting, had produced *Ghosts* in Paris. Encouraged by the Norwegian vice-consul H.L. Braekstad (who proposed establishing an Ibsen Fund to produce the play), Elizabeth was keen to play Mrs Alving. To discuss these plans she contacted William Archer, the eminent theatre critic and translator of Ibsen's plays into English. Impressed by her interpretation of the role of Martha Bernick, Archer obliged and on 10 June 1890 they met for the first time at Gatti's vegetarian restaurant in the Strand (with Elizabeth's dresser Becky) to discuss this risqué play. Archer was supportive but realistic: 'Do you know, Miss Robins, you are treading on dangerous ground? Do you know there are many good people who foam at the mouth when Ibsen is mentioned!'

The spring of 1891 has been called 'perhaps the most momentous period in the history of the modern British theatre'.[17] In February Florence Farr appeared in a single and not very well-reviewed production of *Rosmersholm* at the Vaudeville. March saw the staging of *Ghosts* by the Independent Theatre. It had been refused a licence for public performance and prompted an unprecedented wave of revulsion and protest. Elizabeth did not act in it. She did, however, play the leading role in the Ibsen play of the following month and proved the truth in Archer's warning. She was Hedda Gabler, the character (a term she preferred to 'role' when describing Ibsen's creations) with whom she became most closely associated. The women who take on the egoistical General Gabler's daughter tend to become identified in popular imagination with the character they portray. For example, when Juliet Stevenson played Hedda at London's National Theatre in 1989, one journalist described how his interviewee 'paced and paced about the set … when the words came … They sounded like Hedda Gabler's'.[18] It was emphasised in the press that Ms Stevenson was a brigadier's daughter.

Elizabeth once wrote, 'I came to think of my early life as divisible into two parts: "before or after Hedda"'. She had already witnessed more dramatic changes in her twenty-eight years than many do in an entire lifetime but Hedda truly represented a watershed not least because it was at this juncture that she ceased to be solely involved in the acting side of the stage. With Marion Lea she now undertook joint management (something most actor-managers they had encountered would never have contemplated for themselves). Although American, Marion had studied at the Margate Academy founded by Sarah Thorne of the Margate Theatre Royal. The decision to work together not only helped them as individuals but it also, as Joanne Gates has argued, 'may be credited with changing the course of English drama'.[19]

At first they hoped to find a theatre to stage Ibsen's *The Lady from the Sea* (in which Elizabeth never acted) but, spurned by commercial managers, they resolved to go it alone: 'We raged, dreamed, & then more or less awake began to consider ways and means.' Having begun by talking about management 'as we might have talked about going to the moon' they soon acquired the requisite audacity, cheered by news that Ibsen's new play had a woman's name for its title and two good female parts. They determined to execute *Hedda Gabler* themselves.

The story of the translation and acting rights is convoluted.[20] The ambitious young publisher William Heinemann had offered Ibsen £150 for the publishing rights of *Hedda Gabler*. As a result of the recent international copyright law, Heinemann could, by publishing a few copies of the Norwegian text in Britain, acquire not only first publication rights but also exclusive English rights. Archer, who was known and liked by Ibsen, was thereby unable to publish his promised translation for the Walter Scott Prose Drama series to which he was contributing, since the other major translator of Ibsen into English, Edmund Gosse, had been commissioned by Heinemann. When the latter's translation appeared, Archer rubbished it in the press. Yet the two were reconciled and both got their translations. This came about through Archer's connivance with Elizabeth and Marion.

Particularly worrying for the two women was the realisation that Heinemann had also secured the acting rights. The journalist Justin McCarthy had agreed to stage the play. To make matters worse, McCarthy, and even Archer, had in mind an actress like Mrs Langtry for Hedda, something which made Elizabeth temporarily revise her high opinion of Archer. Determined to succeed, the actresses raised a loan of £300 from Marion's half-sister using Elizabeth's Colorado gold (a wedding present from her father) and Marion's gold bracelet as securities, a detail the press loved. Seeing that they were in earnest and recognising a means by which he might get his translation after all, Archer now blithely proposed that they ask Heinemann for the right to produce the play using Gosse's version but with some necessary modifications for the production. They would, of course, omit any reference to Archer being involved, 'do nothing to show that it is *not Gosse's* translation' and even advertise his name on the playbill.

Archer would, in effect, make his own translation. As Elizabeth observed, 'It was the prelude to an amount of secret diplomacy worthy of a major political crisis.' The English translation was actually 'in great part rewritten not once but several times by three hands, Marion's, mine and mainly, though unofficially, William Archer's'. Marion and Elizabeth worked at their own copies (Heinemann obligingly supplied two sets of page proofs). They then compared notes and consulted with Archer. There was 'plenty of argument and some irreconcilable disagreement'. Elizabeth recalled also the excitement the play produced, 'We read with jeers, we rolled with irreverent laughter; then brought up short by a thrust at our vitals from the Ibsen rapier, blinked, stared at each other and ended in a state of demoralized excitement'. Having won over Heinemann, Archer was now also going ahead with his written translation for the published series. He recognised the value of collaboration and was showing Elizabeth this work.

The women were clearly playing a crucial role in turning the script into acceptable spoken English for the stage. One of the striking features of Ibsen's work is the extent to which his characters speak everyday colloquial speech. This in itself made his plays unappealing to traditionalists who felt that Art and Romance were being sacrificed to mundane contemporary dialogue. Elizabeth's knowledge of Norwegian would have helped the enterprise though it is impossible to ascertain exactly how proficient she was at this stage. In a note after the play had opened, Archer had written the common Norwegian expression '*Tak for sidst* [Thanks for last time]' and added 'does your Norwegian go so far as that?' which hardly suggests competence. Yet she was an able linguist and had spent a summer in Norway. Certainly by the following year there is evidence of her ability to translate. She translated at least some of Björnson's *Stöv, Mors Haender* and *Magnhild* for Heinemann. On finishing the last she sent it to her friend Florence Bell in the hope that 'you'll *pepper* it with a few commas'. Florence may well have helped with more than grammar.

Archer was certainly involved in such translations. In another letter to Florence Elizabeth explained that she was in the midst of reading more Björnson but wouldn't translate it 'for it only means that Archer has to do all the difficult bits over again & I don't like asking him'. A diary entry also shows her working on *Mary Stuart in Scotland*, another play by Ibsen's contemporary and sparring-partner, Björnson.

The text of *Hedda Gabler* was ready by mid-March. It won Gosse's approval.[21] Indeed, in print he dismissed the changes as 'a few highly judicious alterations, with the entire approbation of the translator made for working purposes and to avoid the crudity of the original'. Not only was he minimising the extent of the alterations but he was also ignorant of the part played by his erstwhile traducer, the wily Archer, and the tireless negotiations by Elizabeth and Marion. The women got three years of acting rights from Heinemann (fortunately McCarthy had never started his project). This cloak and dagger drama had involved 'kid-glove' handling but had paid off. The official translator may have played down his alterations, not wanting to attribute too much to the American women, but the translation used for the production of *Hedda Gabler* and, it would seem, to a certain extent, Archer's own printed translation, owed more than history has until recently acknowledged, to the aid given by Elizabeth Robins and Marion Lea.

From the start Marion had visualised Elizabeth as Hedda and herself as Mrs Elvsted. Archer suggested Scott Buist for Tesman. Arthur Elwood played Lovborg and Charles Sugden was Judge Brack. For total immersion in the play Elizabeth and Marion retired to a cottage on Richmond Hill. Elizabeth (in her twenty-ninth year like the character she was to play) explained how she came 'closer & closer till I had Hedda in my bones'. She persuaded the Examiner of Plays (censor) E.F.S. Pigott to grant a licence though he couldn't resist adding that all the characters looked as though they had escaped from a lunatic asylum. They rented the Vaudeville. Known as an 'unlucky' theatre it was cheaper than many but seated over 700. The experienced George Foss became stage-manager with the task of obtaining an extant set and props. Fortunately for pioneers in 'fringe' theatre, the action of Ibsen's plays was frequently restricted to one room inside one home thus reducing costs. Elizabeth wore a gown of 'serpent green' at the start but made her final exit in a black evening dress. The feather boa she wore became the fashion of the season, a fitting symbol of *fin-de-siècle* decadence. Stage directions were carefully studied. As Postlewait has pointed out, Ibsen was one of the first dramatists to supply very specific information on staging and the actresses and Archer followed this carefully.[22] A prompt book was prepared and advance publicity secured.

A prompt book cannot be an exact guide to how a play was actually performed. We cannot tell whether specific instructions were implemented. Productions of any sort will anyway change from performance to performance, neither can we ever retrospectively 'read' an audience as a collective entity. Nevertheless, a prompt book can give us vital clues about the *intentions* of those who prepare it. And Elizabeth's prompt book shows her understanding of how guilt enables evasive and euphemistic speech. Michael Meyer sees Ibsen's use of double-density dialogue as one of his great achievements.[23] For actors used to direct, often wordy, expositions, it must have been difficult to adapt to the need to explore the psychology of a character and the essential subtle reading of the subtext and then convey this to an audience equally unfamiliar with such an approach. Mary Gay Gibson Cima has shown how Ibsen's plays prompted the development of an introspective gesture, known as the autistic gesture.[24] Elizabeth's prompt book shows how she used facial expressions and her hands, and modulated her voice to help the audience interpret a complex character like Hedda who might say one thing and mean quite another. Hedda was herself a consummate actress and the audience had to be helped to appreciate this. The actress Stella Campbell (Mrs Pat) argued that the peculiar quality of Elizabeth's dramatic gift lay in the 'swiftness with which she succeeded in sending *thought* across the footlights'.[25]

What impressed Elizabeth as she began studying Ibsen's work in detail was the extent to which he colluded in all of this, helping her task. He subtly collaborated with the sensitive actor, enabling her or him to pick up his clues and so express the character's emotions. In *Ibsen & the Actress* (in itself a significant title as Jane Marcus has observed), she wrote how, much more than others, he 'comes to the rescue of the actor', never deserting you as long as you trust him.[26] Although notoriously uninvolved with the productions of his later prose plays, Ibsen had learned all aspects of stagecraft as a young man in the theatres of Bergen and Christiania (Oslo). Even though stage conditions in Norway in mid-century were somewhat archaic, Ibsen had been visually imaginative and gained vital experience which informs his playwriting.[27]

He was uninterested in the grand soliloquies which actor-managers so assiduously cultivated. His plays required instead ensemble playing. This and his focus on family and home, in a manner which totally subverted the usual domestic dramas, confused both on and off the stage and often depressed spectators who expected high drama only in high places and for drawing-rooms to produce formulaic farces. To make matters worse, much of the action of his plays lay outside the drama on the stage. It was essentially retrospective. Ibsen intervened, as it were, when the past had already appeared to seal the fate of the protagonists. The past continually impinges on the present and the present can only be understood and renegotiated in the light of the past. Audiences familiar with clear narratives and the unfolding of dramatic sequential events or neat 'cup and saucer' dramas who now watched an opening scene of an Ibsen play might be forgiven for presuming they had walked in after the interval. A lot had to be explained concisely, requiring audiences to concentrate hard especially since Ibsen's concern was with the *inner* life of the characters. Elizabeth felt them to be much more than stage figures—he worked himself 'into their beings'. He may not have aided his audience but he helped the sensitive actor.[28]

Yet, for those theatregoers (with an able cast and production) who were prepared to make an effort, it could be very rewarding. These late Victorian productions of Ibsen helped change not just the stage but also the commitment of the playgoer. Elizabeth took her audience seriously. Taking advice from a man in the audience, she never appeared again for a curtain call after the premiere of *Hedda Gabler*, thus adding to the realism of Hedda's final act. In an article in *The Times* in 1928 Elizabeth credited Ibsen with bringing intelligent people back to the theatre.[29] In the main Ibsen was performed at matinées with a high attendance of women, many of whom felt they could identify with the stage figures.

The Robins-Lea Joint Management held a fortnight of rehearsals. To help the actors achieve as natural an effect as possible, William

Archer attended daily. It paid off: 'No posing, no ranting, no trickery, all rigidly and intensely natural' declared the *Lady's Pictorial*.[30] The first matinée took place on 20 April before a galaxy of artistic figures including Hardy, Kipling, George Meredith and Henry James. James's influential essay 'On the Occasion of *Hedda Gabler*', written after watching three performances, finally acknowledged his full conversion to Ibsen and proved an influential weapon in counteracting opposition. Eleanor Marx who also translated Ibsen and was Nora in a private reading of *A Doll's House*, declared of Elizabeth, 'We have in her a really great artist'.[31]

Many critics were still wary of the foreign dramatist who so shockingly and frequently defied convention. The *Saturday Review* believed Ibsen's study of a 'malicious woman of evil instincts' to be wholly out of place on the stage. Some reviewers used medical metaphors to express their distaste. For the *Observer* the play was 'A contribution to the drama of disease' whilst the *Pictorial World* saw it as 'a bad escape of moral sewage-gas … Hedda's soul is a-crawl with the foulest passions of humanity'.[32] Interestingly, after a performance the following year, Elizabeth wrote to Florence Bell appropriating the same language of disease and diabolical possession as the anti-Ibsenites but in relation to herself:

> I've been rather Hedda-ish the last few days & not very Lisa-like whatever that may be. Do you know I think it's some kind of nervous *disease* that descends upon one with the grasp of such a part. I know quite well I'm not Elizabeth Robins any more than I'm Queen Victoria. I'm *possessed*—some mocking, half-pathetic demon gets into me & whirls me along without help or hindrance from me.

The character of Hedda was especially unsettling for the late Victorian male since she challenged not only what was felt to constitute a feminine woman but even the newlywed. Critics tried therefore to question her very identity. For *The Stage* she was 'not a woman but a thing; a beast degraded from womanhood; half an idiot and very much of a devil'. Another paper felt her to be '"possessed" by a demon of malignity'.[33] She both repelled and fascinated. In language redolent of sexuality she became a she-cat, a serpent.

Clement Scott expressed his fear of Hedda's power to corrupt and recognised Elizabeth's skill in conveying and transcending this. She had

> made vice attractive by her art. She has almost ennobled crime. She has stopped the shudder that so repulsive a creature should have inspired. She has glorified an unwomanly woman. She has made a heroine out of a sublimated sinner. She has fascinated us with a savage.[34]

And so magnetic was her acting that 'No one could move their eyes from her'. Elizabeth's response (some years later) was:

> Mr Clement Scott understand Hedda?—any man except that wizard Ibsen really understand her? Of course not. That was the tremendous part of it. How should men understand Hedda on the stage when they didn't understand her in the persons of their wives, their daughters, their woman friends?[35]

Elizabeth could not see Hedda as one-dimensional. She did not seek to whitewash her, recognising her 'corrosive qualities' (when she said 'I did it for your sake, George', the audience hissed) but neither was she to be simply condemned. Elizabeth saw another side. Hedda had been denied the opportunity to use 'her best powers'. William Archer commented that Elizabeth 'never forgot that Hedda is neither a hypocrite nor a fiend'.[36]

In today's theatres Ibsen's later prose dramas are vehicles for a multitude of interpretations. Some favour using them as modern fables. Those seeking to be faithful to his period provide what are seen as traditional representations of his plays. Yet we conveniently forget just how very novel those late nineteenth-century productions were at the time. Their audiences were not seeing 'costume drama' but topical plays, whilst the actors and actresses creating the first interpretations of characters by a contemporary playwright had a remarkably fresh and challenging responsibility.

Like the character of Hamlet, how to play Hedda has aroused considerable debate. *Hedda Gabler* has become one of the most popular of Ibsen's plays in Britain and we must not minimise the significance and difficulties of its first English production. At the world premiere in Munich (January 1891), the audience signalled its displeasure by whistling. An ineffective Hedda had acted in an inappropriately declamatory manner. By April the play had been performed in Helsinki, Berlin, Stockholm, Copenhagen, Christiania and Gothenburg. Elizabeth had seen none of these performances. She was therefore neither hampered by the demands of comparison and emulation (she chose to see Hedda as 'a bundle of unused possibilities')[37] nor helped by hints of what might be most effective.

And although Shaw aptly commented that Elizabeth had made Hedda 'sympathetically unsympathetic',[38] when it came to understanding women's behaviour, Elizabeth bracketed him with Clement Scott. Determined to tell her what the character meant, he bombarded her with his response, providing detailed criticisms of the translation and interpretation of certain words and phrases. Elizabeth noted in relation to Shaw's unease about Hedda's handling of Judge Brack's advances: 'He couldn't be expected to understand the as yet, unusually Independent Woman' though she did feel he might have better divined his own sex:

> He just didn't know that side they so commonly showed the other sex, & never dreamed, I think, what a lot of social history was bound up in woman's use of the handiest as well as the most quietly effectual means of warding off complications.

At this time Elizabeth and Marion were not, as Michael Meyer claims, 'ardent feminists'.[39] They would not have accepted such labelling then. Yet the experience of acting and producing Ibsen's plays and the reactions to her work helped to transform Elizabeth over time into a committed supporter of women's rights.

Archer prudently waited over a week before giving his public endorsement. It was, in the light of his feelings towards Elizabeth (see Chapter 4), hardly an unbiased statement. Yet this respected critic was not the sort of person to have published a glowing report in *The World* unless he felt it to be entirely justified. He wrote:

> In rapidity and subtlety of intellect, I find it hard to think of a woman in the whole range of the drama who can rival Hedda Gabler; and Miss Robins makes us feel throughout that her own

mind could work as rapidly as Hedda's. She played upon her victims with the crisp certainty of touch of the consummate virtuoso.
Behind every speech we felt the swift intellectual process that gave
it birth … I do not hesitate to call her performance in the last
act the finest piece of modern tragedy within my recollection.
Sarah Bernhardt could not have done it better: and it is long since
Sarah attempted a scene so well worth doing.[40]

The British press tended to collapse actresses into two types, the sexual
and the intellectual. Known to spurn sexual advances, Elizabeth was
unproblematically slotted into the latter category, deemed particularly apposite since she was identified with anti-establishment views
and serious European drama. An anonymous reviewer in *The Theatre*
called her 'a remarkably *clever* actress', adding that her career had
been stunted by her enormous appetite for Ibsen.[41] Stella (Mrs Pat)
Campbell recalled that Elizabeth was 'the first intellectual I had met
on the stage'.[42] Elizabeth periodically worried that she was perceived
as excessively cold and cerebral but her genuinely intellectual interests, lack of staginess (she once described a Beringer party as a 'huge
crush, terribly and ferociously theatrical') and serious approach to
work only served to further this identification. When Lewis Waller
proposed that she act in *Antigone*, Elizabeth promptly began studying Greek. In 'Katherine Fleet' (part of 'The Coming Woman'), the
actress Della Stanley is 'incoherent, untaught, unheralded' but has
'that divinity in her keeping that lights up life'. The eponymous
heroine, well-bred and ambitious, knows the theory of acting but
in comparison with Della (Stella Campbell or Elizabeth's alter ego),
she pales into insignificance.

   Patronisingly described as 'Two plucky little American girls',
Elizabeth and Marion helped produce a triumph for the non-
commercial theatre. The initial five matinées were repeated, then
the play ran in the evening for four weeks (and Saturday matinées,)
gaining the support of both the pit and gallery audiences. Tracy Davis
has estimated that over 21,000 people attended during these thirty-
eight performances, making *Hedda Gabler* easily the most significant
production of 'the Ibsen year'.[43] Although £281 had been made from
the matinées, they had agreed to pay the cast of the flagging play
(ironically named *Money*) which they were replacing in the evenings.

Yet simply covering expenses was no mean achievement especially given the joint management's lack of prior experience. They also received the compliment of having the play parodied in J.M. Barrie's first stage production. Irene Vanbrugh studied Elizabeth carefully for her role in this skit.

By the time of the second portrayal of *Hedda* in October 1892, Elizabeth had seen Martha Brandes in a not very subtle version of the play in Paris.[44] She had also assured Archer that she would restore cuts she had previously made. Her revival was in Brighton where she also played once more Christine Linden in *A Doll's House*. Janet Achurch was Nora (Marion had returned to America). The following year Elizabeth took *Hedda Gabler* to New York. It was her only return to the American stage and the first production of Ibsen's play there. She hired the Fifth Avenue Theatre where she had last appeared in the mid-1880s, producing and acting in one matinée.

Elizabeth and Marion had intended building up a repertoire of plays. After *Hedda Gabler* they had discussed with Henry James adapting his *Roderick Hudson* for the stage. James also helped sort out legal complications surrounding their proposed production of an English version of Dumas's *Denise*. None of these plans materialised. The women also wanted to perform *Twelfth Night*, Elizabethan-style, at the Middle Temple but the press prematurely published their plans before the Benchers were aware of them and 'the old gentlemen of the Temple as good as told us to run away and play somewhere else'.[45] In need of income, Elizabeth now reverted to a melodrama, *The Trumpet Call* at the Adelphi. Not only did this play seem shallow after Ibsen but Elizabeth had also become branded as a particular type of actress. Reviewers detected too much of the 'Hedda Gabler cleverness' and not enough of the foolish, confiding manner of the Sims and Buchanan character. Hedda was not just a beneficial influence.

Fortunately a better opportunity arose with Henry James's own adaptation of his novel *The American*. To Elizabeth's astonishment, however, James who had been impressed by her Mrs Linden at his first encounter with Ibsen on the stage proposed that she play the old housekeeper, Mrs Bread. Elizabeth was determined not to seal her destiny as a 'portrayer of old women thirty years before my time'. Fortunately Mrs Compton's pregnancy meant that the leading role of Claire de Cintré became vacant for the London stage (the play had toured the provinces). Starring Elizabeth, it opened at the Opéra Comique on 26 September 1891. For once she had been able to negotiate a reasonable contract.

Elizabeth had first met her compatriot Henry James in January of that year at Genevieve Ward's. Her immediate reaction was to 'like this man better I think than any male American I have met abroad. He is *delightfully* grave and without the Yankee traveller's thin pretence of cosmopolitanism. This meeting is a ray of sunshine in a dark day.' James, however, rarely exuded sunshine. If she had a cold and felt a little sorry for herself, Elizabeth would call this 'feeling a little Henry James-y'. He was 'a good kind person—but oh the clouds drop down as he enters the door'. Six months after meeting Elizabeth, his sister Alice recorded in her diary that her brother had pronounced Miss Robins to be 'the most intelligent creature, next to Coquelin' with whom he had conversed about the stage.[46]

Unfortunately *The American* was not a great success. Alice James attributed its problems to the fact that it was a disastrous season for all theatres and the Comptons were relatively unknown and impecunious managers, though C.C. Hoyer Miller recalled in a book published in 1937 that Elizabeth's love scene with Edward Compton was the most perfect he had ever witnessed on the stage and lingered on in his memory.[47] Leon Edel argues that, although Elizabeth had 'an adequate bag of tricks' as an experienced actress, she was 'constitutionally incapable of creating so shrinking a flower as Claire—a woman all renunciation and passivity'.[48] Such a judgement surely relies too heavily on Elizabeth as Hedda, ignoring her many and varied other roles on both sides of the Atlantic over the past decade. James had given the play a new, happy ending and written up Claire's part especially for Elizabeth. Yet his *forte* lay in novels that could be read and savoured rather than in writing for the stage. Nevertheless, despite James's sense of failure, the play ran for seventy nights, bolstered temporarily by the attendance one night of the Prince of Wales.

Typecast as Ibsen's 'High-Priestess'—one reviewer thought she had invested Claire with 'the hysterical manners of Ibsen's morbid heroine'—Elizabeth's best hopes lay in his new play. In early November the prolific playwright obliged. Thanks to Heinemann, three copies were sent in instalments to Elizabeth, Archer and Gosse as fast as they rolled off the Copenhagen press. Its arrival in 'very small, violently agitating spurts' added to confusion and initial disappointment. The second instalment made Elizabeth 'think the old man's stark mad'. She told Florence of a young woman 'sprung upon us—but she doesn't smile at me—I'm horribly afraid she's the heroine! How I *hate her*!!!' At this time it was necessary to read a play on stage to secure copyright. The first rendition of the play was therefore held on 7 December at the Haymarket with seven people (including Heinemann and Elizabeth) reading the Norwegian script aloud.

It is due to Elizabeth Robins that *The Master Builder* was produced in England. On 20 January, despite warnings by Archer not to court disaster (he later acknowledged his mistake), she signed an agreement with Heinemann to produce the play: 'I'm now the owner of this wretched bone of contention.' She was, nevertheless, finding 'a strange, wild charm' in the character of Hilda Wangel though she did have some initial misgivings about playing a twenty-three-year-old in mountain costume (she was thirty). Tree offered to put it on, provided that all the characters became English and he played Solness as a sculptor! He even suggested that Wyndham, currently Elizabeth's pet hate amongst actor-managers, might produce it.[49]

Back in August of the previous year, Elizabeth had proposed to Heinemann that she and Florence Bell translate Ibsen's next play. Not surprisingly, Archer had demurred. Elizabeth wrote to Florence explaining:

He takes it with amazing kindness. Says it's an excellent plan but advises me not to let my name appear. Perhaps he's right, he advises our carrying out the scheme just as you & I had planned—I working at it with you & sharing in the profits (by the way are we to have Gosse terms?) but not appearing publicly in the matter. WA thinks it would unnecessarily emphasize my Ibsen proclivities. Besides giving them a chance to say 'Let a shoemaker stick to his last' etc.

Had anybody else reacted thus to her ambitions, it is unlikely that Elizabeth would have conceded so willingly but William Archer was not anybody. The collaboration was to be 'a deep deep dark secret'.

Even Hugh Bell must not know. 'I shall never *never* admit it—no
matter how many lies I have to tell' wrote Elizabeth to Florence,
'but probably no one will ever suspect'. Always a relisher of secrets,
she was pleased to 'help with the work' and keep the play from
Gosse, adding: 'So the next great literary earthquake will tremble
to the theme of … Henrik Ibsen translated by Mrs Hugh Bell.
'Won't it be heavenly?' Interestingly Elizabeth does not include
herself here as the co-translator. How much all this was building
'castles in the air' is impossible to tell. Florence was never a seeker
after publicity. Archer showed Elizabeth his early drafts and some
contemporaries noted Americanisms in the stage play. Heinemann's
publication of the play in February 1893 was in the name of Archer
and Gosse.[50]

   Elizabeth now had to proceed without Marion yet needed financial backing. Herbert Waring with whom she had acted in two plays
came to the rescue even though he was aware that producing Ibsen
entailed the risk of being labelled as 'a "crank" and a "faddist"'.
He secured a backer—'Waring has a capitalist by the coat-tails'—
and agreed to co-produce and play Solness. The Trafalgar Square
Theatre was leased for £50 for a week of matinées. Once again
Archer was indefatigable. He was armed with a block of paper for
comments, and Elizabeth saw him as 'a kind of Recording Angel'.[51]
Together, as Postlewait has noted, they developed a co-operative
rather than an autocratic style of directing.[52] Meanwhile the Gosses
and James gave unsolicited advice on costume. James also prepared
the public for the play, stressing in the *Pall Mall Gazette* how Ibsen
was valued as a player's playwright and representing Hilda as the
heroine most characteristic of its creator and most free of offence, a
Hedda reversed.[53]

   The play opened on 20 February. The week became a fortnight
then an evening run at the Vaudeville followed until the end of
March and Holy Week. Elizabeth had carefully orchestrated her
words and movements, numbering even her laughs and planning
careful, almost mesmeric, eye contact.[54] The inveterate theatregoer
Florence Bell wrote: 'I don't think I've ever seen anything that has
moved me to more frantic enthusiasm and delight than to watch you
through every movement of that play.'[55] Elizabeth's performance was
highly praised. Stella Campbell pronounced it 'the most intellectually

comprehensive piece of work I had seen on the English stage.'[56] Yet
with its 'upper-storey of symbolism on a ground floor of realism'[57]
(something Archer appreciated), many found the play bewildering.
At the time Elizabeth 'thrilled to it as poetry', playing down its
symbolic significance but, like Archer, she did this knowingly as
a bid to get it accepted, understanding that a play so recondite in
its symbolism was likely be seen as opaque and pointless.[58] In later
years she saw her portrayal of Hilda as her greatest achievement.
Virginia Woolf once asked her to a performance of the play. Elizabeth
declined. Her explanation characteristically conjured up the past and
simultaneously liberally reinvented it: '*I'm* Hilda. I'm the person it
was written for.'[59]

In her unpublished autobiography 'Whither & How?', Elizabeth
wrote that the record would show less how she did plays than how
she didn't do them. The best-known example is her surrender of
the part of Paula Tanqueray to Stella Campbell. Pinero had initially
been unable to secure the latter for *The Second Mrs Tanqueray* despite
feeling that she was perfect for the part. He therefore offered it to
Elizabeth but unexpectedly Mrs Pat was released from her Adelphi
commitment. Elizabeth 'with the most remarkable and characteristic generosity' according to Stella Campbell's memoirs, surrendered
the role.[60] Her motives have been interpreted in various ways,[61]
ranging from sisterly sincerity through dramatic gesturing to self-
interest (fear of competition) and personal uncertainty about her
own ability to play a passionate woman. Elizabeth's letter offering
the part makes clear her (correct) understanding of the enormity of
the sacrifice: 'There is to my mind no woman in London so envi-
able at this moment, dear savage, as you.' It is interesting, though, to
note her words to her confidante Florence Bell: 'Don't you see I
want to *act* & don't want to vindicate Pinero and the English drama
& Elizabeth Robins. It's too much.' Whether this was her genuine
belief or whether she wanted Florence and perhaps even herself to
assume she saw it this way is impossible to tell. What we do know
is that this 'woman with a past' play triumphed in the West End and
'made' Stella Campbell.

Elizabeth had worked with Stella Campbell in *The Trumpet Call*
and they would both act in *Little Eyolf*. Before that there were two
exhausting weeks (six matinées, six evenings) acting and directing

an ambitious Ibsen Series in May 1893 at the Opéra Comique. J.T. Grein of the Independent Theatre Society was managing secretary of the Subscription Fund. The trustees were Elizabeth's legal friend Sir Frederick Pollock and Mrs J.R. Green (Alice Stopford), widow of the eminent historian and herself a medievalist and historian of Ireland. During *The Trumpet Call* Elizabeth and Mrs Green had rented a cottage on Wimbledon Common as a retreat. Two circulars were produced displaying support from prestigious names such as Sir Edward Grey, James and Wilde and announcing details of the five-guinea subscriptions (£5 5s, or £5.25). 'Carnival time among the Ibsenites'[62] involved productions of *Hedda Gabler* (with Lewis Waller as Lovborg) and *The Master Builder* but also *Rosmersholm* and the last act of *Brand*, Elizabeth directing but once again working closely with Archer.

Her portrayal of Rebecca West was pronounced superior to Florence Farr's earlier interpretation. Archer thought it Elizabeth's 'largest, finest, most poetical' work to date though Shaw felt she rather overdid the grief.[63] Elizabeth has not written much about this play with its study of the unconscious, save to acknowledge in *Ibsen & the Actress* written some years after Freud's analysis of the characters that *Rosmersholm*, along with *The Master Builder*, was a play which she could not be dispassionate about. Some critics felt that her performance was subdued as a result of her watching Eleonora Duse in *La Dame aux Camélias* on the London stage. Elizabeth admired the great Italian actress who cultivated a natural style and abhorred theatricality. A number of people remarked on their physical similarities[64] (more noticeable in later years).

The decision to stage the fourth act of *Brand*, that tale of the interior of a human soul bereft of love, was a brave one. Ibsen had not written this long epic poem with an eye to its staging. When it was first produced in its entirety on the (Stockholm) stage in 1885, the performance lasted six and a half hours. Recognising that the fourth act 'forms a little drama in itself', the committee now presented it to London theatregoers.[65] Elizabeth played a somewhat meek Agnes. In 1908 she provided an interesting critique of *Brand*, pointing out that Ibsen's preoccupation with the Individual Will prevented his realisation that Agnes's submission and sacrifice of her son constituted an arraignment of the woman's love for the child. He failed to see that 'any mother worthy of the name would take the dying child away' to give him some chance of recovery.[66]

She played two more Ibsen characters. The first was Asta in *Little Eyolf*. This play also arrived in instalments (in 1894) but ones which impressed from the start: 'no one else has the grip & power of that old grey wolf of the North'. Henry James's immediate reaction was that 'It's a masterpiece and a marvel; and it must *leap* upon the stage'[67] though he was disappointed with the final act. A copyright performance was held in December with Elizabeth as Rita. She also played in the same programme the part of Lizzie in William Heinemann's *The First Step*.

Yet Ibsen's play was not produced until 1896 due to a number of factors. Elizabeth was suffering from nervous exhaustion. At one stage she turned production rights over to the Independent Theatre but, largely due to Shaw's involvement which antagonised amongst others, Heinemann, the agreement was scrapped. In the event Elizabeth and Archer decided to go ahead after all and to raise subscriptions, also putting on José Echegaray's *Mariana*. Circulars advertised the Ibsen—Echegaray Series. Although Elizabeth considered the leading role of Rita to be 'one of the most magnificent acting parts ever written', to Shaw's relief Janet Achurch was given the role and Elizabeth was Asta.[68] The Avenue was secured for a week of matinées. Three weeks of evening performances followed. Even those who disparaged Ibsen's 'dismal drama' had to admire Elizabeth's enterprise (£67 profit was divided between herself and the subscribers) though those dazzled by prospects of commercial success remained puzzled by her constantly seeking the hard route, sacrificing such 'brilliant prospects on the Scandinavian altar'.

The production of this subtle play was remarkable for bringing together Elizabeth, Janet Achurch and Stella Campbell (as the Rat Wife). Shaw observed that 'When in a cast of five, you have the three best yet discovered actresses of their generation, you naturally look for something quite extraordinary'.[69] He questioned whether Elizabeth was able to exhibit the full extent of her powers in her part, criticising her nervous restlessness and propensity for pathos though he conceded that this was better controlled in later performances. The pregnant Janet was replaced when the play went into the evening slot by an ill-prepared Stella. Florence Farr became the Rat

Wife and Elizabeth was left to pick up the pieces, unsuccessfully trying to appease Janet.

At the end of 1896 a weary Elizabeth wrote to Florence Bell in search of 'no reponsibility *no Ibsen*. Dear one what an advantage it is that you don't want to discuss the master all day and all night.' Although Elizabeth was the first to praise the parts Ibsen provided for the acting profession, there were times when she was wary about being labelled. When interviewed in New York in 1898 she is reputed to have told a newspaper reporter: 'I am so anxious not to be set down here as an Ibsenite. No, I am an actress' and, when pressed, 'I come here with no mission. I am not trying to convert my country-women to Ibsen.'[70] She was only too aware of how the press could use what she said and conscious that it could be damaging to be solely identified with one school of thought. She may also have been especially cautious in her native land. She was anyway increasingly concerned with widening theatrical opportunities and the scope of European drama. The English version of the Spanish play *Mariana* made her study Spanish and work closely with Henry James in get-ting James Graham's translation right for the stage. Archer especially enjoyed her acting in this 'love-tragedy' in which the controlled intellectual actress showed passionate emotions. But it was not a success and closed after five performances.

From the experience of mounting *Little Eyolf* and *Mariana*, a subscription society called the New Century Theatre (NCT) was launched.[71] Elizabeth, Archer, Alfred Sutro and H.W. Massingham formed the management committee. Elizabeth had explained to Florence how she had become interested in providing a 'kind of little theatre for the Minority which will year by year (for a few weeks or a few months) give a series of performances of plays not to be expected at the regular theatre.' The NCT sealed the professional collaboration of Elizabeth Robins and William Archer. It sought to provide plays of intrinsic interest which 'find no place on the stage in the ordinary way of theatrical business' and to pave the way for a permanent national institution. Elizabeth recognised that 'for the Powers in Possession' it was 'privately an irritant and publicly a reproach'.[72] When Shaw reviewed what he called the 'real history' of the drama over the last decade he acknowledged the part played by Elizabeth and other 'Impossibilists' who clearly turned their backs on commercial theatres.[73] Following in the footsteps of the Independent Theatre Society, the NCT was a brave attempt to provide challenging, artistic, non-commercial European drama for the British intelligentsia. Its European counterparts were the Théâtre Libre in Paris (founded in 1887) and the Moscow Arts Theatre (started in 1897). Two years later, with the demise of Grein's Independent Theatre Society, the Stage Society began.

The first NCT production was *John Gabriel Borkman*, that Ibsenite study of 'the coldness of the heart'. Elizabeth's performance as Ella Rentheim the estranged twin sister of Mrs Borkman seems to have been the least successful of her Ibsen roles. Shaw, for one, felt her to be 'too young and too ferociously individualistic' for the part of the white-haired Ella and Elizabeth admitted to Florence that 'I didn't feel that I was *quite* in it'. The production was not helped by Genevieve Ward playing Mrs Borkman. Part of the 'old school', she was not sufficiently alert to Ibsen's 'prompting' yet in other ways the production was modern. Its naturalistic use of lighting (with candles and lamps) probably owed as much to realism as to economy though it was dismissed at the time as gloomy.[74]

In late 1897 the NCT produced *Admiral Guinea* by Robert Louis Stevenson and W.E. Henley based on *Treasure Island*. Elizabeth directed and read the one-page rhyming Prologue specially composed for the opening by Henley.[75] Stevenson, who had died three years earlier, had a valued critic in his fellow Scot, William Archer. Elizabeth had never met Stevenson but greatly admired his work (her copies of the volumes of his selected letters are heavily annotated), his love of travel and ability to cope with ill health.

In these years there were also plans for other productions which never materialised. These included Shaw's *Candida* and *Captain Brassbound's Conversion*. Elizabeth never acted in any of his plays though he had stipulated that she should have the lead should the NCT produce his work. He had also suggested Elizabeth as a possible co-director of the Independent Theatre on Grein's departure. The NCT put on H.V. Esmond's *Grierson's Way* at the Haymarket in 1899 but more time was spent considering plays than producing them. *Peer Gynt*, complete with music by Grieg, never got beyond the proposal stage. Another plan, worked out with Florence, was to stage Rossetti's 'Ballad of Sister Helen' with a Burne-Jones set and

Grieg's music. Elizabeth consulted the Welsh composer Dr Joseph Parry who thought the plan rather ambitious. Grieg was therefore approached to supply merely a musical prelude but even this came to nothing.

When Ibsen's final play *When We Dead Awaken* appeared in 1899, Elizabeth and William Archer were disappointed. They took part in the copyright reading but their Ibsen decade now came to an end. So too did their public sharing in experimental theatre though as late as 1904 the NCT sponsored Harley Granville Barker's productions (in a modernist style) of Gilbert Murray's translations of Euripides. *Hippolytus* was one of Elizabeth's favourite plays. She praised Murray's version, admiring 'the fresh beauty of the old poem'. Elizabeth had advised Murray on his own *Carlyon Sahib*, an ambitious play inspired by *Peer Gynt* but set in India.[76] She had turned it down for the NCT though a revised version was staged in June 1899 and panned in the press. Archer nevertheless included it in his list of plays for a proposed National Theatre.

For some years Elizabeth had sat through readings by eager playwrights. Dr Edward Aveling, for example, used to appear with a suitcase full of plays, and rather more elevated playwrights such as George Moore, Thomas Hardy and Harley Granville Barker were amongst those eager for her to star in their works. With the new century she became more interested in writing them herself and would soon be working with Barker at the Court Theatre as a playwright. Both Barker and Elizabeth actively opposed stage censorship. When Laurence Housman's historical play *Pains and Penalties: The Defence of Queen Caroline* was refused a licence a Caroline Society was formed specifically to organise a performance by the Pioneer Players.[77] At this event staged at the Savoy Theatre on 26 November 1911 Elizabeth brought Barker on to the stage to address the audience on the subject of censorship.

Barker's name is associated today with the development of a National Theatre, a concept which did not actually materialise until the 1960s. Peter Whitebrook's biography of William Archer (who co-authored with Barker *Scheme & Estimates for a National Theatre*) shows how Archer should also be credited for his part in its genesis.[78] His first plea for an endowed theatre in England was at the age of seventeen.

Elizabeth's diary for 16 August 1891 had expressed her vision of a theatre, 'a glorious Temple of art' where 'ability would be the one open sesame' fusing the best in the world of literature, painting, music and 'honest loving criticism' as the popular home and school of culture. As well as her pronounced and progressive views on gender and theatre management, she believed in a disciplined democracy with actors having some freedom to develop parts as best suited them and their fellow actors. Remembering those endless performances of *Monte Cristo* in the States, she also opposed long runs. She felt that the intelligence of the general public was greatly underestimated, that people wanted to be challenged rather than fed vapid entertainment. Yet she did not see her vision of a 'Theatre of the Future' fully realised. She had discussed it with Wilde in 1892 but these two individuals never quite empathised with each other's aspirations and despite sympathetic noises, he took the idea no further. In 1904 in response to W.T. Stead's request that she write about the London stage for his *Review of Reviews*, Elizabeth referred to the 'small but waxing chorus that cries "National theatre!" "Subsidy!" or "Municipal support"' characterising the theatre as 'easily first as an engine of popular education'.[79] Here she also poured scorn on what she saw as the Foreign Office's half-hearted enquiry into European state support for the arts, questioning how seriously the British took the theatre. In contrast, Europe (she was mainly referring to France and Germany) was far more impressive. She described seeing a Parisian audience inspired by Antoine's production of *Les Tisserands*. At a time of labour disturbances this translation of Hauptmann's historical play about Silesian weavers took on a new significance. So evocative was it that the next day the play was officially suppressed. Elizabeth applauded the idea that the theatre should make people think.

In 1929, many years after leaving the stage, she contributed to a special issue of *Drama* devoted to ideas about a national theatre. Her contribution was to urge giving women a voice on the executive of such an organisation 'and not only this or that middle-aged or old woman. The theatre would die but for the young. They ought to play a part in the life of the Theatre not only before the footlights.' In the meantime some of her hopes for women on the stage had been realised through the feminist Actresses' Franchise League (see Chapter 7). The Edwardian stage had also seen some of her progressive ideas developed by imaginative women such as the tea heiress Annie Horniman at the Gaiety Theatre, Manchester. She promoted young, unknown playwrights, resisted the star system, advocated short runs and a naturalistic style of acting.[80] In February 1914 Bernard Shaw proposed, and Sir Herbert Tree seconded, a resolution (passed unanimously) that Elizabeth become an Associate of the Academy of Dramatic Art which later became RADA. This she accepted.

Although Elizabeth was associated with the *avant-garde*, for every role she cherished, there were others she preferred to forget. They included her part in the melodramatic *A Woman's Revenge* (1893) and in *Mrs Lessingham* a year later. There was also *The Sixth Commandment*, a lamentable Buchanan adaptation of *Crime and Punishment*. Here Elizabeth witnessed the economic exploitation endemic in her profession: five weeks of rehearsal with no remuneration and salaries only guaranteed if the run lasted at least a fortnight. It was extended. Yet in this Elizabeth was able to act with Herbert Waring, Lewis Waller and Marion Lea. It was Marion who began calling her after the name of the heroine: '"Lisa" has lived on the lips of my English intimates & their children & grandchildren.' She became known as 'Lisa of the long hair' and 'Lisa of the blue eyes'.

As Countess Zicka in a revival of *Diplomacy* (an adaptation of Sardou's *Dora*) she toured Birmingham, the north-west and Scotland, replacing Olga Nethersole. Her irreverent account of the Royal Command performance at Balmoral before Queen Victoria and Empress Eugénie points up neatly the contrast between Elizabeth and her more traditional fellow actors,[81] showing her scorn for the sycophantic cast and her republican credentials. Neatly turning the tables, she portrayed the royal household as a piece of theatre. The elderly queen, a dumpy yet dignified figure, played the leading part with a thoroughly trained company of retainers stage-managed to perfection. Elizabeth's own cast which included Forbes-Robertson (who had refused to act in an Ibsen play), Squire Bancroft and his wife, and Hare—all three men were eventually knighted—viewed their invitations and presentation as a wonderful privilege, another vital step in the growing respectability of the stage. In contrast Elizabeth felt she was being transported back to the middle ages and found it especially pathetic that professionals as experienced and skilled as Mrs Bancroft (an actress since childhood and an accomplished manager) should view this cramped performance as their crowning glory.

Later, in the 1920s, Elizabeth was represented in Queen Mary's Dolls' House library along with other well-known writers. The twentieth century saw her move away from the stage. After visiting Alaska she played only two more professional roles, both in 1902. She found the part of Lucrezia in *Paolo and Francesca* especially tough not just because she had been very ill but also because she disagreed fundamentally with her manager, her old adversary Alexander. She confessed to Florence that only her faithful dresser knew how she nearly didn't play night after night. Reverting to control by others did not suit her: 'Of course I made a failure of it. I have never been stage-managed into a success.' She saw her performance as 'against the grain & against every instinct & perception' and wrote (but may not have posted) a five-page letter to the playwright Stephen Phillips explaining how her interpretation fundamentally differed from the one imposed by Alexander.

Her final professional appearance was in Mrs Humphry Ward's *Eleanor*. The novel had earned its author record advance sales but the play was not much of a success.[82] Marion Terry had the lead, Elizabeth preferring the small part of mad Alice which she felt could not wreck the play even if she failed. Unlike many, she did not try to hang on to the limelight. She bowed out on 15 November 1902 aged forty.[83] This may well help to account for her being less well remembered today than those actresses who chose, against great odds, to persevere beyond this age. In her years on the stage Elizabeth had gained experience in many aspects of theatre work, comprehending both sides of the curtain, helping to shape the direction of drama. It was, however, Ibsen's new plays which had provided her with real novelty, depth and scope. Once they ceased there seemed little left for her on the British stage and increasingly it was writing that absorbed her energies.

Nevertheless, after retiring from the stage, her ideas about drama still found expression, both in writing and in occasional public appearances. At a lecture at the Philosophical Institute in Edinburgh in 1908, two years after Ibsen's death, Elizabeth entered the debate which still rages today: whether he was primarily a poet or a philosopher-cum-reformer. She argued that he was first and foremost a poet and by now was prepared to challenge his maxim, expressed most clearly in *An Enemy of the People*, that the strongest man is he who stands alone. This, she claimed, paid insufficient attention to the Collective Will. She believed that 'the outstanding fact of our time is that progressive ideas are barren and without effect except in so far as they are diffused and held in common'. Ibsen's strength lay not so much in the profundity of his judgements as in the way in which he 'transferred material for judgement to the mimic scene'.[84] Some of the implications of this therefore reached further than he himself realised but this did not detract from his being 'the most stimulating influence the Theatre had to give us'. This talk barely mentions the parts which had made Elizabeth so famous, demonstrating instead a familiarity with Ibsen's lesser-known works such as the historical drama *Lady Inger of Østraat*.

Later, in a BBC broadcast on Ibsen in 1928, the centenary of his birth, she alluded to the 'something enigmatic' in all his plays which had generated such a literature about his work. She referred to his capacity for 'sly fun' when confronted with serious students of symbolism. She now submitted that *The Master Builder* had weathered best the test of time: 'It has clarified with the years—or rather our vision has.' She also gave a Centenary lecture, part of a series organised by the British Drama League, which was published as a Hogarth essay. Here she declared that 'no dramatist has ever meant so much to the women of the stage as Henrik Ibsen'.[85]

For many years it was primarily as an interpreter of Ibsen that Elizabeth Robins was remembered. The diplomat and writer Douglas Ainslie saw her as 'the only person able to convey the quality of emotion peculiar to Ibsen—perhaps the very kernel of his genius, of which others reach only the outside, with much trouble'. The journalist Henry Nevinson claimed in his autobiography that he had seen all the greatest actresses of the last fifty years, but that 'none of them produced upon my mind and emotions such an overwhelming effect as Miss Robins'.[86] And the great twentieth-century actress Dame Sybil Thorndike has described how, even though she never saw Elizabeth act in an Ibsen play, the two of them would go through scenes together, 'Lisa with those eyes of fire, and voice haunting and vibrant, making me almost leap in the air with excitement'.[87]

On their final meeting when Elizabeth was eighty-nine, Dame Sybil told her, 'If it had not been for you, we might not have seen Ibsen—anyway not so soon.' Elizabeth's answer was: 'There is always someone to start a new chapter, and I am lucky to have taken part in that revolutionary chapter of the theatre.'

4

THEATRE AND FRIENDSHIP

In her unpublished autobiography 'Whither & How?' Elizabeth acknowledged her Hedda as the active force which shaped her existence from 1891, adding, 'Primarily she brought in her train two great friends.' She had many close friends during her long life but in the 1890s two stood out above all others, providing professional and emotional sustenance to the newly settled American in England. They were William Archer and Florence Bell. What they offered sustained her in different yet equally important ways. She met both of them at the beginning of the 1890s and their deaths in 1924 and 1930 respectively caused more grief than most who knew her could ever have guessed.

'Archer is tall & dark. Looks about 30 is probably 38 has big honest eyes that win confidence & friendliness; is *most* courteous' wrote Elizabeth after their first meeting (to discuss *Ghosts*) in June 1890. He was actually in his thirty-fourth year, a six-footer with aquiline features. This meeting not only marked the beginning of what was to become an important and productive working relationship but also led to a love affair which helped Elizabeth to come to terms with her tragic history and loneliness without sacrificing her ambitions.

Living in digs where guests were constantly coming and going and leaving work late at night increased the vulnerability of the working woman on her own in London. Elizabeth soon found it too risky to wait in Piccadilly for an omnibus so had to pay instead for a cab. Her father, anxious about what he called her 'wanderings about the modern Babylon', had written to warn her that 'There are hours & places of danger there, more than in New York'. The largest city in the world, London was daunting for all newcomers. Henry James described himself as 'an impersonal black hole in the huge general blackness' on first arriving but it also offered him immense possibilities: 'I had complete liberty and the prospect of profitable work; I used to take long walks in the rain. I took possession of London.'[1] Elizabeth's language could never be so confident. She was propositioned by strangers in the street and had to be on her guard in her lodgings where men would lurk on the frugally lit staircase leading to her room. Meals were taken communally at her Duchess Street digs and on at least one occasion she asked to be reseated due to pestering from a guest. She did strike up a friendship with one lodger, the American Edwin Jaquith (Mr X in *Both Sides of the Curtain*) who pretended that he was not married.

Her diary emphasises just how much women were judged by their looks. When Lewis Waller whispered on stage during *The Sixth Commandment* that she was a goose for not coping well 'with such a pretty face', she was so furious that 'I jerked my hand away fr. [sic] him before the audience when I should have clung to him most affectionately.' In fact Waller (the hero), Waring (the villain) and Marius (stage-manager) were amongst those she felt she could most trust in the profession. There were others with worrying reputations. Wyndham, for example, was known 'for his ways with women & his disposition to turn the Theatre into a Harem'.

The long-limbed, red-haired Tree dominates Elizabeth's published account of 1889–90 but her diary reveals a less public and accept-able face. Whilst she dined with him hoping for a part, he seems to have had a liaison in mind. His name has been excised in a number of places from her diary and he later becomes H (his first name was Herbert). He bombards her with telegrams and invitations for dinner. Her diary after one such dinner is staccato and cryptic—'A page of the Past' and 'A struggle, a fainting' and when he proposes placing her in a little house in St John's Wood, a district renowned for its courtesans, she writes: 'a time of peril! Home very sick at heart—never has Despair so mastered me.' In one of her stories the actor-manager Le Grange places Della Stanley in a flat. 'My genius will develop further in a flat', says Della knowingly.

As Elizabeth had found in America, the actress was always a limi-nal figure. She was set apart yet presumed to be available, a woman

in a public position who became off stage another private individual, crossing from fantasy to reality. Professionally concerned with
assuming roles, she was (and still is)[2] seen as never 'off duty' and has
therefore been perceived as somehow immune from 'real' feelings
with her pursuer correspondingly exculpated from responsibility. Frequently Elizabeth's men friends would adopt the name of
a character she played, thereby enabling an intimacy which they
could not otherwise so easily assume. Thus W.T. Stead, moralist and
religious crusader, who had never entered the theatre until Elizabeth
persuaded him to do so at the age of fifty-five, could write to her in
the guise of Hedda: 'Oh Hedda Hedda Darling don't you know how
I rejoice in your success how I glory in your triumph.'[3]

One way of warding off complications was via male relatives.
Elizabeth paid for her younger brother Vernon to come to London to
complete his pre-medical education. The plan was not an entire success: Vernon was utterly uninterested in the theatre, seemed provincial
and shy, was studious but not yet ready for London University. The
University Registrar, Horsburgh, came to the rescue. Like many men
he was clearly smitten by the beautiful actress and was soon sending
Elizabeth sentimental poetry. He also arranged private coaching for
Vernon. Elizabeth found it expensive looking after her brother but
she appreciated being with one of the family and Vernon's presence prompted her to get her own flat. When he first arrived in
the autumn of 1890 Elizabeth was in unsuitable digs in Culworth
Street, Regent's Park where the landlady (an ex-artist's model) held
rowdy parties. So a third-floor flat was found at 28, Manchester
Square Gardens, Dorset Street and nicknamed 'Morocco' since it was
reached by an outside flight of seventy-four steps. For £50 annually
Elizabeth now had some space: two bedrooms, a bathroom, kitchen,
dining-room and study. The study had cool green walls, a rug, a writ-
ing-table, easy chairs, a divan and palms and flowers. Elizabeth was
living here when she began working on *Hedda Gabler* with Marion
Lea and William Archer.

Archer had been born in 1856 in Perth, Scotland. The eldest of
nine children, he experienced a very strict Protestant upbringing. A
significant part of his childhood was spent on the Norwegian coast,
his paternal grandfather having moved there. As a young man he travelled round the world. He had become acquainted with Ibsen's work

in the early 1870s and although he studied at the Middle Temple after Edinburgh University, he became not a lawyer but a journalist specialising in drama. A theatre critic for almost five decades, he was the regular reviewer for *The World* and, by the beginning of the twentieth century, the most influential critic of English theatre. From a radical Liberal and international background he 'fought for realism to become the dominant theatrical form but remained hypnotized by the romance of the stage'.[4] A passionate advocate of a national theatre, he energetically defended the New Drama, opposing restrictions on freedom of expression. For example, it was only Archer and Shaw who publicly opposed the censorship of Wilde's *Salome*.[5] As a translator and interpreter of Ibsen he was revered. His fellow critic Walkley wrote in 1901: 'What Mr Archer does not know about Ibsen isn't knowledge, and what the rest of us know we for the most part owe to him.'[6] His translations formed the standard Ibsen texts in Britain until the 1930s.

In 1884 he had married Frances Elizabeth Trickett, an intelligent, well-read Englishwoman he had met three years earlier at a *conversazione* in Rome. They had one child, Tom, born the following year. They moved to Surrey but Archer spent much of his time staying at his base in Queen Square, London. Frances is credited with the translation of two of Ibsen's plays in the Walter Scott edition he edited.

Like Ibsen, Archer 'wore the mask of rectitude and judgement over a depth of emotion'.[7] The same could be said about Elizabeth who once wrote, 'No woman had ever greater power of control with such capacity for Passion as I.' William Archer and Elizabeth were also well travelled and well informed, discreet and private people who nevertheless made their living by communicating with the public. They began working together in 1891. There is no regular diary entry for this period since they later decided to burn these diaries and letters. However, some notes and letters escaped along with yearly summaries from 1894. There also exist some tiny engagement books from 1892. Work on Charles Dickens's coded pocket diary for 1867 has revealed the time he spent with his mistress the actress Nelly Ternan.[8] Elizabeth's little engagement books with their perfunctory entries show her frequent meetings with Archer, indicated by the sign α.

The autumn of 1891 appears to have been significant in the development and expression of their feelings for one another. For a number of years they celebrated 30 September. On that date in 1893 Elizabeth wrote: 'Two Years ago!!' In 1897 the date is marked 'Birthday α 2 and to dine. Get roses' (Archer's birthday was 23 September) and in 1898 simply '*our* evening'.

Yet her experience with George and her memories of him had made her wary. In another notebook she wrote on 5 November 1891:

> Even W.A. my strongest anchor to good cheer & wholesome activity is coming to demand too much of me of time and of regard. It wd. not be hard for me to love this man not wisely but too well & I must guard my poor life against a curse like that. For soon after I had acknowledged him the one being in the world for me he wd. possess the supremest power to pain me, and unconsciously and inevitably he wd. use his power. Not that he wd. *wish* to, not that he wdn't try to avoid it, but he wd. be as helpless as I.

The following year she wrote a long account frankly acknowledging her sexual desires, arguing with herself the pros and cons of her complicated situation. Then or later, she sought to distance herself or, rather, to suggest to potential readers that this was fiction by giving this writing the title of 'Notes for a woman of 30 who is loved & resists & what she thinks of herself'. Yet despite the removal of self implied in such labelling, her direct references to her grandmother, use of the first person, age (she was thirty) and timing, all conspire to betray its initial purpose.

Here she questions why she resists so desperately since she pays a dear price for celibacy. Is she a coward? Having 'contracted the habit of a nun' she has become 'deathly afraid of the common heritage. I wd. like to escape from every consequence of youth & sex. I loathe being "loved" & yet there are times when every fibre in my body cries out.' In asking why she is so afraid to 'be natural' she is not concerned with conventional morality, observing that a healthy sexual relationship can be said to enhance a woman's well-being whilst denial is clearly taking its toll: 'Am I not an idiot?—repressing

& wrestling with the natural healthy hot-blooded woman until she looks like a spiritless old crone?' Resisting 'a few maddened men' is no problem but then 'comes one who has his revenge'. She is 'on fire I am being tortured—lashed and bitter—like an acid it eats into my flesh & I resisting grow sad eyed and sick.' Although she is '*master* of these red hot stirring times' she is not sure how long she can take her midnight regret, 'I am very human & passion is a fire that spreads & devours.' She has already been 'badly scorched'.

According to Archer's most recent biographer Peter Whitebrook, his marriage had been celibate for some years.[9] The engagement books show very frequent, sometimes daily, meetings between Elizabeth and W.A., as she called him, between 1892 and 1898. They may also have spent some time abroad together, possibly on a cycling holiday in 1897 and in Paris in the autumn of the next year. They needed to keep their meetings secret since W.A. was married but both were private people who did not wear their hearts on their sleeves. Shaw, whose early career was guided by W.A. and with whom he indulged in the kind of bantering relationship only enjoyed by those who understand and respect each other deeply, once called him 'a man in whom dissimulation had become so instinctive that it had become his natural form of emotional expression'.[10] In March 1895 when ill, Elizabeth wrote: 'The most extraordinary & illuminating experiences of my life I have not attempted nor wanted to pass on.' She acknowledged that 'Just one person knows me as well as any one being may know another. That one will have few doubts on any matter touching my brief memoirs, and that one will not be able to speak.' Since she was not writing in the past tense, it may be presumed that she was referring to W.A. rather than to her husband.

It has been suggested by Thomas Postlewait that Elizabeth may have become pregnant with Archer's child, most likely in 1895.[11] This claim is based on her lack of stage work in that year, delay in the production of *Little Eyolf*, reports that Elizabeth was suffering from nervous exhaustion and her later financial support for 'several children'. This last reference presumably alludes to her living at a later date with her friend Flora Simmonds and their joint raising of the young David Scott. But David was not Elizabeth's child (see Chapter 7). It is possible that Elizabeth became pregnant and had a miscarriage or abortion but here again there is no real proof.

She was definitely not pregnant during the second part of this year since between July and December she was using the symbol # to denote the start of her monthly period. This symbol, which could perhaps also be taken as an indication that she was enjoying an active sexual relationship during this time, appears first in her tiny engagement diaries in July 1892, though the paucity of entries before this time means that not too much can be made of it. The symbol also occurs in February and June 1895 and regularly in 1894 and 1896. The lack of entries for some months in 1895 might be significant. It might, however, simply mean that she was not bothering to be as punctilious as usual. We know that she was ill in March 1895, apparently with a particularly nasty bout of influenza. She suffered from colds and 'flu for many years. All we can say for certain is that if she were pregnant, she did not want to make the fact known to her contemporaries or to posterity. Neither can we prove whether or not she and W.A. slept together. More to the point, they appear to have cared deeply and tenderly for each other and to have shared as much time as they could salvage without ultimately threatening Archer's marriage or their public reputations.

Although Elizabeth was very close to Florence Bell, she does not appear to have confided in her about the nature of her relationship with W.A. She wrote to Florence, 'You are the only woman in the world I would give my very heart of hearts to for safe keeping.' After Florence's death her letters were returned to Elizabeth who added to this one '[& yet how far I was from doing it]'.[12] In her correspondence she joked with Florence about W.A.'s apparent lack of emotion and enthusiasm. Describing her performance as Hedda at Brighton she recounted how he declared the last act to be 'utterly beautiful' and 'his eyes grew quite misty—I was surprised'. She would not reveal the 'other' W.A. though her friend discerned something of the depth of her feelings for him. When he died, Florence wrote, acknowledging that what for her was a personal sorrow, must for Elizabeth be a disaster.

Some notes, poetry and letters from W.A. to 'Bessie darling' have survived, either because Elizabeth could not let herself destroy all traces of their relationship or because some escaped her periodic censoring of her papers since they were tucked in with manuscripts rather than amongst correspondence. Such scraps indicate something of the passionate side of W.A., so well camouflaged from the world. When Duse played Cleopatra he joked about her stage kisses, 'the coldest perfunctory little conventions you can imagine. Dearest love, we could give her lessons in that, couldn't we?' When Elizabeth was working at the Garrick in the spring of 1894 he wrote in his untidy scrawl, so unlike his sharp mind, 'Believe me, darling, the last thing I want to do is to hamper your work or stand in the way of your career, and in the meantime what you have clearly got to do is to devote yourself body and soul—& I am part of your body & soul—to Mrs Lessingham. So until that is over I shall try to remember nothing of yesterday except how dear and loving you were to me my own—especially in the cab … my darling, my darling, I love you with all my heart.'

Yet this is the same woman who apparently flung W.A.'s friend Shaw out of a cab into the mud. Elizabeth has been represented by Shaw and others since as an aloof kill-joy, disparaging the male sex. Used to flirting via epistolary relationships and impressing actresses, Shaw found that his verbal gymnastics and comments on her attractiveness fell flat with 'Saint Elizabeth'. Although he admired her work, especially her Hilda, he parodied her defensiveness. In the 1940s he recalled his encounters with the Ibsen actress: 'Elizabeth was interested in me as an Ibsen specialist; but when my reciprocal interest threatened to develop into something warmer she threatened to shoot me and dropped me for many years.'

His attempts to charm stung her into angry retorts which only encouraged him to persevere in his presumptions. Although she could admire his talent as a dramatist and critic and later acknowledged her own 'prickliness', at the time Shaw spelt trouble for her, both because she resented being patronised and because his comments about her and W.A. sometimes, without his necessarily being fully aware of it, actually hit the nail on the head. He outraged Elizabeth professionally and personally by boasting 'no living woman shall turn my head as you have turned Archer's' and suggesting that she publish an essay in the *Fortnightly Review* on 'How to get at William Archer: by one who has done it'. His joking about how the critic Archer had been won over by 'one flash of your dark eyes' clearly unnerved her and reflected his own consciousness that with himself Elizabeth only acted as a 'perverse devil'.[13]

William Archer writes to Elizabeth (facsimile) in the 1890s

Connected to the Irish gentry, Shaw could understand this ambitious outsider yet as a 'very Marxist young man' he was dismissive of her cultivation of society, accusing her of being too much of a 'Lady'. There was some truth in this. When provoked, Elizabeth tended to become aloof and somewhat formal but she was ever-sensitive to the liberties people assumed with actresses. When Shaw used familiar terms she responded: 'My name for you is Miss Robins; and I do not see that the fact of my being an actress entitles any one to call me by any other name.' What Shaw did not know was that W.A. helped frame part of this response, toning down some of Elizabeth's language. W.A. tried to placate Elizabeth, acknowledging that Shaw '*is* an ass' but also 'has one of the keenest intellects I ever came across'.

Shaw's biographers have tended to present Elizabeth through Shavian eyes. George Parks's suicide is given heightened drama by making him *wear* the suit of armour that he used to weigh him down. Elizabeth is made humourless, a woman of 'prim intensity'.[14] Such a reading is encouraged not just by the Shaw correspondence but also by *Both Sides*, written much later and investing Elizabeth's recounting of the 1890s with a strong feminist consciousness. Michael Holroyd suggests that Elizabeth was convinced that 'all men were potential rapists' whereas Margot Peters sees her as 'squeamish' about sex, preferring to 'fascinate rather than gratify' though she does acknowledge that Shaw's habit of attracting yet evading women caused pain for all concerned.[15]

Henry James's biographer Leon Edel argues that she feared and detested Shaw.[16] Why, then, did she choose to open her published autobiography with her correspondence with him?[17] In later years they maintained a witty, affectionate friendship from a distance, helped by age, by their shared memories of theatre and people from the past and by the fact that W.A. could no longer come between them. Elizabeth wrote in one letter: 'Did you ever realize how immensely helpful as well as *stirring*, you were in those turbulent days? I think of you with much affection.' They sent each other works they wrote and Shaw advised Elizabeth on a manuscript about Annie Besant.

In Edel's view Elizabeth represented the classic actress–seductress with the innocent victim: 'the actress had a way of disarming those who talked with her. ... She was all attention; she turned on them her lustrous blue eyes.'[18] He returns, time and again to these 'large liquid eyes'. His picture does not fit easily with Elizabeth's comments on her fondness for Henry James as an intellectual companion. Edel tells us how Miss Robins

> could serve him cocoa in her rooms amid a smell of powder and
> perfume and greasepaint, and talk about the men who fell in love
> with her. He [James] had watched this calculating actress, in the
> world of fakery and illusion—so intelligent about the stage and

about Ibsen, so interesting a sexual object—use poise and appearance to impress and advance herself.[19]

Edel suggests that the friendship was rather one-sided, that Elizabeth created 'an atmosphere of deep and cherished intimacy'. Yet not only did James play an important part in advising Elizabeth on translations of scripts and providing detailed comments on her own play *Votes For Women!*, but he also wrote the scenario for *The Promise* which became his novel *The Other House*, with her in mind. His many letters to her demonstrate the affinity, affection and humour of a friendship based on mutual respect.[20] The novelist Marie Belloc Lowndes who knew both of them well, even wrote that Elizabeth was 'said to be the one woman whom he had ever cared for sufficiently to wish to marry'.[21] Although they did not see much of each other after 1900, in 1914 James wrote to 'My Dear Old Friend' hoping they could meet, 'the sound of your beautiful voice will be a joy to your all-constant old Henry James'.[22]

One friendship which became complicated was that with William Heinemann. A year younger than Elizabeth, he had started his own publishing house in Bedford Street, Covent Garden in 1890. His firm's publications included translations of Ibsen and Elizabeth's early novels. A centenary history describes Elizabeth as 'the woman whom Heinemann loved more than any other'.[23] He proposed to her a number of times over a seven-year period. She acknowledged his genius for friendship and 'I care for him very much but *marry* dear God no'.[24] Anxious not to trifle with him she suggested they keep their distance but Willie, as she called him, found this difficult. Mindful of her past tragedy, Elizabeth was helpless. After a final refusal in 1899 he married a translator and writer, Magda Sindici, but they later divorced. In 1903 he told Elizabeth 'I have often wondered if I ought ever to have married at all, when I knew that you could not join me.' The following year he urged her to

concentrate every nerve on writing the love story which it is the regret of all my life (and the cause of its failure) I am unable to make you live. Ah, Liza, you will never know the truth of it all and the bitter struggle I went thro' for you because I have loved you and worshipped you more than I knew at the time.

Ironically, Elizabeth had written a love story which had some bearing on her life but behind this pseudonymous tale *The New Moon*, published by Heinemann, about a married doctor and his love for a young woman, can be discerned her love affair with W.A. Just after his death, she wished, as always, on the new moon (with silver) and recalled 'W.A.'s New Moon & mine—that little book he thought too well of'.

In 1899, the year that Heinemann married, Elizabeth's relationship with W.A. seems to have changed gear. Her identity as author of *The Open Question* had just been revealed and their Ibsen partnership had run its course. In the summer she travelled to Switzerland with another Elizabeth, Lady Lewis, wife of the eminent lawyer. Ironically, the dramatic ending of *The New Moon* took place in Switzerland (see Chapter 5). There was some sort of personal crisis and an anxious exchange of letters between Elizabeth and W.A. On 12 August Elizabeth wrote, 'I've kept all my most private & most absorbing life out of this record as is fitting but today *that side* of existence swamps all the rest.' She delayed sending a letter. The following day she got stuck on a mountain but her description of how she extricated herself says as much about her personal fears as it does about her finding her way home. She felt 'profoundly unhappy *cannot* go on like this. Life is simply unlivable at this rate.' By the 19th she was feeling marginally better and showed some humour in her *double entendre*: asking whether 'the cloud—the Scotch mist' was lifting.

Elizabeth saw W.A. far less frequently in the 1900s. In the summer of 1901 he left his London quarters to join his wife in south London though nine months later he returned to the city. Yet Elizabeth and W.A. retained until his death in 1924 a very special friendship. They had always respected each other's intellect and their sharing of stage work and writing provided an important dimension to their relationship. They collaborated as playwrights. W.A.'s version of one of her draft plays, a ghost story about the stage, suggests that the crisis of 1899 may not have marked quite the end of their intimacy. Archer's opening scenario concerns a young doctor who contracts typhoid and goes to South Wales to recuperate. Elizabeth, as we shall see, had typhoid fever on her return from Alaska and recuperated in the west country. Her subsequent novel, *The Magnetic North* (1904), dealt with her travels. In W.A.'s account the narrator says, 'My mood was magnetic in so far as it picked out the iron of life and ignored the gold', all of which suggests that he is writing in the early 1900s. Accompanying it is a note written with the old familiarity: 'Dear one I hold you to my heart & bless you & bless you. 3. 30 sweetest one—I kiss your eyes & lips.' On the other side he explains that this is the beginning of his 'Stall E. 22' story and 'I love you my own sweet & thank you for all your love'.

At times of crisis for either of them they were reunited. When Elizabeth returned from Alaska desperately ill, W.A. visited her and arranged for her to see a consultant he knew, though in a letter to William Stead he characteristically claimed that he had little influence with Miss Robins in such matters. He acknowledged that she looked thin but, assuming a casual manner, added: 'I have not a keen eye for these things.'

He was also circumspect about their joint ventures as playwrights. They worked together on several plays but when Elizabeth admitted to Florence his contribution to the play 'Benvenuto Cellini', he was very perturbed: 'I have besought you all along to say nothing of my share.' He had also advised her against consulting Tree (who fancied himself in the lead role). W.A., who tried, somewhat unrealistically, to compartmentalise his life, was always concerned to appear the impartial critic and not one with a vested interest. He continued to give advice, as he had always done, on Elizabeth's novels. She stated that 'I should not have been a writer but for him'.

Although frequently abroad, W.A., would continue to write to Elizabeth. He did not visit her much in Sussex but they sometimes met in London at restaurants such as Kettner's. Elizabeth records quarrelling with him on 'suffrage matters' one Valentine's Day at Gatti's. He had tried to dissuade her from abandoning her writing and getting involved in the 'monomaniac' tactics of militant suffrage.[25]

What Frances Archer knew or thought of W.A.'s relationship with Elizabeth is not clear though it seems that one way in which she coped with her semi-detached marriage was through developing her interest in ways of alleviating stress through massage, fresh air, positive thinking and the regulation of breathing. She had begun at their Hertfordshire home a successful residential practice known as the 'Nerve Training Colony'. In 1918 the Archers' only son Tom went missing in action. W.A. then wrote Elizabeth a letter 'of the old time sort more or less'. She saw him for the last time after he had given a lecture in London on 5 November 1924, noted that he seemed tired and had a cough. On 17 December he wrote to tell Elizabeth that he was going into hospital for an operation to remove a tumour on a kidney and confessed to a horror of surgery. His letter had opened with the poetic statement that he was 'taking time by the forelock'. In *The Open Question* Elizabeth wrote that during her first, deliriously happy months with Ethan, Val had taken 'Time and Fear by the forelock'. Before signing off, W.A. wrote '*tak for alt*' (thanks for everything).[26] He enclosed a new red diary, his annual present.

He never recovered. His brother Charles wrote to Elizabeth the day after W.A. died but she had already learned of his death in an especially hurtful way, through reading *The Times*. Ill with influenza which soon turned to bronchitis, she sent a wreath to the funeral with the words 'Hedda and Hilda in grateful memory 1891. Dec. 1924'.

His death upset her badly. These two very private people had shared a commitment to the stage, to writing and to each other. Elizabeth was now leading a life-style markedly different from the years when she and W.A. were so frequently in each other's company. Yet she could still confess to Florence Bell that 'William Archer's death haunts me with a sense of a large part of my own life being swept away'.

Florence was her other great 'sounding board', a devoted friend for whom the theatre and fiction were also indispensable features of life. The deep mutual admiration and love the two women felt for each other is all the more remarkable because their friendship seems at first sight to be so unlikely. In age, nationality, wealth, social standing, life-style and many attitudes—most notably towards women's suffrage— Florence and Elizabeth seem poles apart. Eleven years Elizabeth's senior, Florence grew up in Paris during the Second Empire where her father, Sir Joseph Oliffe, was a physician at the British Embassy. Yet Florence's married life was spent in the markedly different English business world. Her husband Hugh Bell was an extremely successful Middlesbrough ironmaster. Today Florence is best remembered as Lady Bell, author of a classic social investigation of 1907, *At the Works*, a study of her husband's employees and their families in a town which had belatedly and dramatically plunged into industrialisation.[27]

Hugh's civic honours were many. His offices included being Lord Lieutenant of the North Riding of Yorkshire and he was knighted in 1904. As the employer's wife Florence was a key figure locally. She was also stepmother to his two children from his first marriage, Maurice and Gertrude (later famed for her eastern travels). The Bells had three children of their own, Hugo, Elsa and Molly. Florence also cut a figure in London society. Unlike Elizabeth, she had no need to earn a living.

Yet despite their leading such very different lives, it was to Florence that Elizabeth wrote, 'I will show you with every year of my life how dear you are to me' and 'I love you all the hours of the day'. And Florence wrote in a similar vein, 'I love you dearly, best of friends. I believe that at this moment the reason I want to be in London is simply a wild longing for you' and 'I love you dearly dearly—because I've taken yr [sic] life into mine—and all its concerns—my blessed friend'. Such language surprises us today but was common currency between close women friends of the time. It nevertheless appears striking coming from Lady Bell who was known to be somewhat formal and could appear formidable. The voluminous correspondence between these two women friends exudes intimacy and care. They exchanged letters several times weekly for the best part of four decades. Florence would sign herself 'Yours inseparably' or as Elizabeth's 'Familiar' and nicknamed her '*min lille soster*' (Norwegian for 'my little sister' which became the American title of one of Elizabeth's novels).

They shared a commitment to the theatre and to writing. This overrode other differences and is a useful reminder for us not to assume that because people have espoused different beliefs they have necessarily compartmentalised their affections accordingly or refused accommodation over time. Elizabeth acknowledged Florence as the one woman in the world 'whose criticism weighs with me … you make me think, make me care, make me see with new eyes'. She could win her 'theatre-heart' like no other, being the first to demonstrate to her how much an actor might learn from the non-professional. She 'understood the theatre beyond any other I had known'.[28]

From a child Florence had loved the theatre. Her father had encouraged theatregoing though a career on the stage was not even contemplated for Sir Joseph's daughter. Even a wish to study music (another great passion) at the Royal College was refused. Instead she turned to fiction, writing plays and numerous stories, many for children. In 1887 Coquelin performed in one of her French farces and her friend Sybil Thorndike acted in many of her later plays on the London stage. Elizabeth captured the clandestine attraction of the world of the stage for this lady: 'I love the very *smell* of Behind-the-Scenes, she once said sniffing it up her fine high nose.'[29]

The first letter Elizabeth received from Mrs Hugh Bell (as she initially knew her) was in May 1891. It was full of praise for the actress's performance as Hedda. It also requested Miss Robins to recite at a Chelsea charity bazaar. Politely but firmly Elizabeth declined, explaining that the role of reciter alarmed her, requiring what Hedda would call courage and being far removed from her own profession. Yet the correspondence and the friendship soon flourished. The ten-year-old Molly Bell recorded in her diary that Miss Robins came to dinner on 20 May: 'We all like her *very* much'.[30] Soon she was accompanying them on outings and in July stayed at their windswept home Red Barns at Redcar, designed by Philip Webb and boasting over a dozen bedrooms and a big garden, Molly begging Elizabeth to pronounce it Redca, not Redcâh. By October Florence was talking of writing a play for Elizabeth.

She had already acted in Florence's comedietta *A Joint Household*. Gertrude had reported to her mother that 'Miss Robins was excellent' at the March matinée at the Steinway Hall.[31] Soon Elizabeth was helping her with *Karin*, translated from Alfhild Agrell's Swedish play. She also played the leading role in the two matinée performances in May 1892 at the Vaudeville under the Robins–Lea joint management. It centred around a woman with a corrupt husband and a child who dies. She is only prepared to save her husband from prison if he frees her from her marriage and grants her the right to bury her child. Contemporaries compared the subject-matter to Ibsen's and the acting was highly praised. In a letter to Shaw Elizabeth described *Karin* as a 'dramatic changeling', not born under a Haymarket or Criterion star and 'wedged in a wilderness of scratch matinées'.[32]

Interspersed with Elizabeth's most famous Ibsen roles came her performance in another domestic tragedy of Scandinavian origin. Unknown to its audiences *Alan's Wife* was by Florence Bell and

Elizabeth Robins. Elizabeth had previously read it to Tree who maintained that women could not write but, unaware of its author-ship, he had been impressed. Performed on the afternoon of 28 April and the evening of 2 May 1893 at Terry's Theatre it produced from theatregoers cries to shake the author both by the hand *and* by the throat. Even Grein whose Independent Theatre produced it, appears to have been unaware of its authorship. In the printed edition he described it as 'one of the truest tragedies ever written by an Englishman'.[33] Not until the 1920s did Florence admit to him her involvement.

The original Swedish story was called *Befriad* meaning 'Released' or 'Set Free', the title Florence would have preferred. The more innocuous-sounding title *Alan's Wife* (not to be confused with Rider Haggard's 1889 short story, 'Allan's Wife'), denoted possession, as did the title of Elizabeth's novel *George Mandeville's Husband*. It recast Elin Ameen's story in northern England with Yorkshire names. Reprinted nearly a hundred years later in 1991 as one of four 'New Woman Plays', this tale of working-class infanticide and its impact on the male critics of the day has attracted some interest from modern femi-nists.[34] It has only three scenes. In the course of the first scene Jean Creyke, played by Elizabeth, learns that her handsome husband Alan, 'a Hercules', has been killed in an accident at the works (Gladstone had called Middlesbrough an 'Infant Hercules'). Her baby is born a cripple, the antithesis of his father before all went wrong, and after baptising him Jean smothers her infant to spare him and punish herself. In the final scene set in prison, she does not repent since she is convinced about the wisdom of her action and, like Hedda, finally displays courage: 'I've had courage just once in my life—just once in my life I've been strong and kind—and it was the night I killed my child!'[35] She has to face a death sentence.

For much of the scene her words are not actually spoken but are written out for the actress to convey the feelings, emotions appar-ently 'speaking' for themselves, Jean's feelings transcending everyday speech and theatrical conventions. The stage direction 'silent' is given in brackets eleven times yet in most cases written words follow; for example:

Jean: (*silent—stares vacantly into space*) I can tell him nothing.[36]

Here is illustrated Elizabeth's belief in the power of women's silence, and a technique which could well have been prompted by her appreciation of Ibsen's use of the unspoken text between the lines in his plays. The play is bold in its assertion of Jean's choice: against her mother who had wanted her to marry the puny minister, in her acknowledgement of the sexual attraction of Alan and finally in the act of infanticide. Its celebration of the healthy and strong at the expense of the weak and disabled—the fittest may not literally survive but his naturally mutilated offspring is condemned—makes us uneasy today. It needs to be seen in relation to Elizabeth's interest in heredity and the concerns she would soon be exploring in *The Open Question*.

Yet it was with Ibsen's *Ghosts* that contemporaries drew comparisons, another play which to many appeared to defy all decency. *Alan's Wife* both puzzled and disturbed, clearly justifying the decision of the society lady and eminent actress to remain anonymous. Infanticide was then and still remains a delicate subject, raising fundamental questions about the delineation and labelling of the 'bad mother'.[37] It had become a matter of some concern in the 1860s though much of the interest and resultant legislation concerned unmarried mothers and the regulation of childminding after several notorious cases of baby farming. Although in England and Wales capital punishment did exist for infanticide, there was extreme reluctance to use the death penalty and from 1864 commutation of the death sentence was recommended when a woman was convicted of murdering her own infant. It was felt that such a crime could not be a rational act by a child's mother. Citing temporary insanity produced by childbearing became a convenient loophole.[38] So, in the final scene the Colonel asks whether Jean's mind was affected at the time. The ending with Jean condemned to death does not therefore reflect the tendency of the time but serves a melodramatic purpose. However, Jean's mother's denial of her daughter being temporarily insane effectively removes the usual excuse of puerperal mania (even though some critics still muttered about this). It also provides Jean with absolute responsibility for her actions. The *Sunday Sun* voiced contemporary fears denouncing it as another dreary study in sexual dementia portraying the 'various phases of feminine hysteria and insanity'.

The drama critic W.B. Walkley not only denied that the play possessed any intellectual quality, lying outside 'the region of art', but also tried to exert his opinions over its very creation 'I submit that this play ought never to have been written.'[39] So disturbed was he by Jean's action which lay so far beyond the acceptable boundaries of prescribed motherhood that his revulsion at the destabilising effects of the play caused him to imagine that he saw on stage both the disfigured bloody figure of Alan on the stretcher and the mangled corpse of the strangled baby. In print Archer denied the possibility of both claims.[40]

Yet whilst Archer publicly sided with supporters of the play and wrote the Introduction to the published version, it can be claimed that he also tried to appropriate some of the authority for and of it. His Introduction was forty-three pages long, almost as long as the play. He asserted that he was 'in great measure responsible for the existence of the play, and it is only right that I should put on record my complicity before the fact'. Perhaps he was trying to protect the anonymity of its authors. Archer knew of Elizabeth's part in its development (Shaw claimed that he tried to mystify him as to the sex of the writer). He constructed an elaborate story in which he talked to Elizabeth about the story and she offered to consult 'two clever and ambitious young dramatists'.[41] Whatever his motives, he was at pains to stress how he would have treated the subject differently; for example, by developing dialogue around the ethical issue rather than presenting emotional drama. He claimed that his idea for a play came from reading Ameen's story in a Swedish magazine and that Elizabeth read it in a German translation but did not see it as a subject for the theatre. Elizabeth's own version differs: she first read a summary in Stead's *Review of Reviews* and wrote on 6 May 1893 that she *had* seen a play in it.

It is impossible to be clear about exactly what and how much she contributed to the translation and alterations. Shifting it to northern England with Yorkshire names was probably Florence's idea but what about substituting a minister in place of a doctor? At the front of her 1929 collection of essays, *Landmarks*,[42] Florence is listed as the author of *Alan's Wife* written in collaboration with Elizabeth Robins. Their correspondence mentions Florence working on the last scene with Elizabeth's advice and constant suggestions. Florence clearly found it a powerful experience: 'the mere thought of that play makes my heart leap and burn within me.' They considered whether Sarah Bernhardt might perform 'that dear play of ours' in Paris but this came to nothing. In one letter Florence confessed to the play being 'so little mine'. This may be a reference to the extent of Elizabeth's input though it could, alternatively, be an acknowledgement of the original work of Elin Ameen. In a letter to Shaw written in 1899 Elizabeth told him that 'The real author of that play [*Alan's Wife*] would not be at all obliged' to him for crediting her with a work in which she had 'only a small share'.[43] This could have been the case but again Elizabeth may simply have been seeking once more to mystify.

At home in Sweden and plagued by severe headaches, Elin Ameen was unhappy about the situation. Since there was no copyright agreement between Sweden and England and anyway nothing to prevent a story being dramatised, she had no legal grounds for complaint. She did, however, resent the lack of prior consultation and her rambling letters to Elizabeth display her resentment at exclusion (both in terms of money and publicity) from association with the play. Not until the 1900s did she know for certain that Elizabeth was a co-author. The latter played an elaborate game, claiming to be the intermediary between the Swedish woman and the author. Ameen had always wanted her story to appear in English so the publication of the play rather stole her thunder and she pleaded for some acknowledgement since the original and central idea was hers. In retaliation she translated the play into Swedish without prior approval, reverting to the original ending of imprisonment since Sweden did not punish infanticide with hanging.

Florence and Elizabeth often signed their letters to each other with the names of the characters they were creating on paper and, in Elizabeth's case, acting. Thus in May 1893 the latter was signing herself as Jean. Florence frequently provided advice on costume, hair and props for her different roles. They commented extensively on each other's written work and Elizabeth referred to Florence's 'neverfailing godmothering of my projects'. The latter wrote of her play *Angela* about gambling amongst the wealthy, 'There is not a line in which you haven't a part'.[44] Florence wrote a parody of Elizabeth's novel *The New Moon*. Her triple-decker tale *The Story of Ursula* (1895) with its heroine caught between the different cultures of France and England, was dedicated to Elizabeth whilst *Come and Find Me* was in turn dedicated to Florence.[45] Not insignificantly, the work by

Elizabeth which Florence most approved of was her one children's story, *Prudence and Peter*, written with Octavia Wilberforce. Florence reviewed it for *The Times Literary Supplement* and sent out over 2,000 copies of notices of the book all over the country.

As well as often seeing her friend at her mother's Knightsbridge home, 95, Sloane Street, Elizabeth made frequent and lengthy visits to the Bells from 1892 onwards, first staying at Red Barns and then from 1905 joining them at their new home, the three-storey Rounton Grange near Northallerton with its sweeping lawns and space for family, friends, fellow Liberals and business colleagues. Elizabeth tended to spend several months including her birthdays with the Bells in the summer and was often the only non-relative there over Christmas and the New Year, even after she acquired her own home. She called them her family and within a couple of years of meeting her, Florence was stressing: 'Remember that there is a very happy home here, with a father and mother, and troops of children—'who feel that you absolutely belong to them so it's no good your saying you don't.' Elizabeth encouraged young Molly Bell to write, told her stories she was composing and even talked about her marriage to George Parks.

Being in the bosom of someone else's noisy family was not always Elizabeth's idea of relaxing yet there were times when Yorkshire provided a vital escape route, initially from the stage and emotional pressures especially since her own relatives were thousands of miles away. In September 1892 she wrote: 'coming along the wet gas-lit street this evening, I was suddenly overwhelmed with a sense of infinite loneliness—London seemed the emptiest spot on earth— of course it won't last. I know in my heart I am singularly fortunate being unencumbered but a woman is an unaccountable animal!' Increasingly, as years went by, it also became a means of recharging the literary batteries and recuperating from illness with all creature comforts. In the summer of 1906 Elizabeth wrote from Rounton that 'being a little overdriven I flew to this haven' and returning home after two months reflected on its 'atmosphere of pleasant purpose combined with a maximum of ease & beauty of life'.[46]

Elsa's daughters remember her as Lisa, quoting literature and reading heavily accented tales of Uncle Remus out loud.[47] She is recalled as Granny's friend, very kind, slightly scatterbrained—always misplacing her jewellery—intense but never frightening and refreshingly different from the Yorkshire cousins. Both Florence and Elizabeth tended to dress in sober tones but Lisa was less of a stickler for correct etiquette. Florence Bell was formal even by Victorian standards. She never approved of Elizabeth's calling Hugh by his first name, even after knowing him for over twenty years. She corrected Americanisms and slips in grammar: 'Lisa, you must not mix up your shalls and wills, we have discussed that before.' Her daughter-in-law Frances Bell (née Morkill) has recalled her first meeting with Hugo's mother, how she held court from her armchair:

> with a veil over her head and long flowing skirts, very much the Grande Dame and I was introduced to her and first thing I had to do was to talk French to her … she wanted to know what my accent was like.[48]

Hugh Bell, somewhat less formal, was the director of Bell Brothers (in which Elizabeth invested £1,000 in 1899) and involved over the years not only in iron, steel and coal-mining but also in railway insurance as well as Liberal politics. Elizabeth enjoyed discussing politics with him and if he was in town on business without Florence would accompany him to the theatre. Florence also had commitments such as local schools and improving facilities for Middlesbrough people most notably in her scheme for 'rational recreation', the Winter Gardens. Elizabeth occasionally went to the pioneering Gardens with Florence.

Elizabeth and Gertrude Bell found much to admire in each other. Elizabeth respected this historian, archaeologist, linguist, mountaineer and diplomat. They spent a holiday together in Scotland. In 1927, the year after Gertrude's death in Baghdad, Elizabeth gave a BBC broadcast on her life, pointing to how she had contracted 'a habit of success' from an early age and tracing her Arabian exploits and part in the development of modern Iraq.[49]

In the 1890s Elizabeth had described her as 'simply the most manysided and wonderful person of her sex *in the world*'. She later wrote a long appreciation of her books *The Desert and the Sown* and *Amurath to Amurath* calling her a 'law-lover and law-breaker', a 'reactionary passionate for freedom'. Gertrude praised Elizabeth's work and confided in her about her tragic love-life. Yet, despite mutual respect and appreciation of the pioneer spirit, they espoused radically different views about women's rights. Gertrude the intrepid travel-ler, received in the Middle East as a 'malc' guest who seems to have bothered little about the women's lives, was chaperoned as a young woman in England and later sat on the committee of the National League for Opposing Woman Suffrage. In 1907 Elizabeth joined the committee of the Women's Social and Political Union. Yet the 'Anti' and the Suffragette tried to be fair to each other. Gertrude wrote to 'Beloved Lisa' acknowledging that *The Convert* had convinced her 'That the spirit of the whole movement is really such as you have represented it' but neither she nor her stepmother could sympathise with its opinions. Florence felt it a pity that art was sacrificed for spe-cial pleading and tried (in vain) not to ridicule its political idealism. Yet she found plenty of positive things to say about it and *Votes For Women!*[50] The depth of their friendship was touchingly demonstrated when Elizabeth confessed that if her friend had disliked it 'mortal much' she would never have published it. Occasionally the situation was reversed. Elizabeth criticised a playlet Florence had written for the Women's Institute, arguing, to Florence's chagrin, that the char-acters were too slavishly subservient to be plausible.

Florence was never as implacably opposed to women's suffrage as Gertrude and indeed works like *Alan's Wife*, *At the Works* and a later essay called 'Women at the Works—and Elsewhere' at least suggest some recognition of the need to listen to women's voices. Yet it is to women as mothers that she makes her appeal and her reaction to the feminist Anna Martin's articles on working-class women was that they were 'marred by the obvious holding of a brief for the women as against the men, which makes me SICK'.

As early as 1899 she had poked fun at women's suffrage in her adaptation of La Fontaine's fables. Parodying the frog's desire to be as big as the ox she hopes

Que chacun garde son role: C'est plus avantageux
Et le monde ne s'en trouvera que mieux.[51]

It became especially awkward when Elizabeth found herself staying at Rounton in what Christabel Pankhurst called 'a perfect nest of antis'. The subject of women's suffrage was anyway as a 'red rag to a bull' as far as Hugh was concerned (and Maurice was less enlightened

than his father). In August 1908 Elizabeth found herself in the company of some prominent 'Antis' including Lord Cromer who, as she
remarked to her radical sister-in-law Margaret, had just given the
bill for old age pensions 'a black eye in the House of Lords'.[52] In
this letter to Margaret Elizabeth conveys something of the tensions
she faced in reconciling herself to the paternalistic and increasingly
anachronistic world of Rounton:

> Here I fall into the mid summer [*sic*] flower show and prize-giving
> for villagers and tenantry—all the curiously persistent and in some
> ways very beautiful feudal manifestations which strike so strange
> a note upon the ear attuned to the new music.

Even more incongruous was Gertrude, of a younger generation yet
a 'pillar of the Antis', a movement 'gathering force among the old
encrusted Tories'. Elizabeth's unease rested partly on being personally
pulled in different directions by having a foot in very different and
hostile camps and therefore at times being somewhat two-faced. It
also arose from her appreciation that her hosts were actually amongst
the more liberal and intelligent of their sort. Most importantly, she
knew just how deeply privilege ran in Edwardian England and how
much was at stake:

> there is a bitter battle ahead—my suffrage friends don't altogether
> realize fortunately, what a flint of opposition they'll have to over-
> throw. The more we win friends, the fiercer are our foes … so
> much is involved in it besides 'votes'. It is really a pulling out of
> the chief cornerstones of privilege. Ibsen saw that years ago.[53]

She tried, unsuccessfully, to reason with the obdurate Gertrude, made
excuses about leaving early and, as the Humphry Wards arrived,
packed her bags. Mary Ward had written Elizabeth's last professional
stage role. Elizabeth admired her as a social activist but she currently represented a leading spirit of the 'Antis' (in 1908 she had
become first President of the Anti-Suffrage League). The next day
Elizabeth joined Mrs Pankhurst at the Newcastle by-election. Her
conscience cannot have been eased by the chairman of the meeting
she addressed pointing out that many women who lived sheltered

lives in country houses did not want the vote but 'were a few country house ladies, and a few countesses, headed by Mrs Humphry Ward, to be regarded as expressing the opinion of the women of England?'[54] Two years later, after quarrelling with Gertrude about trade unions and feeling the strain of alienation from the household's views on suffrage, Elizabeth asked herself (in her diary) whether she would be returning in the future to Rounton as there no longer seemed any reason to do so.

The most strained period was March 1912 during the coal strike, also a time of heightened militant suffrage activity. Florence began a letter to Elizabeth by stressing her own ability to see both sides of questions but also denouncing the 'unbalanced and vindictive' manifestations of militancy.[55] Uncharacteristically addressing her friend Lisa as 'Elizabeth', the letter became personal and pointed. She was now carefully cast as a foreigner, at a time of 'national peril' when 'the country (not your country, mark) is faced with disorder'. Florence was shocked that, when 'utter balance, sanity, patriotism are most needed, *you*, a woman of your fine nobility of outlook, should also go headlong into the excitement and write incendiary letters inciting others—whose country it is—to add to the disorder'.

These 'incendiary letters' were not mail set on fire in pillar boxes (a Suffragette tactic) but Elizabeth's correspondence with the press. On 7 March she had had a long letter printed in *The Times* defending militancy and commenting that 'many of us have come to read of broken glass with an intensity of relief'. Florence saw such statements as 'little less than criminal', an abuse of her position and, after a further reminder that Britain was 'the country of your adoption', the letter ended with 'I feel as if the whole world were on a lower level and it makes me miserable'. One way of dealing with her friend's behaviour was to portray her as taken over by 'second rate persons' who 'infest your house and use you as a tool and seem to have hypnotized you'. The language of spells, disease and betrayal resonates through another letter.[56]

Remarkably, the friendship survived though both had to work hard at this. Caution was exercised on both sides. In September Rounton was to receive guests from the Church Congress. Florence shifted responsibility on to Hugh who, she wrote, was 'very definitely of [the] opinion that he wouldn't like *any* suffrage activities

to be connected with this house during that time (or indeed at an
time!)' so perhaps Lisa could postpone her visit? She obliged. Yet
in May 1912 Elizabeth wrote Florence a letter which summed up
their friendship:

> We have always had our separate windows out of wh. [sic] each
> looked at life, seeing as folk must whose windows are not the same
> a different aspect of the scene. I give you my word I do not have
> to pretend there's no gulf. When you were so ill, when I had you
> in my heart every hour of the day I did not find myself thinking
> of any difference—but of long years of a very unusual & beautiful
> relation of all things you had taught me, of what I owed to you &
> … how very much I loved you.

In the 1920s not only did Elizabeth continue to stay at Rounton but
Octavia also visited (and learned to drive there). There were visits
to the Trevelyans in Northumberland (Molly had married Charles
Trevelyan). Florence wisely abstained from reading Elizabeth's feminist polemic *Ancilla's Share*. Its anonymity may have made her feel less
vulnerable through association. What they shared rather than what
divided them was stressed now though their differences emerged in
little matters. When the Dean of Ripon talked to Florence about
woman's mission as submission and put his arm around her, both
women were outraged: Elizabeth's feminist principles were offended
whilst Florence was displeased by such lack of manners.

In 1921 Florence suggested that Elizabeth move to Rounton. In
the same year she achieved the well-nigh impossible, persuading her
to act the part of Lady Fairfax in the Middlesbrough matinée of
her play *The Heart of Yorkshire* to raise money for the Five Sisters
window in York Minster. It focused on three periods in the cathe-
dral's history suggesting that during the Civil War the city archives
were saved by a woman, Anne Fairfax.[57] Elizabeth felt that the praise
she received for her acting was unjustified.

The mid-1920s were tragic years for the Bells. Florence became
increasingly deaf and the great Bell fortune began to crumble. In
1926, the year of Florence and Hugh's golden wedding anniversary,
Hugo, a married clergyman with small children, died of typhoid
on his way home from South Africa and six months later Gertrude

died 'in her sleep' in Iraq. The General Strike helped precipitate the closing of Rounton and the family moved to the more modest Mount Grace. Here, in 1927, largely as a form of therapy (though it had originally been planned for the previous year) Florence developed her plan for a pageant in the grounds of Mount Grace Priory. She had asked Elizabeth to produce it but to the latter's relief Ellen Terry's daughter, Edy Craig, founder of the Pioneer Players, came to the rescue giving Elizabeth a chance to reminisce with her about the suffrage days. Florence, 'frail and indomitable', wrote the script which told of incidents in the history of the Carthusians between the eleventh century and the Dissolution of the Monasteries. It was an ambitious venture involving 118 people excluding the principals and at a time of dwindling income it cost £1,800. Elizabeth, now sixty-five, delivered the Prologue dressed as the Spirit of Time. When she had protested about taking part Florence had simply ignored her 'hoity toity letter'. The pageant was performed for three days. At one dress rehearsal there was an audience of 390 and the queen and Princess Mary briefly visited. Once it was over Elizabeth and the Bells watched it on the news at the local cinema.

Although Hugh was seriously ill in 1929, he lived on for two more years. Florence died in London in May 1930. Elizabeth recorded her death in her diary. Her writing was unusually small. Hugh told her: 'I believe you were more to Florence than anyone.' She accompanied the family to the funeral. The previous year Florence had republished her generous tribute to her friend (originally in *Time and Tide* in 1920).[58] It acknowledged her 'unswerving truthfulness, her passionate intolerance of authority, and her irrepressible dramatic gifts'. The lady of great expectations declared her friendship with Elizabeth to be 'a privilege, an incentive and a standard'. Elizabeth, with 'despair now raging in my heart', wrote in *The Times* obituary about Florence's 'Genius for social intercourse'[59] (echoing her friend's description of herself: 'The greatest of her possessions is her art of human intercourse'). It ended: 'Those who had her friendship had a treasure, and in her death know a loss that leaves them dumb or stammering.'

Yet Elizabeth's most lasting tribute to Florence lies in her book *Theatre and Friendship*. Published in 1932, it is ostensibly about the friendship between Henry James and Elizabeth. Leon Edel has acknowledged it as 'a record of a triangular theatre-friendship'[60] but it was in reality much more than this. Compiled in 1931, it reflected Elizabeth's loss and was her way of circumventing the fact that Florence had not wanted her biography to be written: 'I reflect she did not say she would object to having some of her letters printed.' Here was a means of acknowledging Florence Bell's artistic talents yet in a suitably subtle manner through the letters of the three individuals. She is mentioned on all but three pages of the introduction which ends discussing her. Elizabeth admitted that working on this gave her a sense that she and Florence were once more 'building'. Over half the book is actually about Florence Bell.

It was appropriate that the late Henry James should provide this opportunity. Not only did the theatrical friendship between Florence and himself predate Elizabeth's coming to London but in 1891, the year when the friendship between the two women began and immediately after Elizabeth acted in his play *The American*, he had written a short story, 'Nona Vincent'.[61] The main characters are thinly disguised Jamesian representations of Florence and Elizabeth. Mrs Alsager who had 'an infallible instinct for the perfect' saves a playwright by showing his young leading actress Violet Grey, via a ghostly revelation, the way to become a fine actress and so transform herself and the play. Elizabeth knew her own mind, and her acting ability was not derived from Florence Bell but she did cherish what she gained from this unlikely yet very special friendship. She once wrote to Florence, 'I always have the feeling you'll take better care of me than I could of myself.'

PART III

C.E. RAIMOND AND I

5

COME AND FIND ME

I have a strong conviction that when my acting days are over—my writing days may begin. I shall always have to *do* something—I cd. not live otherwise. So it is my duty like a wise husbandman to lay by for the future a store of enlightenment—glimpses into men and character (—my own and other peoples [*sic*]—) bits of 'acted drama' written down in the flush of a first performance and even the dry details of daily living that I may put my hand on my hard winnings when I don't any longer remember where I got them and how and thro' what man or woman or in what land I found them. If I write when I am too old to act, my best capital next to sympathetic observation and an unaffected style wd. be a diary of my own life.

Although Elizabeth took her own advice, proffered in 1891, and assiduously developed her own 'store of enlightenment' for the future, writing proved to be not only a life assurance policy which could, through prudent garnering, be realised in older age but also something for the present. The Elizabeth Robins of the 1890s was known as an actress and this is how she has been remembered. Her career as a writer has tended to be associated with the years after she left the stage. Yet in practice her professions were not so divided. The 1890s proved to be crowded, creative years for Elizabeth in which she actually juggled her roles as both actress and author.

Even before leaving the United States she had started to look beyond the stage. The tragedies of her life must have already made her more aware than many of the precariousness of life and need to plan. In October 1887 on the Barrett–Booth tour she had written to a friend about 'my new scheme for earning money (by my pen)'. In Kansas City, New Orleans and Cincinnati she wrote Travel Letters for the press. Undeterred by a lack of interest, she believed her pen could be 'a possible staff'. Journalism had been one of her father's many occupations and two of her aunts had been writers.

On tour in Texas in February 1888 she turned to fiction though her short story 'Him and Her' leaned heavily on her family's own history. It tells the story of Helen Raven (another bird surname, which was also the assumed name of an actress with whom she had worked). Helen lives with her grandmother and brother and accidentally learns prematurely of her father's first wife who had absconded with another man, as had Charles Robins's first wife. Several American magazines rejected the story though the editor of the *Home Journal* acknowledged that its author possessed genuine talent and knew how to write literature rather than merely recite a case.

Although she reworked this story when first in England, it was never published, neither was a literary effort based on her London experience, 'Letter from an American Actress'. Probably encouraged by her new friend Frances Hoey (Mrs Cashel Hoey) who had written for an Australian newspaper for twenty years, Elizabeth was keen to become a correspondent for an American paper.

The prime motivation was economic. The average income of performers lucky enough to work forty weeks in the year was a mere £2 a week.[1] 'When, in 1889, Elizabeth received a kind letter from the playwright Pinero, she wrote in her diary, 'oh Father in Heaven I need something more than "recommendation".' Theatrical life was one of 'hard suspense' with far too many gaps between parts. Neither was there necessarily any handsome pecuniary reward when there was work to be had. Elizabeth's contemporary Fanny Brough received only £12 to £16 weekly for many years for her actual performances. Although at the height of her success Elizabeth commanded a good salary—£50 weekly for *Little Eyolf*—her preference for non-commercial theatre and short runs meant that her years on the British stage were ones when she was continually seeking to supplement her income. Thus, she wrote in March 1890 of her writing: 'I will take

up my new work with no illusions—it is to be for a *purpose* & that
end must consecrate my work.' The actress Fanny Kemble provided
a valuable role model. By the mid-1870s she earned £300 annually
from the *Atlantic Monthly*.²

Writing, particularly journalistic articles and short stories, could be
fitted into spare time. The short story had evolved in Europe in mid-
century and was now popular in England. It seemed an especially
promising way of securing the cash she badly needed to help her
family back home. It did not require capital yet offered opportunities for her to exercise her powerful imagination and draw upon her
own travel and experiences. Yet Elizabeth did not find writing an
easy alternative route to a good income. Her early short stories paid
only between £10 and £14 apiece. As she wrote to Florence Bell
when negotiating one such story, 'What on earth is the good of *my*
scribbling if I don't get decently paid for it.' She did, however, enjoy
writing and, thanks to her diary, was well practised. The diary helped
her to work through and legitimise her actions and contradictions,
providing both material and a dry run for her fiction. She also jotted
down incidents and story-lines which might be handy for the future.
She had long been a careful observer of people. She felt that her
keen eye for detail owed something to the habit of collecting for
the specimen cabinet she had begun as a teenager in the Colorado
mining camp.

The spring of 1889 found her still waiting for parts and determined
to try 'my hand persistently at short stories or novels'. She utilised her
experiences from her journey of 1888 to Central America in what
she called a 'novelette' (see Chapter 10). A year later she was acting in
Dr Bill but with little enthusiasm and the worry of getting 'my own
bread & butter' when the run ended. She was ever-conscious of time
running out and, to her horror, had just detected her first grey hair
(for much of the following decade she would dye her hair). Behind
all her actions lay her awareness of family responsibilities, especially
her mother's needs:

> If I am to accomplish anything helpful & worthy for my people
> I must not depend upon the precarious living afforded me by
> the stage. I must write Letters if the opportunity comes if not
> novels—not that I think I can make 'a name', not that I have

confidence in my ability 'to deliver a message' to my generation only that it is clearly my duty to take some surer way to help my people than leads thro [*sic*] a stage door. Lots of stupid women write books & make money—I shall not, cannot be worse than some & if I write a passable story & follow it with others & can make a home for my mother & take my brother thro college I could be happier & richer in gratification than if I'd written the *most* clever book of the day & benefitted no one.

Just under 4,700 books had been published the previous year and Elizabeth was determined to add her pen, if not her name, to this list. She dreamed of the time when she would no longer have to ride on an omnibus late at night, only too conscious that 'someone at home needs these shillings'.

When involved with stage work she found little time to write except perhaps on Sundays: 'I live in the Theatre & reach home at night too tired to hold a pencil let alone write new stuff.' Her most productive writing periods—for example, the year 1895—were the least busy in terms of acting and stage production. Yet she reiterated her vision of writing as a long-term 'As men will lavish all their keen devotions on some unresponsive mistress & at the last content themselves with some more grateful if less loved woman—so will I try literature loving acting ever the best.' At a later stage she annotated this diary entry with the words 'how completely I changed'.

Acting had been her original choice. Writing, developed out of exigency, became her habit. Yet she graduated from the apprenticeship of her early journalism and fiction to a position where she became a respected, prolific full-time writer, committed to a profession which lasted for the rest of her life.

In the spring of 1890 Elizabeth began a novel which has not survived. It was set, at least in part, in Norway and at one stage called 'The Curse of Marriage'. Some of her material and ideas most probably found expression in her epic novel *The Open Question* as did an early sketch of her grandmother. Elizabeth now tried concentrating on writing about the stage since 'nothing can be so well described as a recreation or occurrence recently freshly experienced' but neither her stage novel 'The Coming Woman' nor her tales 'Scenes behind the Scenes' were published. There was one exception to the latter,

'La Bellerieuse' (published in the *Pall Mall Magazine* [for details of Elizabeth's publications see Appendix 2]), a romantic story about a Rachel-like figure from the gutter who becomes Europe's greatest light opera artiste.

The stage also influenced her writing in other ways. An avid reader herself, her ideal was to do for fiction what Ibsen had done for drama. Recognising that she had 'no more hope of inventing a new plot than I have of discovering a new colony', she stressed in her diaries and notebooks that she was

> never so interested in an author's dissecting of character … as I am in discovering the character myself from what people do & say.

She remarked that Ibsen 'never tells anything' about the consummate female characters he created yet somehow 'they themselves show us themselves with amazing simplicity'. This is what she sought to achieve. She was also critical of 'the artistic verity of omniscience' disparaging those writers who believed they could

> lift the veil of semblance & pretend to tell the world what is. No one knows anything more than what seems—& after all what seems, is better material for art—let the scientists say we <u>know</u>.

She published some non-fictional material about the stage. Ten years after her article about the Barrett–Booth tour, the *North American Review* printed her account of Sarah Bernhardt's Hamlet. This considered the actress's assumption of a masculine role and praised her poise but was more a tribute to Booth than a study of Bernhardt. Not having been professionally trained, and having such painful personal memories of the Boston years, Elizabeth tended retrospectively to see herself as Booth's protégée. Her tour with him was elevated into a very significant development in her acting career.

Still interested in travel-writing, Elizabeth wrote about perhaps the most famous of all amateur stage productions, the Oberammergau passion play. Encouraged by the journalist W.T. Stead, she briefly turned her back on the London stage and visited Bavaria in the summer of 1890. Thanks to Stead's contacts she lodged with the man who played Herod and was treated to a privileged behind-the-scenes tour.

She observed how the drama in the Roman Catholic service con-tributed to the massive, committed spectacle mounted by 'peasant players'. Although several drafts of her account exist and the story is retold in her autobiography,[3] Elizabeth's impressions of the passion play did not appear in print at the time. Yet this journey of an unbe-liever was nevertheless influential in shaping her attitudes towards writing and acting: 'At last I had seen that these players take their Art sandwiched between their daily bread. It is neither pastime nor trade. It is Life itself. So would I be content to take mine.'

Stead was to be one of the people who encouraged Elizabeth as a writer (see Chapter 6). Another journalist who had a major influence was, of course, Archer. From December 1890 Elizabeth was installed in her own flat in Manchester Square Gardens. She generously acknowledged that it was from here that she 'went to school with WA & learned what I know of writing'. He 'steadied & guided my early steps in the direction of novel writing'. She jotted down themes and settings in her diary and notebooks and discussed ideas with him. Although Archer was ever-willing to listen, it can be argued that he was not always sufficiently prepared to allow Elizabeth's own style and views to emerge. He could be quite intimidating, 'a ravening Herod with a sword ready for all infant ideas'. When she finished working on the first act of the play 'Benvenuto Cellini', Elizabeth told Florence that she wouldn't dare tell Archer that she had writ-ten it so quickly. More than one work was abandoned as a result of Archer's critical appraisal.

Nevertheless, with his experience and contacts in the publishing trade, Archer could offer much practical advice. He also secured Norwegian translation work for Elizabeth which helped to pay the bills. For working on a translation of the explorer Nansen's work she got £50. Archer advised her about placing articles, about the reserva-tion of rights and appropriate fees. After *Alan's Wife* Elizabeth worked on a number of plays which never saw the light of day, not least because they touched on subjects which were viewed by many as taboo. One was 'The Mirkwater', set in the north of England. Vague northern settings enabled Elizabeth to use her personal knowledge of the north-east without being committed to specific locations. The play dealt with breast cancer and suicide. As in *The Open Question*, Elizabeth validated the taking of one's life in extreme circumstances:

'It is worthy only of the brutes to cling to life for mere life's sake, after joy and usefulness are done.' Parts of this three-act play using the Ibsen technique of the retrospective were written by Archer though Elizabeth did the suicide scene. In another play of the mid-1890s, 'The Silver Lotus', containing alterations by Archer, we can see some of the ideas which would find fuller and more confident expression in Elizabeth's feminist play *Votes For Women!*, ideas about women's percipience and betrayal. Like the later novel *Camilla*, this play provides an avowal of woman's sexuality. Yet it is ostensibly a study of female alcoholism.

It was, however, the very different 'Benvenuto Cellini' which appeared to hold out the greatest promise amongst Elizabeth's plays pre-1900.[4] The larger-than-life Renaissance sculptor, gold and silversmith appealed to her romantic imagination. In Norway Edvard Bull had told her how his brother Ole had once played a violin carved by Cellini. The play is a somewhat uncharacteristic historical melodrama set in the French court of Francis I. Archer worked on it with Elizabeth in 1899–1900 and Alexander, Wyndham and Tree were consulted about production. With some reservations about its length, Tree accepted it but his option for exclusive rights was withdrawn after disclosure of the authorship. Archer had been especially anxious that his involvement should not be detected. Abortive discussions ensued about a New York production and in France Coquelin rejected Florence Bell's translation, feeling that the play was too close to a French novel on the same subject which Archer (not Elizabeth) had read.

Elizabeth did not use her own name for her early fiction and drama. Her insistence on anonymity was intrinsically related to her position as a well-known actress. In her early days in London before becoming established on the stage she was less secretive than later. In fact she took her manuscript of her 'novelette' to a couple of publishers, lent it to Frances Hoey, sent it to the drama critic Clement Scott and left it for Oscar Wilde to read. As Elizabeth became acclaimed for her acting so she sought to hide her identity as a writer. In an interview with the press in 1910 she explained that if she had appended her name to her stories people would have treated them as mere curiosities, making it impossible to judge whether they actually possessed any literary merit. Here and elsewhere she argued that an author's personality intrudes between a critic and the author's work. She had sought to avoid this, wanting to be judged as a novelist rather than as an actress who happened to write novels.

Her love of secrecy and corresponding fear of revealing too much of herself also help to account for the hiding of her true name and for her acknowledged interest in blurring fact and fiction. She once toyed with the idea of writing a fictitious journal of an 'un-famed but capricious introspective person' like Marie Bashkirtseff which she would publish not as fiction but 'simply as a true diary'. She added that she respected truth but did not want 'that white light turned on *me* for the benefit of others' amusement or pity any more than I could stand naked in the market place'.

Elizabeth's story 'Him and Her' had been signed 'Saxton', her brother's name. It was, however, under the *nom de plume* of C.E. Raimond that she was first published as a fiction writer. The actress who had camouflaged herself as Clare Raimond in America rein-vented herself in Britain as a writer using an amalgam of her father's initials (some manuscripts are signed Charles E. Raimond) and again a fancy spelling of her brother's name. One of her literary aunts had used the pen-name of Sidney Russel.

A pseudonym had other advantages. Elizabeth was increas-ingly concerned about the difficulties women writers faced from the public's insistence on identifying them with their heroines. As chairwoman at the Women Writers' Club Dinner at the Criterion in London in 1899, she criticised the way the heroine could so easily be 'hung round the neck of the author'. Although she later modified this to concede that when ideas were consistently expressed through many characters over a series of books, it was justifiable to deduce an author's viewpoint, she still recognised the indefensibility of peremptorily identifying a character's opinion with the writer's.[5] Recognising the difficulties women also faced more generally in being treated as professionals and understanding people's expecta-tions in terms of gender, Elizabeth saw that a pseudonym which people would presume to be a cover for a male writer might at times be convenient.[6] As she explained in her article 'Woman's Secret', so conscious is the woman writer that it is '*his* game she is trying her hand at, that she is prone to borrow his very name to set up on her title-page'.[7]

William Heinemann, who published Elizabeth's early novels, never shared her penchant for a pseudonym, protesting 'there's no money in a shadow … The public like a personality.' C.E. Raimond in fact went to considerable lengths to confound her readers and disguise her identity. She refused to sign the usual contract for publication of her first novel, instead persuading Heinemann to send her a personal letter agreeing to terms. This was locked in the office safe.[8] For at least one short story Archer wrote in ink over her proofs to disguise Elizabeth's handwriting from a potentially inquisitive editor. To complicate the situation further, another American writer with her name, married to the lithographer Joseph Pennell was now in England and knew Elizabeth. This led some people (after Elizabeth's own identity had been revealed) to confuse the two women. Thus, for example, the *Green Room Book* for 1907 claimed that C.E. Raemond [*sic*] was the real name of Elizabeth Robins Pennell. The latter wrote biographies and in the mid-1880s in Boston had published a life of Mary Wollstonecraft.[9]

Elizabeth used her pseudonym to great effect in her first published novel in 1894. Its deliberately provocative title *George Mandeville's Husband* draws attention to gender, naming and identity.[10] It concerns a second-rate woman novelist who becomes a great success. Having adopted a male pseudonym she then reveals her identity and holds a weekly salon where her husband, whose name we do not know at the outset, is simply introduced as George Mandeville's husband. George had of course become a popular assumed name for women writers. The fictional novelist is inspired by George Eliot and George Sand (mentioned by their real names) whilst Elizabeth's contemporaries included the New Woman writer George Egerton (Mary Chavelita Dunne) as well as the playwright George Fleming (Constance Fletcher). Elizabeth was the leading lady in George Fleming's play *Mrs Lessingham* in the spring of 1894. She also knew personally contemporary male writers such as George Moore, George du Maurier and George Meredith. Of Meredith she once wrote, 'God how the man can write'.

During the course of the 219-page novel, George Mandeville adapts a novel for the stage. Elizabeth paints a picture of an overbearing woman whose talent has been exaggerated and whose husband's and daughter's lives are sacrificed for the dubious sake of her art.

She exposes the farce of play-readings, the heart-breaking difficulties of getting plays accepted. This, the less glamorous aspect of her work, is characteristically assigned to Wilbraham her long-suffering husband. She pokes fun at the pretentious and hangers-on and indicts matinée performances where no thought is given to the performers and scenes are rewritten at the last moment: 'What are actors for but to exercise their memories?'[11]

The central focus is, however, the damage to the family. It is possible to read the book as a wry exploration of role reversal. All that the husband has to endure is what is usually commonplace for wives: to live vicariously through the provider, to be denied even your own name and to be valued, if at all, for your position as the spouse of the acclaimed. Wilbraham's role is to support, whether it be at the salon or in nursing his wife's ego after a troublesome review. They move from Paris to London for her career. He gives up his painting—'dabbling'—and she retreats to the study. He is relegated to the box room where he paints in secret until even that tiny room of his own is taken over by his wife's friend. He is the child-rearer. The daughter Rosina is afraid of her mother and spends her time with her father who devotes his energies to her well-being. When she falls ill he nurses her, blaming himself for her fever. When the illness becomes life-threatening the mother takes over. She is the only one there when the child dies and after the tragedy she even appropriates memory, her neglected child becoming increasingly like one of her own literary heroines. Throughout the words 'he' and 'she' could be transposed.

Yet surely Elizabeth's intention is more subtle than this? Crucial to her representation is her *own* use of the male pseudonym. She knew that readers would presume C.E. Raimond to be a man. Though not written in the first person, the book would nevertheless be read as a male perception of the situation. It can therefore be argued that Elizabeth was seeking to present and deride how the male sex tended to envisage the consequences of women liberating themselves from the domestic 'ideal'. The story exposes a man's fear of what happens when a woman succeeds and acquires power. She becomes a gross (and she is literally presented as physically very large) caricature of femininity, neglecting her role as mother and emasculating her husband. She calls him a 'dear, stupid boy' but 'he held his ground like a man'. He likes women *in* literature but not producing it. He is terrified lest his daughter becomes like his wife and his nightmare is of

> the woman horde advancing—taking by storm offices, shops, studios and factories, each fighting with desperate success for 'a place', whether in a learned profession or on the top of an omnibus, competing with men in every department of industrial life, jostling them in the streets, preaching to them, clamouring against them.[12]

In stressing 'a dozen womanly things' rather than Rosina becoming a career woman, Wilbraham so succeeds in stultifying her ambitions that all she can think of doing is repairing other people's clothes. When she dies she utters 'man must make and woman must mend', which readers would have recognised as a parody of Charles Kingsley's famous line 'For men must work, and women must weep'.[13]

Ironically, Elizabeth's insistence on preserving her own anonymity took the sting out of her tale. Because she did not reveal that the novel was actually a woman's reading of how a man might project his fears about female success, contemporaries were unable to appreciate her intentions and the nature of her parody. She was able to enjoy a joke at her readers' expense but in the process she actually divested the story of some of its potential strength. Not surprisingly critics took C.E. Raimond at face value. The author was presumed to be criticising the 'short-haired woman' and praising womanliness, even marking the beginning of a reaction against the New Woman novelist. Even modern assessments have fallen into this trap, portraying the book as a satire on pseudo-intellectual novelists especially George Eliot. One critic believes that she 'evidently detested George Eliot's moral rectitude' whilst a feminist literary critic has seen the book as mounting 'a full-blown malicious attack on the pretentious woman novelist usurping the masculine role'.[14] This surely was as a means rather than as an end.

Although it is possible to argue that Elizabeth who had been married to an actor called George was here coming to terms with some of her guilt about his lack of success and subsequent suicide, the story needs to be seen as a tongue-in-cheek representation from an assumed male-eye view, full of attendant warnings about how very differently men and women see the world. Far from detesting George Eliot, Elizabeth was a lifelong devotee. 'What a capacious and clear intelligence that woman had! I must say I admire her tremendously' she wrote on rereading *Middlemarch* in 1896. Shaw recognised the debt she owed to Eliot though characteristically managed to turn his perception into a complaint about 'Saint Elizabeth'.

Elizabeth did, nevertheless, poke fun at those who hero-worshipped the leading women novelists of the recent past. The foolish heroine of her unpublished story 'White Violets or Great Powers' reveres the memory of Charlotte Brontë her 'patron saint, even her closest friend' (she knows her only through her books and Mrs Gaskell's biography). Yet Elizabeth's concern here is to show that writers are better being true to themselves than imitating others and she is at pains to stress just how much women need fiction. Moreover, her real target in both stories is the man who cannot recognise that there have been great women novelists since he won't appreciate what writers have done for women in presenting the woman's view. Wilbraham can see George Eliot only as 'three parts man'. In his view a woman's success is necessarily predicated upon the loss of womanliness. Yet, as Elizabeth makes clear at the start of the novel, men and women might deploy the same language but invest it with very different meanings. It didn't occur to either George Mandeville, alias Lois Wilbraham, or to Ralph Wilbraham that they should 'make sure that womanhood meant the same thing to both of them'.[15]

So, far from being simply an indictment of successful woman writers or an amusing satire on the mannish woman and the New Man of the 1890s, Elizabeth's novel marks a development in her exploration of the construction and maintenance of notions of femininity and masculinity and a consideration of how, in her view, men envisaged change. When an actor appears at one of George's gatherings, Lady Ballantyne calls him an 'effeminate-looking man'. Wilbraham prefers to designate him 'a masculine woman'. It is no coincidence that at puberty Rosina faces her crisis and fails to survive precisely when she is becoming a woman. At a time of debates about homosexuality and sexual identity, about the role of the New Woman in literature, on the stage and in contemporary society and when the institution of marriage was being re-evaluated by some, Elizabeth Robins was beginning to provide via fiction a critique of society which would find full expression in her feminist novel *The Convert*.

Both *George Mandeville's Husband* and Elizabeth's second novel *The New Moon* were published under the name of C.E. Raimond in Heinemann's Pioneer series. The latter was completed in October 1894 and appeared the following year. Written in the first, male person, it concerns a husband Geoffrey Monroe (the same Great Man initials!) and a wife Milly. There are some similarities between the couples in the two novels. Both are ill-matched; the husbands see themselves as intellectually superior and each despises his wife's interests and use of infantalising pet names. In *The New Moon* Milly is an ailing, intensely superstitious woman, 'with her, superstition was a cult; it stood her, instead of poetry, learning or friends. She had a sign for every event of life, and an omen for every dream'.[16] She not only is the opposite of everything her successful husband finds attractive in Dorothy, the young woman with whom he becomes obsessed, but also represents the antithesis of his beliefs, thus positing superstition versus science, the spirit presiding over the rational. In contrast Dorothy admires biology and devours technical books. Her superb health appeals to the doctor who spends his life fighting disease and comforting his wife. In a somewhat contrived and melodramatic ending with a fire in Switzerland, Geoffrey is forced to decide which woman's life he can save. His wife wins.

The relationship between Monroe and Dorothy is, however, presented sympathetically. Dorothy scorns 'the conventional concern of a girl's friends to get her married at all costs' and, written at the time of Elizabeth's friendship with Archer, the book acknowledges the 'other woman' in a positive light, stressing that 'Most women grow up and marry and die, and they never in all their days have so much as touched the hand of their heart's true comrade'.[17]

The story disturbed. For one critic 'It is practically a defence or apology of a married man's love for a maiden; the subject is therefore vulgar … we do not like the book'. Yet in writing about the problems of marriage Elizabeth was in tune with contemporary writers such as Gissing and Hardy whose *Jude the Obscure* had been published the previous year. Yet whereas Gissing's later fiction such as *The Whirlpool* (1897) represented a retreat from the advanced views which had informed his novel *The Odd Women* (1893), Elizabeth's work was to become increasingly committed to feminism.

The previous decade had witnessed a number of attacks on spiritualism by medical men, usually neurophysiologists and psychiatrists, seeking to link it to the origins of mental illness. Elizabeth's fiction posited orthodox medicine practised by men against what today we call alternative medicine and/or spiritualism representing the female side. She suggested a humanising of the former, the profession her father had wanted her to follow, and this in time became a passionate plea for feminising medicine. She also sought greater understanding of the latter.

Her short story 'The Threlkeld Ear', first published in 1898, is set in a rambling house in which the old retainer (as in Ibsen's *Rosmersholm*) warns the woman now inhabiting the ancestral home that this is not a place for the young. Whereas doctors attribute her son's death to excitement, sleep walking and heart failure, the Threlkeld folk know better: the Christmas ghost has returned to claim its rights. The mother is seized by the power of the 'occult in physical Nature' and realisation of how little we know about 'the soul of things'. Similar tensions can be observed in the story of a doctor, *A Dark Lantern* (1905), which was originally called 'The Black Magic Man', and in *Where Are You Going To … ?* (1913) where the doctor experiments in his laboratory and Aunt Josephine, steeped in her Biosophical Theory, bombards her nieces with letters about the essential harmony between 'soul states' and the health of the body.

The interest in superstition and spiritualism evinced in her fiction was matched in Elizabeth's own life. Since her own youth in America she had turned silver in her palm and wished on seeing a new moon. One of Florence Bell's grandchildren has recalled how her granny and Lisa were being taken for a drive at the time of the new moon. Florence called down the speaking tube to the chauffeur, 'White, will you stop and see if the moon is out.' White promptly did so, announcing, 'The moon, my Lady.'[18] The two women got out of the car and curtsied three times to the moon. It was the new moon that was a presentiment for Milly of evil to come. Milly's life revolved around portents and Madame Estelle's predictions. As a young woman on Staten Island Elizabeth had spent time with women mediums such as Mrs Andariesi and it had been at a seance with Madam Dis De

Bar that her career as a successful actress had been foretold. After her husband's death she had, however, become somewhat sceptical of the spiritualist belief in communicating with the souls of the dead through seances though she remained curious about this practice which particularly appealed to women and channelled knowledge via the powerful female medium. Like her father she was interested in experimenting and in London joined the newly formed Society for Psychical Research which sought to submit spiritual phenomena to the scientific test.[19] In the 1890s she attended several meetings held at the home of Frederic Myers, a prominent psychical researcher in London who developed the theory of the subliminal self.

In Boston she had frequented the homes of people who believed that the spirit existed independently of matter. One such person, Clara Erskine Clement Waters, a believer in esoteric Buddhism, was in London in 1890. Mrs Waters and Elizabeth visited Madame Blavatsky, co-founder and matriarch of the Theosophical Society. Theosophists connected with occultist traditions and got their inspiration from the Far East, cultivating the inner life and the hidden potential for the human race. The Society for Psychical Research had, in 1885, produced a damning report representing Blavatsky's theosophy as fraudulent. Although close to death, this amazing, somewhat androgynous bohemian who claimed to be directly inspired by the Mahatmas, remained 'terrifying in size and effect'. Watching her roll cigars and denounce enemies, Elizabeth was fascinated: 'What an actress she would have made … A marvellous personality but I would not trust her.'[20]

By this time Elizabeth's chief interest in the claims of theosophy and spiritualism more generally seems to have been in getting material for her writing. She used this in various ways. In her unpublished novel 'White Violets or Great Powers' the Brontë-obsessed authoress Selina Patching believes she possesses powers and participates in seances. When Elizabeth began this novel she had just read a life of Harriet Beecher Stowe who claimed to have conversed with the spirit of Charlotte Brontë. Selina also reads the proceedings of the Society for Psychical Research. Here Elizabeth reveals how people can be duped or hypnotised into believing what suits them. In *The New Moon* the large languorous figure of Milly appears at first like a rather cruel caricature of a silly superstitious woman lacking any independent will and logic. Yet not only is this how her husband chooses to see her but it is Milly alone who actually correctly anticipates events and the scientific mind is incidentally shown to possess its own fears and fatalism notably in matters such as heredity.

The New Moon was number seven in the Pioneer series. The following number was *Milly's Story*, also published in 1895. This told the tale from the wife's viewpoint. Contemporaries and later intimates such as John Masefield believed both books to be by the same author. Indeed, the British Library still attributes *Milly's Story* to C.E. Raimond. Yet had Elizabeth chosen to present the woman's side it is more likely that she would have told Dorothy's story (Florence Bell did just this). *Milly's Story* was a 171-page parody by Blanche Alethea Crackanthorpe who had read Elizabeth's story in manuscript.[21] Few knew the truth. It filled out parts that the first book had not dwelt upon. Elizabeth knew 'BAC', as she was called, socially but did not regard her as a close friend. Her husband, an eminent barrister, had accompanied Elizabeth on psychical researching whilst BAC had published a couple of sensational articles in *The Nineteenth Century* (1894) advocating professional training for unmarried girls and attacking the 'matrimonial hunt'. Elizabeth was not pleased that Heinemann accepted BAC's book. She was, however, fond of her 'gifted and lovable' twenty-six-year-old son, the talented writer Hubert Crackanthorpe who was found drowned in the Seine the following year after his wife had left him for another man. Both Elizabeth and Hubert had published short stories in the *New Review* of 1894.

Proud to publish 'the newest of the new', this journal produced by Heinemann had begun a new policy in January 1894. Each month a short story would be selected without regard to any previously gained reputation of the author. The first such story was 'A Lucky Sixpence'. Elizabeth was the author but it was published anonymously so that it stood on its own merits rather than being 'suspected of assistance from the considerable position occupied by its author on another platform'.[22]

Women writers on both sides of the Atlantic welcomed the concision of the short story, its scope for earning money comparatively quickly, and the opportunity it offered to innovate, especially in exploring relations between the sexes. For example, George Egerton who had lived in America and Norway and later became a drama agent published two collections of short stories in Britain in the early 1890s, *Keynotes* and *Discords*, both of which look at relationships from the woman's perspective. The latter even takes up the issue of infanticide which had just been tackled in the play *Alan's Wife*. Elaine Showalter sees the short story providing the missing link between the golden era of Victorian women writers and the later era of feminist modernism.[23] Elizabeth appreciated how the short story gave her scope to sketch out ideas and episodes in untraditional ways.

Two of her short stories for the *New Review* concerned the production of fiction and originality. 'Dedicated to John Huntley', published anonymously in June 1894, revolves around writing, plagiarism and trust, providing a useful vehicle for discussion of the ownership of ideas and the role of the artist as creator, suggesting that we borrow from each other continually and that 'Our opinions, if not echoes, are little more than modifications of those we've heard'. Although the artist may be merely providing a new treatment for an old theme it is argued that we are invariably and understandably proprietorial about that very treatment. The American writer Edith Wharton also wrote short stories about the tension between art and life and about the troubled triangular relationship between writer, publisher and public. For example, in 'The Descent of Man' (1904) she presents a professor who has written a skit on the popular scientific book. This fools the publisher who then deliberately deceives the public.[24]

In 'Miss de Maupassant', using the C. E. Raimond by-line, Elizabeth satirised publishers who sought to capitalise on new, risqué novels.[25] The author is revealed to be not only a woman, thus confounding the publisher's gendered concept of delicacy, but also a plagiarist. Elizabeth's editor persuaded her to alter the name of the fictional publisher from Merriman and Street to Merrimen and Streake lest John Lane, publisher of the first *Yellow Book*, took offence. Aubrey Beardsley had briefly considered using Elizabeth as the model for one of his *Yellow Book* 'eccentricities'. The *Yellow Book* also contained the writings of Crackanthorpe (known as the English Maupassant). Another contributor, much influenced by Oscar Wilde, was the poet and journalist Richard Le Gallienne whose married sister became Hubert Crackanthorpe's lover. Le Gallienne inspired Elizabeth's (unpublished) satire 'Valentine Cobb', which, like 'White Violets', exposed the absurdity of hero-worship. It also displayed the egoism, romanticism and pretensions of the precious poet juxtaposed to the practical woman copyist.

Much of Elizabeth's writing is concerned with London society, which is hardly surprising given her extremely well-connected social life as an eminent actress and friend of influential people. Readers of her fiction might be forgiven for believing that Britain lacked much of a middle class since in her British-based novels her concern is overwhelmingly with titled society, politicians and other powerful figures. She seems to have conducted a love/hate relationship with this society. It provided her with material she wanted and it appeared to welcome her. Yet she knew that in the last resort she remained emphatically an outsider and the literary exposés of some of its values and concerns by this American actress must have left some of those who entertained her feeling that they had been used. Sometimes her sketches were only thinly disguised.[26]

In her novel *A Dark Lantern* the English socialite Kitty Dereham provides a damning indictment of English society with its 'chaffing patronage of men and women whose ideal of accomplishment was to ride, dance, play certain games, know what to wear, what to say, and above all when to smile. The prevailing note was ridicule.'[27] Yet behind this world where laughter was all that was socially safe and being serious was akin to a crime, lay a darker side as revealed in Kitty's opium-sodden father. The late Victorian period is contrasted with the previous century 'when fine ladies strung rhymes as they strummed the harp, when Lady Mary Wortley Montagu could cap verses with Pope' and when Kitty's own poetic aspirations would have been cultivated rather than crushed.

Elizabeth had become interested in Lady Mary Wortley Montagu through her aristocratic friends. In 1898 she stayed at Ripley with Lady Caroline Grosvenor and here saw portraits of this eighteenth-century traveller and woman of letters. She was given Caroline's grandfather's edition of her life and letters and read of her living in Turkey and Italy and supporting women's education. On Caroline's prompting she did some research with a view to writing 'a magazine study'. The result was a long, somewhat ponderous article in the first number of Lady Randolph Churchill's *Anglo-Saxon Review* (1899). Entitled 'A Modern Woman' it assumed, slightly naïvely, that few readers knew about Lady Mary and informed them of her achievements.

Caroline was the widow of the Hon. Norman Grosvenor who had died in 1898. The organiser of People's Concerts, he had been one of Elizabeth's financial backers for Ibsen productions and auditor for the New Century Theatre. Caroline, who later chaired the Women's Farm and Garden Association and founded the Colonial Intelligence League for Educated Women, spent much of her time in Europe. In the spring of 1899 Elizabeth joined her and her daughters in Dresden. In her diary she recounts how here and elsewhere Caroline made it apparent (though never in so many words) that Florence Bell was not of her class. Florence's father was a surgeon and her mother part of the wealthy Cubitt family of London builders. Although Hugh Bell was highly respectable and would be knighted a few years later this eminent ironmaster was nonetheless 'in trade' and as Lady Charlotte Guest, wife of another ironmaster, once observed, 'in this aristocratic nation the word Trade conveys a taint'.[28] Elizabeth was both fascinated and infuriated by the manifestations of the British class system and sought to explore the presumptions of the privileged in her fiction.

The year 1899 was a productive one for both writing and travelling. In the summer she accompanied Betty (Lady) Lewis, wife of her solicitor, to the Alps. It gave her a taste of the rest cure, something she would turn to in the future. It also provided the kernel of a new story which she finished in September 1899 though it was not published for some years. Originally entitled 'The Glacier Mills', the novella 'The Mills of the Gods' tells how an ageing Italian playboy, a satanic figure of a count, woos a young woman who finally agrees to marry him. Her weapon is her silence. Several themes emerge here which would be developed in Elizabeth's later work, most notably the importance of woman's silence and the need to expose man's capacity for brutality. Elizabeth told Florence that she did not want her tale seen simply as a ghost story.

She did, however, write several ghost stories. For example, 'A Masterpiece the World Never Saw' concerned a painter infatuated by an image of a young woman he had glimpsed in the American South. Here Elizabeth is making fun of the romanticism of artists. 'The Father of Lies', written in October 1895, also uses a portrait as a key device in the unfolding of the story. A son has to decide whether or not his father—an imperial hero—had in fact taken credit for another man's success.

Although Elizabeth also wrote about the working class, her fiction seems to situate workers only in relation to the ruling class. Her third book was a collection of sketches of domestic servants published by Heinemann in Britain in 1896, entitled *Below the Salt*. Whistler designed the jacket. In the United States the collection had the less esoteric title of one of its other stories, *The Fatal Gift of Beauty*. Some of the nine short stories had been published separately over the past two years. The subject-matter was relatively unusual. Florence clearly found it distasteful and told her friend that one of the incidents she related was 'entirely revolting. I hate those details—do you know all those things shock me horribly.' When Elizabeth was seeking a subtitle which would underline the '*humanity* these people share in common with their masters' she told Florence that this 'is I believe not sound doctrine from your point of view'. Some reviewers were also wary. The *Norfolk News* saw 'A Lucky Sixpence' as 'more powerful than pleasant' but of course it belonged to 'the very modern school'. Years later a sub-editor recalled how his editor had been 'very much afraid of the story' but Heinemann insisted on publication.[29] Elizabeth was, however, asked to reconsider one incident thought likely to offend and duly did so. Its realism still provoked some 'vehement protests'. Yet its fine writing was also acknowledged and there was even speculation as to whether George Moore was the author.

Originally entitled 'Hester', this first story had been written on tour in Liverpool in 1893. It tells the common enough tale of a young maid seduced by her employer but points up his scheming and her innocence, presenting her side and giving her some voice of her own. The pregnant maid is forced to lie about her liaison to save her employer's marriage. The only positive alliance is intra-class, between the maid and the older and wiser servant who lives next door. Hester is turned out of the house, the last line marking the servant's one defiance of her master: 'She went out softly without closing the door.'

Elizabeth was conscious of how servants were perceived as available. When walking alone on Redcar sands one day she became aware of the sound of footsteps remorselessly following her.

Her one thought, itself testimony to her own class assurance, was 'What if he thought I am a servant.' At the same time she was impatient of some of the conventions of polite English society. She described a train journey in which the man sitting opposite was watching her. It crossed her mind, 'What a bore it was that we were too well behaved to do more than steal covert glances & get what scant confirmation we cd. [*sic*] in that sneaking way instead of saying something about you—who are you? etc.' An old man entered the carriage then a woman with a child. Immediately the old man asked her where she was going: the very question she had longed to put to her companion but which her class and position as a woman (rather than mother) prohibited.

In 1911 the American feminist Charlotte Perkins Gilman published a short story on a similar theme to 'A Lucky Sixpence' but with a more radical edge. In 'Turned' the two wronged women ultimately decide that it is the man who is superfluous.[30] When he returns from his business trip he finds that he has lost his wife, his servant and the baby: 'And the woman who had been his wife asked quietly: "What have you to say to us?" In Elizabeth's play *The Silver Lotus* written in 1895–6, it is the woman and the servant who can see the tragedy. The only one who cannot understand is the husband.

The eponymous story 'Below the Salt' and 'Confessions of a Cruel Mistress' take the perspectives of the employing class. The former concerns the servant of a clergyman and his wife. They recognise the need to treat servants as human beings yet are shocked when their servant exercises what she sees as her prerogative, helping herself to writing paper and items which ironically aid her own son in becoming a Nonconformist minister. Elizabeth's servant stories are broadly sympathetic to their subjects but today the effectiveness of several of them is reduced by the device of adopting a patronising use of phonetical spelling and malapropisms when recounting the servants' own words.

The story which links most clearly to the author of *The Convert* is ''Gustus Frederick' in which a Lady Bountiful is dismissive of an unmarried working-class woman who chooses to have a child without any means of support yet cannot accept the single state and childlessness of her own sister with whom she dutifully visits the poor. The sister observes how it is apparently fine to breed in one class yet inconsiderate in another. Elizabeth scorned those who married because of societal attitudes. In 'A Lost Opportunity' she shows the anger of a single woman and expert on educational theory who is pitied by a mother who feels she lacks the 'natural instinct' which can only come with motherhood. When she declares 'You've never had a child' the single woman neatly replies 'How do you know?', challenging the one presumption and exposing another. Elizabeth was always conscious of her equivocal position as a woman on her own. Her fiction reveals how the unmarried and motherless women are seen as threats and on more than one occasion, as in her unfinished story 'Poppy and Mandragora', argues that marriage can cut short love rather than confirm it.

For ''Gustus Frederick' she had utilised Florence's account of a young Middlesbrough woman 'who had her child so blithely without the formality of marriage'. Many of the anecdotes and representations of servants had a source closer to home. Elizabeth's own servants relayed some of the incidents to her and even became the basis of characters in her tales. They included Rose Turner, 'poor old Anne' who turned to drink and a C. Kohler who worked for Elizabeth in the early 1890s. The latter's affectionate letters to Elizabeth are very similar in spelling and tone to the words used in 'Vroni', one of the most dated stories which uses 'broken English' and takes the form of an extended conversation (rather like a playscript complete with stage directions), telling the tale of a servant from the Rhine. Elizabeth does not seem to have deceived herself about the shortcomings of this story, telling Florence Bell that she could never rid herself of surprise 'that these amusements have a market value'.

Elizabeth's own connections with her servants do not, on the whole, seem to have ended when they left her. The most enduring relationship was with another German woman Karolina Gardner whose marital misfortunes may have helped inspire the stories known as 'The Portman Memoirs'. Karolina was Elizabeth's cook in the mid-1890s. Heinemann was then persuaded to advance a couple of hundred pounds to help her buy a bakery in Bermondsey. In later years Elizabeth appealed to the Home Secretary and to the British-German Foundation on the family's behalf. Lady Lewis paid for music lessons for Karolina's daughter. Mother and daughter stayed with Elizabeth twice a year. The outbreak of war and riots in

Bermondsey created fresh problems and Karolina and her children returned to Germany. They were still in touch with their former employer in the 1930s. Young Elizabeth Gardner, who had become a music teacher, had also studied *The Convert* carefully.

Although Elizabeth believed in the theory and practice of employing servants and expected them to work hard, she also supported any educational aspirations and, in the Edwardian years, interest shown in suffrage feminism. Her servants were given theatre tickets and copies of her books. Two were sent to hear Mrs Pankhurst in Brighton. They returned 'galvanized'. One was a young Danish housekeeper, Laura Alkjaersig. She later wrote to thank Elizabeth for being 'one of those who gets others growing'. She went on to college, translated Elizabeth's suffrage essays into Danish and eventually became principal of a Danish Labour college. She was still in touch in the 1920s when she spent some time at Ruskin College, Oxford investigating opportunities for working women.

The identity of the author of all these servant stories remained unknown until revealed by the *Daily Chronicle* after the publication of *The Open Question* in 1898. Elizabeth informed the newspaper's editor that, 'No doubt unintentionally you did me a grave injury'. Yet this novel both marked her acknowledged advent as a writer (to Heinemann's relief he was able to use her name for the second edition) and signified her first real literary triumph as well as her first book set in America. She had expended much energy on this bulky tome. It paid off. It was easily her most moving and accomplished work to date. Although critics felt it to be too long, it was well received. Arnold Bennett's journal describes it as 'quite first rate and notable'. Hugh Walpole pronounced it 'a masterpiece of courage, humour and authenticity' whilst her compatriot Mark Twain extolled its

> depth & truth & wisdom & courage; & the fine & great literary art & grace of the setting. At your age you cannot have lived half of the things that are in the book, nor personally penetrated to the deeps it deals in, nor covered its wide horizons with your very own opinion—& so, what is your secret? how have you written this miracle? … I have not been so enriched by a book for many years, nor so enchanted by one.[31]

Her secret was that she *had* personally experienced more travel, tragedy and variety than many women in their thirties, certainly more than those who knew her could divine.

The Open Question helped Elizabeth financially. She received a £200 advance, compared to £50 for her previous book, and it sold over 1,500 copies in less than three weeks. It was reprinted the following year when it also appeared in Germany. There was an English Tauchnitz edition and it was serialised in Germany and America. Although still constrained by the need for 'small and trifling economies', she could now rely on an income of about £120 a year thanks to her investments in Bell Brothers and in the United States and she reckoned that she needed to make about £280 annually in order to live comfortably and help her family. The stage, geared towards the young actress and lacking in financial security, held little future. Elizabeth would devote herself to writing and to developing her 'mental muscle', reading philosophy and other serious subjects daily 'as other women do their prayers'.

So, where and how can we situate Elizabeth as a writer of literature? Her early writing has, with the exception of *George Mandeville's Husband*, unfortunately been forgotten and to modern readers she is identified as a feminist novelist and playwright of the Edwardian period. Yet this work needs to be set in the context of her writing of the 1890s when she experimented with form and subject-matter and sought to establish herself as a writer. By the time her identity was revealed she had become more sophisticated though her very early work is enjoyable, not least for its sense of irony and the fun it pokes at the world around her.

Elizabeth's female literary acquaintances ranged from Mrs Humphry Ward to Olive Schreiner and she knew personally the key artistic figures of the day. *The May Book* published by Macmillan in 1901 in aid of funds for Charing Cross Hospital contained contributions from sixty-seven eminent writers, artists and musicians including Hardy, Meredith, Henry James, Evelyn Sharp, Burne-Jones, Sarah Grand, W. E. Henley and Elizabeth Robins. Elizabeth's offering did not show her at her best: it was a somewhat cloying children's story called 'Geen Baceler' (Green Bracelet) about a missing bracelet and a misunderstanding between a boy and his grandmother.

Yet in many of the subjects she tackled over these years and through her identification of the sexuality of men as the key site for exploring problems in relationships, Elizabeth can be seen as one of the New Woman writers of the 1890s.[32] This was a term used satirically at the time as in Sidney Grundy's play *The New Woman* (1894) though Elizabeth was not a fan of the popular writer Sarah Grand, the person most closely associated with the serious New Woman writer. And Elizabeth's exploration of male sexuality was to become much sharper *post* 1900.

In fact Elizabeth defies too neat a pigeon-holing. She continued writing short stories alongside substantial novels for many years though increasingly her feminism came to the fore, giving her work a much sharper edge. Nevertheless she can be identified with those boldly criticising marriage and even motherhood from the early 1890s. Some of her writing, most notably her major work *The Open Question*, appears quintessentially *fin de siècle* with its leitmotif of suicide and discussions of degeneracy and Parisian life.[33] Yet this novel also needs situating in relation to Elizabeth's American upbringing and literary heritage. And although she became known as an Edwardian feminist novelist, she needs to be located alongside both the New Woman writers of the 1890s and those earlier women writers, dubbed by Elaine Showalter the 'Feminine Novelists'.[34] They frequently identified with their fathers and had either lost or been alienated from their mothers when young. As a writer Elizabeth admired the style of George Eliot (Shaw dubbed her the American George Eliot) but in some of her less conventional subject-matter she was more in tune with developments in short story writing in America. She must also be seen in the context of European drama.

It is possible to trace in Elizabeth's writing from the 1890s onwards an emerging feminist critique, clearly, but only partly, influenced by the psychological realism of Ibsen, which would find most confident expression in 1907 in her justly celebrated novel *The Convert* (see Chapter 7). Yet Elizabeth's love of experimentation and wide-ranging life-style preclude narrow compartmentalisation. Who would have predicted that *The Open Question* would have been followed by an adventure story in the genre of the male quest romance set in Alaska, with the strength of the story lying in the author's personal familiarity with the terrain? Moreover this novel, *The Magnetic North*, was a best-seller and the book for which Elizabeth Robins was most praised in her lifetime.

6

THE MAGNETIC NORTH

It was not the prospect of finding gold which drew Elizabeth to Alaska in 1900. Unlike the crowds who had rushed to the Klondike in 1897, Elizabeth's search was unconnected to pecuniary gain. At its centre was her concern about her youngest brother Raymond. She had seen little of him since her early days at the Old Stone House but (partly because of this) he had become the focus of many of her hopes and fears.

Born in 1873, Raymond was eleven years younger than Elizabeth but the eldest and youngest of the Robins children were the most determined and ambitious of the family members. In her mother's absence Elizabeth had looked after the small boy who was sent to live with his grandmother. Later, the brother and sister would dwell on and romanticise the few years they shared together in Ohio. In 1938 Raymond wrote to tell Elizabeth how she was 'the only one in all those yesterdays of my early youth in the family home, who was not touched with the *doom* and always VICTORY seemed to sit eagle-winged on your crest'. Elizabeth would reminisce about the 'early winter evenings, sitting with the three little boys by the dining-room fire, eating red apples and shell-bark hickory nuts, while the stories were told'[1] and it was always Raymond who was her favourite. She was his early mentor though as an adult Raymond preferred to see himself as her guide.

When he was eight his mother observed, 'He inherits the fateful gift of genius. I tremble for the future, I have never known it to bring happiness to its possessor.' Within months Raymond developed terrifying convulsive seizures which appear to have been a form of psychic epilepsy.[2] Such behaviour only confirmed the family's worst fear about heredity. Elizabeth witnessed some of the early attacks, noting on 13 January 1881 how Raymond was 'taken alarmingly ill', demonstrating symptoms of brain fever. She stayed with him all night. At this point she was acting as housekeeper and giving her brothers lessons but soon after left for New York and the stage. The boys were sent to Dr Bodine in Louisville and, when well enough, their mother (living nearby in a boarding house) looked after them. Dr Bodine felt that Raymond's only hope of escaping an asylum was the routine of work. So school was abandoned and he became a cash boy in a local store. Ironically, given her fate, Hannah told Elizabeth of her 'unconquerable opposition' to her son being institutionalised. At first the attacks continued and Raymond almost lost his job but by the summer of 1883 his health had recovered. Then he ran away to Frankfort, Kentucky hiring himself out as a brickyard water boy for $1.25 weekly. He was not yet ten. The police were sent to find him.

Raymond's relatives sent him to join his married cousin Lizzie (née Bodine) and her husband Zach McKay at their orange grove near Brooksville in central Florida. Living at Bodine Grove Raymond received some months of formal schooling then tuition from a local businessman. In his mid-teens he joined his father and brothers who were now living in southern Florida. The man who would become a preacher and a human rights activist and would debate politics with Trotsky, Lenin and several American Presidents, had a succession of jobs in his youth. Raymond later recalled being a cowboy, storekeeper at a phosphate mine and coal-miner in Tennessee and Colorado where he also became a union organiser. His biographer Neil Salzman has, however, pointed out that these experiences have been documented only by Raymond and *post* 1905.[3] He suggests that they were 'apocryphal mosaics' based on contemporary accounts of others which gave Raymond useful credentials for his work in the labour movement. Repudiating his parents' pedigree, Raymond appears to have retrospectively constructed an image of himself as a struggling working-class youth, thus enabling him to empathise with those he later sought to help. Elizabeth (who was prone to stress the gentility of her background) was impatient with Raymond's fanciful notions though, as we have seen, she chose to embellish her family's opposition to the stage in her reminiscences. When in 1935 Raymond described his childhood as one where he lived in a room which opened on to stairs and a crowded back yard leading into a noisy alley, Elizabeth was shocked: 'What in the name of heaven does he mean? This curious transformation of truth this defilement of what had every right to be a beautiful memory ...' She was thinking of the Old Stone House: he meant his mother's lodgings. Even though he probably chose to exaggerate the poverty of his surroundings, the experience and his propulsion into working life seem to have scarred him.

As a young man Raymond's prospects were good. He worked in real estate then, with a little timely help from Lloyd Tevis, became a prospector in the Florida phosphate business. Success in mining speculation enabled him to study law with a firm in Florida then to become a law student in Washington, DC. By the age of twenty-two he had a law degree, achieved in one year, and, from 1897, his own practice in San Francisco. Rapidly succeeding as a lawyer he now sought to share his life once more with his sister. Flushed with success from a Supreme Court victory and confident in his ability to become a great lawyer, he does not seem to have realised that Elizabeth might not wish to surrender her own successful career and life-style to cross the Atlantic to join him.

The relationship between these two was always intense. They wrote long, impassioned letters to each other throughout their lives but, perhaps because in certain respects they were too alike and each too dependent on the other, they frequently engendered disappointment. Both were committed people, 'workaholics' with vivid imaginations, a degree of stubbornness and often unrealistic expectations of others. When Somerset Maugham met Raymond in Russia his reaction to this non-smoker, non-drinker who worked all hours was 'He isn't human'. Leonard Woolf who described Raymond as a 'strange, gifted, wayward character', felt that he possessed the same mercurial vitality as Elizabeth.[4] There were physical resemblances too, especially around the eyes. Gertrude Bell was struck by their similar mannerisms: 'He's rather like Lisa, talks like her throws back his head and speaks in bursts of eloquence—He is a very striking person; I fancy he's going to be a big power'.[5]

As a child 'the Great Soul'd Girl who taught me Greek mythology and the multiplication tables!! and dreamed dreams with me of the glory that the coming years would bring' had solemnly agreed with Raymond that they would never marry but would share a home together. In 1891 Raymond confessed, in a letter Elizabeth cherished for decades, that 'There is no one as near to me in my purest & noblest moments as you darling & though my letters may be few & unsatisfactory you are as a star in the east leading me onward & upward too [*sic*] larger & higher aims'. Salzman believes that Raymond's decision to join the gold rush in Alaska can be explained only by Elizabeth's refusal to live with him in California. She herself later admitted that, had she given up her London life, he would not have gone north. As Salzman puts it, 'Her refusal was a denial of his success'.[6]

Yet there were additional reasons why Raymond found Alaska attractive. He sensed that lawyers would be welcome in the raw societies of individuals motivated by gold fever and his 'Klondicitis' was encouraged by a huge gold strike near Dawson City. Although the Robins family did not mention it, Gertrude Bell noted another incentive. In 1898 she met Lloyd Tevis who told her that he had encouraged Raymond to go to the Klondike.[7] Saxton provided a further impulse: Although older than Raymond, this brother with 'the beautiful voice and the wanderlust spirit, spoiled darling of a broken mother and a broken HOME' seemed to be one of life's losers. In Raymond's words, 'Never did he find his way in this hard world.' Raymond and Elizabeth found his aimlessness incomprehensible. Uncle Morrie initially held out some hope for Saxton though even this was linked to the family history: 'You boys are the result of inbreeding and physiology teaches that wonders may come in this way.' There is little evidence of what Saxton himself believed. He was the opposite of his sister: written communication was not his strength. Accounts of his behaviour tend to be filtered through the somewhat censorious Raymond who failed to appreciate that his brother might actually prefer not to be in the limelight.

It does, however, seem that Saxton was prone to depression. In one of his rare (undated) letters to Elizabeth he described how there were moments when 'things look *black, black, black* & I feel like letting go and drifting again, but so far I have been able to over come [*sic*] this terrible fascination—it I realize is *fatal*'. Raymond cautioned Elizabeth: 'We must be very careful with him & do all in our power to hold him in the track … I know that you & I will always be strong & independent.' Raymond worried his sister with tales of Saxton dirty and hungry working as a night clerk at a low lodging house in Denver where 'thieves, street jugglers and the sub-merged and dissolute of all classes in a mining city congregate'. In retrospect Elizabeth wryly noted that Saxton was actually 'without a vice except the chain-cigarettes and black coffee'[8] but in the eyes of Raymond (who would later work for such people but not be *of* them) Saxton was evidently not the fittest in terms of moral fibre. His prospects seemed 'as dark as a dream of Dantean hell'. Raymond subsidised his brother in the mistaken belief that Saxton was studying law. He then persuaded him to come to San Francisco where he could keep a closer watch on him.

Saxton was the first to be dazzled by Klondike gold which he saw in the window of a bank. Taking off into the unknown appealed to this loner and for once Raymond thought his brother's plan worth pursuing. In a letter to Florence Bell written in August 1897 Elizabeth explained quite casually that Raymond had just gone after gold. Years later she added, 'How little I made of what to me mattered a 1,000 times more than anything else … And my intimates think they "know" me.' In fact she underestimated her friends. Even sixteen-year-old Molly Bell noted that Lisa 'has 2 brothers at Klondyke and is dreadfully anxious about them'.[9]

Arriving in St Michael on the west coast of Alaska, Raymond and Saxton faced a harsh endurance test. Much of their first Alaskan winter they were stranded with several other men on the lower Yukon river 1,700 miles (2,735 km) from the Dawson gold-fields. Their cabin life and Raymond's subsequent intrepid journey by foot then dog sled up the frozen river to the Klondike (with a Colonel Shulte) formed the basis of Elizabeth's novel *The Magnetic North*. Saxton waited in camp with the others awaiting the thaw and took the first boat upriver in the spring. The brothers met up again in Dawson City but all the best claims had already gone.

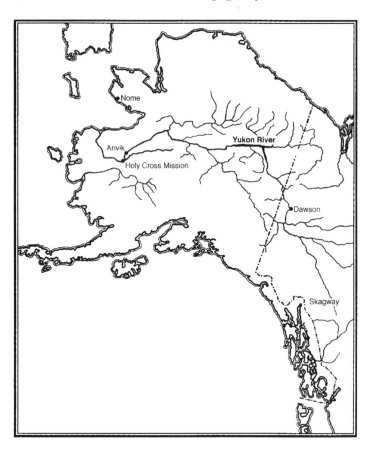

Map of Alaska and Yukon

Raymond had, however, begun to find something else. Less dramatically than some accounts suggest, he was being converted into
a lifelong committed Christian. After nearly a year with no news
Elizabeth finally heard of Raymond's rescue on the trail by Indians
and help at the Jesuit Holy Cross Mission. Knowing that her brother
did nothing in small measure she now feared that he would become
a Jesuit priest. This helped goad her into her audacious plan to make
a personal trip to Alaska. Although she had acknowledged (at the
time of writing her Oberammergau article) that she had a 'wealth

of artistic & sympathetic interests in the church', Elizabeth also confessed to finding nothing else there and wrote to W.T. Stead with an
'unpremeditated confession of un-faith'.[10]

After briefly visiting California for supplies Raymond returned to
Alaska not as a Catholic but as a somewhat unconventional Assistant
Superintendant of Alaskan Missions for the Congregationalist Church
(licensed to preach) in the newest and most northerly mining camp
in the world at Nome on the shores of the Bering Sea. A seminal text
in his espousal of the social gospel was Professor Henry Drummond's
Natural Law in the Spiritual World (1884). Inextricably linked was a
commitment to social justice. Raymond's other mentors were the
radical thinkers Henry George and Tom Paine. He now became
a community leader, literally and metaphorically cleaning up the
new boom town, advocating sanitary development and stamping out
corruption in church and what there was of local government.

Ironically, the person who prompted the agnostic Elizabeth to undertake her journey was the 'most unflinching follower of Christ I have ever
known'. William Stead had helped Elizabeth to visit Oberammergau.[11]
He succeeded in getting at 'the heart of many things & many people he
got at my till then hidden thought'. Stead was fascinated by Elizabeth.
He flattered her, claiming that she led the most interesting life of any
of the many women he knew. Possessing what Elizabeth called an
'incorrigible Puritan view', he had for many years viewed the theatre
from afar as a manifestation of hell. Although Elizabeth enlightened
him, he 'expended much eloquence trying to save me from the hide-
ous dangers of ordinary theatrical life'. Over lunches at Gatti's in the
Strand they now debated the pros and cons of her proposed trip. Stead
realised how much it meant to her and his opposition gave way to firm
support. Elizabeth wrote, somewhat dramatically, 'I owed my brother to
Stead.' He advanced her £300 which, together with her share of the
sale of the Old Stone House and royalties, made possible the temporary
abandonment of paid work and the making of the journey. Stead wrote
to editors in London and New York and undertook to take and place
articles Elizabeth would write about Alaska. A seasoned investigative
journalist, Stead sensed some good stories here. Any profits after his
reimbursement would be shared between them.

Had Ibsen still been producing masterpieces, it is questionable
whether Elizabeth would have gone. As it was, her theatrical career

seemed past its height. It was the beginning of a new century and, as she admitted many years later, she felt a strong sense of restlessness. Now she had the chance to be with her brother having made her own decision and there was an opportunity for social reportage and material for future novels. It was, nevertheless, an extremely bold move to travel many thousands of miles to an unknown land, three times the size of France, to join a society of men clamouring for gold. She would be leaving behind a charming fishing cottage at Itchen Abbas, Hampshire (lent for rest and writing by Sir Edward and Lady Grey).

Elizabeth's timing was perfect: she saw Nome at the height of its popularity, gold having been discovered on its beaches in July 1899. Before leaving she did some research[12] and wrote a short piece for Stead to use as an introduction to her Letters. Here she explained that Nome had until recently been home only to small numbers of Eskimos during the seal-fishing season. Gold transformed everything. The population shot up to 18,000 and by early 1900 an estimated 65,000 were planning to seek their fortunes there in the spring. Brother Vernon cautioned Elizabeth against joining these numbers and she received no reply to her request for Raymond to cable London that he wished her to come. Nevertheless she left England at the end of March.

She kept a detailed and carefully crafted diary of her Alaskan adventures which she dredged over subsequent years for literary purposes.[13] Beginning it on 5 April 1900 at the sumptuous Waldorf-Astoria on Fifth Avenue, Manhattan as the guest of Mrs Erskine Waters, Elizabeth was demonstrating the ultimate contrast to the life she was about to undertake: Here she met socialites such as Edith Wharton's former sister-in-law. She also made the acquaintance of a lugubrious fellow traveller who had already staked claims in Nome. A former private detective who had worked on the infamous Lizzie Borden axe murderer case, he was destined to become a character in Elizabeth's novel *Come And Find Me*.

At the Boston Institute of Technology she tried her hand once more at assaying. Then she headed for Canada. In Seattle she arranged her passage and stocked up on provisions including Heinz foods and crème de menthe. The fortnight's sea voyage was a revelation for the erstwhile star of the stage and a far cry from the comfort of transatlantic staterooms. As a writer Elizabeth watched carefully her fellow passengers, most of whom she would never have encountered personally in London society. She was impressed by one of the women with whom she shared a cabin, a middle-aged stenographer who had been the first woman notary public in Colorado. She was also the first woman voter Elizabeth had met—in 1893 Colorado had been the second of the United States to grant women full suffrage. This plucky woman now sought a new life in Alaska where women would eventually be enfranchised a year ahead of the first British women. Elizabeth wrote, 'This life and character do more (together with the gradual "widening" of the years) to make a woman suffragist of me than any argument I ever heard.'

Elizabeth was not the only woman aboard who would write of her exploits close to the Arctic Circle. Neither were these women the first to make such journeys. In 1879, for example, the American Libby Beaman had been the first white woman to visit and live on the northern Pribilof Islands off Alaska.[14] Given her British connections, Elizabeth wished to explore and report on the Canadian Klondike but her primary target was far from there, on the other side of the boundary in the vast Alaskan territory the Americans had purchased from Russia. Elizabeth would 'find' her brother in Nome.

In fact Raymond came to her. The first sight of Nome revealed a beach crammed with tents. Elizabeth was ready to pitch hers and start the life of a pioneer. Then 'A slender young man, with a soft hat and a long mackintosh, dark eyes and dark smoothshaven face, is coming toward me. "Raymond", I say, and he "Sister".' Elizabeth's twenty-six-year-old brother led her to his base, the three-storey hospice where she had a room of her own, was cooked for and ate as well as, if not better than, in London. Nome itself was more basic as Elizabeth's description of a street shows:

> An irregular passage between the rows of tents and sheds, a waste of sticky black mud, up slippery bill and down slimy dale, with people and dogs laboriously zigzagging to keep out of the worst of the slough or from falling into the two or three pools of muddy water made by those who were rocking out gold.

Over the following weeks she became reacquainted with Raymond. He told her that 'no one was ever such a power in another's life as you have been in mine' and indulged their old fantasy of creating a home together. Yet he also admitted that he was considering marrying a woman who was helping the mission. Much of the time he was simply too busy to raise or dash Elizabeth's hopes. He was 'a magnet … to the eyes and minds of the Nome inhabitants'. People looked to 'Brother Robins', a term Elizabeth loathed, to intervene in disputes and solve their spiritual fears. Elizabeth later described Raymond as 'the most idolised human being I have ever known'. In her diary she deplored the way he was sacrificing himself 'for a bit of muddy tundra'. She pleaded with him to leave. During her few weeks in Nome she did dissuade him from proposing marriage and Raymond told Elizabeth that she was his 'magnet and the goal'.

She became a reporter, taking photographs, interviewing miners camping on the beach and walking miles across the tundra. All of this was recorded in detail in the diary and in a number of articles. A trip with a judge to Grantley Harbor near the Siberian coast involved sleeping on a boat with a biscuit tin for a pillow. *En route* they passed Port Clarence which must have reminded Elizabeth of the faraway Bell Brothers ironworks at another Port Clarence on the north side of the River Tees opposite Middlesbrough. Elizabeth's account of Grantley Harbor, the latest gold-field town in the making, was published with an introduction by Stead in his *Review of Reviews* in July 1900.[15] This was the only article he actually published (he was sent at least seven) though he helped to place some of the others. An article on Cape Nome in the *Pall Mall Magazine* the following year was carefully tailored to its British audience. The trading store run by the Alaska Commercial Company was described as the 'Whiteleys of the North' (Whiteleys of Bayswater was London's first department store). To Elizabeth's annoyance the article was, however, doctored and erroneously claimed that she went to Alaska because her brother was ill. The *Seattle Post Intelligencer* published her account of the hopes and despair of gold-seekers staking claims, the claim-jumpers and those combating lawlessness.

Not all her articles on Alaska were written on the spot. Over Christmas 1901 at the Bells' Elizabeth wrote an article on 'Pleasure Mining' for the *Fortnightly Review*, tracing the lure of gold from Greek myth to modern placer (surface) mining. This somewhat technical piece was, significantly, preferred by Raymond to Elizabeth's more personal Alaskan accounts. It generated £13 13*s* which were duly repaid to Stead. The *Fortnightly* also published Elizabeth's account of the royalty tax in the Klondike.

She had gone on to the Klondike after forty-two days in Nome. Now the more intrepid part of her travels began since she no longer had Raymond to provide material or emotional comfort. Leaving Nome on 26 July Elizabeth sailed with strangers down Norton Sound for St Michael then travelled by river steamer to the Klondike. She continued her interviewing. The captain of the boat told her all about sealing. On the way to St Michael she wrote an article about the imposition of quarantine after a smallpox outbreak on a ship arriving at Nome. This was never published, neither was her account of the Anvil Creek 'clean-up'. Some articles may have got lost in transit.

Elizabeth now retraced some of her brother's steps on the long trek. Being summer, conditions were entirely different. At Anvik, a Yukon trading station, she met her brother Saxton whom she had not seen for many years:

> I see before me a thin, haggard, and yet not sickly-looking man of 31, long face, stubbly moustache, dark red-brown almost black in some lights, unshaven for the rest, and I think unwashed.

He had, however, risen very early and rowed 23 miles (37 km) to Elizabeth's boat. She noticed that his hands trembled. He told her that he 'liked the life, the freedom and the "big chances"' though he seemed far from securing the last. Whereas Elizabeth savoured the moments Raymond spent with her, after only a few hours with Saxton 'I suddenly feel with a sinking of the heart that I have no more to say to this poor brother of mine'. She confessed to feeling 'full of sorrow for him—but I feel helpless—at a deadlock'. He had not even known that their mother was still alive.

In fact both Hannah Robins and her son Saxton were to die the following year within a few months of each other. In her diary summary for 1900 Elizabeth had referred to 'the madness & suicide by wh. [*sic*] we were menaced, bound, dogged from generation to generation'. Saxton committed suicide not long after this was written. After their reunion she described Saxton's life as one 'that always just "misses" it'. Remembering him years later in *Both Sides of the Curtain* she chose to present a young, somewhat different Saxton in Florida, the eldest of the Robins brothers with a 'highly social disposition and humorous alert mind', casting his brother Vernon into the shade.[16] After their final meeting he had written to his sister telling her how much their reunion had meant to him and confessing that his last six years had been ones of hardship, drifting from job to job and illness which led him to 'the border'. In response to a second letter in which he alluded to a breakdown, Elizabeth had written, 'I conjure you to make courage a matter of course in your life.'

Elizabeth's subsequent journey took her inside the Arctic Circle. She spent her thirty-eighth birthday on the Upper Yukon. At Dawson the tables were turned and she found herself interviewed by the *Klondike Nugget*. On a trip to nearby creeks she was forced to take the only available accommodation in the Gold Hill Hotel, a gambling joint full of drunks and 'town' women. She was told that the men were so little accustomed to seeing 'decent' women that they hardly knew how to treat her. In Nome she had insisted on visiting 'gambling hells' such as the Gold Belt.

She later worked such places into her fiction. The short story 'Miss Cal' opens at a fashionable London dinner party. The urbane politician and arbiter of good taste, Noel Berwick, has suggested that a young American singer he has met should entertain the gathering. The story's narrator recognises her. She had grown up in Nome, 'the gathering place of the nations, Mecca of the derelict, the dumping heap of the world.'[17] Her father had died when she was small and she had been raised by the proprietor of the Golden Sands gambling saloon, a former bank robber reputed to have killed fourteen men. Yet when the narrator confesses to knowing about her past, this ingenuous young woman, so unlike Berwick and his world, displays a fond remembrance for her upbringing, naïvely recalling the kindly Nome folk. This rather sentimentalised tale applauds the inherent goodness in the 'rough' men who gave their money to provide a better life for the talented girl.

From the Gold Hill Hotel Elizabeth travelled by steamboat to Skagway then south to Juneau. On 26 August on the way back to Seattle came her first mention of 'feeling wretched'. She took medicine and visited a salmon cannery. One of her last actions before the diary petered out three days later was to buy $5-worth of gold dust from Magnet gulch. At some point on this homeward journey she also drafted a letter to Raymond (which was never sent) acknowledging that he should leave Nome only when he really wanted to do so and not because of her pressure. She also stressed that he should marry only when it was right for *him*. The letter ended with a vision of the 'Road House', the home that they would some day share.

What happened next can only be pieced together from later accounts. On reaching Seattle at the end of the month Elizabeth learned that Raymond had contracted typhoid fever in Nome. Unknown to her, he had resigned his mission post two weeks after her departure. She had been feeling unwell for several days. A doctor diagnosed a feverish cold but on 31 August she was admitted to Seattle General Hospital. She too had typhoid fever and would spend the next two months desperately ill in hospital.

For thirty-three days Elizabeth could not take solids. Salmonella typhi had entered the bloodstream through the intestinal wall, causing fever, headaches then a rash and diarrhoea and extreme lethargy. Raymond was taken out of Nome just in time—on the last boat before the winter freeze—but he faced a nightmare sea-journey to Seattle. He arrived at Elizabeth's bedside on 17 October: 'At first sight I think he looks like Christ.' By the end of the month both were sufficiently recovered to travel by train to Louisville. Elizabeth saw her mother for what proved to be the last time. Raymond had not seen her for eighteen years but Elizabeth made sure that he did not spoil his memory of her or disturb Hannah by a visit.

She arrived back in London on 21 November. The ensuing months found her very weak with almost unceasing headaches and loss of hair. She suffered from post-typhoid symptoms for two years and although she experienced longevity, her health would, from now on, be a constant worry. Illness (including a thrombosis) soon drove her to Soquel, a nursing home in Paignton, Devon. At first she seemed to grow worse. On 19 January 1901 Raymond arrived and stayed for over a month, for once devoting all his energy to her. After consulting a nerve specialist in March Elizabeth tried her first rest cure at Ventnor on the Isle of Wight. Her period of enforced isolation found later critical expression in fiction (see Chapter 9).

She did return to Soquel briefly in the autumn but she also recuperated at the Lewises' Norfolk home, the Danish Pavilion at Overstrand, and sought to regain vigour by going abroad. In May she stayed with Caroline Grosvenor in Florence: 'I had always felt that to see Italy could make a broad mark of division over one's life—that existence would never be quite the same again.' Then she travelled on to the Swiss and French Alps staying for five weeks at Aix-les-Bains, taking the waters and building up strength. In this most unlikely of places in the south of France Elizabeth began writing what became her best-selling tale of the frozen north. Even in January 1904 after it was finished she was still not fit and asked herself, 'Was ever a book before wrought out of so much pain?' On publication that spring she was so concerned about her health that her diary records her consumption of charcoal biscuits rather than her book's reviews.

Inspired by the Yukon diary smudged by 'finger and fish oil' which Raymond had shown her, Elizabeth had begun writing short stories at Soquel. They were turned into her novel. One story, originally part of the novel, was then taken out. 'Monica's Village' first appeared in print in 1905. It provides a more critical treatment of issues of race and gender than most of her Alaskan work, including a comment on the treatment of native Indians:

> The white man has not even set these people on his map, but they shivered in the white man's cheap cotton, having bartered their costly furs. White traders and prospectors have slaughtered caribou by the herd, and left them to rot on the hills.[18]

Elizabeth's characters the Colonel, his young companion and an Alaskan commercial agent discuss the treatment of women. The Colonel displays a chivalric attitude but it is the young man whose views are most reactionary. All this is a preamble to tales about the powers of a woman who runs a nearby village. When they finally reach Monica, 'A tall woman stood there, with an air of majesty'.[19] It seems that, like Rider Haggard's Ayesha, she must be obeyed. She is the arbiter of justice for the Indians. The white men are relieved to hear her perfect English since they can only conceive of this embodiment of civilisation as of their own race. Yet her ethnic origins are not what seem to matter to the Indians. There is a vagueness about where she came from and she has been there 'All the time'. The story ends with the words 'Monica is Mother of her People'.[20] This woman who cures the sick is seen as possessing magical powers. She is revered as a sorceress. The Colonel's response is echoed in Elizabeth's later writings: 'Every woman's a sorceress who doesn't too diligently explain away her mystery.' Monica is reputed to have bucketfuls of gold but if there are mines nearby '*She* would never tell'.

Elizabeth's story is a neat amalgam of scenes she had witnessed and been told about by Raymond and a parody of Rider Haggard's popular novel *She*. At a camp close to Dawson Elizabeth had herself come across an 'impossibly old' Indian woman she had labelled '*She!*'.

Although her contemporaries do not appear to have made the connection, *The Magnetic North* invites some comparison with one of the best known quest tales concerned with imperialism, Joseph Conrad's *Heart of Darkness* published in *Blackwood's Magazine* in 1899, then in book form in 1902. Although one is set in Alaska and the other in Africa, and Conrad's book is more sophisticated and complex, both are voyages of self-discovery, involving the penetration of unknown territory and the unconscious. They explore much more than journeys upriver in far-flung foreign lands, examining man's capacity for both good and evil and whether savagery will 'out' when civilisation (as it is defined by the dominant culture) is removed. Both are also by writers immersed in, yet not originally from, imperial England.

Elizabeth's tale was essentially Raymond's story of that first winter in Alaska in 1897–8. Raymond's unfinished diary (which has not survived) became what she called her 'handrail' for Yukon sketches which were eventually turned into a lengthy novel aided by oral testimony from Alaska and information gathered by Raymond's partner Albert F. Shulte. Raymond commented on Elizabeth's draft manuscript but his only suggestion was that she should eliminate a reference to the men eating doughnuts! Whereas he saw 'Monica's Village' and a story called 'The Esquimeaux Horse' as gems and acknowledged the power of his sister's 'terrible imagination', he had reservations about the novel which was rather too close to reality for his liking: 'Frankly I lack sympathy with this work, despite its rare beauty and unquestioned power.'

It begins with a Denver bank clerk, a Canadian ex-schoolmaster, an Irish-American lawyer, a Kentucky 'Colonel' (who had never fought) and 'the Boy' (who is twenty-two) arriving in Alaska bound for the Klondike. The weather forces them to set up a winter camp on the Yukon. Just under half the book is set at the Big Chimney camp where this motley crew become resourceful and learn to endure each other in adverse circumstances. The characters are based on the men Raymond and Saxton had met at sea and camped with during the harsh winter. Raymond is Morris Burnet, the Boy an amalgam of Uncle Morrie's name and that of Charles Robins's half-brother;(Raymond had also visited Burnet, Texas and written to Elizabeth from there). The Colonel and the Boy whom some critics saw as representing the author set out together to conquer the elements, travelling along the frozen river. Here and in 'The Caribou Stand', a thriller with the same two characters, Elizabeth explores fraternity pushed to its most extreme.

In the classic quest genre the heroes of *The Magnetic North* meet frequent obstacles along the way. Although they nearly starve, encounter snow blindness and temporarily harbour murderous thoughts towards each other, in the end their better natures prevail. They reach their destination and are all reunited in the Klondike. Yet the Colonel dies whilst the Boy's experiences of being received and revived at the Russian Holy Cross Mission and transfixed by a lone cross in the snow, have turned his quest for gold into a search for spirituality. In a somewhat enigmatic ending (Elizabeth never quite came to terms with her brother's shift to religiosity), the Boy appears to be on the point of turning back to Holy Cross.

The Magnetic North was very popular.[21] Yet it is not easy for us today to appreciate this. Even though the bonding of 'real men' in the rugged outdoors has some late twentieth-century parallels, the men's restrained language and delicacy when, for example, encountering the few women in the novel, make it seem unconvincing. The sentimentalised representation of their dealings with the young Eskimo boy[22] and depiction of natives as uncivilised primitives jars whilst the portrayal of the intense friendship between the forty-year-old Colonel and the Boy cannot be accepted so innocently. Names like Mac and a Kentucky 'Colonel' are more reminiscent of fast food than of adults surviving in a part of the world which now boasts package holidays. At best *The Magnetic North* reads today like a good adventure story for boys, full of suspense, an able yarn. It can also be seen as an imperial Gothic tale,[23] invoking moral idealism yet reinforcing stereotypes through its representation of white men 'going native' in an undeveloped land which is labelled 'the Great White Silence'. In 1904 it was welcomed as adult fiction and appreciated for its 'portraiture of life'.

There is some evidence that Elizabeth was not entirely satisfied with this product of so much physical pain. When Mark Twain congratulated her on her great work she commented in her diary, 'how odd that it shd [*sic*] seem so to the people who ought to know that greatness is not spun in so loose a webb [*sic*]' She believed that she could write a great book but had not yet done so. Yet within four years the book was in its seventh reprint. Its depiction of a cold, silent, faraway land had a chilling effect on its readers. Octavia Wilberforce had a friend who had read it 'on the hottest summer day in a hayfield and it had made her shiver'.[24]

Alaska was topical. The previous year Jack London's *Call of the Wild* had also been published by Heinemann. This American socialist had, like Raymond, joined the Klondike gold rush in 1897 and his Alaskan story had proved immensely popular. Gold-hunting made for a romantic story. David Belasco's melodrama *The Girl of the Golden West* (the basis for Puccini's opera) opened on the New York stage in 1905. Set in a Californian gold camp it was also very successful. Elizabeth's use of authentic details, such as making cabin windows out of glass jars, and occasional Yup'ik Eskimo terms, aided what one critic called the book's 'almost appalling veracity'.[25] Her writing was compared to Zola's in its attention to detail. She had in fact been reading Zola on the last stages of her Yukon journey.

Contemporaries were unaware that the teenage Elizabeth had lived in a mining camp neither could they appreciate that this book was about her own 'heart of darkness'—'how far I had to go to find Raymond'—but they did recognise the allegorical journey exploring the inner self. Quest novels are usually written by men about men and in this book in which all the main characters are male, Elizabeth was appropriating the form and providing something radically different from her earlier and later work. Her decision to deflect attention from herself and focus on her brother's experience was not unconnected with her understanding of publisher and reader expectations and would have freed her slightly in her use of language.[26] Yet Elizabeth was constrained by the fact that her identity as a writer was now known so that ironically this, her most 'masculine' of novels, was the first which readers knew from the outset to be by a woman. Critics handled the matter of female authorship by suggesting that it was conceived 'in the masculine spirit' and by expressing surprise that a woman could have written it. The fashion designer Worth congratulated Elizabeth on a novel which he could hardly believe to be 'the outcome of a woman's brain'. It is not surprising that she later railed against the concept of the exceptional woman.

When *The Magnetic North* was published, tongue in cheek, the *Daily Chronicle* commented, 'Nothing remains for women now but to find the North Pole'. Elizabeth later published a 'sister' volume called *Come And Find Me* which was partly about the struggle for the Pole (by a man). Once again her timing was impeccable. Although written in 1905–6, it was published in book form early in 1908, the year that, Dr Frederick A. Cook reached the North Pole.[27] Hildegarde, the heroine of the new story, goes to Alaska on her own to find her father. Here was a version of Elizabeth's own experience and a further subversion of the male quest story. Apparently it was Florence Bell who encouraged Elizabeth to turn her travels into a novel though in a letter to Heinemann the author explained that she had received a number of letters asking whether *The Magnetic North* was based on first-hand knowledge so she felt she should now write her own story. The book was dedicated to Florence who declared, 'Dear, I think this Book is simply a Masterpiece.' In the 1920s Florence drafted a synopsis hoping the novel would be turned into a film.

As in Ibsen's social dramas, the action on which the story turns has largely taken place before the novel begins. Nathaniel Mar had discovered Alaskan gold in the 1860s (in Nome Elizabeth had been told how the true discoverer of Anvil gold had been cheated out of it). He has become a disappointed American banker who hankers for the life and gold he left behind. He is as apathetic about his daily life as his wife is energetic. Mrs Mar never wastes a moment. Even on a train journey she reads a biography and crochets for dear life (this description is based on a busy English woman Elizabeth once encountered on a train). The doughty daughter Hildegarde and her spoilt friend Bella both long for the young explorer, Jack Galbraith. After about 150 pages in the cluttered claustrophobic Mar household, there is sudden action. Mar has finally taken himself back to Alaska and Hildegarde goes in search of him. Elizabeth is at pains to stress that women can be 'doers' too but that they so often lack opportunities: 'the reason women aren't more use in the world is because they don't have a chance … they don't have education.'[28] In 'Woman's Secret' Elizabeth later wrote: 'We find the chief difference between ourselves and men to lie in the fact that men are expected to struggle against adverse circumstances, whereas they have made it our chief virtue not to struggle.'[29] Her novel showed what could be achieved. It drew heavily on her diary (passages designated for the novel were marked in blue crayon).

Jack Galbraith's fate brings us back to *Heart of Darkness*. Hildegarde finds him dying in a hut on a lonely Alaskan shore. He burns the coloured crayon sketch which is his proof of having reached the Pole. Elizabeth signals her reservations about the implications of man's conquest of the world but as a personal traveller who had helped translate the work of the explorer Nansen she also understood the ambition and appeal of

> the terrible, beautiful place that would still go luring men with its lying legend on all the maps, crying out in every tongue in Europe—

> UNEXPLORED REGION
> COME AND FIND ME![30]

She quotes Captain Cook's wish 'not only to go further than any one had been before; but as far as it was possible for man to go'.

This book never won the applause of *The Magnetic North*. It includes some indication of Elizabeth's evolving feminism. At sea Hildegarde learns from Etta (based on the Colorado stenographer) that 'Even the best men haven't got so far as to want the respect of all women'[31] and it is Hildegarde who tells Cheviot, the young banker who has followed her to Alaska, that she loves him. Yet such gestures would not have appealed to many of those who had warmed to her previous Alaskan novel. At the same time the ending and contrived meetings make it ultimately little more than romantic fiction enhanced by sentimental drawings. This would have been disappointing to readers of *The Convert*, published in 1907.

The most factual account of Elizabeth's travels came in her documentary book *Raymond and I* published posthumously in 1956 by Leonard Woolf. It used the diaries and correspondence between Raymond and Elizabeth and also drew on her letters to Florence. Raymond had forbidden the publication of such a personal account during his lifetime. Elizabeth had anticipated opposition. In 1933 she told her friend Marie Belloc Lowndes that

> It is such an unveiling (the letters part of the book) of the development of a young man's thought & life as I do not think has ever seen print

She also admitted that there was 'dynamite' in the last quarter of the book.[32]

The Alaskan material was also adapted for children. The 'Go to Sleep Stories' were loosely based on Eskimo legends. Elizabeth used the device of an old storyteller relaying tales on long winter nights, drawing on the magic powers of animals and birds such as the crow. Yukon creatures also featured in her children's play 'The Bowarra' (bow and arrow) in which the central character is Kaviak the child from *The Magnetic North*. Despite some interest and reworking by Granville Barker in 1909, the play was never produced neither did her 'Go to Sleep Stories' get into print. Nevertheless, in the main, Alaska served Elizabeth well as a writer.

Its personal legacy was a renewed commitment to sharing a home with Raymond. Still physically weak and convinced that her acting career was ending and her future a literary one, Elizabeth was keen to settle. After many years of rented accommodation and months of sick beds in alien surroundings she was tired of being 'harried & hunted from room to room, from city to city from continent to continent'. Adept at encouragement from afar, Raymond wrote how they would go in the springtime to the woods and mountains and find a home, 'we are of one blood, bound together by the invisible fabric of a great love woven by the loom of time … we will do this thing. I pledge you in the name of the Everlasting Father.'

Elizabeth had therefore returned to America in the autumn of 1902 seeking a home for them both. She felt that she had rescued Raymond and believed him to be the one family member who still depended on her: 'I have created a claim here & I must look to it that I am faithful to the obligation. But for me he wd [*sic*] be lying in an Alaskan grave at this moment.' Since returning to the States Raymond had thrown himself into labour politics, negotiating for the United Mine Workers during the 1902 anthracite strike. He was now superintendent of a municipal lodging house in Chicago.

Elizabeth waited for him to join her in Virginia for their search but his 'tramps & thieves' kept delaying him. They snatched a little time riding together in the Shenandoah Valley in early August but Raymond was heading for a breakdown and Elizabeth was in delicate health. With nothing settled and having spent more time with Mrs Erskine Waters than with her brother, Elizabeth reluctantly returned to England in September and another two months in a nursing home.

The following year her dreams looked like coming true. Raymond returned briefly to Florida. As a lad he had been teased by the boys of the Snow family who lived in the big house on top of one of the state's few hills. He had resolved that he would one day live there. In December 1904 he saw the Hernando County estate once more. This would be their home. They would call it Chinsegut, an Eskimo term signifying the spirit of things lost and regained. Elizabeth loaned Raymond $5,000 saved from royalties and her grandmother's legacy. The house had been built before the Civil War and was now badly in need of renovation. Sixty acres (24 hectares) were purchased on the crest of the hill with 120 acres (48.5 hectares) surrounding it. On Easter Sunday 1905 Raymond wrote to Elizabeth, 'My Beloved— This is the resurrection morning! Chinsegut Hill. I write under our own roof & on our own land.'

In a highly charged letter he told Elizabeth that

Against all other men and women in the earth the secret chambers of my Soul are barred and locked, and I can bid them keep their distance but you O Bessie can open every door, and each deep hidden chord throbs responsive to your touch. I love you blessed One, I love you to the utmost limit of my heart's devotion, joy and hope.

But this was not a romantic tale with a predictable happy ending and when he wrote these words Raymond had not met Margaret Dreier.

On 9 April Raymond was returning from preaching on the social gospel at the Plymouth Church, Brooklyn. He was introduced to the eldest daughter of the millionaire Dreier family of German descent, now settled in Brooklyn. Thirty-seven-year-old Margaret was five years older than Raymond and equally devoted to social progress and Christianity. Raymond wrote to his sister: 'I have just had a vision.' He went on to explain that 'next to Jane Addams [Margaret] is the best incarnation of the social conscience I have yet seen'. She had worked for the Women's Municipal League and was now active in the Women's Trade Union League (formed in 1903) which helped working women organise themselves into unions, providing support and cash and putting pressure on employers for improved wages and conditions.

Margaret became the centre of Raymond's devotion, the emotions previously lavished on a faraway sister now finding an immediate and willing recipient. The following month they became engaged and in June they married. Raymond was now the chief resident of the Northwestern University's social settlement in Chicago, a city which boasted over a dozen settlement houses.

Within half an hour of hearing that her brother was to marry, Elizabeth had written to Margaret, signing herself Elizabeth Robins Parks. Margaret's reply included the words 'Make my home yours when you come.' For the rest of her life Elizabeth would feel that Margaret had actually taken away *her* home, Chinsegut. It became a retreat for Margaret and Raymond and later their main home. Over the years Elizabeth would stay there but as a guest. Margaret's account of how her heart 'stood still when we reached the top of the hill' can hardly have calmed her new sister-in-law who had not yet even glimpsed Chinsegut.

For years Raymond had carried around the world a photograph of his sister in *The American*. Now he handed it over to Margaret: 'Bessie was my great light until I found my own beloved one.'[33] Soon the couple were spending money lavishly on Chinsegut, another bone of contention for Elizabeth over the years. Nevertheless she attended the wedding in America, sailing back to England in July 1905. She now accepted that she had to find her own place. Within the next few years Elizabeth discovered a house in Sussex in southern England and this county became her home for the rest of her life.

PART IV

ELIZABETH ROBINS

7

THE CONVERT

In the years before the First World War Elizabeth campaigned for the vote for women. In March 1912 after attending the Conspiracy trial of suffragettes she addressed 12,000 women at the Albert Hall, urging fairer treatment of suffrage prisoners. She then returned to the calm of her Sussex home, 'all so pretty & pacific'.

Until 1907 her English home had been London. Her first sustained experiment in English country living was, however, in a secluded, wooded Surrey village. On 18 April 1907 whilst London was applauding her play *Votes For Women!* (see Appendix 3 for Elizabeth's publications on women's suffrage), Elizabeth visited Woldingham and saw Blythe. She called it a 'cottage' but like many romantic urban dwellers she was using the term to describe a rather substantial building. She wasted no time in surrendering her lease on her current flat at 24, Iverna Gardens, Kensington and became a tenant at Blythe, joining her new friend Flora Simmonds there for the best part of two years. Flora was an art critic and linguist who did translation work for Heinemann. The household consisted of Flora, Elizabeth, David Scott (Flora's young ward who was probably her son)[1] and a Danish cook, Nancy Jorgensen. Here Elizabeth wrote what is today her best-known work, *The Convert*.

In a short story about women's suffrage Elizabeth described a fairly young widow living in an old house in the country and 'the need to make some corner of earth smile—to make some spot perfect before you die'.[2] Anticipating the publication of *The Convert*, Elizabeth told Florence Bell that she now had dreams of buying a house with a garden: 'How satisfactory to make some acre or two of this English land to smile because of me before my efforts cease.' Now that the Chinsegut dream had turned sour and with the Blythe experiment a success, the entire household, including Hi the dog, moved to West Sussex where Elizabeth leased a house for £30 per annum. It was Mildred Buxton, wife of the Postmaster-General (whose home Newtimber Place was close by) who showed Elizabeth the beautiful L-shaped Backset Town House standing on its own amidst fields yet only a stone's throw from the village of Henfield. A former farm-house, part of it was thought to date back as far as 1350. Elizabeth slept there for the first time on 3 April 1909. She had signed a fifteen-year lease with an option to buy after two years. 'There's an atmosphere of beauty and graciousness about the house already'[3] she wrote after one week. Thanks to royalties and American investments within a few years she had bought the house, now known as Backsettown, and land surrounding it, and had renovated the interior.

Elizabeth became a well-known figure in the village of Henfield. During the school holidays she read and walked with David. She also lent some support to the Henfield suffragists, moderates organised by a local vicar, and took part in their suffrage concert. She was, however, known to be one of the militant suffragists, labelled suffragettes.

What had turned this woman in search of a quiet life into a suffragette? Some contemporaries felt that the militant suffrage organi-sation, the Women's Social and Political Union (WSPU), founded in 1903, provided women with the freedom and excitement lacking in their lives.[4] Yet this could hardly be the case for Elizabeth though her very independence, endorsement of Ibsen and first-hand experience of the difficulties facing women in the theatre made it likely that she would endorse feminist views. Soon after arriving in England she had met socially feminists such as Emily Faithfull and the secretary of the Central London Society for Women's Suffrage had even asked her to a meeting in 1889. She had accepted but did not attend it.

Yet although she was to attribute to Ibsen an awakening of interest in the 'woman question' she was, by her own admis-sion, at first an ignorant opponent of women's suffrage, too ready to accept the grounds 'advanced so complacently by those ladies who tell you that they have all they want and so feel at liberty to condemn the less fortunate—or less self-centred'.[5]

Above: 1 The Old Stone House, Zanesville, Ohio, *c.* 1880; this is where Elizabeth spent much of her childhood

Right: 2 Elizabeth aged eight

3 Grandma Jane Hussey Robins

4 As Clare Raimond in America

5 Husband George Parks

6 The first glimpse of Europe—
Ole Bull's summer home in
Norway

7 Elizabeth the actress in London, 1891. This picture was given to the Bell family. On the back was written '"One isn't always mistress of one's thoughts" *Hedda Gabler*'

8 William Archer in 1891

9 The Edwardian Elizabeth

10 Florence Bell, Lady Bell

11 Chinsegut, Florida today

12 Mary Dreier, Raymond Robins and Margaret Dreier Robins

BACKSET TOWN HOUSE
HENFIELD

Above: 13 Backsettown,
Henfield, Sussex

Right: 14 Elizabeth in 1907

15 Elizabeth as an older woman

16 Elizabeth and Octavia Wilberforce haymaking at Backsettown

Where she did advocate change it was of the incrementalist kind, particularly in the form of improved education for women. She was, as she later admitted, full of 'masculine criticisms'.[6]

Her shift towards a more specific goal, that of the vote for women as a beginning rather than as an end in itself, almost parallels the development of women's suffrage in Britain. On 1 November 1905 Adela Cort, secretary of the Kensington branch of the larger and slightly older of the two main suffrage societies, Mrs Fawcett's umbrella organisation, the National Union of Women' Suffrage Societies (NUWSS), wrote to invite Elizabeth to address a draw-ing-room debate on suffrage—on the opposing side. Adela Cort did, however, add that she was 'Not quite sure whether you stake your straw in the opposite camp firmly enough to do this'. Elizabeth's immediate reply made her position clear. She was then hailed as 'a most welcome convert to the cause of women's suffrage'. Perhaps the former actress would like to present to the branch her former objections and present converted views? Conversion was to become a subject for her fiction, but the confessional was not Elizabeth's personal style. There is no evidence of her 'telling all'. Nevertheless this correspondence is significant in that she had not only resisted opposing suffrage but had actually *named* herself as a suffragist.

A few days earlier her diary had recorded a dinner held by the Lewises. This was not one of her diurnal entries but rather the care-ful shaping of a recalled experience into a scene which might be of use in fiction. It tells how the radical MP Henry Labouchere regaled guests with an account of women bombarding Parliament for the vote. Elizabeth added, 'Quite heroically, I thought in my simple way.' They had demanded an audience with Labouchere but he had refused to face them:

> I couldn't have done it for worlds' he said with a comic look of terror, 'but I sent another fellow. He came back & says he 'You're quite right my dear fellow … don't you go, it's appalling to look at 'em. There isn't a week-ender among 'em'.[7]

This story was later used almost verbatim in *Votes For Women!* and *The Convert* though the words were put into the mouth of Sir John Greatorex MP, rumoured to tell 'such good stories at dinner'. In her diary Elizabeth recounted how Labouchere indulged in jaded jibes about women in politics being old maids or having short hair. When she objected, his response was 'You don't mean to say you … You don't look that sort.' Elizabeth's attendance at polite dinner parties seems to have played a part not only in supplying background and speech for writing but also in helping convince her of her own developing views and need to articulate them at a time when the suffrage message was becoming more prominent.

There was a sense of theatre in the suffrage movement. This is not to subscribe to George Dangerfield's portrayal[8] of it as demonstrating elements of brutal comedy—he belittled its achievements—but to recognise the appeal of its impassioned oratory, pageantry, costume and self-sacrifice. When Sybil Thorndike first heard Mrs Pankhurst she was struck by 'what a lovely part she would be to play'[9] and per-haps Elizabeth was responding to her appreciation of performance.

In 1906 she began writing suffrage drama. The actress Gertrude Kingston was setting up her own company and wanted Elizabeth to write her a play. She appeared to have unlimited funds and to be open to suggestions. Elizabeth told Florence how Gertrude had been pelting her with invitations to dine so, impressed by her ability and eagerness, she began working on a play called 'Judith', loosely based on the French 'Tragic Muse', the actress Rachel. Yet high drama was unfolding closer to home in the name of women's suffrage so she shifted her focus to the present and 'The Friend of Woman'. This was done 'at white heat' in the autumn of 1906 but at Harley Granville Barker's suggestion it was renamed *Votes For Women!*[10]

It gives the woman with a past both a present and a future, showing how the struggle for the vote is relevant to all and how 'The Personal is Political' is far from being an invention of the modern women's movement. We learn that the heroine Vida Levering had, ten years earlier, become involved with the Hon. Geoffrey Stonor, a family friend who had offered help at a difficult time. From a privileged background but taking offence at 'an ugly thing that was going on under my father's roof', Vida had tried, unsuccessfully, to earn her own living. Adapting the words of Clara Collet, a (non-fictional) expert on women's industrial employment, Vida later explained to the naive Jean Dumbarton (called Beatrice in the stage version): 'Some girls think it hardship to have to earn their living. The horror is not to be allowed to—.'[11] When Vida had become pregnant, Stonor, only too aware of his father and his own political career, had advised an abortion. Vida had reluctantly accepted this.

A decade later and throughout the course of the play, she is a suffragette. She also moves in society circles where she encounters the charismatic Stonor, now a Conservative MP, and his fiancée, Jean. The latter is drawn to Vida's views especially after hearing her speak at a women's suffrage rally in that symbolic and commemorative centre of public urban space, Trafalgar Square. Although treated like a child by Stonor and society, Jean understands soon enough that he and Vida had once been lovers and confronts him. It is Vida, however, who enables Stonor to have a life with Jean through an agreement that the MP, whose parliamentary seat is vulnerable, espouses the cause of women's suffrage. Whether or not he, as well as Jean, is genuinely converted or merely grasping at a machiavellian solution, is open to interpretation. What is clear is that a fallen woman can be redeemed and dedicate herself to a cause which can be her and other women's salvation. The man who served one woman ill will now serve hundreds of thousands of women well. For those believing in women's suffrage, it was a happy ending but it was far from the conventional closure. Death does not signal the end, nor does emigration or marriage, but Jean has found a political voice. Women's suffrage had a new role model in Vida. Well-dressed, thoughtful and dedicated, her common-sense reaction to the conversation of her peers exposes to them and to readers their own lack of understanding, thereby effectively challenging media images of suffragettes.

The process of researching and writing this play turned Elizabeth from being one more woman in broad agreement with women's suffrage into a committed suffragette publicly identified with the cause. She began it after a summer at Rounton and in the same month, September 1906, that the WSPU moved their headquarters from Manchester to London. On 16 September Elizabeth met Mrs Pankhurst to discuss the play. She was anxious to have it performed as soon as possible not solely on account of pressure from Gertrude Kingston but also because of its topicality and the opportunity to 'ventilate the cause'.[12] She was also spurred on by the fact that a male playwright had been making enquiries to the WSPU about information for a suffrage play so 'I have seldom in my life worked at such pressure'. On 3 November she read a draft to Molly (Florence Bell's suffragist daughter) and her husband the Liberal MP Charles Trevelyan. Molly noted in her diary that Elizabeth had been 'tremendously fired' by suffrage, 'is hand in glove with them—& this play is a sort of tract. It is very good, we thought'.[13]

Where had Elizabeth obtained her information? In her autobiography Hannah Mitchell explains how the writer had attended the Huddersfield by-election 'to get the atmosphere'.[14] Hannah relayed a few incidents to her and in return received some hints on writing. The second act of the play which consists of an open-air meeting in Trafalgar Square details suffrage speeches with remarkable authenticity. Amongst Elizabeth's personal papers are over twenty-six pages of typed notes detailing eight suffrage meetings held between July and October 1906 and these, based at least in part on events that Elizabeth personally witnessed, form the basis of the suffrage incidents and speeches in the play and subsequent novel of 1907.[15] Much of the bantering amongst the crowd is based on actuality and the same goes for the speeches, some of which Elizabeth also read up in the press.

It is possible to identify the stage characters. Ernestine Blunt is modelled on Teresa Billington-Greig who caused a stir at the Hyde Park meeting of 8 July though in *The Convert* (but not in the play) Ernestine becomes a lawyer, perhaps to deflect attention from the association of Christabel Pankhurst LLB with Vida which had worried the Pankhursts. In fact Elizabeth changed her original first name of Christian to Vida. As Mrs Pankhurst put it: 'Now Christabel has no past still many people might torment the imaginary with the real & say that Christian's story is Christabel's. We should not like this to happen, should we?'[16] When Vida makes her 'maiden' public speech, it is based on comments about the police court given at a Hyde Park speech. Mrs Baldock seems to have been the model for the fictional working-class woman who is a Poor Law Guardian. The typed account of a Battersea Park meeting opens with Elizabeth pondering on what the Bells would have thought had they seen her there with Mrs Pankhurst, 'I, if you please, carrying propagandist literature, pamphlets etc.' The scene is described in *The Convert* and was in turn praised for its verisimilitude by Sylvia Pankhurst in her book on the suffragettes' history.[17]

The following year Elizabeth explained to a New York magazine that it was the personal effect of attending a suffrage meeting in Trafalgar Square out of (quote) 'shamefaced curiosity' which had spearheaded her into suffrage activity.[18] This sounds remarkably like her own creation Vida in the novel which Elizabeth was then writing. The novel extends the narrative back to Vida's pre-suffrage days, tracing her conversion. Given the fact that by the time of the Trafalgar Square meeting (1 October) Elizabeth was already working on the play, a more pragmatic explanation can be given for her attendance than 'curiosity' suggests: she needed 'copy' for her play.

In the process of acquiring this, the observer became participant. On 23 October Parliament reassembled and after a protest in the lobby of the House of Commons (the Prime Minister had refused to pledge the government to introduce Votes for Women), eleven women were arrested. Elizabeth followed this up by attending a meeting chaired by Mrs Pankhurst at Caxton Hall the next day. She also went to the police court and was shunted into a side room marked 'female witnesses' and deliberately kept out of court. This personal indignity she felt keenly. The next day she attended the annual conference of the National Union of Women Workers at Tunbridge Wells and was shocked to discover that they accepted the 'extraordinarily and flagrantly untrue' press accounts of the suffragettes. This somewhat inappropriately named organisation was composed of rather genteel ladies, most of whom had little direct contact with trade unions. For the first time Elizabeth was sufficiently roused to make an unscripted intervention outlining what had actually happened in court. Claiming that only six weeks earlier she had 'strongly disapproved' of women's suffrage (not the impression she had given Adela Cort a year earlier), she now earnestly advocated helping 'struggling sisters'. She denied that any of the women were 'wild and hysterical'. Mrs Fawcett the society's vice-president asked her to convey to those in prison their sympathy (official messages contravened the society's rules). Elizabeth did just that. Sylvia Pankhurst later recalled her surprise at a visit from 'this brilliant creature'.[19]

Elizabeth wrote to thank Mrs Fawcett for her generous treatment of women who 'in ways you do not approve, are trying for the thing you have fought for by the dignified tactics that the world is forced to admire'.[20] She also confronted the source of misinformation by writing to *The Times* complaining about the 'outrageous lies' the press had told about the women.[21] The first of a number of defences of women's actions in the press, it opened modestly. Elizabeth described herself as a foreigner long accustomed to English hospitality who had come to see the necessity of women's suffrage. 'Her heart must have been hot within her' wrote Margaret Dreier Robins to her sister Mary.[22] In December Elizabeth proposed a toast to the cause at the Prisoners' Banquet at the Savoy, chaired by Mrs Fawcett.

By February 1907 she was acknowledging that her sympathies were 'so entirely with the movement that I would be very glad to serve either the old party or the new in any way in my power'.[23] Some reviewers of the play suspected that Elizabeth favoured the NUWSS. Yet although she admired Mrs Fawcett whom she had first met socially in 1889, Elizabeth's letter to her had also suggested an increasing unease with the moderates' approach: 'the women who work on "constitutional lines" cannot always reach and stir the larger public.' This belief was to commit her to the WSPU. She admitted: 'I am as yet rather ignorant about it all, but I mean to be less so.' In the following February when the first 'Parliament of Women' met at Caxton Hall Elizabeth witnessed mounted police riding down little bands of women trying to reach the Commons. She was herself driven off the pavement three times and in danger of being trampled under horses' hooves. She told Lady Strachey that until then she would not have believed that such things could happen in England.[24]

Nevertheless, she viewed her pen as her most powerful means of influence. *Votes For Women!* she saw as 'the first thing I shall have written under the pressure of strong moral convictions'.[25] There was, however, a slight hitch. Despite having commissioned a play, Gertrude Kingston now had a new part. She was also increasingly concerned about the sensitivity of Elizabeth's subject-matter (one manager refused to deal with the topic) and procrastinating. Elizabeth was released from the contract and turned with relief to the bolder Barker of the Court Theatre who had already seen an early draft. Much advice was now proffered. Henry James penned fifty pages about the first part of the first act! He favoured fewer characters but Elizabeth would not let him thereby depoliticise it: 'I have *got* to have as much of the woman movement as shall put the ignorant in possession of its main facts.'[26] J.M. Barrie and Shaw were encouraging and even Archer went the 'reckless length of saying stoutly that "it is all right"'. Elizabeth did, however, admit that she had some personal reservations. The play was 'too much in monochrome' and somewhat humourless. Barker helped polish the script and, with his skilful stage-management and a highly professional cast, it became a powerful production by the Vedrenne–Barker management.

Elizabeth attended the final rehearsals. It opened on 9 April, attended by, amongst others, Stead, Barrie, Pinero and the Pankhursts. Florence, no friend of suffrage, nevertheless came to London for the occasion, sitting in a box with Elizabeth, who was apparently 'modestly concealed'. In line with the Court management she was opposed to playwrights taking curtain calls and did not appear at the end, despite cries for her to do so.

The play proceeds from the familiar to the startling. Act I is set in a country house using stock melodrama devices such as the significant dropping of a handkerchief. It contains what Sheila Stowell has called 'A grab-bag of conventions recycled for feminist ends'.[27] Each act seems to represent the stages of development in English theatre since Elizabeth arrived in England. Act II, hailed as 'the finest stage crowd that has been seen for years' (*The Sketch*),[28] utilised experienced Court performers rather than 'supers' and could be compared with the open air meeting in Ibsen's *An Enemy of the People*. In showing how all women entering male arenas were subject to the male gaze, Elizabeth was demonstrating what brought women together rather than what divided them. The final act was both the most personal and the most progressive, disturbing critics. It probed personal relations and the man, rather than the woman, made restitution for the past. Archer was alarmed by 'the ferocious Vida of the close. Oh Lord! oh Lord!'.[29]

In the same year Barker wrote *Waste* yet was asked to eliminate all references to abortion.[30] He pointed out that he had recently produced Elizabeth's play in which the plot turned upon 'a criminal operation which was quite openly referred to on stage'. Yet his piece in which a prominent politician seduces a married woman was seen as a potential embarrassment to political leaders. He refused to alter it. The Stage Society put on one performance attended by Elizabeth who was also one of seventy playwrights who signed a letter to *The Times*, penned by Galsworthy and Archer, condemning the menace of censorship. Yet not until 1936 was Barker's play allowed to be performed in public. Stowell has questioned whether the granting of a licence to *Votes For Women!* was 'whimsical inconsistency' or evidence of 'a patriarchy so smug as to be unperturbed at the possibility of any real threat from specifically women's agitation'.[31]

Despite annoying those who disliked seeing theatre used for such personal and political issues, Elizabeth's 'manual of realism' (*Morning Post*)[32] was a success. Originally accepted for eight matinées, it was given two more and an evening slot. It closed in June after thirteen evening performances because the Vedrenne–Barker management ended. Katherine Dreier, Margaret's sister, had attended a matinée and seen scores turned away. People were standing three rows deep and she marvelled at the play's effect on conversation. On her train into London she overheard people discussing 'the extraordinarily clever woman' who had written this play.[33]

Elizabeth's acquaintance Mary Cholmondely wrote a futuristic play called *Votes For Men* in which women had the vote and men were disenfranchised. Yet the suffrage drama which flourished in the wake of *Votes For Women!*, such as Cicely Hamilton's *Diana of Dobson's*, was not restricted to concern with the vote and encompassed a range of social and economic concerns.[34] Elizabeth was one of 400 who attended the inaugural meeting of the Actresses' Franchise League at the Criterion Restaurant on 10 December 1908. Edith Wynne-Mathison who had played Vida and three others in the *Votes* cast also joined it. When the president Gertrude Forbes-Robertson invited Elizabeth to speak at a meeting, she characteristically declined but attended and suggested names of actresses who might join.[35]

The two main suffrage societies received a quarter of Elizabeth's fee for *Votes For Women!* For the first week this amounted to £7 4s 10d (£7 24p) each.[36] Elizabeth perceived this distribution of her royalties as one of the few rights women already possessed. The cause also benefited in other ways. The play was produced in New York and Rome in 1909. When Marion Craig Wentworth did a reading in Chicago to the Political Equality League, Margaret was deeply moved. 'Oh Elizabeth, I have no words for that play—for the tender, deep insight into the human suffering of the thousands & thousands

of our sisters.' According to Margaret the audience was largely composed of the ignorant rich who predictably began giggling in the
wrong places. However, they soon became 'deeply interested'. Agnes
Nestor, international secretary of the Glove Workers' Union, told
Margaret, 'It isn't only trades unions, and it isn't only votes, is it? It
is just the whole question of woman.'

Some contemporaries criticised the British women's suffrage
movement for being too single-minded, seldom discussing 'the fun-
damentals of progress among women'.[37] As Agnes Nestor recognised,
in her play (and even more so in *The Convert*), Elizabeth opened up
wider issues about motherhood, work and sexuality. Some of these
concerns had been raised by the women writers of the 1890s but
now they were being harnessed to a political claim.

Originally fearful that her play might never get produced, Elizabeth
had decided to extend it into a novel knowing that 'however much
a firebrand', her reputation as a novelist would help publication.
Although Heinemann was keen, Methuen's contract was more
attractive so was accepted. The novel came out in Britain in October
1907 before the published version of the play. Mrs Pankhurst read an
advance copy, starting it at midnight and finishing the 300 or so pages
the next morning. Her verdict was that Elizabeth had again done the
impossible, making the 'political part absorbingly interesting'.[38]

In September when Elizabeth was working on the proofs, Mrs
Pankhurst visited Blythe. The brakes had failed on Elizabeth's bicycle causing her to crash into a bank. The dye from her stockings
then poisoned her ankle and she could barely hobble. This was not,
however, a sympathy visit to the invalid. The previous day, after serious differences over the running of the WSPU and concern about
its relationship with the Labour Party, there had been a major split
and key figures including Charlotte Despard, Teresa Billington-Greig
and Edith How Martyn had left the Union to form the breakaway
Women's Freedom League. For the Pankhursts, who recognised
the value of having a well-known propagandist on the Committee,
Elizabeth seemed an obvious choice. '"*Do this for us*" begged Mrs
Pankhurst. I at last agree' but 'not very willingly'.

It was one thing to allow her name and picture to be used as one
of four 'Prominent people in favour' in the card game 'Suffragette'
but quite another to agree to work with the Pankhursts.[39]

Elizabeth knew this would mean considerable commitment just when she was settling into country life. Moreover she loathed public speaking. Her diaries are studded with entries such as 'ill at the thought of speechifying' and 'oh the rapture of being done with lecturing'. She believed that she was not 'equipped for politics', couldn't speak extempore and lacked her sister-in-law's superb physical strength and private means. Over the last year she had refused many invitations to 'harangue the public since my quite unprecedented little speech at Tunbridge Wells'.[40] Mrs Pethick-Lawrence had been one of those who had hoped to secure her to address a meeting. In the event, the guests at a lunch in Holborn had to make do with a letter from the writer who was suffering from an (expedient?) illness in Woldingham. Elizabeth maintained that there were heaps of admirable speakers but few commercial feminist writers of fiction 'who can reach the mass'.[41] Researching, writing and delivering talks were time-consuming and, on the whole, did not earn her money. Used to delivering other people's lines not her own, the former actress felt 'naked in the withdrawal of the magic cloak of invisibility'[42] and she frequently learned by heart her suffrage speeches. In March 1912 she sat under a tree in Green Park before her Albert Hall speech, trying to 'look idle while I put myself thro' the first pages'. The mass meeting was a great success. A record £10,000 was taken for the cause.

Despite her own misgivings Elizabeth was highly effective, accomplished in the skills of how best to appeal to an audience, how to use language, cadence, pauses and presence to maximum effect. The journalist H.W. Nevinson who resigned from his position on the *Daily News* because of his support for suffrage, described Elizabeth as 'one of the finest speakers and writers for the cause'.[43] One observer was convinced that she surpassed Mrs Pankhurst in her 'power of sweeping an audience along with her and in her great gift of quickening the spirit and urging it upwards to the heights of an enthusiasm that does not quickly die'.[44] And Mrs Pankhurst herself assured Elizabeth that she possessed 'the gift of personal magnetism in a far greater degree than I have by nature'.[45] Evelyn Sharp was one of those inspired by her. 'The impression she made on me [at Tunbridge Wells] was disastrous. From that moment I was not to know again for twelve years, if indeed ever again, what it meant to cease from mental strife'.[46] Elizabeth later wrote a two-page introduction to the wartime edition of Evelyn Sharp's witty sketches entitled *Rebel Women*. Others such as Jean Hamilton (wife of the soldier Sir Ian Hamilton), and the writer Margaret Hadwen (Zoe) attributed their suffragism to her.

Talks involved travel. 'Shall Women Work?' spawned 'a new crop of the horrid things' in 1909: talks in Bradford, Brighton, Leeds, London and Manchester. The previous year she had replaced the imprisoned Mrs Pankhurst on a punishing Scottish speaking tour resulting in illness in Glasgow. Never having fully recovered from typhoid fever, she found that her major talks were frequently followed by several days of illness. Katherine Dreier stayed with her in 1909 and told Margaret how she suddenly collapsed and 'how painfully delicate she really is'.[47]

Elizabeth's initial reticence about the Committee was compounded by reservations about the (in)famous occasion in October 1905 when Christabel Pankhurst and Annie Kenney had audaciously interrupted the Liberal Party meeting in the Free Trade Hall, Manchester. As Jane Marcus has argued, they demonstrated the 'real violence of militancy, the assumption of verbal power'.[48] Elizabeth later declared that she had 'little understanding of and no particle of sympathy with the first militant act'.[49] This was a somewhat disingenuous statement. Not only did the record show that she was prepared to defend militant tactics which were far more threatening for those at the receiving end but she was also well aware of the importance of this challenge to male political discourse through asking for the vote and thereby breaking the habit of woman's silence. This very subject of woman's silence was the basis of her article 'Woman's Secret'. What disturbed Elizabeth was not what was done or how it was done but to whom. The intervention had come as Sir Edward Grey was appealing for the return of a Liberal Government. Sir Edward was one of Elizabeth's cherished friends.

It was to the Greys' fishing cottage at Itchen Abbas, Hampshire that Elizabeth had retreated at weekends during *The Master Builder* and she later wrote there. The Greys knew the identity of C.E. Raimond and read *The Open Question* manuscript. Sir Edward was the same age as Elizabeth, they had married in the same year and both been prematurely widowed. Dorothy Grey had inspired confidence when Elizabeth lived in London on her own, teaching her that 'to please

is no more woman's business than man's'. She was a formative influence in shaping her views on relations between the sexes.[50] She
also told Elizabeth that she ought to be an orator. Politics would
enable her to use her brain and give her a real cause. Dorothy died
in an accident early in 1906 and the Liberal Foreign Secretary Sir
Edward Grey, described by G.M. Trevelyan as 'remote, firm and sadly
serene',[51] reminded Elizabeth how much Dorothy would have 'taken
in what you are doing'. Elizabeth helped Louise Creighton with her
memoir of Dorothy Grey and kept a photograph of her at the foot
of her bed.

In so far as she identified with the major political parties, Elizabeth's
sympathies lay at this stage with suffragist Liberals like Grey. She
had attended the first meeting of the Liberal League in Chelsea
Town Hall (formed in February 1892 to promote Rosebery's political views and supported by Grey and Asquith).[52] The tragedy for
women like Elizabeth was that it was a Liberal government which
they found themselves opposing throughout the years of active
campaigning for the vote. Although H.H. Asquith, Prime Minister
from 1908 was an 'anti' (Elizabeth claimed that the women had 'lost
a weak friend [Campbell-Bannermann] and gained a determined
enemy'),[53] since 1867 the Liberals had more than doubled the size of
the Conservative vote in the Commons in favour of women being
enfranchised. Yet with such promise came greater disappointment
when they proved to be so illiberal, failing to make votes for women
a reality. Increasingly suffragettes despaired of what Elizabeth dubbed
the 'Perfidy of Sympathisers'. One of the themes of her talks and
articles became Liberal hypocrisy.

She found herself in a very delicate position. Faced with increasing attacks on Grey—Christabel was soon calling him 'culpably
weak'—her loyalties were stretched. She nevertheless tried to exert
influence on the political figures she knew by personal lobbying and
written communications. When Mrs Pethick-Lawrence urged her
to stir up people against the prison treatment of the Pankhursts, she
dashed off a letter to Grey. He read her articles on suffrage and wrote
to her at some length, initially counselling patience and deriding
the tactics of 'personal annoyance'.[54] Inevitably their views became
more divergent over time. Grey was juggling with competing political discourses, one developed within the parliamentary tradition in

which he and his Prime Minister were sometimes at odds with each other, the other fundamentally challenging male-orientated values. As early as October 1908 he was expressing concern that either he or Elizabeth were seeing the situation 'crooked': 'If you are right I ought to resign at once; if I am right you are not being fair to the Government.' He failed to appreciate the parallax and that one perspective inevitably rendered another 'crooked'.

Over time Elizabeth's commitment to the militants increased. Although Rosen has claimed that the WSPU committee created in September 1907 never met,[55] Elizabeth's diary shows that there were weekly meetings at this time at the WSPU headquarters at Clement's Inn. Her own attendance was, however, sporadic. Her first appearance was in mid-October when she was asked to write an article for the new WSPU newspaper, which had the same name as her play, and to lecture at the Portman Rooms. She attended two further meetings then in mid-December sailed to America for a few months. Mrs Tuke the joint secretary presented her with flowers in the WSPU colours of purple, white and green on her departure.

Although she often had to be cajoled into speaking at WSPU events, in the autumn of 1908 Elizabeth promised Christabel that she would 'give a great deal more time in future' to the movement.[56] She was immediately pressed to attend a WSPU breakfast. The value of business breakfasts was felt long before the late twentieth century. They were 'excellent for giving people an insight into the real character of our movement, and for rousing their interest in the question of Votes For Women'.

When an urgent call came in September for additional helpers for the Newcastle by-election, Elizabeth joined Mrs Pankhurst for a few hectic days at the end of which the Liberal lost his seat to a Conservative shipowner. At one meeting she sat on a lorry in the wind: at another in a public house she heard Mrs Pankhurst address striking members of the Amalgamated Society of Engineers.[57] Her own contribution came at a crowded afternoon meeting of ladies at the Town Hall where, feeling unwell, she delivered a 'maimed version' of her speech. She also helped to electioneer in Croydon and at the Haggerston by-election.

The WSPU held over 20,000 meetings in 1909 alone. Yet as Martha Vicinus has argued, what was particularly revolutionary about the suffrage movement was its insistence on a female presence in male places.[58] Elizabeth went on the 1908 autumn deputation to the House of Commons having declined to attend the previous spring and she went to Westminster for the Women's Parliament of the following year. In this same year Elizabeth made a will in which she bequeathed money 'for the advancement of women's influences upon a direct participation in Public Life in England & America'.

She combined her profession and feminism via the Women Writers' Suffrage League (WWSL) founded in 1908 by Cicely Hamilton and Bessie Hatton. Its aim was to obtain the vote on the same terms as men. Its methods were 'the methods proper to writers—the use of the pen'. Independent of any particular society, its qualification for membership was to be a published author. Members included Olive Schreiner, May Sinclair, Sarah Grand and an old friend Constance Maud (in the 1890s Elizabeth used to stay with her family at the Rectory in Sanderstead, Surrey). Elizabeth was the WWSL's president from its inception. At a Waldorf Hotel reception in May 1909 she lectured on the importance of Mary Wollstonecraft and considered gendered perceptions of the 'Good Woman'. She attended some of the monthly At Homes, wrote to the Home Secretary on behalf of prisoners denied writing materials and did a reading from *The Open Question*.

Zoe Hadwen, (whose Chelsea garden was planted with flowers in the WSPU colours) gave Elizabeth yellow irises and madonna lilies, the WWSL colours, for the 1911 Coronation Suffrage Procession. At Mrs Pankhurst's request Elizabeth helped in 'booming' this event in advance through an article in the *Westminster Gazette*. The press had declared a boycott of news of the procession and Elizabeth had to negotiate carefully with her editor. Although Sylvia's work mentions Elizabeth taking her turn in carrying the WWSL banner at the NUWSS demonstration of 13 June 1908, the latter's diary shows her watching events from a window and later going by cab to the Albert Hall. She was definitely a participant in the gigantic WSPU demonstration eight days later, joining the procession at Euston and driving behind Mrs Pankhurst in a cab (which included the writer Mona Caird) to Hyde Park.[59] Elizabeth had purchased a scarf in WSPU colours and her hat was trimmed with purple (dignity), white (purity) and green (hope). Her account of this spectacular event, said by some to exceed 250,000, appeared in the *Daily Mail*. She missed the June 1910 demonstration as she was in Dresden for a cure but joined the western half of the procession of 23 July which focused on Victory and Justice and sported a Roman theme. In Hyde Park she heard Laurence Housman, H.N. Brailsford and Lady Constance Lytton.

Anxious, as were many women, to challenge the dowdy caricature of suffragettes as the 'sexless monstrosities' epitomised by Miss Miniver in H.G. Wells's novel *Ann Veronica* (1909), Elizabeth dressed as she had always done, with style. Yet she and other feminists emphasised that they were dressing fashionably to please themselves, not men.[60] She had a white satin dress trimmed with violets which she wore on appropriate and even inappropriate occasions such as a dinner party where Asquith was present. His response was: 'You're looking very hostile'!

It is not difficult to criticise Elizabeth's socialising with key establishment figures. Rather than jettison her society friends whom she had known rather longer than the suffragettes, she played a delicate balancing act with all the tensions, charges of duplicity, hypocrisy and irony this could engender. Arriving for one dinner party held by the Cabinet minister Lord Buxton (at which Grey was present), she found policemen outside to ward off suffragettes. We have already seen how her support for women's suffrage threatened her friendship with the Bells and sometimes she tried to compartmentalise her interests. When a guest at Rounton began talking of *The Convert* she hushed him: 'Nothing gained by discussion of *that* here.'

From her early days in London Elizabeth, like the actress-suffragette Lillah McCarthy, was much sought after on the social scene. Her close friends included not only liberal-minded lawyers such as Sir George Lewis and Sir Frederick Pollock and their families but also government politicians, some of whom she had met through the Bells. It is perhaps too easy to suggest that the ex-actress enjoyed playing roles or simply being different but without too much difficulty she does seem to have straddled rather different worlds. Other suffrage supporters, connected by blood or marriage to aristocratic and/or government circles, must also have been placed in not dissimilar positions though possibly as a professional writer, and an American lacking formal and familial ties to the English class system, Elizabeth enjoyed greater latitude than her women friends.

Both sides appear to have recognised that there were not only draw-backs but also some potential advantages in knowing such a 'well-con-nected' person. Christabel continually pressed for useful names and addresses, begging Elizabeth to 'do your best with such Cabinet Ministers as you know, will you not!'.[61] She asked her to bring certain items in the feminist press to their attention. From the start Mrs Pankhurst, who wished that Elizabeth could 'shut out the opinions and doubts' of her world and influence them rather than vice versa, was unashamedly frank about Elizabeth's potential usefulness:

> I believe that you could do more for the women's movement if you could let yourself go a little more than you do. You have influence with many people which could be made useful if you make those people who admire you and believe in you feel what people who know Christabel and me feel about us.[62]

Christabel was delighted when Elizabeth supplied her with 'some really weighty names' as possible supporters.[63] When she stayed two nights at Henfield she elicited a list of all the MPs Elizabeth knew. And did Elizabeth know Lady Gwendoline Cecil of the Primrose League which had been 'so disgracefully inactive' about women's suffrage? What could she tell Christabel about Sir Frederick Pollock? Who ought to attend the big procession and Albert Hall meeting in June 1910—'I mean people of special influence who might be interested and impressed by the sight of so immense a gathering'?[64] She thanked Elizabeth for Sir Hugh Bell's letter, 'the most important production of all'. We do not know whether Elizabeth had been sent this letter or whether Sir Hugh knew of its ultimate destination. On one occasion Elizabeth told Christabel that the Buxtons were having a ministerial dinner party. 'I have promised to go there at 5 tomorrow & hear any news. Shall we meet in the evening?' She completed her conspiratorial note with 'Do not say to anyone what I've told you.'[65] Elizabeth also picked up some potentially valuable information about the government's attitude to deputations at a luncheon held by Lady Arundel and asked if she could convey this to Clement's Inn. Permission was not given but she wrote to the source of information Lady Frances Balfour (of the NUWSS and friend of Asquith) in the vain hope of some news.

Soon after joining the Committee Elizabeth dined with the Prime Minister and his family. Reginald McKenna, who would become Home Secretary in 1911, and Grey were among the guests. Four days later Asquith replied to a letter Elizabeth had written him. Marked private, his reply was handwritten from his Scottish home. In it he stressed the impossibility of asking the present government to pass a measure of women's suffrage, suggesting that the majority who were opposed to it could resign. He added that the probable results of women's enfranchisement were, in his view much exaggerated and he doubted the effectiveness of any crusade of organised violence.

Increasingly aware of Elizabeth' own stance, her politician friends must have become wary of what they said on social occasions and may even at times have fed her information they wanted conveyed to the WSPU. Her thinly disguised parodies of polite society in novels such as *The Convert* must also have concerned some though the vivacious Elizabeth Robins continued to be welcomed to country houses and dinners in town. Her character Vida spoke to male politicians and social acquaintances 'from the depths of her womanhood'[66] and realised that she was talking a foreign language to the likes of Lord Borrodaile. She disparagingly refers to the 'narrow lancet of the medieval tower which was his mind'. So, increasingly, must Vida's creator have had moments when she found it difficult to maintain her equanimity. When Evelyn Sharp, Emmeline Pethick-Lawrence and a particularly close friend, Lady Sybil Smith (sister-in-law of Mildred Buxton), were released from prison in July 1913 after hunger-striking, Elizabeth wrote, '*What* a good thing I'm not dining wi [*sic*] Cabinet ministers!!' Her worlds could get uncomfortably close. When, in 1914, Henry James's portrait at the Royal Academy was attacked, she simply noted that it was done by a suffragette. Admittedly by then she was herself less involved with the movement but even if she knew the perpetrator it was probably less painful to make such an act seem as anonymous as possible.

Elizabeth was also anxious not to become simply a conduit for relaying information to the persistent Pankhursts. Emmeline and Christabel's somewhat instrumentalist use of her talents placed her in an invidious position. She maintained some integrity by refusing to accede to all their demands. She wrote in her diary of her resolution to help the cause but 'without letting myself be swamped, or my own view of things to be coerced or to be denied by me'. This was not always easy. Although not as dazzled by Christabel as Sylvia later claimed,[67] Elizabeth found her very persuasive and admired her mind and utter commitment. Never an instinctive committee person or prepared to be dictated to by others, Elizabeth uttered her own views from the start. Just a few days after joining the Committee she refused to sign a statement against the seceders. Later when Mrs Pankhurst was imprisoned and Christabel in France she was careful not to sign WSPU office instructions. Yet she had joined an organisation which increasingly required dedication. She once described a painful scene between Lady Grove and Mrs Pankhurst in Caxton Hall: 'Mrs P. extinguished her & Christabel sweeps what remains of her out of the hall!' Emmeline Pankhurst she respected as 'one of the Great People of the time and she is noble. But Lord! What a force behind that frail refined face!'[68] Elizabeth's admiration for the Pankhursts and their power of persuasion militated against dissent. Putting aside paying work and going to London for a WSPU committee meeting with two articles to write and a talk to deliver, Elizabeth then spent all day with Mrs P. 'and the things she made me promise make me aghast'.

Sometimes she got caught in the middle of her conflicting loyalties. The crisis over the Conciliation bill encapsulates Elizabeth's dilemma and perhaps an inflated sense of her own role in shaping political deci-sions. An all-party Conciliation Committee which included Grey had, in 1910, proposed a compromise of giving the vote to single women householders (but only to wives if the house was in the wife's name). This bill held out some hope for suffragettes and led to a truce. It received a majority of 139 votes in July on its first reading and the following May passed its second reading. Yet the Chancellor of the Exchequer Lloyd George was soon arguing that the bill was not demo-cratic enough and in the process imperilling its chances by seeking an amendment to include the wives of voters. Elizabeth pointed out at a talk in Crowborough that he failed to understand that women were anxious to secure the principle of their right to vote. Amending the bill now, even if it did seek to widen considerably the numbers entitled to vote, might well jeopardise its success. What Elizabeth most resented was the inability of men like Lloyd George to 'look at the matter from the point of Woman Suffrage as a whole'.

Then in early November a new Reform bill was announced, a *Man*hood Suffrage bill. Having announced that an amendment to the Reform bill would allow some women to get the vote, the government was confirming women's votes as merely supplementary to giving votes to men. This move also effectively scuppered the chances of the Conciliation bill (though Elizabeth and other suffragettes seem to have underestimated the significance of the swing in the tactical Irish Nationalist vote from support for the 1911 Conciliation bill to voting against it the following year).[69] Asquith had now to face a Deputation from suffrage societies.

Back in late October Christabel had begged Elizabeth to 'invoke' Grey. When she had talked to him privately he had advised maintaining the integrity of the Conciliation bill and had assured her that there was no danger of a Reform bill being introduced. The Liberals in turn had persuaded Elizabeth to talk to Christabel 'about holding up the storm of vituperation'. The two women met at Elizabeth's club (the Ladies Athenaeum) and after a long talk, agreed that Lloyd George could be given eleven days' grace. The very next day Elizabeth learned in a frantic note from Christabel that a Manhood Suffrage bill had been announced. The two women met again. In a letter Grey told Elizabeth: 'It seems heartbreaking to me that every statement made should be so misconstrued & drives me to despair.'[70] After worrying about whether or not to attend the Deputation to Asquith and Lloyd George, Elizabeth finally compromised. She would go so long as she could remain silent and reserve her independence as to further 'steps', an arrangement which seems to sum up her ambivalent position.

From the Deputation (which consisted of herself, Christabel, Mrs Pethick-Lawrence, Annie Kenney and Lady Constance Lytton from the WSPU and representatives from eight other suffrage societies) she went to Clement's Inn, then dashed off a long letter to *The Times*. This was not printed (and possibly not sent) but a draft exists. Here she argued that the government considered a political abuse unworthy of serious attention 'unless each abuse presses upon electors'.[71] Nevertheless she suggested that Asquith was unaware of the full implications of his action and later maintained that, had he foreseen the effects of his step, he would not have taken it. Finally, and this may have caused her to withdraw the letter, she attacked those friends who remained silent in the name of Cabinet solidarity. Their silence signified 'a misuse, a debasement of loyalty'.

After writing this letter Elizabeth felt it pointless to keep her prearranged meeting with Grey. He, however, insisted on talking and, in her words, put the situation in 'A quieter new light', explaining that Lloyd George had agreed with him to back the amendment and bring in married women. Grey stressed that this would enfranchise seven rather than one million women. Elizabeth explained how thoroughly dissatisfied the suffragettes had been after their Deputation. She then went through 'rainy, dirty streets' in futile pursuit of Christabel.

The next day she turned to fictional drama, composing a scenario for a short story entitled 'Discretion'.[72] Ostensibly concerned with the wife of a Cabinet minister who brings the government to the verge of collapse by her revelation of a Cabinet secret, it also focuses on a personal scandal surrounding the minister which is effectively hushed up, the man's constant indiscretion being discreetly handled. The government is saved. This was never published but a short story of militant suffrage 'Under His Roof' appeared in sixpenny pamphlet form in 1912 (proceeds were divided between the WWSL and the WSPU). Here Elizabeth created a macabre tale rich in symbolism about an old house with a raftered ceiling. Esther, widowed in her mid-thirties, is visited by Miranda who had once been engaged to the man Esther finally married. Believing that she is helping her and salving her conscience since she knows that her husband really loved Miranda, Esther now wants to share her home with her. Miranda does not wish to be patronised. She has gained a new strength and freedom, through her commitment to women's suffrage. When Miranda proposes instead that the two women stand side by side braving mounted policemen, Esther recoils. Not prepared to change she remains at home where the real danger lies and she is crushed by her collapsing roof. Backsettown had a roof of Horsham stone which Elizabeth had raised so that the oak beams would be exposed (her bedroom, the upper part of the original medieval hall, became known as 'rafters'). From her new home she was warning of the dangers of living a life refracted through a man's decisions, encompassing both his perspective and his vote, and the perils of living in the past.[73] Perhaps she was also reminding herself of the false attractions of retreating to the home rather than braving the world.Yet the story's celebration of militant suffrage as the pana-cea for all ills lacks the subtlety of *The Convert*.

Although there had been sporadic window-breaking earlier, a new phase of militancy began in the autumn of 1911, fuelled by what Elizabeth called Asquith's 'blind step into the hornet's nest of manhood suffrage'. Government, office and shop windows were smashed in the West End and further mass destruction of plate-glass followed early in March 1912. Mrs Pankhurst and many others were arrested and there were now nearly 200 suffragettes in prison. Despite being anxious about going to London after reading of the arrest of members and 'fearing stones', Elizabeth did accompany her friend Zoe to Whitehall for two hours on the evening of 4 March when window-smashing took place. Although not close enough to see very clearly, they witnessed a number of arrests. On the 7th the uncompromising letter by Elizabeth appeared in *The Times* which deeply disturbed Florence (see Chapter 4). Her habit of surrounding militancy with eloquent words, making it appear reasonable, infuri-ated readers like the anti-suffrage Violet Markham who resented the claim that the suffragettes voiced the moral consciousness of the nation. In a reply to *The Times* she hinted that Elizabeth was once more play-acting and asked:

> When women take to rioting is it necessary to dignify the pro-ceedings with such fine phrases as those of Miss Robins's letter … the militant suffragettes … smash windows, but, like Hedda Gabler, they wish 'to do it beautifully' and fortify themselves with a high moral atmosphere. They play with anarchy and appeal to the lowest passions of the mob, but these manifestations must be justified as the product of a lofty spiritual ideal.[74]

Elizabeth had dared to claim that, through suffering, the women's ideal had become a religion: 'No other faith held in the civilised world today counts so many adherents ready to suffer so much for their faith's sake.' At the end of that month the Conciliation bill was defeated by fourteen votes.

Her stance on militancy was both clear *and* problematic. In the press she espoused the militant tactics, praising the irrefragable spirit of the suffragettes and portraying them as fighting for what she called 'the final triumph of civilisation'.[75] She exposed the irony of men actively engaged in preparations for war yet aghast at the breaking of windows. The word militant implies combative, bellicose behaviour yet Elizabeth saw militant activity as a means rendered necessary by the violence of others. She understood that militancy by women was especially feared because of the dysjunction between perceived notions of how to treat women (which were bound to be at least in part upheld by those claiming to respect law and order and to value 'ladies') and the desire to repress and contain expressions of militancy. She distinguished between the suffragettes' militant, symbolic acts which she presented as the natural concomitant, the only logical step left to secure their rights—'apathy is the arch-enemy of reform'—and the violence which was the cowardly response of the authorities. So inflammatory was her article 'Touchstone' (known as 'The Perfidy of Sympathisers' in *Votes For Women*) that the editor at the *Westminster Gazette* refused it, arguing that not only would its author be charged with conspiracy but that he could also find himself in trouble for printing it.

The titles of her talks and articles suggest the shift in tone and purpose from the interrogative 'Why?' of 1909 to later assertive titles such as 'Woman's War'. When published in America,[76] the latter was illustrated with photographs of hunger-strikers and emblematic weapons such as a hammer concealed in a woman's stocking. Here Elizabeth provided a devastating account of the unprovoked violence of the authorities and crowd in Lloyd George's native North Wales when he had opened a Village Institute at Llanystumdwy in 1912. Her account was based on the experience of the suffragette sister of one of her Henfield neighbours. On holiday in Wales she had joined the protest against a professed suffragist minister 'offering the public a gift, when an overdue public debt remained unpaid'. Her clothes were torn off her whilst her friend's hair was pulled out.

'Deeds not Words' was the WSPU motto yet Elizabeth used words as her weapons to incite others to deeds. She was careful to keep her physical distance. She had been present in 1910 when suffragettes encountered police brutality on what became known as Black Friday but she had not been one of the women trying to reach the Commons. Instead she cruised the area in a cab picking up exhausted women and carting them off for cups of tea. She saw enough, however, 'to send me away sick and shuddering' but self-sacrifice was not her *modus operandi*. She remained an investigative journalist but one who believed passionately in the justice of the cause she wrote about. Yet she was painfully aware of her equivocal position and the gap between her own inflammatory writings and lack of personal participation. She once confessed that she would rather die than face prison.[77] In her unpublished letter of November 1911 she admitted to 'constitutionally abhorring strife & loathing violence' though she threatened that people like herself might now be forced 'to walk the roughest way' by the government's own actions. She argued that not all were fitted for the same service, trying, not very convincingly, to persuade herself and others that those who *did* choose to engage in militant acts, go to prison and hunger-strike, those whom she saw as more heroic, would have the greater rewards in the end. She had admired the fictional Hedda's courage and envied the pluck of the hunger-strikers who protested against the government's refusal to grant suffragettes political prisoner status. Many of those she knew well, understanding that their aim was the sublimation of self yet also knowing that she was not prepared to take the very steps she advocated in print.

In the meantime she chose verbal attacks and passive resistance such as refusing to complete her census form in 1911, writing across it 'The occupier of this house will be ready to give the desired information as soon as the gov [*sic*] recognizes women as responsible citizens'. She visited suffrage prisoners and was the first to greet Evelyn Sharp at the gates of Holloway on her release. She wrote a circular letter to over 100 'big wigs', pressing for First Division treatment of prisoners, appealed to actresses for support for Kitty Marion the imprisoned music-hall performer and contacted the bishops about the iniquities of forcible feeding.

It can be argued that although she did not put herself on the line in the sense of personally throwing stones, making or placing incendiary bombs or even deliberately inviting arrest (over 1,000 women went to prison for the cause between 1906 and 1914), her outspoken defences of militant tactics and insistence on her own voice in a largely hostile establishment press were equally brave. She was *not* a British subject and thus ran the risk of being deported. And despite the phenomenal self-sacrifice and hardship displayed by some women who heretofore had been law-abiding, respectable and respected people, the suffragettes themselves still seem to have applauded Elizabeth's position. Mrs Pethick-Lawrence who had personal experience of prison told her: 'You who have not to go through the bitter test, you are free to show what it really means.'[78] Mrs Pankhurst understood that Elizabeth was being militant in her own way and she and Ethel Smyth read Elizabeth's 'Sermons in Stones' in prison and thought it splendid.[79] Although a charismatic orator, Mrs Pankhurst was, by her own admission, no writer and Elizabeth's role was therefore all the more important.

Brian Harrison's analysis of suffragette militancy focuses on the leaders and the led.[80] In-between were individuals like Elizabeth who were not executing militant acts to order but were attempting to provide some kind of rationale. It did not amount to a consistent ideology since her writings on militancy were largely reactive and shifted over time but it did represent a persistent and insistent presence in that thermometer of the British establishment, *The Times*. Christabel believed that Elizabeth excelled in explaining and expounding militancy to a press[81] which was intent on labelling the suffragettes as hysterical hooligans and deviants.

The risks Elizabeth took were evidenced by the fact that her mail was intercepted by the police. When Christabel disappeared it was rumoured that Elizabeth was harbouring her in Henfield. Flora who, as Elizabeth put it, was 'not sound on the suffrage', took fright when a policeman appeared at Backsettown one day in May 1913. Mrs Pankhurst had just been sentenced to three years' penal servitude for inciting others to blow up Lloyd George's (empty) house and was on hunger-strike. Elizabeth had sent £10 to the cause and received letters from Mrs Pankhurst and Christabel. All the policeman wanted was a contribution to the cricket club.

Yet despite Elizabeth's outspoken printed words, her connections still counted. In the 1930s she met again Mary Neal who had sat with her on the WSPU Committee. Mary asked Elizabeth if she remembered saving her from prison. According to her story, she and Elizabeth were arrested in one of the suffrage raids and their names taken 'but they heard you were a friend of Sir Edward Grey's so they wouldn't proceed'. It is impossible to tell how well Mary's memory was serving her. There is no mention of such an event in Elizabeth's diary.

Yet whether or not founded on fact, it was clearly the perception of others that she was ultimately 'protected'.

To date it has been Elizabeth's promotion of suffrage ideas via drama and the novel which has been recognised as her contribution to the women's suffrage movement and made synonymous with her views on the subject. Yet this work was written before she joined the WSPU Committee and before the most active years of the movement. Not only does her fictional work need to be set alongside her non-fictional output of 1906–13 but it could also be argued that she has an equal claim to fame as interpreter *par excellence* of militancy, showing to those outside suffragette circles in particular the significance and likely consequences of both government and suffragette action. Worried about misrepresentation she sought to enlighten and warn. In *The Spectacle of Women* Lisa Tickner has observed that

> The effectiveness of militant propaganda had at some point to be determined by the extent to which it could retain the status of *political* representation and activity, and not be reduced—the cause and its adherents along with it—to the category of feminine hysteria.[82]

Elizabeth seems to have understood this, presenting votes for women as a rational and logical demand. She looked back, drawing on movements such as Chartism which sought to enfranchise men, and stressed that the foundation of a civilised society lies in its relations between men and women. She argued that there had been demands for the vote for many years but unlike the constitutionalists who tended to see these years as formative, her purpose was to contrast the forty years of hope but little concerted action with the vital difference that effective organisation could make within a few years. She also drew on the past to show how people had once needed to fight for what was now taken for granted (for example, the founding of the Bank of England). She stressed the excitement of joining a great moment in the world's history with 'the Tendency of the Time on our side'.[83]

She delighted in turning presumptions on their head. 'Sermons in Stones' opened with the provocative declaration that 'The great majority of Suffragists of all societies are lovers of peace'. In 'Woman's War' she argued that the marvel was not women's impatience but that 'so many for so long repressed impatience'. In 'Why?' stones did not signify violence but were made expressions of moral indignation at the abuse of physical force.

These and many other articles, speeches, letters and lectures were published in 1913 in Britain and the States in a collection of over 350 pages called *Way Stations*. Using an American term for a local station in a transportation system for her title, Elizabeth seems to have wanted to present herself as only a minor player or traveller in the movement stressing in an Author's Note that she was never one of the 'more active participants' in the events. She was actually prolific in print in encouraging others but here the intention was for the WSPU rather than Elizabeth Robins to be on show, hence the deliberate disclaimer. It provided a cumulative record of the distance the WSPU had travelled between October 1905 and June 1912 yet despite her personal downplaying inevitably presented her own subjective interpretation of events and journey of enlighten-ment. As with any railway system, *Way Stations* was accompanied by a time-table. Between each article (some in print for the first time) were several pages headed 'Time Table', detailing key events in the history of the WSPU up to mid-1912. Continuing her railway metaphor, Elizabeth billed her book as 'the only succinct account in existence of the main line of the Militant Suffrage Movement'. Yet today this collection is virtually unknown.[84]

Elizabeth had begun collecting suffrage material with an eye to a collection as early as the summer of 1909 when her American agent Paul Reynolds suggested this but it was not completed until early 1913 when she was in Florida. It is dedicated to Margaret Dreier Robins. One important source was Sylvia's *The Suffragette* (1911), the only published history of the militant movement then available. Another source was *Votes For Women*.

The book's first article 'Woman's Secret' served also as a Preface. It had been first published by the WSPU through the Garden City Press. The Union saw the publication and dissemination of literature (via its Woman's Press) as a key part of its work. Elizabeth began 'Woman's Secret' on 2 October 1907. It appeared in print only two week later, one day before *The Convert*, and called upon women to find their own spoken and authorial voices. Here and elsewhere Elizabeth was at pains to stress that men should not be blamed for all injustices, not all women were 'Angels of light' or men invariably 'Princes of Darkness'. In a speech carefully tailored to the broad-based WWSL, she attributed her own support for suffrage to the hope that through political equality, society would reach 'a true understanding and a happier relationship between the sexes'. Yet whilst she praised men's support for the movement, she warned against those who explained away women's evident ability by labelling a woman achiever as an 'exceptional woman'. And she was emphatic about the need for women to make decisions for themselves. In *The Convert* Ernestine Blunt declares, 'Men tell us it isn't womanly for us to care about politics. How do they know what's womanly? It's for women to decide that.'[85] The book also explores the implications of a denial of motherhood (it opens with Vida visiting small children in a nursery) but she also suggests that women who accept such responsibilities, which can mean a wider group than natural mothers, have indeed a grave duty. It has been suggested that the ending of the play can be interpreted as a feminist response to the finale of *A Doll's House* by recognising the difference between Nora the wife leaving her husband and Nora the mother leaving her children.[86] At the same time Elizabeth does not suggest that all women are cut out for motherhood. In an unpublished part of 'Shall Women Work?' she argued that those who rightly value motherhood would 'no more insist that every woman must be a mother than that every man must be a hunter or house-builder'. And in *The Convert* she points up the importance of those who do not have maternal responsibilities in leading women's struggle.

Elizabeth also displayed an international approach to women's suffrage. This was especially evident in a two-part article in *Votes For Women* named after Thomas Carlyle's essay of eighty years earlier, 'Signs of the Times'. It opened with the latest election news from Denmark. Elizabeth also entertained Australian suffragists in Henfield and when an American journalist descended to discuss suffrage, 'I give him tea … and indoctrinate him'. A number of her articles in the American press were designed to illuminate the British situation. An affectionate sketch of Christabel (*Harper's*, 1913) humanised the leader, stressing that she did not always wear 'the militant face'.

As an American Elizabeth helped foreground a valuable international dimension for the movement, arguing that 'the battlefield is English Soil, but the issue belongs to the human race'. She observed how the Americans 'have taken fire from the English torch.'[87] Her sister-in-law Margaret's sister Mary Dreier and her friend Frances Kellor were key figures in the American Labour movement and through them Elizabeth helped forge suffrage links. By 1907 Margaret was president of the American Women's Trade Union League and dubbed 'the American Pankhurst' in the press. Elizabeth brought Margaret and Mrs Pankhurst together and provided useful written Introductions for the latter on her American tours.

On her own trip home in early 1913 Elizabeth and her suffragist friend Pippa Wells heard the renowned settlement worker 'Saint Jane' Addams speak at a National Woman Suffrage Association meeting at Carnegie Hall. The next day at a private club Elizabeth met Theodore Roosevelt. They discussed militancy and disagreed. She noted how he was anxious to be popular and 'sympathetic' yet also keen to lay down the law. She disliked his 'suffrage superficiality' and misguided stress on chivalrous behaviour. A few days later she attended a Women's Labor League meeting of shirtwaist strikers.

Margaret was keen for Elizabeth to encourage the working women of Chicago where she was based. Elizabeth considered a pamphlet akin to her lecture 'Shall Women Work?' but feared that it would be too discursive. This was, however, published in the *Metropolitan Magazine* (New York) as well as in Britain. In it Elizabeth sought to demolish the arguments of those seeking to remove women from employment by protective legislation, arguing instead, as had Mrs Fawcett for many years, that women needed the protection of the parliamentary vote. Whereas Cicely Hamilton in *Marriage as a Trade*, also published in 1909, concentrated on middle-class women, Elizabeth at least gave some voice to the working class here though in her suffrage novel working-class speeches turn upon humour rather than argument. She was realistic enough to point out that women did not find the drudgery of mill work enjoyable but did it to earn vital money for their families. She ridiculed arguments that women lack physical strength and whilst appreciating that they enjoyed little freedom at present, she resented attempts to see poor women, and married women in particular, 'legislated out of such liberty as they now possess'. On more than one occasion she exposed John Burns's attacks on married women's work, arguing that women resented not being consulted about what was best for them. It was for *them* to decide between 'the greater evil of semi-starvation and the lesser evil of confiding their young children to an older child'. Adapting Kingsley's verse she wrote: 'Men must work and women must work, or else both will have good cause for weeping.' She saw a minimum wage as a way of abolishing the more flagrant forms of sweated labour.

Elizabeth also argued that women frequently worked excessive hours so appreciated the value of some regulation as opposed to abolition of jobs and she maintained that unorganised working women particularly needed the vote to ensure that laws were properly enforced. How the one would result in the other she did not make clear. Unlike many women of her class, she was critical of the 'charity habit', the condescension inherent in so much of the work with the 'less fortunate', believing that the goal should be eliminating the need for charities rather than boosting them. In *The Convert* she inverted the usual invasion by the wealthy into working-class life by having Vida insist on intruding her experience of a tramp ward into the 'spacious quiet' of Ulland House gentility. In this novel Elizabeth also underscored the power of motherhood through the denial Vida faced.

Six years later in 'Woman's War' she chose to emphasise difference, by stressing 'that mother-instinct which rules in the spirit as well as in the body of our half of the world'. Yet elsewhere she was critical of the 'Madonna picture', stressing that not every woman has children, hence women should not be considered only as mothers. Moreover children grow up so women should not be dismissed from consideration as workers once they have borne children (Hamilton's book assumed that women must choose between marriage and employment). In a draft version of 'Shall Women Work?' Elizabeth had even suggested that the best mothers were not those who never had time for anything but their own children.

Elizabeth's emotive descriptions of women brickmakers, pit-brow lasses and Cradley Heath chainmakers were culled from other people's observations. Sylvia might visit Wigan and other northern industrial towns but Elizabeth learned about the English working class from her reading (for example, Cadbury, Matheson and Shann on *Women's Work and Wages*) and attending conferences such as the National Union of Women Workers conference in Manchester in 1907 where she heard Mrs Cadbury and Clementina Black speak. With the exception of the evidence cited in 'Why?', her examples of women's work were largely located in the industrial north. Although she did mention sweated labour and in 'Why?' recounted a tragic story about a tailoress, missing from her accounts is any detailed attention to or analysis of the newer forms of employment for working women. Little mention was made of shopwork, waitressing and clerical work which expanded so rapidly for women. Between 1851 and 1911 the number of women clerks escalated from 2,000 to 166,000.[88] Elizabeth projected a somewhat narrow picture of working-class women, one which focused overwhelmingly on manufacturing industry and the most depressed and exploited, more dramatic figures than the typists and shopgirls she encountered in London.

Much of her fiction focused on the most privileged groups in society with some attention to those who serve them. She was also interested in the medical profession but not, in the main, concerned with the middle class. There is an anti-bourgeois thrust in her writings. In her efforts to document and stress the need for the vote she tended to pity and generalise working-class experience (for example, 'Prison is *real* to the poor')[89] and ignore the 'respectable' working class. In her zeal for suffrage she was sometimes dismissive of working-class men's struggles. She protested that those who threw stones at windows in 1912 received harsher punishment than striking miners who attacked people. Moreover, despite her relatively progressive views on some aspects of protective legislation, she did not appreciate some of the complexities surrounding the issue such as the internal dynamics and degree of unionisation of particular trades. Despite her American connections Elizabeth had little direct contact with British trade unionists at this time. Moreover her advocacy of the healing powers of the vote must have sounded hollow to many. Indeed Lady Murray who described herself as a 'keen suffragist and a quasi-socialist radical' questioned in a letter to Elizabeth[90] not only the militants' lack of control, adding 'you do too, I know' (which Elizabeth underlined in blue crayon!) but also their lack of prior politicisation and failure to understand that the effect of suffrage on women's labour would necessarily be slow and indirect.

In 'Why?' which was published in Britain and the States Elizabeth examined the reasons for women wanting the vote. Its style is reminiscent of Engels's *The Condition of the Working Class in England*. It presented the state of the militant suffragists in the 1900s and was amply documented with facts, figures and laws to authenticate its arguments which were dedicated to changing a system. In contrast 'Mr Partington's Mop' dealt with the flaws in the arguments of the anti-suffragists. Christabel persuaded Elizabeth to write this. During the reform agitation of 1830–2 the figure of Mrs Partington had been created, trying in vain to hold back the tide of change with her broom. In 1910, the year of Elizabeth's article, Ernestine Mills published a postcard of 'The New Mrs Partington' (of the Anti-Suffrage Society) trying to push back the tide against waves of women. On the horizon was the sun and Votes For Women.

At the end of 'Woman's War' (which also concluded *Way Stations*), somewhat uncharacteristically, Elizabeth drew on nature to suggest a brighter future. She compared militant suffrage to an irresistible natural change, sinking 'the old high places under inrushing seas'. She closed the book with a dramatic image: 'so have the deeps of the submerged sex been upborne to light, to the bright danger of the peaks, by those very forces which sought to hold her down.' Her book was published in March 1913 before another kind of war took over and five years before any women in Britain gained the vote. And by the time of its publication Elizabeth had resigned from the WSPU Committee, leaving in October 1912 with the 'Peth–Pank' split.

This split chiefly concerned the new direction in which militancy was moving. Adherence to a militant programme brings with it an inexorable escalation of activity when measures fail to produce their desired effect. Although the suffragette approach might encompass personal martyrdom it was not in the business of indiscriminate killing and threats to specific human targets were never officially condoned. Nevertheless by the autumn of 1912 with the older militant tactics no longer novel and the continued intransigence of the government, the situation was changing. According to Evelyn Sharp, Frederick Pethick-Lawrence was deeply concerned about isolated acts of violence 'calculated to take human life'.[91] He considered them both wrong and inexpedient. Differences between the Pethick-Lawrences and the Pankhursts surfaced and resulted in the former leaving the Union.[92] They saw themselves as still militant, always defining militant action as wider than direct breaches of the law, but were firmly opposed to inciting violence and concerned about the primacy of educating the public before escalating action and thereby losing support. Elizabeth's views were broadly in line with the Pethick-Lawrences'.

Since July 1912 Christabel had been directing secret arson attacks. In that month Helen Craggs was arrested for attempting to set fire to Nuneham Courtney House, home of the anti-suffragist MP, Lewis Harcourt. Dr Ethel Smyth was also arrested on the same charge though her case was dismissed. On 23 July *The Times* and other papers published a letter signed by twenty-six eminent men and women supporters of women's suffrage deploring the WSPU's 'provocative and bellicose' position, arguing that with a majority currently pledged to support suffrage and an amended franchise bill, it was foolish to alienate support at such a critical moment. They claimed that those who persisted in militant methods were actually the most serious enemies of the cause. Four days later a lengthy response appeared from Elizabeth prompted by a plea from the WSPU. Here she rubbished the notion that any genuine supporter would be lost since 'women care about this question more than they care about peace or praise'. Then, for the first time in public she attacked Grey directly. He and Haldane had headed the list of signatories to the letter. Elizabeth deflected attention from the letter's plea by criticising these men's silence in recent debates. Did either of them care enough to be prepared to give up office if the amendment were not carried?

This letter camouflaged Elizabeth's growing doubts. She had been shaken by the letter of 23 July which had been signed by a number of her friends including Gilbert Murray and Lord Robert Cecil, as well as veteran suffragists such as Millicent Fawcett and Elizabeth Garrett Anderson. Some years later in a letter to *The Times* (1921) reflecting on pre-war militancy Elizabeth maintained that violence, even towards things inanimate, was antipathetic to the nature of women.[93]

From 1912 militant suffrage appeared to be taking on new meanings, attacking private as opposed to public property and in practice endangering life. Country houses and works of art impinged too closely on Elizabeth's 'other life' and values. As the apologist for militancy in *The Times* she was placed in a difficult position. Yet she understood that the new, more extreme acts of militancy (which would find clearest expression in 1913) were increasingly likely to antagonise the public without seriously threatening the government and made likely even harsher retribution for the suffragettes. It was becoming easier to represent them as 'fanatics' and harder for Elizabeth to talk about logic and rational behaviour. Her personal belief was in the efficacy of strong words accompanied, if provoked, by symbolic actions. But others had moved beyond this.

From the vantage point of 1924 she reflected on the way in which moral force degenerated into material force and took the real power out of militancy: 'Minds whose ascendance had been based on constructive faculty, wasted their energy on devices for destruction.'[94] When she ventured to express her misgivings about the Nuneham Courtney House incident at Clement's Inn, an argument ensued. When her letter appeared in print she read it 'fearfully' though Mrs Pankhurst and Mrs Tuke expressed their approval. There were also some other divergences becoming apparent between Elizabeth and the leadership. For example, Elizabeth was very moved by the writings and personal testimony of Lady Constance Lytton. She reviewed her *Prisons and Prisoners* in *Votes For Women* and was increasingly critical of the way Mrs Pankhurst pressurised her to remain active even though she was severely physically incapacitated after her prison ordeal. Years earlier on her visit to Balmoral Elizabeth had met her mother, a lady-in-waiting to Queen Victoria.

Sylvia claimed that Emmeline Pankhurst told the Pethick-Lawrences that 'If you do not accept Christabel's policy we shall smash you.'[95] Whether or not Mrs Pankhurst uttered these exact words she nevertheless succeeded in engineering their exclusion. When ninety-four businesses whose windows had been broken sued the Union and won, the Pankhursts could not pay and the wealthy Frederick Pethick-Lawrence would not pay. He was therefore bankrupted. Mrs Pankhurst now argued that property owners, insurance companies and the authorities viewed him as a means of profiting and saw his wealth as a political weapon through which to attack the militants. The man who had been so generous to the Union was now made a liability.

Elizabeth was faced with conflicting personal loyalties. She met Mrs Pankhurst for lunch on 10 October but could not forget that Mrs Pethick-Lawrence had given her an especially warm welcome when she had first joined the Committee. 'I like them all too much' is recorded in her diary.

Elizabeth's first visit to the new WSPU headquarters at Lincoln's Inn House, Kingsway was a memorable one. She spent 'a strange & moving hour' with Mrs Pethick-Lawrence, 'I feel very tenderly towards her.' Emmeline Pethick-Lawrence deplored intrigue but was angry and upset at the ways in which the bonds of loyalty and friendship, so valued by suffragettes, were now being challenged. She claimed that in comparison with this, 'fighting the police, being imprisoned being forcibly fed is nothing'. Elizabeth was shown a copy of a 'business' letter sent by Mrs Pankhurst, Mrs Tuke, Annie Kenney and Christabel to Mrs Pethick-Lawrence in which it was suggested that Mrs Pethick-Lawrence might take over the Imperial Suffrage Movement in Canada! Two days before the Committee meeting that would decide their fate Elizabeth received a 'pathetic' letter from Mrs Pethick-Lawrence, begging her to attend.

When she got there on 14 October and even before the couple arrived Mary Neal cried out to Elizabeth 'the Laurences [*sic*] are leaving the Union'. Elizabeth noticed that when they arrived they did not shake hands with those who had signed the letter. Everyone was strained. Mrs Pankhurst began by declaring that where confidence no longer existed, working together was impossible. She was against allowing Mr Pethick-Lawrence who was not an official member of the Committee to make a statement but was overruled. After his defence and discussion they were asked to leave the Union. Several members protested and Elizabeth expressed her astonishment and regret, urging that such a disaster was not irrevocable and that all should reconsider. '"When people no longer trust one another" said Mrs P. & the more I saw of the tension the more I saw I was too late.' Mary Neal and Elizabeth appeared to be the most concerned but Mrs Pankhurst put them in their place by telling them that they had not attended meetings very often and had 'deliberately neglected to inform ourselves'. The Pethick-Lawrences then walked out.

The next day Elizabeth was at Backsettown but 'All my thoughts in London'. She wrote to Mrs Pankhurst and resigned from the

Committee but as Emmeline Pethick-Lawrence's memoirs show, the former from now on dispensed with the WSPU Committee. Speaking at the Albert Hall Mrs Pankhurst called for support for the new militancy. A statement appeared in the press about the split and the Pethick-Lawrences put on a brave face, telling Elizabeth three days later that they were full of hope for the future. She remained friendly with them for the rest of her life, following with interest Fred's career as a Labour Cabinet minister. Elizabeth believed that in repudiating co-operation the Pankhursts failed. The final outrage was severing the Pethick-Lawrences from partnership: 'The value of the man and woman who had laboured and sacrificed … given … steadiness to the Pankhursts' force and fire, the Pankhursts alone failed to realize.'[96]

In her resignation letter Elizabeth had explained to Mrs Pankhurst that she did not 'resign any smallest part of my affection for you & Christabel'. She had attended the Conspiracy trial and Mrs Pankhurst whilst in prison had entrusted her jewellery to Elizabeth, who had also visited Christabel in hiding in France. Elizabeth told Margaret that 'There is no sort in England, man or woman so well hated & so well loved' as Mrs Pankhurst.[97]

Resigning gave her the freedom to speak her mind. In November she sent Christabel in France sixteen pages detailing her misgivings about the running of the WSPU.[98] She questioned Christabel's idea of leadership, asking if she could wisely be the sole judge of what was best: 'If the Captain is too far in front of his forces—he isn't leading them … he is merely following an impetuous "inside feeling".' Using a theatrical metaphor she commented on the waste of force. The Union needed binding together, 'if the Chief actors spend their time in prompting the walking ladies what becomes of the *scène à faire*?' She criticised Christabel's running of the newspaper and argued for the importance of personal platform power. Echoing Archer's words to her but inverting them, she stressed that thousands of women could write but 'Nobody living has the power you & your mother have as public speakers'. She claimed that she had begged Mrs Pankhurst to have a stronger inner circle of advisers. Taking into account others' views would make a committee more amenable and thus make it easier to carry the rank and file. She questioned Mrs Pankhurst's model of the Salvation Army, arguing that this could not work since the emancipation of women was 'eminently a rationalistic *enterprize* faith'. The Salvation Army drew on ignorance and sentimentality and so the analogy was inappropriate.

Christabel's even longer reply dissected specific words and statements in a legalistic manner. She stressed that it had always been understood that she decided political matters. The complexity and delicacy of the situation meant that she didn't want people jogging her elbow. She deliberately missed the point about collective decision-making. If people wanted to contact her they could, 'There are only 16 hours in a day available for work you know.' She drew a diagram to show how the organisation enabled people to set others to work:

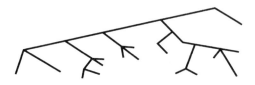

Some of her responses were somewhat glib. On the issue of having a strong council she replied, 'The world is our council.' She maintained that she did take other views into account and confessed to thriving on objections but added, somewhat disingenuously, 'It is a strange thing that so few of our critics are constructive critics.' She wondered whether Elizabeth had been harbouring such thoughts for a long time and advised her to wait until she saw what Mrs Pankhurst could do before making premature judgements. In another letter in early December she stated that it was difficult to explain 'what makes me feel it right to be an "*autocrat*"—though you know I am not so regarded by the people who work with me—All I do is try & open doors & illuminate paths.' Elizabeth received only two brief mentions in Christabel's memoir *Unshackled*.

Despite the split (and Elizabeth also resigned her presidency of the WWSL in October 1912), she remained an active supporter of women's suffrage. Christabel praised her 'Woman's War' article which was written in December 1912 after the split. In a letter to Florence Elizabeth explained that she and Sybil Smith felt that the WSPU was now 'passing into another phase' but that she and 'a legion are where we were'.

Elizabeth contributed a piece on the Cat and Mouse Act (Prisoners' Temporary Discharge for Ill Health Act 1913) to *The Suffragette*. In the summer of 1913 the paper (edited by Christabel) published criticisms by a number of famous people of this law which enabled temporary release of hunger-strikers under special licence and reimprisonment once deemed appropriate. Elizabeth urged repeal of the Act, stressing that its immediate effect was to discredit authority and encourage rebellion. She also pointed out that in addition to inflicting medieval cruelty, the government was actually uniting its enemies. She alluded to Emily Wilding Davison's death at the Derby and the effect of this on public opinion. If an unknown woman *giving* her life could produce such a reaction 'what passion of feeling' would sweep the country if life were to be cruelly *taken*, especially if that woman were a well-known leader? Yet Elizabeth was careful to stress that different suffrage societies were equally concerned about the consequences and that those working for repeal were friends of law and order, anxious not to see such a stain on the name of Liberalism.

Elizabeth's *Way Stations* Time Table ends in mid-1912. In contrast to previous years, Elizabeth's diary for 1913 and 1914 contained only sparse references to suffragettes. Mrs Pankhurst asked her to speak at the Albert Hall in April 1913 but she refused. One of her American relatives wrote from Zanesville in May, having heard with relief that she had left the militants and suggesting that she now read St Paul's advice to women! Elizabeth sent a message of support to a Votes For Women Fellowship meeting organised by the Pethick-Lawrences and on the eve of war discussed with Lady Henry Somerset, former President of the British Women's Temperance Association, the value of a monster suffrage petition amongst the non-militants and prom-ised to speak to Mildred Buxton (who was in contact with Lloyd George) on the subject. Lady Buxton had, however, had enough of women's suffrage by this point. In her opinion 'all suffragettes were obsessed and could talk of nothing else'. She did, though, observe that Elizabeth seemed to make nonsense of such a theory.[99]

Although, as we have seen, militant suffragism did matter to Elizabeth, particularly between 1907 and 1912, the five years when she sat on the WSPU Committee, Mildred Buxton was right in that even in her most active years, it was never Elizabeth's sole com-mitment. Mrs Pankhurst once explained, 'We are possessed by this

Cause … We live by & for it. It is this that gives us the power over other people's minds.'[100] Not so for Elizabeth. In June 1912 after her speech at the Albert Hall, she was relieved to 'fly back to my novel with a sense of speaking my own language after stumbling in a foreign tongue'. Despite her effectiveness as a political propagandist, she appears to have primarily defined herself, even at this stage, as a creative writer. She would comment how she was trying to 'do a little pot-boiling again' and that suffrage was woefully expensive. During this time she was working on a romantic novel called *The Florentine Frame* which, although concerned with a mother and daughter, was far removed from being a feminist polemic. It was 'well nigh impossible to get on with this. Oh the difficulty created by these breaks.' She had also met the poet John Masefield and from this very personal relationship came a novel about the white slave trade which she was researching at precisely the same time as she was grappling with the politics of militant suffrage.

8

WHERE ARE YOU GOING TO ... ?

During the Edwardian period Elizabeth became acquainted with a number of literary men who professed to support women's suffrage. One was H.G. Wells whose views on women were, in her eyes, antediluvian. She was not afraid to state this publicly. In *The Convert* Vida discusses Wells's *In the Days of the Comet*, pointing out that 'Even in his most rationalized vision of the New Time', the author 'can't help betraying his old-fashioned prejudice in favour of the "dolly" view of women'.[1] What infuriated Elizabeth was that 'a profoundly interesting person & a genius' had falsely convinced himself that he understood women. His vision of social progress was fundamentally impaired by his failure to confront the nature of woman's desire which, as Susan Squier has pointed out, lies at the centre of *The Convert*.[2]

When, in 1909, *Ann Veronica* was published, Elizabeth and other feminists were outraged at Wells's selfish advocacy of free love.[3] She argued that 'thinking people won't endure free love' since 'love can't ever be free for women & never free except for the meaner sort of men'. She resented his depiction of suffragettes. Yet when she told Wells 'Until I read *Ann Veronica* I did not know how meanly you thought of the movement', he replied, 'There's absolutely nothing in *Ann Veronica* against the suffrage only a quite kindly criticism of the suffragette side of it.' Learning that the WWSL had invited him to give a reading at a reception she used her power as president to protest, arguing that he had abused his position and ridiculed suffrage and its workers. To his annoyance he was replaced.

Wells's conduct in his affair with Amber Reeves lowered him further in Elizabeth's estimation. She was friendly with Maud Pember

Reeves, who begged Elizabeth to try to discourage her daughter and Wells from seeing each other. She told Elizabeth of Wells's 'outrageous proposals' that Amber should, after divorcing her husband, live in a cottage close to him and his wife and type and drive for him to earn her keep. In the meantime Elizabeth had obtained her former home, Blythe, for Amber. After Amber's baby was born she also stayed briefly with her little daughter at Backsettown. Yet Wells persisted in seeing Elizabeth as a kindred spirit and confidante, believing that there was 'a sort of freemasonry between us people of the imaginative life'. She in turn told him what she thought of his behaviour. Scraps of draft letters to him survive. The posted versions may, of course, have been less frank. These fragments throw an interesting light on Elizabeth's thinking at a time when she was the subject of considerable attention from another writer, John Masefield. Elizabeth warned Wells that although he had previously been able to dominate other spirits, he was now facing shipwreck, having muddied the souls of his wife and Amber. She wrote:

> Everything that is most beautiful in life grows out of sex & every bit most evil. You have shut yr [*sic*] eyes to this last fact. Yr lack of self control is not only making misery for other people & misery for yr self—it is corroding yr brain. You can't see straight anymore.

She was glad that society was now more tolerant of the illegitimate child and emphasised that she was 'a believer in love' but 'not in the corruption of character that you confuse with sex expression'.

She was especially incensed when Wells told Heinemann that he was not the father of the child: 'He finds it inconvenient now to be so advanced … sickens me.' Wells accused Elizabeth of being hypocritical, wrongly believing that David Scott was her son. He longed to know 'What makes *you* so bitter with men?' Elizabeth became more and more convinced that Wells was simply 'sex obsessed', and felt her belief to be confirmed by *The New Machiavelli*. In an anonymous work in 1924 she called him 'the literary Grand Turk', a figure who saw women existing primarily to provide physical satisfaction for men.[4] Yet when he publicly declared that 'Miss Robins thinks she is at war with men; she is really at war with sex' the feminist paper *Time and Tide* trumped his remarks by stating that Elizabeth was actually at war with that attitude which made it possible for Wells to write in such a way about women.[5] Wells came to epitomise for Elizabeth much of the sex antagonism she so condemned in the 1920s.

Her friendship with the rising literary figure John Masefield was very different. The journalist Gerald Cumberland observed in his cameo sketches of artistic figures that the poet's mind was 'cast in a tragic mould'.[6] Here was a man who did not laugh. Three years earlier Elizabeth had read Masefield's second novel, *Multitude and Solitude*,[7] as diversion from toothache. 'This is an attractive noble sort of mind' she wrote, adding, 'If he had humour he'd go far.'

The future Poet Laureate did of course go far though his early life had smacked more of distant travel than literary and public achievement. He was born in Ledbury in the English border country in 1878. His mother died when he was only six and after miserable spells with relatives and at boarding school, he joined HMS *Conway*, a training ship for future Merchant Navy officers.[8] His unhappiness in another all-male institution prompted illness then desertion though his early seafaring life provided the material for much of his later verse. He worked in Manhattan in a Greenwich Village bar when seventeen then spent two years upstate at a Yonkers carpet factory. Here he cultivated what he called his 'faculty of mental story-telling'[9] before returning to England and another inappropriate job as a bank clerk. As with Elizabeth, the new century presaged a change of direction. He became a freelance writer, moved in circles which included Yeats and when twenty-four published his *Salt-Water Ballads*.

Gerald Cumberland's sketches included Elizabeth.[10] Here was another figure who possessed 'the gift of tragedy'. He recalled meeting her just once: the impact of her physical presence was such that, 'like an ashamed school boy, I walked speechless and fuming from the room and kicked myself in the passage'. Masefield was also to find Elizabeth's influence overwhelming and sexually very disturbing.

On 17 November 1909, the day after first mentioning Masefield in her diary, coincidentally Elizabeth received a 'fan letter' from him. He had been reading *Votes For Women!* His first play, *The Campden Wonder*, had also been staged at the Court Theatre in 1907. He declared hers to be 'so splendid, so noble and so full of beauty that I would like to thank you for it. It is the one play of our time truly inspired by a spiritual passion. It is the one heroic play.' This was the first of over 260 letters Masefield wrote to Elizabeth over the next six months in his relentlessly neat hand.[11]

The intense relationship between these two artistic temperaments appears to have been, in the main, an epistolary affair. According to Elizabeth's diary they met eleven times in the half year during which they corresponded so fervently (and on three of these occasions his wife was also present). The first of Masefield's two visits to Backsettown took place just over a week after his first letter arrived. Elizabeth described him as 'grave big-eyed intensely quiet'. According to her diary, he came to lunch, insisted on getting the 2.33 p.m. train home but missed it so came back. They went for a walk, returned for tea and, in Flora's absence, Masefield offered to write an article about Elizabeth. She unselfishly tried to dissuade him: 'It would do this generous creature no good to be singing my praise upon so high a note … he must not get himself labelled uncritical.' He left soon after 5 p.m. Elizabeth's diary entry closes with 'Flora and I both like him.'[12]

Writing to her on his return home, Masefield called it a 'white letter day. You give me so much. You awed me. It was like your soul talking. I have a strange feeling that I have been in the presence of a spirit who has been telling me of the possibilities of life, and of all its beauty and wonder.' Yet his recollection of the afternoon was markedly different from Elizabeth's. In March 1910 he wrote down his version of that first meeting, expressing surprise at her physical appearance. The black dress trimmed with lace was clearly a sober contrast to the publicity photograph he had seen of the actress with its direct gaze and elaborate stage costume. In Masefield's narrative Elizabeth makes him miss the train by taking him up into the gentian room 'where the ice was broken thoroughly'. This blue room was Elizabeth's bedroom.

Yet there is a danger in seeing his account as simply a fantasy which conveniently shifts the emphasis from the spirit he so much admired, to the flesh. We know that Elizabeth was more than capable of self-construction through narrative and at times deliberately sought to confuse any possible reader by compression or omission, though the presence of Flora for most of the time and the fact that it was their first meeting, reinforce the likelihood of Masefield building upon the developments and desires of the last few months to shape the start of this story. A few days before, recollecting their first meeting, Elizabeth had sent him some of her own jottings in which she described how she sat at breakfast in her silent raftered room *feeling* that he was alone there with her. She added, 'I am glad to think no other man has ever sat down in this room with me.' Masefield may well have translated such suggestive imaginings into an imagined past.

Trying to piece together both sides of the relationship between Elizabeth Robins and John Masefield takes us on to a difficult and potentially prurient path. Intimate letters written between two individuals were intended for their consumption alone (though Elizabeth later chose not to burn Masefield's letters even though he advised this). Not only can we never entirely decode them but there is also a temptation to see the expression of passion as timeless and so forget that it too is shaped by customary conventions, language and understandings particular to an age and mediated by class, culture, generation and gender. Yet whether Masefield's love-making (this word alone has markedly different meanings at different historical moments) amounted to more than an adultery of the mind and page,[13] is not really the point. What is significant is that both he and Elizabeth were, for a number of months and for very different reasons, intensely preoccupied by their concern for each other. Their respective behaviour provides an insight into the power relations of gender and expectations surrounding notions of manliness. Their correspondence also gives us a glimpse of an Elizabeth less firmly in control than in her diaries though we still need to guard against viewing her love letters as necessarily spontaneous outpourings. This episode in her life played a crucial part in the making of one of her most popular novels *Where Are You Going To ... ?* and had an effect on Masefield's own literary achievements.

Elizabeth was seventeen years older than Masefield. He was already married to a woman over eleven years older than himself. The Masefields had a young daughter, Judith, born in 1904. Most significantly, for the entire period of his relationship with Elizabeth, his wife was pregnant.

On their country walk during that first meeting, the two writers had sat on a tombstone in a local churchyard. Elizabeth had outlined her plan for a novel based on the story of two girls, one of whom had been lured into white slavery. Flattered by her confiding in him,

Masefield offered to help. His contribution was to be based on his knowledge of 'the wild beast in man'. He thus provided a device through which he could validate from a distance the eroticisation of his friendship. Masefield was soon writing letters at least several times daily. On one day alone in January 1910 he sent her nine letters. Each letter detailed the precise minute of writing and, given the frequency of postal deliveries then, not much time elapsed between the writing and receiving of letters.

By mid-December and his tenth letter, Masefield was unburdening himself with stories of prostitution and life at sea which he would hesitate 'to discuss even with a man'. He asked Elizabeth to trust him and let him write frankly. Although we do not have her side of the correspondence before late January (and her diary entries do not betray much), she appears, from the tone of his writing, to have agreed to let him write freely. Initially anxious to make the subject seem scientific and detached, he explained that he was investigating different governments' attitudes towards prostitution and would report his findings. The formal soon shifts to the personal: 'I will then tell you from my heart exactly what torment sex can be to a man.' Wanting to emphasise his qualifications for imparting such knowledge yet clearly anxious to distance himself from the men he was condemning, he became the convert, repulsed by his previous association with a debased society. He recalled a fifteen-year-old girl in Cardiff who stopped him on his way back to his ship, offering him her body for 6*d* (2½p). He turned her down and confessed that the memory of this encounter had haunted him ever since.

In the name of the projected book he provided a simple taxonomy of prostitutes' clients, delineating on lined exercise paper included with the letters the three groups of 'manly worth' who resorted to prostitution and providing detailed case studies of ten men, each identified by an initial. He spared nothing: describing various sexual perversions, sexually transmitted diseases and forms of prostitution. He provided reports on brothels in Japan, France and Belgium: 'And then, *if you like* [my italics], I'll tell you about normal temptation, the struggle which a man has. The facts will be my own, the sort of things one never tells to anybody.'

His confessional account, hinted at earlier but now in mid-March elaborated, told in intimate detail of schoolboys, sailors and himself masturbating (this form of 'beastliness' accompanied by Victorian forebodings of consequent insanity), mastery and enforced submission in homosexual acts and instances of bestiality. He outlined the functions of the male sexual organs, described man as consciously taking advantage of woman and presumed that sex is primarily a 'supreme surrender' for the latter. He recalled an attempted assault on himself on board ship. Not only did the recounting of such intimate details clearly exceed any line of duty in undertaking research but both writer and recipient knew that such detail was superfluous. Publishers, the public and the censor (the original format for the white slavery story was a play) would not have allowed it. None of this deterred Masefield who suggestively added, 'Let us talk of it, and see if any sparks will fly from the contact of our two minds.'

One of his poems, later called 'CLM'[14] (his mother's initials), was sent to Elizabeth. It deplores men triumphing over women and trampling their rights, ending with the observation that men's lust 'roves the world untamed'. Through focusing on their lust he found a means of expressing himself in sexually explicit terms which provided a short-cut to an intimate relationship or, at least, a substitute for one. It also made it more difficult for Elizabeth to object since they both knew that by replying she was colluding in the arrangement. There were times when he urged her to write formally, to address his wife as well as himself since he did not want Constance to be upset. Thus he confirmed Elizabeth's complicity and controlled her reactions to some of his more outrageous writings by requesting formal replies.

Why did Elizabeth condone and even sustain this relationship? There are several possible explanations. Initially she appears to have been flattered by the attention of this rising poet, in his early thirties, an attractive and sensitive man who had travelled and even lived in America. His affirmation of her sexuality came at a crucial time since Elizabeth was going through the menopause. In her customary written review of the past year she wrote on 1 January 1910:

> One great drain of vigour no longer carries away the life force. This 'change' women have superstitiously thought proclaims the end of all their best powers. But in this maybe they were hypnotized by man's sex-view of woman's use in the world. But if she,

too, is a human being as well as a possible parent she comes at my age to her majority.'

She speculated whether 'it might be that I am come now to my true intellectual harvest time' and 'at this benighted stage of the world's history' pondered the possibility of a woman *beginning* life in her forty-eighth year. This was immediately followed by 'A few weeks ago came along John Masefield taking fire and promising to help with Docet Umbra …'

When Masefield told her how happy she made him, she responded: 'I am grown very sensitive to people's saying I make them unhappy.' Whatever her inmost feelings, she knew from bitter experience the possible consequences of trifling with a man's passion. He also knew how to express what she called 'Beauty of feeling and beauty of words'. He read her work avidly and claimed that *Votes For Women!* made him want to burn all his own books and start again. Not surprisingly, one of his favourite novels was *The Florentine Frame*, concerned with the growing relationship between a young man and a much older woman. He suggested collaboration. Elizabeth had memories of working constructively with William Archer. W.A. was no longer an active presence in her life and was in fact abroad when Elizabeth first met Masefield. Her correspondence with Masefield was an antidote to her suffrage work, an inspiration to her own creativity and, importantly, he enabled her to encourage a romantic figure who had, until recently, been dealt some harsh blows. Raymond's commitment to Margaret made her feel superfluous so far as her little brother was concerned. Here was somebody who palpably needed her to aid him. Masefield's letters were undeniably frank but at least such words came from a distance. She was anyway used to an outpouring of passion in her brother's letters. Dealing with a poet was, she felt, likely to involve some hyperbole: he was in love with the poetry of words.

Through his written conversations with Elizabeth, Masefield appears to be trying to make sense not only of his past but of his own masculinity. In the outline of a thinly disguised unpublished autobiographical novel, 'Lost Things',[15] he described the character John as sensitive and weak. The meticulous Masefield who loved order, precision and cleanliness lived the supposedly effete existence of an artist yet had to cope with the paradoxes of an earlier life which included the sailor 'picking up' women on shore. Whilst he described his fellow seamen as the only 'real' men and referred to 'manhood knocked bare at sea', he also had to reconcile this with the knowledge that here he had experienced the sexual encounters which most concerned him. Another poet A.J. Munby, who died in 1910, also questioned the constituents of masculinity and femininity as a means of understanding his own sexuality.[16] Much of Munby's adult life was spent talking to women of another class who either appeared to defy the conventions of their sex such as the trousered pit-brow women working at the top of Lancashire coal-mines or used their sexuality as their trade. Like Masefield, Munby was led by his interest and copious notes to reconsider gender roles and relations. He also conducted a secret and problematic heterosexual relationship.

Elizabeth became the recipient for Masefield's self-exploration. In part his letters were an expiation for what he perceived as his former sins. Religious imagery was used liberally. For example, he wrote, 'Let me kneel to you, and confess, and be absolved' and 'Renunciation is a sharp agony and love like ours is a holy beauty'. He appears to have handled his confusion about appropriate male and female behaviour by insisting on the innate goodness of women and the potential wickedness of men. Men's hearts are 'stables for beasts' but 'women bear the Christ there'. His idealisation of women probably owes something to his love, as a young man, of the Arthurian legends and of the medieval Welsh tales published in English as *The Mabinogion*.[17] He was a great admirer of Rossetti, and his chivalric and Pre-Raphaelite notions of womanhood seem to sit uneasily with Elizabeth's feminism.

Yet Masefield was also a self-proclaimed supporter of women's rights. Like many of his contemporaries, however, his espousal of feminism, despite some claims to the contrary, appears essentially to have sought equality via a celebration of female difference. Much of his language concerned the service which he wanted to perform *for* women. Nevertheless, Elizabeth recognised his potential usefulness and in February 1910 after her objections to H.G. Wells speaking on women's suffrage at the Queen's Hall, London, she turned to Masefield after Thomas Hardy, Henry James and George Bernard

Shaw all declined to speak. She did not attend the lecture though read a draft of Masefield's *My Faith in Woman Suffrage* (which was published by the Woman's Press in 1913). Parts of it were designed to please her—for example, it quoted Ibsen—but most of it was about how men go wrong and lack the 'great reverence' they should have for women. Nevertheless, Mrs Pethick-Lawrence wrote that it 'held us all spellbound'.[18]

By this time there had been a marked shift in the nature of the personal correspondence. The second meeting (over two weeks after the first) had taken place at the Masefields' London home. Elizabeth had taken tea with the family, followed by a hasty dinner with Constance, then rushed off to a women's suffrage meeting. Letters flowed and on 4 January Masefield met Elizabeth at her Ladies Athenaeum Club then accompanied her to the station. He later referred to her hand being in his. Her cryptic use of the word 'Goodbye' in her diary suggests some physical contact. It was on this occasion that she appears to have hinted at a secret in the past. In a letter written the following day Masefield referred to her agony 'in those unknown rooms over there', adding: 'I knew that the miracle of life had begun within you once, just from the look in your eyes; and I knew the day we first walked together that a little dead son was buried in your heart.'

As we have seen, it is possible that Elizabeth became pregnant in the States. It is, however, equally possible that she was not referring to an actual child of her own, though she may have been deliberately unclear. Elizabeth already felt that she had lost Raymond and in her memoirs explained that 'he had been like my little son when I was myself a schoolgirl'.[19] There had been the real death of her half-brother Eugene who was buried on Staten Island (and Masefield infers in his letter that the child's grave is there). She knew too well the difficulties facing a childless woman and was aware of how people speculated about David being her son.[20] She also understood how much motherhood meant to Masefield. In his suffrage speech he emphasised that men were concerned with affairs of life and women with creation of life. Perhaps Elizabeth was referring to a meta-phorical birth (and death) but if so, she now permitted Masefield to interpret her words literally until his fantasising and narratives of self-construction reached a point where she felt she must retreat.

After this meeting, the greeting in Masefield's letters changed from 'My dear ER' to 'Mutterlein' and letters were signed 'Your Grown Up Son'. Elizabeth's diary began referring to SJ (Son John). In the year in which Freud finally spelt out in print his theory of the Oedipus Complex, the mother and son imagery took precedence. It provided a vehicle for Masefield to explore much more personal realms of sexual longing and at the same time gave him greater latitude since he could always protest that all he was expressing was the pure love of mother and son. Thus he symbolically entered her room. 'Might we meet in thought … Might your son come to say his prayers to you, morning and night.' The son needed to atone, not only for his own sins but also for all that men did to women: 'I wonder what men can do to make it up to them?' More particularly he sought to repay the pain that was made most explicit in childbirth. His wife was soon to give birth. His own mother had died a few weeks after bearing her sixth child.

The letters that survive from Elizabeth to Masefield from late January onwards show her colluding in the game. At times she wrote like the scolding mother. Mostly she encouraged by telling him of the comfort and joy of his letters. Both appeared to thrive on the thrill of secrecy. She joined him on several occasions in the British Museum, left notes at K7 (his Reading Room seat) and sealed envelopes at her club. He sent her telegrams signed Johnson! He even watched her from a distance at Victoria Station, ironically the very place where Elizabeth was to locate the meeting between the white slavery procuress (masquerading as an unknown aunt) and the innocent Bettina in *Where Are You Going To … ?* Masefield deployed a secret language, a mixture of French, Spanish, Portuguese and hieroglyphics, in making copies of her personal letters.

His biographer Constance Babington Smith casts Elizabeth in the role of the 'enchantress', referring to her 'hypnotic power', her 'aura of mystery' and 'bewitching charm'.[21] Yet the situation was not one-sided. As for bewitching, Elizabeth wrote to Masefield, 'you conjured me by so new a spell' though she also acknowledged her own responsibility—'I went on & on, at each step more blind than happy'. Nevertheless, she protested on several occasions about his wish for her to spend more time with his family though she did spend one night at their London home, and questioned his proposals for Constance to share their work on the white slavery story: 'I wonder if three people can do this sort of thing.' Only once did she receive her at Backsettown. In February she protested: 'I cannot invite a woman here from whom I am secretly taking something she wd. [*sic*] never of her own free will give to me.' But Masefield's over-identification with the role of a son had already rendered him conveniently oblivious to Elizabeth's misgivings.

When she tried to protest that she had done nothing for him and that he should not claim kinship, he neatly replied that 'All the mother's giving has been given, it is now her boy's turn to give back. Let the giving be all mine.' She began questioning whether he should be sending her good-night letters but he again had an answer. They were written to add something to her life, 'something which I might be adding to my real mother's life, a gentle something'. When she pointed out that all her friends helped enrich her life and put a stitch in her embroidery, he replied, 'I have taken your silk to make your embroidery in my life.'

In some letters he claimed that he was not worthy to be her son, thus preparing the way for further confession. The pictures he painted of men's temptations, whether involving homosexuality (the 1885 Criminal Law Amendment Act introduced penalties against homosexual behaviour in private as well as public) or heterosexual pursuit of prostitution, were carefully separated out from Masefield's own current life-style but still required forgiveness. Masefield's present life appeared markedly different from the masculine image of the seaman. His work, like that of many women of his class, was largely confined to the home and he seems to have been more involved in childcare responsibilities than most of his contemporaries. Yet this caring man was unsettled by his infatuation with Elizabeth whilst his wife was pregnant. He handled the tensions via a mother/son relationship. This appeared to accord Elizabeth power. Yet that power was essentially temporary. Sons grow up. Rather than face the future he sought forgiveness for his past and made a fatal error in seeking to uncover Elizabeth's history. He used his dreams as a means of probing her 'mystery', trying (unsuccessfully) to identify the secret lover to whom she had alluded. Elizabeth only ever revealed as much as she wanted to divulge.

The mother/son language suggests sexual games; for example, he referred to the spanks she owed her boy. Yet Masefield denied that he harboured 'any glimmer of evil thought'. He became increasingly explicit: 'Put your arms about me, beloved, and draw me down, and let my arms pass about you and lift you to me. Let my life beat in your pulse. Let all the beauty in my mind pass into you as we cling together, mingling our nature.' Such was his fantasising that he even hinted at an incestuous relationship. The recent 1908 Punishment of Incest Act had instituted a penalty for incest in civil law. He wrote: 'Dear, you and I, such lovers, must be above the law in all things. Your loving son, dear. Your loving John, your boy.' Such claims hastened Elizabeth's retreat. She scribbled in pencil by the passage about the law: 'Oh dear! Why will he fantasticate like this—it spoils things—We are under the Law. These Poets!!'

When he wrote that he lay awake at night troubled by thoughts of her, she protested: 'It gave me an awful sense of something unnatural, perverted, diseased', all words which *he* had bandied about freely when talking about those he claimed to despise. She insisted, 'It is not for that I have come into your life', presenting herself as standing for 'tranquillity and trust and peace', stressing (rather belatedly) the maternal, desexualised aspect of their imagined role. She wanted him 'strong & happy', armed to do his 'beautiful work that will make the little inner group so proud & all the world the richer', to make a shelter for him and, still partly indulging him, she wrote that she worried about his genius for suffering 'as mothers do'. She had been seeking to bring him some of the things he went without as a little boy: 'sunshine and confident light-heartedness'. Elizabeth now sought to reassert her own physical space, and persuade him (and herself) that it was wiser for him not to come to her house, to meet only at the club 'and as heretofore in the general rooms'. She hoped, though, that he would still need in her the '*true* [my emphasis] Mother-office'.

Yet within a fortnight she was hinting that she might not be writing again and carefully introducing the possibility of leaving the country for a rest cure at Dresden. Always concerned about her health, Masefield could hardly protest about this. By 2 May he was writing, 'You have closed your door.' A few days later Elizabeth met him at the British Museum but then had lunch with William Archer. After mid-May the intimate letters ceased. On 4 July Masefield became the father of a son and on the few occasions that he and Elizabeth communicated again, his letters were formal and his handwriting far less cramped. Reviewing the year 1910 Elizabeth wrote: 'Masefield seems to be lost, for the time being at least. I think of him with tenderness and anxiety … he has a hard road to travel and walks the flint barefooted—poor John.'[22]

Towards the end of 1916 they met again under very different circumstances. Newly returned from Red Cross work in France and about to write his romanticised account of Gallipoli, dedicated to Elizabeth's friend Sir Ian Hamilton who commanded the Mediterranean Expeditionary Force in 1915, Masefield encountered her (in company) in London. She wrote, 'He is less unhappy looking than he used to be. *That* sensitive soul bears the horrors strangely well.'

Since they had last met, Masefield had become a household name. 'The Everlasting Mercy' published in 1911 had, as Babington Smith emphasises, been a turning point.[23] In that same year he also began a long narrative poem 'The Widow in the Bye Street'.[24] The widow Anna had a smile, voice and face which 'were all temptation'. Her husband had taken his own life and she revered his memory. A dead child is mentioned and her wanton past (and present) emphasised. Jealousy and desire are paramount, a mother's jealousy of her son's passion for Anna and the jealousy of Anna's son Jimmy towards Anna's lover. Jimmy meets Anna and seals their unhappy fate at the fair. In February 1910 Masefield had written to Elizabeth, 'Is your door locked against me. If open we'll go to the fair together.' Anna comments, 'Men make this shutting doors such cruel pain.' Anna's control over Jimmy includes her barring him from her home though suggesting they might meet in town. They must not kiss but he can write. Elizabeth recorded reading it 'sadly'.

Masefield once told her, 'I've hidden a lot of my secret life in my books.' His novel *The Street of To-Day* (1911) is an embittered tale of how little the sexes understand each other. It shows how easily marriage can turn sour.[25] One of the characters, Mary Drummond, resembles Elizabeth in some ways. Elizabeth read it 'with shrinking interest', prompted not so much by the delineation of the independent and beautiful Mrs Drummond dressed in black, committed to reforming the public health system and saving the hero's soul, as from a recognition of the symbols and esoteric references they had once shared, now appearing in print. For example, Masefield refers to 'the mills of the Gods' (the title of one of Elizabeth's stories and later, a book) and to 'white violets', another title and the flowers she cherished in memory of her husband. He also describes a country cottage shared by two women friends, one of whom becomes the hero's wife, and Burning Mansions where he and this unhappy wife live in the tower. He had told her that he would include for her the symbol of the tower in a novel. Ibsen's tower in *The Master Builder* was known as a phallic symbol.

Masefield later admitted that he had burned a novel he had been writing. This was probably 'Lost Things' which he had outlined for Elizabeth in 1910. It concerns a beautiful American southerner called Val (the name of the heroine in Elizabeth's *The Open Question*). She leaves her husband and two children for a more stimulating life in New York then London. She becomes a writer and, like many early feminists in Britain, a passionate opponent of the Contagious Diseases Acts of the 1860s which regulated prostitution, humiliating and punishing women but exculpating men. She rediscovers her daughter Lisa in America but it is her relationship with John who had run away to sea, been exposed to vice, deserted and become ill which is crucial. Attracted initially by her personality, they then discover their true relationship to each other and the ultimate need to repress physical passion. John's wife is pained by her exclusion from their closeness and this leads to their pledge to make their spiritual life paramount, to give to the cause of women 'all the passion which life denies in themselves'. The real-life John claimed that Elizabeth made him vow that all his work henceforth would be done for the cause of women.

Masefield also had an impact on Elizabeth's work. It was he who suggested a story based on the oak rafters at Backsettown which became 'Under His Roof'. He also read and was unusually critical of her rambling narrative of 390 pages originally called 'Miss Patching or The New Jane' (later entitled 'White Violets or Great Powers') and even tried writing a descriptive passage for this unpublished novel. Most significant, however, was his scenario of 'Docet Umbra.'[26] When Masefield had first visited Backsettown, Elizabeth and Flora had been trying their new sundial. The motto Elizabeth had engraved on the little grey stone dial was *Docet Umbra* ('The shadow has told') and he selected this as the title for the story about white slavery. Eventually the play they worked on together was transformed by Elizabeth into her best-selling, sensational novel, *Where Are You Going To … ?* (*My Little Sister* in America), a novel which has never been associated with John Masefield.

Before the First World War this novel was seen as an 'epoch-making narrative'. *McClure's Magazine*, a family journal which first published it in America (in two parts, beginning in December 1912), boldly declared that it 'startled a continent', arousing more discussion and stirring more consciences to action 'than any similar document of the last decade'.[27] The ensuing novel *My Little Sister* was in its fourth edition within a month and sales frequently exceeded 1,000 copies daily. It was also very popular in Britain. Yet 'The story you can't forget' has long ceased to be read. Forgotten also is the sense of urgency and the rumours and tales which surrounded its subject matter for many years. An organised international 'traffic' existed, enticing young women into prostitution and shipping them to continental brothels. It was suggestively labelled the white slave trade.

The original idea for a story came from Maud Pember Reeves, feminist, Fabian and author of a study of Lambeth. In 1907 she had told Elizabeth a factual account of two innocent young Englishwomen enticed to a brothel. Elizabeth then told Masefield 'the story I've carried so long in my head'. His scenario for a play centres around Vida Levering (the central figure in *Votes For Women!* and *The Convert*) living at 24, Iverna Gardens, Elizabeth's former flat.[28] She refuses her suitor because of the shadow of her dead sister Muerte, a victim of white slavery. The suitor then confesses his past. The second act is set in a gentlemen's club and the denouement takes us back to a police court where a desperate Muerte fulfils her naming and destiny as the archetypal doomed fallen woman. Elizabeth elaborated on the theme. Her suggestion of including the nursery rhyme 'Ring a Ring of Roses' in the story, connoting danger and disease lurking beneath innocence, was replaced by 'Where are you going to, my pretty maid?'. Whilst Masefield focused on the contrast between the pure young girl and male experience and complicity, Elizabeth developed the other characters. Both Masefield and his wife favoured the novel form which they felt would permit greater exploration of the psychology of the sisters and the 'monstrous tragedy' of it all. This advice was heeded. Yet although at one stage Elizabeth envisaged a working partnership under the pseudonym of E. and J. Wargrave— 'Anonymity lures me as of old'—the breakdown of her relationship with Masefield meant that the book was temporarily abandoned.

When, in mid-February 1912, she resumed work on the white slavery subject, she called her sketch 'What Became of Betty Martindale' (a reference to her friend Dr Martindale, author of *Under the Surface* about venereal disease) and centred it on soldiers returning home on board a ship. This was soon replaced by a refinement of the original story. Two middle-class teenagers are lured to London by a bogus aunt. Taken from the railway station to a brothel, the older sister (the unnamed narrator) escapes but cannot retrace her younger sister Bettina. Her one consolation is that the life of such a victim can only be a short one.

Two months later came the news that Elizabeth's friend W. T. Stead had drowned in the *Titanic* disaster. This haunted Elizabeth for days— 'I am on that ship or with my friend struggling in the icy water' she wrote in her diary and this event prompted fervent concentration on the very subject which had made Stead infamous. Parliament's refusal to raise the age of consent and punish traffickers in vice had, in the mid-1880s, resulted in Josephine Butler, the veteran campaigner against the Contagious Diseases Acts, and Catherine Booth of the Salvation Army, appealing to the journalist Stead. His audacious plan to procure a thirteen-year-old from her family to demonstrate the ease with which a girl could be sold into prostitution and sent to a brothel abroad, paid off. Judith Walkowitz has argued that the sensational case of Eliza Armstrong in the *Pall Mall Gazette* drew upon traditions of melodrama and pornography and simultaneously incited and disciplined interest in sexual danger, constructing it as a national issue for the nation to read about.[29]

Although Stead had a brief spell in prison, the Criminal Law Amendment Act of 1885 raised the age of consent from thirteen to sixteen. The first part of the legislation was originally entitled 'The Suppression of Prostitution' but parliamentary debate reshaped this into 'The Protection of Women and Girls'. It extended procurement to cover the removal of young women abroad and tightened control over brothels. In practice protection could now easily become repression, the law enabling a coercive regulation of sexuality and disciplining of the working-class family. The increased prosecution of brothel-keepers created difficulties for groups of women renting lodgings and increased prostitutes' dependence on pimps. The National Vigilance Association was founded by those known as social purists keen to ensure the enforcement of the Act. A Select Committee of the House of Lords had recently shown little evidence of women who were not already prostitutes going to work in European brothels but enough of a moral panic had been raised to ensure that the spectre of white slavery at least thrived in the popular imagination.

The writing of the story coincided with considerable WSPU activity and the Conspiracy trial where Emmeline Pankhurst's speech from the dock drew attention to white slavery. There was renewed pressure to tighten the part of the Act dealing with streetwalkers and brothel-keepers. At a suffrage meeting at the Albert Hall in mid-June Elizabeth expressed her cynicism at the timing of the new bill, claiming that it owed more to the death of Stead than to concern at the 'abiding horror of women's lives'.[30]

Initial reactions to her manuscript were promising. Flora had never before reacted in such a positive way and even the lady-like Florence Bell was 'spellbound'. William Heinemann cautioned against anonymity, declared the book's effect to be 'rather overwhelming' and persuaded Elizabeth to write more. It was at this stage that she decided to investigate the situation personally and to join temporarily the band of social explorers penetrating the hidden world of London low life. Her involvement was essentially as an investigative writer rather than as an activist in social purity. Yet her motives can be questioned. Since she was writing about white slavery and a protected country girl, why did she feel the need to observe working-class streetwalkers? It would, of course, have been impossible for her to investigate personally brothels such as the one she wrote about and described as 'one of the most infamous houses in Europe'[31] just twenty minutes by taxi from Lowndes Square. Nevertheless the direct evidence she obtained from her nocturnal visit to Piccadilly did not appear in print. Perhaps she reasoned that by undertaking some personal research she gave herself a little credibility in case she was challenged about her knowledge of prostitution. She could hardly divulge her main source, John Masefield.

In 1906 when researching her suffrage play Elizabeth had visited Beatrice Webb and they had discussed women's lodging houses: 'My dear Miss Robins,' exclaimed Beatrice Webb, 'you don't know anything about these things. I do.' Elizabeth asked if she had visited a tramp ward and was told she had not, so she suggested that they went together one night. Beatrice Webb now 'drew in her horns' and made excuses. In 1912 Elizabeth was determined to go ahead and to test once more her acting powers.

On 25 July Elizabeth attended Tower Bridge Police Court, sitting through a number of cases none of which related to prostitution, let alone white slavery. She ascertained that the police kept a list of known brothels, and alluded to this in her story. She then made a midnight trip to the Coventry Street area of Piccadilly. Having obtained permission from Catherine Booth she donned the full Salvation Army costume accompanying General Hillyer to a street outside a public house to observe the women and men. Anxious not to betray her true identity (as several others had apparently done), she initially said as little as possible, taking her cue from Hillyer. She noticed how small the women were, linking this to economic deprivation, and observed what little notice they took of Hillyer. Her notes describe a number of women and their clothes, then focus on one woman with, a 'dignified face' and her conversation. Her story began in a familiar way: raised in an Edinburgh orphanage she became a servant in London, leaving her job because of cruel treatment and seeking refuge with the Young Women's Christian Association. The YWCA, however, abandoned her when she most needed help and it was a prostitute who rescued her from starvation. This attack on organised Christianity (which reads like the modern version of a Bible story) predictably alienated Hillyer and sets Elizabeth's non-judgemental account apart from those of most social investigators imbued with religious and moral purpose. Distancing herself from her Salvationist disguise, Elizabeth (calling herself Mrs Parks) invited the woman to visit her at Zoe Hadwen's Chelsea home the next day. Zoe hoped to rescue her but she never appeared, afraid, as Elizabeth recognised, of being once more 'sermonised'.

The experience left Elizabeth feeling 'bruised mentally by the sights and sounds'. Yet we cannot read her account as a straight-forward reporting of events. Written at the back of her diary it represents a stage in the careful shaping of a narrative. The singling out of one young woman who stood out from the rest and Elizabeth's instant befriending are more suggestive of a literary device and of the author/investigator's beliefs in her own powers of persuasion than of a blow-by-blow account of the hour and a half she spent in Piccadilly. When the woman (never named) was asked about how men treated her, according to Elizabeth 'She gave me a curious quick look full of unconscious eloquence "You don't Know" she said and changed the subject.' This Scotswoman was probably the closest she could come to recreating a Bettina.

A comment made later by Hillyer led to a significant addition to the manuscript. She told Elizabeth that many young prostitutes had been ruined by their fathers. Always interested in the impact of one generation on another, Elizabeth now accounted for the fictional mother's over protectedness towards her daughters by referring to this mother's own troubled childhood and exposure to 'a great deal of evil'. It is hinted that child abuse is the real unspoken tragedy of the story and that the chain of disastrous events might have been avoided had the mother not sought to keep her children in ignorance because of her own tragedy which she could barely articulate. This can be seen both as a plea to appreciate the hidden roots of tragedy within families and as a response to those social purists who sought to blame working-class parents and mothers in particular, for not shielding their daughters from ruin. Wrapping up daughters in cotton wool as Bettina's mother had done, is revealed as a highly undesirable alternative. Yet Elizabeth's emphasis that ignorance does not protect innocence was one which some saw as a dubious manifestation of the liberated feminist even though early twentieth-century society showed greater appreciation of the value of sex education than had the Victorians. A later, abbreviated American version of the book eliminated the passage referring to the mother's past. A play based on the novel emphasises the mother's sudden and awful enlighten-ment as a young woman and (in words reminiscent of Masefield) mentions 'men with the beast in their souls' but does not allude to the possibility of incest.

Elizabeth sent the proofs to Masefield. The woman whose past had played so powerfully on the poet's imagination had focused her fictional story on a fallen woman who was not the architect of her own fate. His 'chilling' response—that her story was more like the first portion of a trilogy than a full working out of the results—was singularly devoid of the old reverential praise and completed his distance from a once-shared venture. Elizabeth sailed to America on the *Lusitania*, arriving in time for a welcome Christmas reception for her serialised story 'My Little Sister and the Gray Hawk of the World'. It was then published as a book by Dodd, Mead and Co. and in January 1913 appeared in Britain as the Heinemann publication *Where Are You Going To … ?* Within weeks of publication over 18,000 orders had been placed for the British version alone.[32] The secret of her success lay partly in the popularity of any topic concerned with a sex scandal apparently based on 'a true story'. Sales were also helped by the book containing descriptions of a brothel. The publishers actively promoted it. Success was also due to a number of other factors: timing, the novel form, international appeal and, perhaps most significantly, the focus on the middle class.

In December 1912 the much debated Criminal Law Amendment Act tightened procedures for contravention of the 1885 law. Throughout this period feminists were not united over social purity. Some were concerned about the threats to civil liberties inherent in the approaches of organisations such as the National Vigilance Association. This highly controversial issue helped ensure that this topical book would be read. In the summer of 1913 the fifth International Congress on the White Slave Traffic was held in London. The book was ammunition for those seeking further regulation of vice. With an established author tapping a rich vein of melodrama, success seemed guaranteed, especially since reviewers presented it primarily as a tract: 'a work of art and a war cry. It is a reproach to inaction and a call to arms' claimed the *Cleveland Leader*. Yet it outwardly and refreshingly eschewed the form of the moral tract (though retained a moral).

Unlike George Bernard Shaw whose focus in *Mrs Warren's Profession* (1894) had been on the economic origins of prostitution and capitalism's culpability for different forms of sex slavery, Elizabeth's emphasis was on the part played by male sexuality in the continued success of prostitution and, beyond that, white slavery.[33] The men encountered in the brothel are represented as predators, powerful individuals and responsible (in both senses of the word). Here she also differed from Stead whose sensational account of Eliza Armstrong being sold into prostitution had, as Judith Walkowitz observes, silenced positive female voices and cast the mother as the villain, occluding the culpability of men.

Literature about the white slave trade in Britain tended to be by those with a crusading zeal rather than in novel form. For example, Olive Malvery had written *The White Slave Market* (1912) explicitly to campaign for raising the age of consent to eighteen. Elizabeth sat with her on the Council of the National Association of Women's Lodgings founded by the Congregationalist Mary Higgs who had disguised herself to visit women's lodging houses.[34] It included an investigation of Whitechapel, with Salvation Army support, and an essay on 'Western Men with Eastern Morals'. Such 'exposures' fed the moral panic and were often deeply xenophobic. Elizabeth's novel avoided the crude depiction of foreign men (Jewish immigrants were frequently a target) but did succumb to a stereotype in the depiction of a French dressmaker colluding in the abduction.

In 1920 an Italian woman who had lived in London published a novel which drew very heavily on Elizabeth's story. Elizabeth had Madame Vivanti's book translated and consulted the Society of Authors. She was advised against taking legal action against such plagiarism given the difficulty of proving any prior claim over the original story on which her tale was based. There had been another novel about the white slave trade but it was set in New York. Richard Wright Kauffman's *The Daughters of Ishmael* was published in 1911, the year after Federal legislation on the subject.[35] It concerns a girl who escapes after being abducted to a brothel but she cannot then eradicate this past. Adapted by A. D'Este Scott for the stage it was performed by Edy Craig's subscription company, the Pioneer Players, in London in March 1914.

American interest was as intense as British concern. The Chicago Immigration League claimed that 1,700 girls were 'lost' in one year between the railroad terminals of New York and Chicago. With her family connections Elizabeth had access to material such as a paper on Chicago's white slave traffic and a report on the public morals of

Boston. Raymond had lectured on vice and VD in Chicago whilst Margaret and Frances Kellor had in practice and print spent some years determining the links between New York City's employment agencies and prostitution.[36] Although she chose to focus on London, Elizabeth's book was relevant to both sides of the Atlantic.

Most shocking to its readers was the depiction of middle-class girls. Implied in the deceptively innocent title is the question 'Where have you come from?' This was neither the tale of a sinful woman who had fallen and received her just deserts nor the usual story of an ignorant working-class girl in need of a moral lesson. Elizabeth later claimed that she wrote the novel to bring 'the horror home to the privileged class, the gently-nurtured',[37] showing that not even they were immune. Not only is Bettina from a respectable rural home but the tentacles of the plot reach back to her neighbourhood. Bettina's friend, daughter of Lord Helmstone, is engaged to a Guardsman—a 'regular' at the London brothel. The book had a powerful effect on its readers. Octavia Wilberforce's mother and brother lectured her on its contents so that 'for about a week I suffered from depression at the rottenness of the world in general'.[38] Her tutor couldn't sleep after reading it. Her uncle Basil, Archdeacon of Westminster preached about it in Westminster Abbey thus furthering the connections between this subject and the older slave trade. Eva Slawson, a legal secretary in London, wrote to her friend Ruth Slate, 'Dear, the book upset me, made me long to move heaven and earth to lessen this evil—it seems to me a problem beyond the power of mere legislation.'[39] When the book first appeared people begged Elizabeth to assure them that it was only a story, 'nothing at all but—a novel'. Without revealing her source, she stressed that its basis was real and that the police and others had corroborated that other Bettinas existed. Christabel Pankhurst was keen for her to reveal the original family.[40] This she never did.

It produced a lot of mail. Letters (some anonymous) came from Hampstead, Exeter, Dublin, Colorado and elsewhere. A San Diego man uneasy (as were others) about the lack of a neat, happy ending suggested the formation of a vigilante group, the Knights of Chivalry, to rescue such maidens. Another reader suggested that the Pankhursts break the windows of brothel-keepers.

Although Elizabeth was concerned about white slavery and pros-titution more generally, it seems to have been some time *after* the publication of the book that she became involved in social action. Her diary and letters suggest that the evolution of the story owed more to her recognition of its potential dramatic force, and Masefield's interest in her, than to a personal crusading interest in exposing a social evil.

In April 1913 *The Suffragette* printed Christabel's 'The Government and White Slavery'.[41] It was suppressed in New York. Elizabeth praised Christabel 'for sweeping aside pretence of fiction & coming out with facts'. She was concerned to enlighten rather than keep young women ignorant about sexuality though whereas Elizabeth increasingly placed the emphasis on better medical knowledge for women, Christabel advocated what some have interpreted as a some-what glib 'Votes For Women and Chastity For Men'. She attacked the forces, arguing that the government was in effect a procurer of women for vicious purposes, and quoting Elizabeth's novel with its reference to 'Government women' kept in tents in India for the army's pleasure and indictment of the British navy cruising the Irish coast in search of women.[42]

Christabel claimed extremely high percentages of venereal diseases amongst British men. In that same year a Royal Commission began investigating the subject. Its results published in 1916 were less alarm-ing and alarmist than the figures used by Christabel. Nevertheless, there was now considerable concern about troops using 'Maisons tolérées' on the French Front. In February 1918 Elizabeth helped the British Association for Moral and Social Hygiene (newly formed from the Ladies' and Men's National Associations). After visiting the secretary Alison Neilans and discovering for herself how Lloyd George and others had turned a blind eye to these brothels, Elizabeth liaised with General Bartlett of the US military.[43] Over the follow-ing months she attended various meetings in London hearing Mrs Fawcett and the preacher Maude Royden speak on the subject.[44] A visit to the US Embassy elicited further facts and figures for the British organisation.

In the early 1920s, as part of the Six Point Group (see Chapter 9) Elizabeth campaigned for a further amendment of the criminal law including increased prosecution of brothel-keepers. Nevertheless she seems to have viewed her contribution to such questions essentially as one of education via literature and after her novel's success she contemplated a play. She was well aware of the delicacy of such a venture. George Bernard Shaw had described *Mrs Warren's Profession* to her as 'this unlucky play of mine'.[45] Not until 1925 could it receive a *public* performance in Britain. In the spring of 1913 Elizabeth was unwell and sought out Cicely Hamilton to adapt her novel. Interestingly Masefield's original contribution towards a play is conspicuous by its absence from Elizabeth's deliberations at this stage. She knew Cicely Hamilton through the WWSL. Like Elizabeth, Cicely came from a respected family but became an actress, active feminist and published writer. Cicely admired *Votes For Women!* and sent Elizabeth a copy of her *Marriage as a Trade*. Elizabeth called this book 'brave and original'.[46] Both were in the Six Point Group in the 1920s, lived long lives and died in 1952. Cicely appears to have been flattered by Elizabeth's appeal and was even prepared to let a play appear without her own name, providing she received some remuneration. Both women were wary of the happy ending sought by theatrical agents and managers. In the summer Elizabeth worked on Cicely's version whilst staying at Rounton.

There were plans to stage the play in New York and in London. The Women's Theatre was to produce it at the Coronet, Notting Hill on 20 July 1914, complete with the original ending. Money was raised by the Actresses' Franchise League but the Lord Chamberlain refused to license the play.[47] Although initially the Examiner of Plays argued that this 'glorified penny-dreadful' was well intentioned and not worth banning, his advisors, including Elizabeth's erstwhile colleague Squire Bancroft, convinced him that passing it would suggest partiality since *Mrs Warren's Profession* had been banned. So it was never produced. However, unknown, it would seem, to Elizabeth, her sensational novel was the basis of an American film in 1919.[48]

PART V

FROM E.R. TO ANONYMOUS

9

ANCILLA'S SHARE

Reflecting on the year 1910 and the departure of Masefield from her life, Elizabeth noted, 'A new friend & very devoted is Octavia Wilberforce. She is interesting & far more gifted than anybody knows except me. She can go far if she makes up her mind.' They had met in early July of the previous year. Elizabeth was spending the weekend with the Buxtons and the twenty-one-year-old Octavia, a friend of young Phyllis Ponsonby, came to lunch. Elizabeth's diary doesn't mention this, yet Octavia, writing in her seventies, recalled it as 'a turning point in my life'. The famous novelist wore a suit 'the colour of speedwell which matched her beautiful deep-set eyes' and 'It was a case of hero-worship at first sight'.[1]

Octavia was the great-granddaughter of William Wilberforce though ironically she felt herself to be 'a bond slave to family life'. Her home Bramlands was nearby and soon Tate, as she was then known, was cycling to Backsettown daily, helping Elizabeth tend her roses and soaking up the cultured atmosphere. Her parents were wary. Miss Robins was said to be a friend of H.G. Wells and George Moore (something *she* would have disputed) and had apparently been uncomplimentary about men in a recent novel. The youngest of eight Wilberforce children had been denied a proper schooling and her parents saw her destiny as marriage. Not so Octavia. She rejected Charlie Buxton's proposal when she was twenty-three and realised that she was '*not* cut out' for marriage, 'the very thought of it makes me shudder and it revolts me'. What did appeal, however, was the idea of becoming one of the second generation of pioneer women doctors. In 1911 only 2 per cent of doctors in England and Wales were women, many of them working overseas. When Octavia told Elizabeth of her hopes she 'looked at me with flashing eyes, with an expression I'd never seen in them before and burst out "Now that *would* be a worthwhile life … It's the greatest profession in the world".' In contrast her mother warned that she would become a discontented old maid. Her father refused to pay and cut her out of his will.

The Buxtons paid for her training, Elizabeth providing the moral support. Octavia had never been taught how to study and despite careful tutoring matriculated only on her eighth attempt. In 1913 she began medical studies at the London School of Medicine for Women then did her clinical training at St Mary's, Paddington which was experimenting in taking women students. Here she got her first paid job on finally qualifying at the age of thirty-three. During those long, struggling years Octavia had to combat the entrenched prejudices of some of the men in her profession. Elizabeth's support was 'protective, far-seeing, ambitious for my success'. Family ambition and involvement (two of Elizabeth's uncles were deans of medical schools and Vernon Robins was a health officer in Louisville), feminism and her own illnesses increased her interest in medicine. In the unpublished part of Elizabeth's memoirs she declared that two professions excel all others in educating women: medicine and the stage.[2]

Male doctors feature in several of Elizabeth's novels, the most arresting figure being the saturnine Dr Garth Vincent of *A Dark Lantern* (1905) who fascinates the aristocratic, sociable Kitty Dereham. It is an attraction of opposites. The doctor with 'the Dark-Lantern face' is dedicated to his work, never attempts to charm, unlike Anton the shallow Prince Charming and is said to walk 'like a shopkeeper'. Elizabeth reveals through Lady Algernon the precarious position of the modern medic: 'in my day, medical men were kept in their proper places. *Now*, the person who has been prescribing for your liver in the morning, may be peering into your plate at the dinner table. Disgusting!'[3] Yet a lack of class assurance was matched by a growth in professional authority. And in dealing with women patients the power was absolute. Overstrained by her demanding, drug-addict father and her princeling, Kitty succumbs to a nervous illness from which Vincent rescues her via a rest cure. Everything is on his terms. She is prescribed total rest for six weeks, denied communication with the outside world, ruled over by nurses in thrall to the doctor. Although in the last resort Kitty could still dismiss Vincent, she is more and more drawn to this 'Black Magic Man' (the original title for the book). Whereas she resisted Anton's attempted seduction, she surrenders her body to the doctor, first as a patient, then, after the cure, as a lover. They live together in the countryside. When they marry he is racked with jealousy, she lives in fear of his earlier dissolute living—always hinted at but never made explicit. Only by exorcising the past through recognising its irrelevance can they face a future together.

The rest cure was well known to women like Elizabeth. Developed by S. Weir Mitchell at his Philadelphian clinic, it was adopted in Britain in the 1880s.[4] It was seen as the solution to neurasthenia, the nervous disorder understood as a manifestation of the tensions of modern urban society on sensitive souls, particularly artistic women (rather more middle-class than Elizabeth's heroine). Like Kitty, they were subjected to rest, massage and a dairy weight-gaining diet in a bid to induce eventual activity as a welcome contrast. The patient submitted to the doctor's omnipotence. Implicit in the process of curing women patients was the belief that they would revert to being traditional feminine women, something Elizabeth queries by making Kitty the one who takes the initiative and propositions Vincent, showing a possible extreme outcome from over-dependence.

Margaret Dreier had, before meeting Raymond, been pronounced a neurasthenic but perhaps the best-known American woman sufferer was Charlotte Perkins Gilman whose story 'The Yellow Wallpaper', first published in 1892, details the progressive insanity facing the patient subjected to the rest cure by her husband-cum-physician. Virginia Woolf also found her rest cures terrifying. In *Mrs Dalloway* (1925) Septimus Smith is subjected to the maddening therapy of rest and more rest, leading to increased weight and loss of mind. Virginia Woolf had reviewed *A Dark Lantern* twenty years earlier. She pronounced Elizabeth 'a clever woman, if she weren't so brutal'.[5] Despite its over-long Prologue, it made compulsive reading. Olive Schreiner has recounted reading it on the steps of her house for some hours until she thought her eyes were failing. She looked up and discovered that the sun had set and that she was trying to read by the moon and stars.

'I greatly fear that there's gun powder in that book' wrote Elizabeth. She knew that her 'wild love story' might offend. Florence praised its originality and daring but implored her to omit some 'simply revolting' bits. Her American publisher insisted that cuts were needed. Elizabeth was, however, more concerned about readers making connections between Garth Vincent and her physician. Although her first doctor in London was Garth Wilkinson who had told her in 1891 that she was overwrought and should go abroad for some weeks for a change, she had recently been treated by Vaughan Harley, an advocate of rest cures and she was anxious lest people think that Vincent was based on him. She consulted her solicitor before publication.

Over the last few years Elizabeth had acquired first-hand experience of rest cures and was not impressed. In *A Dark Lantern* Kitty recuperates in Torquay and Ventnor. After typhoid fever and the Paignton nursing home, Elizabeth had been sent to the Isle of Wight for a six-week Weir Mitchell cure: 'Precisely the wrong thing for me, I being still invincibly determined to live.' One side of her room was glass. The only sound was of the howling winds off the sea. Once released she fled to Italy. Two years later her neuralgia and other ailments forced her to consult several eminent specialists. Neuralgia was then thought to result from a defective blood supply to the brain. They diagnosed that she was simply 'worn out' and advised rest. She protested that she had rested enough. Doctors at a Virginian spa denied that her nerves were the problem, pointing instead to rheumatic and gastric disorders. Back in London Vaughan Harley insisted that she was suffering from shock and must give everything up. 'I rebel—refuse.' Eight weeks and two days later she emerged from incarceration in a nursing home.

Early in 1904 with her doctor pronouncing he could do no more for her (she had abandoned his medicines after a three-month trial) Elizabeth tried Dr Lahmann's Kür in Dresden. There were times when she had noises in her head and now she was losing weight and fearing that she had cancer. She remained in Dresden for nearly four months. Her new vegetarian diet included wholemeal bread, milk, eggs, fruit and vegetables and she was warned that her prescribed meat and bullock's blood taken three times daily had poisoned her. She took no medicines but enjoyed vibrator massages, hot packs and air baths in the forest, going barefoot in the snow. With a healthy diet and hydrotheraphy, first popularised in Silesia in the 1830s, she flourished. She began and 'made great strides' with *A Dark Lantern*.

The Kür became a welcome part of Elizabeth's life, 'baths and betterment' beckoning whenever the going got tough. Elizabeth returned to Lahmann's a number of times, even taking part in gymnastics. In the 1920s she attended a cure at Saltsjöbaden combined with a visit to Flora who was then living in Sweden. She took the water at British and European spas: at a spa in Savoy she discussed American politics with the American journalist Ida Tarbell, wrote some of *Where Are You Going To … ?* and read *Madame Bovary*.

For many years Elizabeth also suffered dental problems, partly due to determination to retain some teeth. Emergency dental treatment in hospital was carried out as far afield as Battle Creek, Michigan. Her most persistent troubles were, however, gastric problems which she called 'the enemy', an old pain over her left kidney and back ache. Doctors warned that Backsettown was too damp and, partly because of this, she spent many winters in London. At the end of the 1920s she had a bad attack of thrombophlebitis but then and later she could at least receive the attention of Dr Octavia Wilberforce.

Elizabeth was in her late forties when they had met and described Octavia as 'more my child than my "friend"'. Octavia's letters are signed S.C. (Sussex Child) and *The Messenger* is dedicated to S.C. Elizabeth's diary descriptions hardly suggest an adult. For example, 'OW fractious a little. But a v. good child really' was written when Octavia was twenty-eight. The older woman sometimes expressed impatience with Octavia's moodiness which was exacerbated by her reactionary family. During her training Octavia lived in lodgings in London then a hostel, seeing Elizabeth whenever possible. Flora left Backsettown in May 1915 and from that time Elizabeth spent long periods in London. During part of the war she stayed at Zoe's 'vine-clad' home writing the novel *Camilla* which, as she explains in the dedicatory note to Zoe, helped provide 'a kind of air-raid shelter for the mind'. From the autumn of 1917 she shared a flat with Octavia in Cambridge Gardens which was handy for St Mary's. Using the military language which pervaded wartime, Octavia described herself as Elizabeth's ADC (aide-de-camp). Qualifying in 1920 she felt 'my devotion to E.R. became more adult. I felt myself more on equal terms.' Although Elizabeth would continue to stay in London and America, the two women made their permanent home in Sussex.

From the 1890s sexologists began to categorise relationships as normal or deviant. The stigmatisation resulting from labels such as 'sexual inversion' (used by Havelock Ellis in 1897) helped prevent many women from admitting their sexual identity.[6] Shortly before this the term 'Boston Marriage' had been used in New England. This described a long-term relationship between two, otherwise unattached women, likely to be pioneers in a profession, involved in work in the community and upholders of feminist values. Lilian Faderman adds that we do not know whether or not such relationships were sexual but that they involved women spending their lives primarily with other women, to whom they gave 'the bulk of their energy and attention', and with whom they formed 'powerful emotional ties'. In many ways the friendship between Elizabeth and Octavia followed such lines. The leitmotif of Elizabeth's life in the twentieth century was her commitment to feminist principles. She had met Octavia during her suffrage years and in their wake continued to be an active champion of women's equal rights. Both of these dedicated professionals led women-centred lives and their friends included couples such as Drs Flora Murray and Louisa Garrett Anderson and Dr Louisa Martindale and Ismay Fitzgerald.

Octavia had led a sheltered life. It was only when a woman student in her hostel became, to Octavia's alarm, obsessed with her that she was told something about lesbianism. This 'came as a considerable shock to my innocence'. She was twenty-eight. At the same time she was writing effusive, loving letters to Elizabeth. After Elizabeth sailed to America, Octavia recalled their parting:

> Kiss me, you said tonight & my heart went out to you in a flood … At the back of my mind I shall be kissing you all yr voyage across & you can't mind that because it will only be in my mind, not the contacts you don't like.

Elizabeth's apparent dislike of such physical contact did not lessen their devotion to each other. Octavia once told her friend Mabel

Smith that 'a lasting and deeply-loving relationship was entirely pos-sible without sex'.[7] For Octavia, Elizabeth had become, and was to remain, the most important person in her life.

Despite Elizabeth's sometimes barbed attacks on male antagonism towards the female sex, her heterosexual history made her less exclu-sively woman-centred than Octavia. Her 'involvement' with John Masefield coincided with getting to know Octavia and it is possible that Octavia never learned of the earlier affair with William Archer. In her late twenties Elizabeth had also had a similar experience to Octavia in her London digs but at somewhat closer quarters. This was one episode which did not get repeated in *Both Sides of the Curtain*. A lodger called Mrs Davis was attracted to the somewhat naïve Elizabeth who commented how 'with singular earnestness' she would kiss her on the stairs and even made her sit on her lap, telling her: 'I love you, some day you'll know how much.' In her diary Elizabeth confessed to being strangely drawn to her, she 'attracts me against my will'. She felt that her influence was 'not *good*, not wholesome, or I could study & sleep better—she has dominated me these few days past—her face is ever before me, her voice sounds in my ears even when she's out of the house'. She was concerned that her acting (in *The Profligate*) was suffering and felt it unwise for anyone to gain so powerful an influence over her. She seemed to 'draw out my vitality with her eyes'. Her friend Miss Ludwig was 'devoured by jealousy' and Elizabeth was told that she had 'heard us talking together last night—swears she heard me making – – – etc. Do you know anything about the French nature. God grant you never may!' Soon after Mrs Davis became ill and Elizabeth who had long contemplated leaving Duchess Street moved to Montagu Place. These digs were, however, so unpleasant that she returned after one night. Mrs Davis seemed a little better but soon after left for that symbol of sexual freedom, Paris. At a later date Elizabeth wrote that 'it makes me creep to remember that woman'.

In middle age Elizabeth's primary allegiance was to further wom-en's opportunities in public life. The youthful Octavia Wilberforce personified this concern. For Elizabeth, Octavia was increasingly a precious and refreshing part of her life. As she gained professional skills beyond Elizabeth's ken, so the latter's respect for her deepened. From 1923 Octavia had her own medical practice in Brighton at the home she bought (with help from the wealthy Mrs Yates Thompson whose father had been the publisher of Charlotte Brontë and Thackeray) at 24, Montpelier Crescent. She eventually became head physician at the New Sussex Hospital. As Elizabeth Robins aged, so their roles began to reverse, with Elizabeth becoming increasingly dependent on Octavia. As we shall see, as an old woman living out the Second World War in the States, Elizabeth felt bereft without her. In her late seventies she wrote to Octavia in Brighton, 'I am parched with longing for you.'

Whilst Octavia pursued her career, Elizabeth publicised the cause of women in medicine. After the First World War medical schools which had cautiously welcomed women students to pay their fees in place of men fighting abroad, now closed their doors again. When in March 1922 the London Hospital announced that it would take no more female students Elizabeth wrote an angry letter to the *Sunday Times*.[8] Two years later St Mary's followed suit, symptomatic of the reaction against feminism which characterised this period. The game of snakes and ladders was wearying. Elizabeth was delighted at the prospect of a Ministry of Health but discovered that the Standing Committee was not in favour of the proposed Women's Consultative Council. In *The Times* she asked how any ministry might achieve its goals without making full use of the 'caring'.[9]

She now had some knowledge of hospital management. From 1912 she was involved with the Lady Chichester Hospital for Women and Children in Brighton and during the war wrote an eight-page pamphlet advocating its work and appealing for funds.[10] Miss Aldrich-Blake was the senior surgeon and Dr Martindale (who eventually became president of the British Medical Women's Federation) one of the three female visiting doctors. Spearheaded by the latter, a more ambitious scheme soon developed for extending this small institution into a fifty-bed hospital run by women for women. Elizabeth was one of its key figures from the start. Her wealthy friends were persuaded to give generous donations. Hugh Bell gave £200 for five years but the greatest financial support came from Mrs Yates Thompson, enabling the purchase of Windlesham House in Brighton. Elizabeth got Mrs Lloyd George to open the New Sussex Hospital at the end of 1921. Elizabeth was one of the five trustees, briefly chaired the Board of Management (Lady Rhondda was a treasurer) and remained on the board until 1928. A ward was named after her. In 1923 Octavia supplemented her income by working as a clinical assistant to Outpatients.

For part of the First World War Elizabeth actually worked at a hospital. She and the novelist suffragist Beatrice Harraden volunteered as the librarians at the Women's Military Hospital at Endell Street, London. Boasting 1,000 beds and thirty-four wards it was run entirely by women to aid servicemen. Dr Flora Murray and Louisa Garrett Anderson, both with experience of military hospitals in France, were in charge. The hospital was hastily converted from a workhouse and the first batch of soldiers arrived two weeks earlier than planned. Elizabeth was there from the start in May 1915. Her diary comments on workmen still hammering whilst convalescent soldiers poured out their tales. She took books round the wards, listened and sometimes wrote letters for the soldiers. Once again, friends such as Dolly Yates Thompson were persuaded to give financial support.

In August Elizabeth visited Rounton where Florence as local president of the Red Cross was now a hospital commandant (for which work she would become a Dame of the British Empire). At the Bells' Elizabeth talked to the woman organiser of the First Aid Nursing Yeomanry working near the firing line in Belgium. This, an earlier conversation with her Endell Street employers and a difficult interview at the War Office with Sir Alfred Keogh about stretcher-bearing for women, prompted her to write an article for the Daily Mail on women's foreign service.[11] Her argument that those women who were fit and willing should, like Belgian women, be given opportunities to serve as stretcher-bearers, produced a number of critical letters in response.

Back in Endell Street Elizabeth found an influx of Australian and New Zealander patients. By the end of the year her own health was suffering and when Raymond suggested a trip to Florida, she responded positively. Her resignation was not well received by the hard-pressed staff: 'You'd think me a deserter who ought to be Court Martialled.' Nevertheless, Elizabeth retained her respect for the Endell Street experiment which she saw as proving the value of enlisting the 'latent power' of untrained women.[12]

Her tasks had included helping to arrange an entertainment for disabled Belgian soldiers. She also served on a committee organising the billeting of these soldiers in the Henfield area. In October 1914 Elizabeth's diary had referred to 'this martyrdom of Belgians that the world looks on at'. Her short story 'The Tortoise-shell Cat' depicts an American woman raising money for Belgian refugees from the safety of the States.[13] In 'Under His Roof' immersion in women's suffrage had been suggested as the solution to an unhappy personal life. Here it was war work. In a story for an American magazine set in Scotland, Ruth is a war victim, the illegitimate child of an Edinburgh medical student and his landlord's daughter.[14] Brought up in an orphanage, unaware of her background and now a nurse, she wants to find her parents. The Hon. Mrs McAlpin who runs the orphanage tracks down the father, a Harley Street consultant. Ruth meanwhile has found a new purpose in life through volunteering for work in a military hospital in France and even hopes to be a stretcher-bearer. Her father just happens to sail with her and is won round, pledging support.

Illegitimacy and claims to parenting are the subject of 'The Frog Baby' serialised in the suffragist *Woman's Leader*.[15] Here is yet another titled lady making herself useful. The childless Lady Terence, bustling with war work committees, brings home a tiny child from an East End lying-in hospital. With her class prejudices and belief that she can own even a child if she so wishes, she reveals herself to be unfitted for the task of raising the boy. The topic was prompted by friends adopting children. Jean Hamilton's Harry had been abandoned in the Paddington crèche of which she was president and after Maude Royden's son died, the feminist preacher adopted a cook's baby in the care of Dr Martindale.

Mrs Pankhurst's replacement of suffrage with patriotism on the outbreak of war is well known, epitomised by *The Suffragette* being renamed *Britannia*. When war was declared in August 1914 Elizabeth wrote to Florence: 'And so peace-lovers as we may be, who can doubt but England has taken the only decent course? But the nightmare is like a palpable darkness.' Like many other women she was concerned about the initial unemployment of women, lectured on war service for women at the Pioneer Club, Brighton and spoke to the Women's Emergency Corps founded by aristocratic ladies and suffrage activists such as Lena Ashwell. It provided a register of qualified women eager for paid war work. In an article entitled 'War Service at Home' (see

Appendix 2) Elizabeth extolled the varied work of the corps—helping refugees, interpreting, the Land Scheme and much more—and in the *New York Times* she outlined the new England she had seen emerge since war began. From a state of stability and unreadiness, there had been a profound change and display of endurance. Although acknowledging her love of German literature and of many German people, in a somewhat unsubtle comparison, she contrasted what she saw as the German tendency to dragoon people into order with the British spirit of voluntary co-operation, epitomised by the German policeman as a symbol of despotism and the very different British 'bobby'. Yet on the outbreak of war her former servant, the German Karolina, had joined Elizabeth in Sussex. Both women had to register at the local police station since the outbreak of war had not prompted Elizabeth (unlike Henry James), to become a British citizen. She was, however, 'beyond words glad … a great burden has rolled off me' when America eventually joined the war.

Elizabeth's attitudes towards war changed over time. She did not follow the Pankhurst route or the patriotism of William Archer who was soon working for the War Propaganda Bureau at Wellington House. From an initial resistance to any exclusion of women from work, she moved towards a critique of war itself. In March 1915 she wrote (in eight days) a story called 'The Centaur'. When Hugh Seaford returns from Florida to his native Sussex with his beloved horse Dixie people are shocked when he refuses to enlist. Yet a wounded soldier admires his courage in voicing his pacifism from the outset. Rather than allowing his horse to be requisitioned, he reluctantly accepts a commission in the cavalry, maintaining that this is solely to look after Dixie, war being 'the most horrible indefensible thing on earth'.

In the same month Elizabeth told Florence that she was considering attending the International Congress of Women at The Hague, the first major European meeting since war began. It was attended by over 1,200 women, though the British government allowed only three British representatives. Its president was the American Jane Addams. Jill Liddington has stressed that it helped establish the principles for a future peace settlement and it is from this event that the international women's peace movement developed.[16] Elizabeth's mention of the Congress was somewhat casual but it signalled an interest in peace and in woman's role in combating militarism which would become increasingly important for her. As a result of the Hague Congress the Women's International League was formed (the words 'of Peace and Freedom' were added to the title in 1919). Elizabeth was a member of this for a while though her subscription had lapsed by 1925 and was not renewed.

In 1917 she became a lecturer for the new Ministry of Food where her friend Maud Pember Reeves was in charge of the women's section. From February 1915 Germany's submarine blockade raised grave fears about how long the food supply could last. A Food Economy campaign was in full swing, encouraging all sorts of ways of making basic foods go further. It is somewhat ironical that Elizabeth who relied on cooks to prepare her food, should lecture on food control. She attended a training session in London in March then plunged into a series of lectures in places such as Ealing, Arundel and Portsmouth. She toured Ireland for two weeks giving twice-daily talks and emphasising her American nationality to combat anti-English sentiment. In the autumn she was chosen as one of a few speakers for London schools. She spoke rather than read her lectures, perused children's essays and reported weekly to the ministry. Visiting London County Council schools in Deptford, Bromley-by-Bow, Fulham, Putney and elsewhere she was pleasantly surprised by the 'women of cultivation and enthusiasm' dedicating their lives to teaching. In Wandsworth warnings of a Zeppelin raid forced her to take refuge with the children in a basement. The headmaster seemed keener on a talk about the Klondike than on war propaganda. After covering two schools daily for two months, Elizabeth was ill for several weeks. She attended a few food lectures early in 1918 but chose not to resume this work.[17]

One significant wartime contribution to food production and conservation was made by the Women's Institutes (WI), a movement which originated in rural Canada. The first British WI was formed on Anglesey in 1915. By October 1918 there were 760 in England and Wales. Elizabeth was a member of the founding committee of Henfield WI, established in 1917 as the second Institute in West Sussex, and she served as president. By 1920 it had 183 members. Backsettown was the venue for WI garden parties and Elizabeth was even prepared to recite and do readings for the Henfield WI.

Two of the leading local WI figures were Helena and Margaret Mack. The latter liked to emphasise her Irish heritage. A Henfield woman recalls her as always dressed in emerald green and riding a green bicycle and she preferred to be known as Margaret Macnamara.[18] As secretary of the Henfield WI and as an ardent believer that 'Nothing short of the Socialist Revolution is really worth working for', she was keen for the Institute to become politicised. It was rumoured locally that it was anyway a Ladies Socialist Club! Elizabeth tried to keep the peace. Interestingly, it was Henfield which put forward and carried the important motion to substitute 'non-party' in place of 'non-political' in official literature at the London conference in 1918, thus enabling WIs to become involved in issues such as housing. Elizabeth liked Margaret Macnamara who also wrote plays. She 'puffed' her *Baby in the Ring* (performed at Caxton Hall for the WI) in an article in the *Observer*. At the end of the war Elizabeth sat on the new publicity committee of the National Federation of WIs whose chairman was Lady Denman (distantly related to Octavia and later on the board of the Backsettown Trust). In 1919 *The Nineteenth Century* published Elizabeth's article 'A New View of Country Life' which praised the WIs as an essential part of the multi-faceted work of Reconstruction.[19] Although she spent much of her time in the city, it was a paean to country living, sounding warnings about social disaster if too many fled to the towns. The WIs were praised as 'little Democracies', self-governing, self-supporting and encouraging all classes to work together. Five years before *Ancilla's Share* appeared, Elizabeth was arguing that the best way in which women could serve the ultimate ideal of co-operation between the sexes was to encourage a preliminary co-operation between women, exemplified in the WI.

Elizabeth commented that the ending of war had resulted not only in the men coming home but also in women having to go back to the home. This she had not foreseen. In a wartime article (*Contemporary Review*, April 1917) she had argued that women were in work to stay and that it was time male trade unionists appreciated this and learned to work with rather than against them.[20] 'Conscription for Women' pointed out how little those in charge knew of working women's attitudes though praised Mary Macarthur of the National Federation of Women Workers. Conscription for men had been introduced in

January 1916 and would, a year after the article appeared, be extended. By 1917 there had been a vast increase in the numbers of women employed—the Woolwich Arsenal, for example, now had 25,000 women munition workers compared to 125 in 1914. Discussion of female conscription appears to have emanated from resentment towards women who were not working rather than arising from a labour shortage. Elizabeth opposed it, arguing that 'you cannot safely legislate for people whose conditions you don't know'. In her view a cavalier use of women as docile and cheap labour placed them in an extremely vulnerable position.

Elsewhere she observed that wartime gave women two major forms of service, one 'to help in providing the means to break men to pieces; and [the other] to help to put broken men together again'.[21] Focusing on the former in her article she showed how women's health was destroyed in munition factories. She warned that without 'a highly organised and well-financed trade union backing, women will find themselves defenceless'. But her chief objection to conscripting women lay in their lack of direct representation: 'there can be no palliation of the outrage of conscripting an entire sex which is forcibly prevented from having the smallest share in making so momentous a decision.' Female conscription did not become a reality and by early 1918 some women workers were being dismissed.

Elizabeth also published in 1917 an article entitled 'Women at Home and Beyond the Seas'.[22] This mentioned the political expediency involved in the espousal of suffrage by the American political parties then turned to Britain where proposals to revise the register of electors were prompted not with women in mind but to prevent the exclusion of those men who had been fighting abroad. She stressed that it was not suffragists who argued for the vote because of women's war contribution. What women required was fair dealing. The refrain 'Set them free!' is repeated several times. Women, it is argued, don't need gratitude but they cannot do without the vote. Later, in *Ancilla's Share* Elizabeth pointed out that once the notion of conscripting women was considered, the old fiction that women lacked voting rights because they were unfit to share in defending the state, collapsed.[23] She maintained that what made possible the limited women's suffrage introduced in 1918 was not the actual war effort. After all, as she and other feminists noted, if that were the case, why did all those young women war workers not get enfranchised? Rather, their work made it possible for the 'man in the street' to understand the need for female voters.

On 6 February 1918 the Representation of the People Act was passed, giving the vote to women householders or householders' wives over thirty. Universal male suffrage was granted. Elizabeth attended celebratory dinners and the NUWSS suffrage celebrations at the Queen's Hall. But it was a muted victory. Not until 1928 did women gain the vote on the same terms as men.

Over the next few years she was involved in various attempts to give women greater visibility. When, in 1920, she received an appeal to express sympathy with a manifesto issued by Russian intellectuals, she wrote to *The Times*, pointing out its one 'grave omission', a failure to include any women.[24] She hoped that the Soviet Union would not repeat 'the old, dreary, foredoomed experiment of running a lop-sided world'.

In an article in the *Fortnightly Review* she explained how, in the final stages of the war, a group of women had met to realise the principle of a House of Commons as distinct from a House of Ladies which had been proposed by opponents of women's full share in political life.[25] She counteracted the worries of those who felt such a body to be superfluous by arguing the importance of pooling different skills and the value of a holistic approach. She knew that what women 'have yet to prove is a fitness for leadership combined with a fitness for co-operation'. In June 1918 she gave the opening address at the meeting for a Women's Parliament organised by the National Council of Women and chaired by Nina Boyle one of the joint founders of the first voluntary women's police force. The Council of Women was the successor to the National Union of Women Workers, a broad umbrella organisation essentially conservative rather than radical in its focus. Elizabeth sat on the Deliberative Council Executive briefly but was uneasy, noting that no pacifists or Labour women were represented. Before the end of the year she stood down: 'I do not feel it to be what I hoped.'

Whereas the pre-war suffrage movement had espoused one goal, albeit with different views about the best means of achieving that end, during the 1920s feminism appeared increasingly diffuse, even defensive.[26] In an unpublished piece called 'Temptation' Elizabeth argued that the old securities were gone and the new ones had not yet arrived. Instead of finding herself free, the modern girl was encouraged to 'patch up a semblance to the old order which people told her was so entirely beautiful and good'. 'New Feminism' as espoused by women such as Eleanor Rathbone (who became President of the major feminist organisation of the period, the National Union of Societies for Equal Citizenship) did not live up to its name, focusing more on difference and the special experience of women as wives and mothers. The very word 'feminism' became generally discredited whilst the decade's legislation which purported to remove legal disabilities proved in practice to be limiting and limited. In the early 1920s the Marriage Bar became accepted for the first time for teachers and this was reinforced by a test case in Wales in 1923.

Elizabeth did not become involved in the campaign for birth control as did some interwar feminists. She was, however, part of the equalitarian group challenging the notion of defining identity through men or through motherhood alone and fighting for equal rights and responsibility. In the early 1920s she was closely associated with the Viscountess Rhondda, Margaret Haig.[27] This Welshwoman personified the belief that women could enjoy an independent role in public life though she was immensely aided by wealth and parental support. The women in her family supported suffrage and she had been the organiser of the Newport, Monmouthshire branch of the WSPU. Her coal-owner, Liberal father made her a company director. When he died in 1918 he had just been promoted to the rank of Viscount. His will made provision for her to inherit his title. Lady Rhondda now hoped, as a result of the new Sex Disqualification (Removal) Act 1919 to be allowed to take her seat in the House of Lords. She soon discovered the limitations of the legislation. Her Petition to the Committee for Privileges of the House of Lords went well until the anti-suffragist Lord Chancellor, Lord Birkenhead, intervened and had it referred to an enlarged committee which now included himself. By a vote of twenty to four, the second hearing rejected the Petition of the 'Persistent Peeress'. Lady Rhondda's mother and Elizabeth had provided moral support, accompanying her to the Lords. Elizabeth now dashed off protests to four leading daily newspapers but discovered that Lord Birkenhead's campaign embraced the press. In 1925 the Parliamentary Qualification of Peeresses bill was defeated in the Lords by two votes. The following year when Lord Astor reintroduced it, Elizabeth was asked to contact peers who might support it. Not until 1958 (after Lady Rhondda's death) when life peerages were created, were women admitted to the House of Lords, taking their seats in 1963.

The 1919 legislation also enabled women to become Justices of the Peace and serve on juries but here again the backlash against feminism showed how legislation unaccompanied by a belief in its efficacy was problematic. There was a popular outcry against female jurors. Elizabeth argued in a letter in the *Morning Post* that this illuminated just how much that profoundly affects women is usually swept under the carpet.[28] The new women jurors showed that men had something to hide and how 'the decent man may dread the decent woman's judgement'.

On holiday with Octavia in North Wales in 1919 Elizabeth asked herself on her fifty-seventh birthday whether she shouldn't now turn aside from fiction just as she had once abandoned acting. Perhaps she should devote her remaining time and strength to 'the Realities', focusing on women's affairs and trying to make 'the better counsels prevail'. She believed that if she put her mind to it she could 'make a place & a centre of New Time influence' in the press. Wasn't this aim more in keeping with the 'Years of Experience'? Early the next year Lady Rhondda organised a deputation to the editor of the *Daily Express* to protest against the unfair treatment of women by the press. Elizabeth agreed to introduce for her a series of six articles on the subject of paternalism. Here she contrasted young men being told of opportunities at the top with 'Newspaperdom's' message to women that 'There's plenty of room at the bottom'.[29] Paternalism, that enemy with the benevolent face, was arranging women's lives for them.

The desire for an independent, non-party press which provided an example by effectively representing women's views resulted in the influential political (but non-party) newspaper *Time and Tide* which sought to treat women and men as 'equally part of the great human family'.[30] Elizabeth's diary first mentioned proposals for a new paper in late January 1920. In a telling statement she supported Lady Rhondda's venture, explaining that she was for "the People" with a completeness and conviction which I find in none of my intimates. Because I'm for the People *therefore* I'm inclusively for that section of the People I know best, the middle class.

She expressed her gratitude that the educated woman would now have a mouthpiece. She became one of the first seven Directors (all women) of the publishing company and purchased £20's worth of shares, attending her first board meeting on 3 March. Then and later she urged delaying the first issue—'I am appalled at the childishness of the preparations. Tell Rhondda a *little* of what I feel.' After due delay it appeared on 14 May, the first issue including the flattering appreciation of Elizabeth by Florence Bell as the first in a long-running series on Personalities and Powers.

Elizabeth attended a number of formal board dinners and meetings at Lady Rhondda's flat. Her main journalistic contribution was the children's adventure story–cum–recipe book *Prudence and Peter* which was serialised in ten episodes from late May 1920. Her co-author J. Woolley Paddock was Octavia who seems, from Elizabeth's diary, to have been chiefly concerned with devising and making the recipes whilst Elizabeth wrote the story and helped eat the experimental meals including an outdoor 'banquet' in the Hazel Alley in imitation of the tale. An early example of non-sexist children's literature with its emphasis on twins, a boy and a girl, both resourceful and fond of cooking, it was published in book form by Ernest Benn in 1928, dedicated to Mrs Yates Thompson and well reviewed.[31] The second half is set in wartime and includes a chapter about a Food Ministry lecturer visiting a school.

Elizabeth did not write regularly for *Time and Tide* though her contributions included some non-attributed articles such as 'A Talk with Mr Otto H. Kahn' (July 1921). This was about the German-born banker who developed the New Theatre, New York (for which Archer was an adviser for European plays) and urged greater co-operation between Europe and America. Although appointed to the 'programme council' in February 1921, she resigned from the board in May 1923 when the paper was just two years old. Some board members felt that her resignation was prompted by her dislike of the young Rebecca West who wrote the theatre reviews.

Anybody closely associated with H.G. Wells faced a hard time with Elizabeth. Rebecca West had attended her first board meeting the previous December. Of this meeting Elizabeth had written, 'I feel I waste my time & do them no good.' There is some unclarified evidence that she was increasingly uneasy about the tone of the paper especially 'In the Tideway' news items. Long before her resignation there were internal tensions. In January 1921 Lady Rhondda had begged Elizabeth to attend a meeting to back up her views, adding that she was prepared to split the board rather than surrender. Elizabeth did, however, continue to make occasional contributions in later years such as an appreciation of Mary Scharlieb 'The First Woman MD of London' (1924). She also wrote both positive and highly critical letters in response to articles.[32]

Time and Tide was the main platform for the Six Point Group which was formed in February 1921. Elizabeth was one of its twenty-two vice-presidents though it did not receive much attention in her diary. It included the new generation of feminists such as Vera Brittain as well as older women like Lady Rhondda and Dame Ethel Smyth. In some respects it was a successor to the WSPU but divested of its brand of militancy and pledged to equal rights and social justice. Like the People's Charter of the 1830s, it drew up six points for action. It became affiliated to the Consultative Committee of Women's Organizations, the umbrella group formed by Lady Astor (the first woman to take her seat in Parliament) in order to co-ordinate attempts by women's groups to put pressure on Parliament.

Elizabeth wrote the introduction to the Six Point Group's Supplementary number of *Time and Tide*.[33] The group wanted 'satisfactory legislation' for the unmarried mother and her child and for the widowed mother. It also sought to combat child assault. Equal rights of guardianship for married parents were demanded along with, equal pay for teachers and equal opportunities for both sexes in the Civil Service. Reform was sought via government legislation rather than by private members' bills. A 'black list' advertised the MPs who were the worst offenders against women's interests, a 'white list' proclaimed the best. A 'drab list' detailed those who had promised but not delivered support. The first of the group's campaigns was centred around an issue of considerable interest to Elizabeth: the Criminal Law Amendment Bill. It was passed in 1922, raising the age of consent to sixteen.

When she resigned from *Time and Tide* Elizabeth also gave up her work for the English committee of the Femina Vie Heureuse annual literary award. She had served with friends such as Lady Pollock and Marie Belloc Lowndes since 1919. During the war she had resumed her presidency of the Women Writers' Suffrage League but helped to disband the society in 1919. Soon, however, she was active in the international organisation P.E.N. (Poets, Essayists and Novelists) and in the Society of Authors. She frequently met other writers at the new Forum Club formed in 1919, was one of its original shareholders and sat on its founding committee. She also attended the somewhat exclusive Give and Take Club, a women's luncheon club started by Mary Cholmondeley in 1910. It met during the season at the St James's Hotel, London. Lady Brassey became a guiding spirit and Florence Bell was a regular.

Unlike many, Elizabeth's views on party politics seem to have got more, rather than less, radical as she grew older. She read Isabella Ford's *Women and Socialism* in 1906 and declared her Independent Labour Party principles to be 'sound'. By 1922 she was congratulating Florence's son-in-law the MP Charles Trevelyan on his Labour victory and becoming increasingly impatient with Maurice Bell's grudge against the working man.[34] Her preface to *Ancilla's Share* (1924) held out hope for the new Labour government, particularly in respect to maintaining peace.[35] A number of factors influenced her increasing preoccupation with peace and the part women could play in this. Although not religious, in 1918 she heard the powerful pacifist Maude Royden preach at the Nonconformists' famous City Temple in London. She was sufficiently impressed to return time and again to hear her, believing her to be one of the greatest forces in Europe in her encouragement of a 'peace mind'.[36] She was disillusioned when the Peace Conference did not include Mrs Fawcett who was already in Paris. When Clemenceau deigned to declare that women representatives of the allied nations might attend those commissions of the Peace Conference dealing with women and children, Elizabeth wrote that women were the 'main peace asset' and that Jane Addams should have sat alongside President Wilson in Paris.

Her brother Raymond was wary of Wilson and critical of the Versailles Treaty and League of Nations, seeing the latter as a disappointing league of victors. Along with friends such as Salmon L.

Levinson and Senator Borah, he immersed himself in the Outlawry of War Movement which sought an international formal treaty making war a crime among nations.[37] He carefully projected himself not so much as a pacifist as concerned with the workings of international law. He wanted Elizabeth to form a committee and be the leading apostle for the Outlawry of War in Britain but she had placed her faith in the League of Nations.

In October 1918 when the League of Nations Union (LNU) was formed, Elizabeth heard Sir Edward Grey lecture on the organisation. She attended a number of LNU meetings, including one of university women affiliates held at Bedford College. Urging arbitration of international disputes and multilateral disarmament, the LNU was the most respectable and popular means for women to express concern about preventing future wars. Membership rose from a quarter of a million in 1925 to a peak of 406, 868 by 1931.[38]

When Lady Rhondda stayed in November 1920 Elizabeth told her about her 'passion for Peace and how it must govern the degree of interest I take in *Time and Tide*'. She did not dare advocate immediate unilateral disarmament but was keen to do her utmost to bring about a real change of heart over the use of physical force and so enable agreement and disarmament. Elizabeth wrote an article on peace for the *Daily Chronicle* and stressed that 'The only lasting eminence as well as only safety—is organised disarmament and education of the peoples'. She told Lord Robert Cecil, president of the LNU, that 'a mass of voiceless people' owed to him their best hopes for 'the triumph of reason'.[39]

By 1924 Elizabeth had become critical of the lack of women on the League of Nations Council and as official delegates to the Assembly. It had, in her view, become a League of Men, served by women in subordinate offices. In 1928 she chaired an Outlawry of War meeting held at the American Women's Club.

Over these years Elizabeth's non-fiction became increasingly polemical whereas her fiction moved in the opposite direction. *The Messenger* (1919) can be read simply as a sensational wartime spy story in the wake of John Buchan's *The Thirty-Nine Steps*. Elizabeth knew Buchan both as a publisher and as the husband of Caroline Grosvenor's daughter Susie.[40] Although *The Messenger* includes accounts of actual wartime events such as the torpedoing of the

Lusitania and is at its strongest when suggesting how the coming of war affects everyday life and mentality, it contains stock ingredients including an uninhabited Scottish island used as a communications outlet by the Germans foiled by a British aristocrat, a German female spy who disguises herself as a Belgian nun, messages in code and invisible ink cracked by a wizard secret service man. Two voices predominate. One is redolent of many espionage tales, involving the demonising of the enemy. The alternative voice, more muted, is that of pacifism. Two young male friends, Gavan, whose chief is Adviser to the Admiralty, and Julian, a passionate believer in peace, fall in love with the same young American woman, the adamantly innocent Nan who bears peace literature to President Wilson. In a scene reminiscent of *The Convert* but ending in violence, Gavan goes to hear Julian advocate pacifism to a hostile crowd at an open-air meeting. The most powerful figure is, however, Greta the spy. Julian eventually drowns after his ship is torpedoed in the Atlantic and the absurd plot of espionage and counter-espionage predominates.

Elizabeth had some difficulty getting the story accepted. Her contract gave her little option but to write it extremely quickly. She had enjoyed Rose Macaulay's *Non-Combatants and Others* and had written to tell her so but a pacifist slant was not considered expedient by her American editor Tom Wells who was concerned about potential sales. He urged Elizabeth to play down Julian's pacifism. Cuts were made therefore though Elizabeth did eventually restore a little of her original material. She was well aware of the weaknesses of the book.

In 1920 she adopted a very different style of writing 'The Book of Revelations' is a close reading of the diaries of the soldier and war correspondent, Lieutenant-Colonel A. Court Repington CMG. They had received considerable publicity and were in their sixth edition. Repington's frank account of life in the War Office, Whitehall and a Mayfair Society scandal outraged Elizabeth. She maintained that its revelations of a crude fomenting of militarism alongside unashamed junketing were a gift to those who believed in revolution.[41] She also wrote of the dangers of 'Preparedness' for war. This meant an invitation to, rather than defence against, fighting. She expanded several articles into a repetitive, disjointed book. Lord Robert Cecil politely declined to write an introduction. Arthur Ransome, the publisher's reader, tactfully suggested that Repington was already over-exposed. Grant Richards would only go ahead if there were drastic cuts and the author's name were given, conditions which ensured that the work remained unpublished.

In February 1924 Elizabeth did publish a book anonymously. Like her analysis of Repington's diaries, *Ancilla's Share* was a committed work written in an adversarial style, adducing evidence, often in the form of lengthy quotes, to substantiate arguments. There are some similarities with the section on 'Woman and War' in Olive Schreiner's *Woman and Labour* (1911) and, as Jane Marcus has argued, in certain respects, it prefigures Virginia Woolf's work, notably *A Room of One's Own* and *Three Guineas*.[42] Yet its staccato style helped to make it less appealing than these famous works. Virginia Woolf saw Elizabeth as essentially a pre-war writer but she was referring to her fiction.[43] In *Ancilla's Share* was revealed the twentieth-century writer. For example, Elizabeth analysed what today we would call sexist language, examining the usage of binary oppositions such as master/mistress, courtier/courtesan, wise man/'wise woman' and the fact that 'he' meant in men's minds what the plain word said and not 'what he assured her that it meant'. This and her exposition of how women have been hidden from history, anticipated feminist writings of the 1970s.

Back in 1907, pondering on the rise and fall of civilisations, Elizabeth had wondered about making her final book

> Notes on Women in History or some such collection of material
> that shall serve to start a wiser better educated sounder brain than
> mine upon some great work that shall serve to show the Nations
> how they may be saved—thro' the Mother Spirit of Mankind.

By the time she wrote such a book, the war had provided an additional urgent imperative so that her study of over 300 pages became one of women, history and the search for lasting peace, with Ancilla the Handmaiden demanding her just share in the future.

Elizabeth argued that war threatened civilisation. Men could prevent war but had failed to do so. A recurrence of such horror was possible only with the international co-operation of women and men: 'Wars will cease when woman's will-to-peace is given equal

hearing and equal authority in council with man's will-to-war'.[44]
The creation of a civilised society must be in stages. An essential
prerequisite is for women to learn to serve the interests of other
women, to co-operate with each other. Here Elizabeth is critical
of the lost opportunities of women's leadership to date, though she
does not advocate a women's party.

Her blunt opening sentence, 'These pages are not addressed
to the masculine mind', and her subtitle, 'An Indictment of Sex
Antagonism', immediately alienated some who did not listen to her
full argument. Here and elsewhere she stressed that her ultimate
aim was for the sexes to work together effectually and in harmony
but only at the point where genuine respect existed would true
co-operation be possible.[45] Exactly how and when the transition
might take place from a successful realisation of the first condition
to the ideal harmony of the sexes is not explored. Indeed part of the
book's poor reception must be linked to the overwhelming focus
on the evils of the past and present and, as a result, a somewhat
pessimistic prognostication.

At times Elizabeth's emphasis on woman's empathy with peace
and need to extend a moral climate seems more suggestive of 'New
Feminism' and a belief in woman's 'natural' qualities than the equalitarian perspectives with which she was associated. Yet her thinking
went beyond a simple equality versus difference equation in that she
incorporated difference into her phased plan for equality. Some of
the material and arguments she had used before, whilst her chapter on the 'Ladies of the College' of Amen-Ra which discusses the
peremptory dismissal of ancient women's abilities by a smug British
Museum 'expert', was based on her brush with the Egyptologist Sir
Ernest Budge in 1922. Her use of history and literature ranged far
and wide: from Sappho to Wells, the one much praised, the other
equally damned. Wells retaliated in print, calling the book an artless
demonstration rather than an indictment of sex antagonism.[46]

Rebecca West noted in 1923 the 'modern timidity about mentioning that there is such a thing as sex-antagonism'.[47] Yet Elizabeth
was prepared to name, dissect and denounce it at a time when for
non-feminists, doing so suggested ingratitude. Even for equalitarian
feminists it implied a worrying subscription to sexual difference and
women's superiority (which Elizabeth explicitly denied). And Lady

Rhondda had her doubts. Whilst generally praising the book she nevertheless took issue with the claim that men's attitudes towards women's work were founded on sex antagonism.[48] Neither did she believe that sexism was as widespread as Elizabeth claimed. Lady Rhondda felt comforted by recent history which, she maintained, demonstrated the acquiescence rather than antagonism of men.

So, contemporaries voted with their feet. In its first three months *Ancilla's Share* sold a mere 300 copies. The publisher Hutchinson warned that 'it won't move without a name' though, according to her diary, a second edition did appear in October and, thanks to praise from the renowned American feminist Alice Paul, it was published in the States. But it was not anonymity alone which accounted for poor sales. Although fascinating for the late twentieth-century reader, Elizabeth's angry, audacious book did not suggest easy solutions to the deeply entrenched views it exposed. In the cautious, economically depressed post-war climate of the 1920s it was less disturbing to choose not to hear, let alone heed, such messages.

10

TIME IS WHISPERING

In March 1923 Elizabeth's new novel *Time Is Whispering*[1] found an appreciative audience. Before the end of the year it was in its sixth edition. Set just after the First World War, this mellow tale of friendship and love in rural England between a gruff old man who has given his best years to the Indian Civil Service and a middle-aged widow who becomes his tenant, seems, in tone at least, a world away from *Ancilla's Share*.

Dealing with the changes wrought by war and how memory is constructed, the book also contrasts the rootlessness of youth with the maturity of later years, the autumn of life (Florence suggested 'Autumn' as a title). It explores how two very different people, Sir Henry Ellerton and Judith Lathom, can so arrange their lives that companionship and harmony become possible. At first the directness and practicality of Judith, epitomised by her landsuit, are a revelation to Henry who seems to belong to another era. The book gently celebrates the development of feelings amongst those no longer young. Although they are shocked by the gossip they provoke and eventually marry, this decision is primarily prompted by their choosing,[2] for the first time in their lives, to use marriage to fit their own demands. By retaining their individual space and control they appreciate being together. The future lies with young women such as Kate, a former 'Government Instructor of Landwomen', and her partner Mary. Henry's former home becomes the basis for a new kind of life in rural England, a training place for women, some of whom will become head gardeners, bailiffs and farmers.

Throughout the book there are descriptions of apple cultivation which had become immensely popular. Elizabeth's own home had once been Becket's Farm and renowned for its Blenheim apples. Judith delights in turning her apple orchard into a livelihood. In 1919 when she began the book, Elizabeth was considering turning Backsettown into a self-supporting cider farm. This never happened but eight years later it did cease to be a private home. By this time, with the aid of her friends Pat Allen and Rachel Sharp who ran the Violet Nurseries on Henfield Common (and whose work Elizabeth would have had in mind when writing about the fictional Kate and Mary's venture), the land surrounding Backsettown had been purchased, adding to its privacy. It now became a place providing a brief 'Rest Pause' for overworked professional women and those with heavy domestic responsibilities.[3] It was Octavia and her close friend Dr Marjorie Hubert who suggested this to Elizabeth. Recognising that over-fatigue could result in serious illness they believed that a timely combination of proper rest and careful nourishment could prevent this. Their original idea even included a children's ultra-violet clinic. Initially sceptical, Elizabeth was soon won over. She had recently considered a mortgage and had been looking for a tenant. Although she wondered 'What would I do without Backset in the background?', there were financial and health considerations. Doctors had warned her about dampness and about chalk in the water. In 1926 she was ill with congestion of the lung.

It was eventually agreed that Octavia and Marjorie would rent the house, gardens, orchard, copse and outbuildings for three years initially, for which they would pay Elizabeth £100 annually. An Executive Committee met for the first time in September 1927 with Octavia's long-standing friend the Hon. Phyllis Ponsonby in the chair. Elizabeth attended the monthly meetings. Patrons included the Buxtons, Denmans, Pollocks, Hamiltons and Sybil Thorndike. Some alterations were made to the house, Dolly Yates Thompson paid for the installation of electricity and a matron and domestics were appointed. On 14 November Backsettown opened as a con-valescent home with a difference. Patients were discouraged from talking of illness. They ate home-grown vegetables and, thanks to the acquisition of a small herd of Jersey cows tended by two 'land girls', fresh dairy produce. The idea of meals on trays in the garden whenever the weather permitted was considered a novelty and aid to the recuperative powers of this tranquil atmosphere. Fees were kept as low as possible, initially between £4 4s and £8 8s weekly. Patients included mothers, nurses, social workers and writers. The first six months saw only sixteen patients but advertisements in the educational and medical press and *New Statesman* helped. So too did fund-raising garden parties and, at a low point in 1933, a Benefit for Backsettown and the New Sussex Hospital at the Theatre Royal, Brighton where Elizabeth's compatriot Ruth Draper performed sketches. At one of the Backsettown Twelfth Night parties Elizabeth recited the Prologue from *Admiral Guinea*. After operating at a loss, during the war Backsettown made a small profit and by 1944–5 had 163 patients. Elizabeth attended her last committee meeting in August 1949 but the Backsettown Trust which included Leonard Woolf continued to run the home as long as it was financially viable. It was finally sold in 1991.[4]

When the Backsettown experiment began Elizabeth bought a London home at 36, Albion Street on the north side of Hyde Park, a location intended to make it an attractive let if necessary. It proved to be too expensive to maintain yet not actually big enough to house all her books and possessions. She sold it as soon as possible and rented a flat at 6, Palace Gate. For the remaining twenty-five years of her life Elizabeth was not content to remain in one place, dividing her time in England between Brighton and London but also staying in America. Far more time than she wished was spent in hospitals and nursing homes in both countries.

The duality of this transatlantic life-style had already been reflected in her fiction, most notably in *Camilla* (1918) which moves in time and space between England and America. Partly set in the home of an old-established north country gentry family—Elizabeth was familiar with, for example, the vast Trevelyan estate in Northumberland—it also describes New York and Florida 'High Society'. Through Camilla's relationship with the all-American playboy Leroy and the quintessentially English Michael, Elizabeth probes national characteristics (the book was written during wartime) and expectations of behaviour. She exposes British assumptions about the vulgarity of the wealthy American and about American use of English, the subject of frequent discussion between Elizabeth and Florence.

It is, however, the English assurance, from centuries of social and cultural dominance, which especially fascinates her. Camilla defies the stereotype of the modern American woman in all but one respect. She is wealthy, never flashy, painfully silent rather than chatty—but she is divorced. Yet this divorce represents no simple equation of new world and new values. Camilla has been devastated by what her husband Leroy and his lover seem to take so lightly. She is a highly moral, even moralistic woman, whilst the English Nancarrows condone the adultery of Michael's sister in preference to the publicity of divorce.

Just before the end of the story Camilla seems to find her independence, to be determined not to live her life through men in future—there is even a brief condemnation of the term 'superfluous women'—yet after Camilla finally rejects the renewed superficial charms of Leroy, the reader is left with the likelihood that Camilla will marry her dependable Englishman. Such an ending came about as a result of pressure from the *Cosmopolitan* magazine which published the story in America. Elizabeth was told that circulation would suffer for months if Camilla did not remarry. 'Oh the quaint child of a public' she wrote in her diary but she knew better than to ignore such warnings. Camilla did not marry again in the novel but by showing her sailing home to England leaving Michael in New York, Elizabeth enabled the more traditional reader to envisage them ultimately in wedded bliss since Michael was bound to return to his own country and do the 'decent thing'. Yet at the same time, she did not totally surrender the enlightened Camilla since the patient Michael had first to wait for *her* to take the initiative and write to him, thus giving other readers some limited scope for an alternative scenario.

'There's something about a Florida pine-wood—well, when you've lived with one, you know' says the author in *Camilla*.[5] The novel describes rides in the woods and the appeal of Florida life. Chinsegut had 700 acres (280 hectares) of pine forest and 70 acres (28 hectares) of citrus fruits. Some of Elizabeth's happiest memories were of riding Dixie amongst the pines and 'through tangles of jessamine-laced live oak and palmetto, down to dim lakes where the cypresses stand in water … and never see a soul'.[6] Yet from her first visit to Chinsegut at Christmas 1905, Elizabeth's time there was also deeply troubled.

Margaret, Raymond and Elizabeth all had forceful personalities and were used to getting their own way. Elizabeth could never quite accept that Raymond had chosen to spend his life with Margaret rather than with his sister and in the process ignored her dream of a shared home. At the beginning of *Come And Find Me* the long dedicatory note to FB (Florence) written at Chinsegut in January 1906 resonates with Elizabeth's disillusionment: 'This was to be a place where my fellow-dreamer and I should not only rest, but having rested, work as never before.'[7] Margaret who, with Raymond, was deeply embroiled in Chicago politics and social work, could not comprehend Elizabeth's desire to stay on at Chinsegut after they had left. She speculated whether she was hard up so could not afford a hotel elsewhere. When Raymond was ill she thought it best not to worry Elizabeth but was then reproached since Elizabeth learned of Raymond's illness through the press. In truth, though, whatever Margaret did or didn't do, Elizabeth was likely to find fault. Margaret and Raymond had a particularly passionate, intense relationship and Raymond, who placed frankness before tactfulness, told his sister that he and his wife were closer than any two people in the world and that if it ever came to siding with one of them, he would be wholly with Margaret. Elizabeth acknowledged that it would be sad if a newly wed husband did not feel thus '& yet loneliness spread round me like a sea'.

Her diary became the receptacle for her embittered feelings. Elizabeth particularly resented the way in which her money was being spent but her repeated outrage at the cost she had to bear represented a way of articulating the loss of her brother as well as financial expense. It had originally been agreed by Raymond and his sister that she would lend $5,000 from her Zanesville bank fund for the purchase of 214 acres (86.5 hectares) including the house. When Raymond and Margaret married, Elizabeth ceded to Margaret by deed half of the original purchase as a wedding gift. She also agreed to contribute to living expenses about $300 annually and pay tax and insurance. Yet although Chinsegut was for many years only a holiday home for Raymond and Margaret, they devised elaborate plans for extension and renovation. In October 1905 Raymond informed Elizabeth that $4,000 had already been spent on work there and it would cost a further $25,000. Margaret had put in $3,000 and it would help if Elizabeth could invest $2,000 more. This turned into $5,000. Elizabeth resented the way that decisions were being made without consultation with her, decisions which she considered far too grandiose for a home which was not lived in for much of the year and was fast becoming a mockery of the simple retreat she had sought. The 'fortress and a sunny paradise' held out by Raymond was an enormous burden 'instead of a refuge from care'.

Margaret had inherited $600,000 from her father, much of this being spent on the Labour movement, yet Elizabeth who had to earn her living and could not visit very often was financing the improvements. Raymond was anxious not to look as though he were living off his wealthy wife (he did not dispel the widespread belief that he had made his fortune in Alaska). Two bathrooms, a kitchen wing, stables, servants' quarters and an observatory were added and more and more land was acquired, and planted. Chinsegut became an estate of 2,200 acres (890 hectares). Over time taxes increased dramatically. When Elizabeth protested at the way her money was being used, Raymond calmly offered to take the place off her hands—'as tho' that wd [*sic*] make all right'. In a long letter written to Florence in January 1906 (but never posted), Elizabeth spelt out her grievances. Margaret and Raymond were 'blithely indifferent to everyone else in the world' and it was indubitably Margaret's, not Elizabeth's, home. During her period of suffrage activity Elizabeth was busy in England but when she did escape to Florida she wondered why she had returned, 'All that I suffered here and thought I had laid aside comes alive again.'

Both Elizabeth and Margaret were respected figures. Margaret was president of the Women's Trade Union League from 1907 to 1922. A later president, Rose Schneiderman, wrote that 'No history of the American Labor movement would be complete without Margaret Dreier Robins'.[8] She became president of the first International Congress of Working Women in 1921 and has been hailed as 'The Progressive era's most energetic and articulate exponent of the rights of unskilled working women'.[9] Margaret's feminism was, however, predicated upon different beliefs and goals from Elizabeth's. She supported essentially separate roles for men and women. She had no child of her own but, according to her biographer, saw motherhood as a metaphor for female nature.[10] Working so tirelessly for the cause of other women, Margaret and Elizabeth were unable to help each other, personal rivalries sadly dogging their relations.

Several times during the First World War Elizabeth braved the Atlantic. Just before her 1915 trip two ships were blown up in the Channel. Raymond suggested buying Elizabeth out but she refused. In March 1917 she changed her mind but no action was taken since Raymond had been appointed acting head of the Red Cross Commission to Russia. There he personally witnessed the last two months of the Provisional Government and the Bolshevik Revolution, discussed American-Soviet relations with Trotsky and Lenin (who became his hero) and returned to America as Lieutenant-Colonel Robins, a convinced believer in co-operation with Communist Russia.

It was another six years before he saw his sister again. Raymond and Margaret were in England briefly in 1923. Elizabeth held a dinner party for them at the Ladies Athenaeum Club. Guests included Gilbert Murray, Lord Robert Cecil, the Bishop of St Albans, Lady Rhondda and Florence. Through Elizabeth they also met Lady Astor, Maude Royden, the Trevelyans, Ramsay MacDonald and the Pethick-Lawrences. Yet there was little chance for a real talk: 'He & I in London—& he might be better at the Pole.'

Two years later Raymond suggested that, at his expense, Elizabeth should bring Octavia to the winter sun of Florida to recover from pleurisy. The Robinses had recently made Chinsegut their permanent home and, anticipating his sister's reaction to changes, Raymond pleaded—'If you *will* to make things hitch they will probably hitch. … Let us try to be happy & simple & not be too critical or too wise.' The visit was not a success. Octavia was not fully recovered whilst Elizabeth was privately mourning the recent death of William Archer: 'Things long dead, as I had thought, rise up & look at me with the colour & inconsistency of life. Would I had been kinder.'

The visitors felt that Margaret resented their presence. The very English Octavia took offence at Margaret's marked pro-German stance and anti-British stories. Little incidents which signified assertion of control over space were magnified into major areas of resentment. In such an atmosphere Raymond's proposal that Elizabeth sell her part of the property (which, after all, she had once thought expedient) was seen as adding insult to injury. In her autobiography

Octavia claimed that she had never witnessed such jealousy or rudeness and begged to leave earlier than planned.[11]

On her return Elizabeth sent Raymond a very long, detailed letter itemising grievances and declaring that the twenty years since her purchase of Chinsegut had brought her little profit and much sorrow. The next few years were even more painful. Heavy financial losses and crippling increases in property tax meant that the most sensible solution for the Robinses was to deed Chinsegut to the nation. To do this a Deed of Quit Claim had to be agreed and signed by Elizabeth. She refused. Lawyers advised on both sides and Margaret's lawyers were keen to go to court but Elizabeth felt unable to take this step. She still primarily blamed Margaret but also had to recognise Raymond's role. Eventually after a year of pressure, agonising and hard negotiations, she signed. The settlement left Raymond and Margaret sole owners in return for the secured payment of $500 every six months for twenty-five years or until Elizabeth's death (one of her lawyer's objections had been that Elizabeth's life expectancy might only be about twelve years!). Gertrude Bell who had little sympathy for Raymond, understood: 'the most awful experience is the crumbling of an idol.'[12]

In the aftermath of the Wall Street Crash, Raymond's struggle to save the First National Bank of Brooksville (he was chairman) and the Depression resulted in Chinsegut being deeded to the Federal Department of Agriculture in 1932 as a wildlife sanctuary and an agricultural, horticultural and forestry experiment station. Today it is run by the University of South Florida. The house and hilltop remained Margaret and Raymond's for their lifetimes.

The settlement shook but did not sever the Raymond–Elizabeth tie. In 1930 after his wife Marie died, the gentle Vernon took an overdose but was revived. This prompted Elizabeth to visit him at Waverley Hills sanatorium near Louisville at Christmas. She saw Raymond briefly in New York *en route* to Kentucky, fearing that Margaret had 'innoculated' him with 'dread of my presence'. She noted that he looked older and more haggard. She was not in good health herself, requiring urgent dental treatment. At this point Raymond had not completed the Chinsegut deal with the government and feared that he would soon be forced to leave his home. He met Elizabeth again just before she sailed. He was profoundly depressed. She remarked on his 'staring eyes & tight mouth', understanding that the real fear was something he could not articulate, 'the thing that had been with him since childhood'. He had suffered a nervous breakdown in 1914 and another seven years later when he contemplated suicide. Now once more Elizabeth comforted her little brother. She was no longer writing novels but her diary description of their parting at the docks might easily be mistaken for her fiction:

> And he was gone into the covered gangway. He kept straight on … I felt dazed. I went back & ran to the deck above & then up to the still higher one—& the further I went the less I could see of the landing stage … I ran down again asking this one & that … I hurried on, crying inwardly & calling Raymond Raymond … people laughing & gesticulating … only no one heard my voice. I stood waving my handkerchief & he his while the ship drew slowly out & slowly turned … & I couldn't see him any more … there were only snowflakes in the air.

Once home, Raymond's letters ('YOU mean to me something apart from all others. YOU have been the longest LIGHT in my pathway, the *hidden treasure* in my heart for the most years') continued to play havoc with Elizabeth's emotions. At such a distance she felt particularly helpless when he wrote about nights full of terror and demons threatening his sanity, 'times of darkness when reason is blotted out'. He was on one of his punishing lecture tours, this one organised by the Allied Campaigners on behalf of the 'enforcement of the Constitution and the Outlawry of the Liquor traffic' and could expect up to four meetings daily. On leaving the platform he would feel numb, the 'mists of collapse around me'. In 1932 in his 179th city with 80 to go, he wrote: 'The release cannot be far ahead.'

It came on 3 September. On that date Raymond Robins disappeared. He had left New York supposedly *en route* to a meeting in Washington DC with President Hoover to discuss prohibition and the re-election campaign.[13] Raymond never arrived neither did Margaret hear from him. Soon 185 Special Agents of the Prohibition Bureau were searching for this outspoken supporter of prohibition. Rumours of sightings abounded. Many believed that bootleggers had got him, that he was being held by New York or New Jersey gangs or Florida rum runners. Some wondered whether Al Capone was holding him to ransom. There were tales of his being made to walk the plank. It transpired that he had received threatening calls in about a hundred of the cities he had toured the previous winter. After a month American and English newspapers reported that his disappearance was as baffling as the mystery of the Lindbergh baby. A desperate Elizabeth refused to face the press. Like Margaret she was convinced that he was still alive. She felt she understood her brother's need to escape, wondering if he had fled to the Soviet Union.

Still with no news of Raymond, on 12 October Elizabeth sailed to America. On board her liner, ten weeks after his disappearance, she received a cable announcing that he had been found. He had been living in the small mountain town of Whittier in North Carolina. Suffering from psychogenic amnesia, he had called himself Reynolds H. Rogers, a miner from Harlan County, Kentucky. He lived at a boarding house and spent his time prospecting and regaling locals with long speeches about world peace and the re-election of Hoover. A twelve-year-old boy recognised him from a photograph. Margaret's nephew John Dreier identified him but in return received no sign of recognition. Lisa von Borowsky, a young German woman who had come to Chinsegut in the mid-1920s as housekeeper, then gardener and became in effect one of the family, has recalled the extraordinary story of Margaret's reunion with her husband.[14] On hearing that Raymond had been found, Lisa drove Margaret to see him at a sanatorium in Asheville. Margaret spent many hours there but he did not know her, simply saying 'She's a lovely lady but she's not my wife.' Eventually Margaret felt that Raymond would be less agitated if she left. She asked him if, before she went, he would shake her hand. Lisa tells how the moment he touched Margaret, Raymond knew she was his wife. His memory returned.

Elizabeth appeared the next day, finding Raymond calm and grave. She also visited Vernon then briefly saw President Hoover at the White House to thank him for his exertions on Raymond's behalf. Once home Raymond recovered rapidly though the publicity of his amnesia was ultimately damaging to his reputation. He resumed lecturing and in 1933 returned to the Soviet Union on the eve of its recognition by President Roosevelt.

During her anxious weeks of awaiting news Elizabeth had turned to the notes about Alaska. Over the following months, with advice from her writer friend Marie Belloc Lowndes, she was 'bent with every good hour of my life' on the personal story of Raymond in those years. Some premonition of the future seems to have prompted her to write on 1 March 1933, 'No doubt now it will be a book unless R. prevents publication.'

In January 1934 Vernon died. The following month Elizabeth and Octavia sailed to America together. Elizabeth was anxious to obtain Raymond's endorsement of her book and secure a contract. The two women wisely stayed away from Chinsegut. According to Margaret's nephew Ted Dreier and Lisa von Borowsky, Elizabeth was deliberately kept away from there for some years.[15] Raymond now feared that Margaret was 'cracking' under the strain of the last few years. Octavia and Elizabeth stayed in Manhattan at the luxurious Plaza Hotel anticipating a handsome advance from Putnam's. Raymond visited, read the manuscript but was strangely silent about it. But on the third day Elizabeth wrote of 'the darkened skies'. Raymond refused to let it be published in his lifetime. An advance of $2,000 and a contract had to be turned down. Octavia described Elizabeth, who had worked on the book for sixteen months, as 'shattered and inconsolable'[16] and tried unsuccessfully to reason with Raymond. The papers announced that the novelist Elizabeth Robins had been called home early and the two women returned to Britain. The Woolfs had already agreed to publish *Raymond and I* but now had to undertake not to do so whilst Raymond was alive. It came out in 1956, Raymond having died in 1954, two years after his sister.

The year after Raymond's rejection of her manuscript Elizabeth was once more roused to concern for him. He fell whilst pruning a tree at Chinsegut, spent two months at hospital in Tampa and for the rest of his life was a paraplegic. Nevertheless, his mind remained active and he continued to express his political ideas verbally and on paper. He communicated with Elizabeth for many more years, increasingly indulging in fond reminiscences of their childhood.

During her visits to Chinsegut Elizabeth had got to know the black servants who kept the place going. In charge until his death in 1924 was Fielder Harris (Uncle Fielding), one of the people Raymond most admired. A former slave from South Carolina he had known Raymond since he was a boy and had awakened in him a lifelong interest in nature. A number of his relatives lived and worked on the estate. He was in the unusual position of being foreman with whites under him, a situation not well regarded in the deep south. The Ku Klux Klan was powerful in Hernando county where blacks outnumbered whites and it made its presence felt at local elections. In 1907 an incendiary fire burned down the stables.[17] Elizabeth noted over the years the undercurrent of hatred and fear which local white folk evinced. Although at times somewhat patronising about the black servants, she spent a lot of time talking to them, seems to have liked them and hoped that they 'might come to like us'. When in 1908 she took Fielder Harris to the races at Tampa she asked him to sit beside her. An official tried to pull him down. 'I have seldom felt more angry or more mortified' she wrote to David Scott. She was told that he could not sit with her. She immediately left and joined the segregated section for coloured people. This embarrassed Harris who left. Elizabeth wrote, 'The more I see of the dark people in these days the more I wonder at their patience with the whites. If our race doesn't mend its ways there will be an awful reckoning one of these times.'

From childhood Elizabeth was aware of the history of slavery and its connections with her family and home. Before her time the Old Stone House in Putnam had held monthly prayer concerts for abolition and in 1835 the renowned orator Theodore Weld, the American Anti-Slavery Society's agent for Ohio, had addressed abolitionists there.[18] A few months later Elizabeth's future home hosted the State Abolition Convention. Unlike Putnam settlers many Zanesville folk were of Virginian origin and although Ohio had prohibited slavery, they were in favour of it. They crossed the river and broke up the meeting. During a further convention in 1839 some damage was done to the Old Stone House and barns were set on fire. Ten years before Elizabeth's birth the ex-slave and best-known black abolitionist, Frederick Douglass, spoke at the local church.

Elizabeth's mother's family had been slaveholders in Virginia and then Kentucky. Her mother's tales of the trouble she had in persuading her trustee to allow her to manumit her slaves and as a young woman saving to buy the liberty of one slave a year, apparently made a deep impression on her daughter.[19] In *The Open Question*

Elizabeth exposes the wage slavery economy of the north as well as the prejudices of the south.[20] The father of the family into which Mrs Gano's son marries is a Bostonian who edited an abolitionist newspaper. Elizabeth has the southerner Mrs Gano visit them and the Ladies Domestic Philanthropic Society (Coloured Registry Office). She exposes their lack of care for the former slaves whom they place but do not employ themselves. Mrs Gano's beliefs are predicated upon an assurance of racial superiority but she prides herself in having been a good employer and resents the north having dictated to the south.

Tensions between north and south surface in several novels. In *The Florentine Frame* (1909) in which the wealthy Isabella Roscoe and her daughter both fall in love with the same young playwright, the latter is from South Carolina. His narrow plantation outlook contrasts with the urbane New York widow. He remains horrified and ashamed that a predecessor had seduced a black servant who then had his child but his shame is not for the victim. He is somewhat taken aback when Isabella does not empathise with his views but shows concern for the 'coloured people'.[21]

In *The Open Question* Mrs Gano had declared *Uncle Tom's Cabin* to be 'A great, bad book'.[22] In 1909 Elizabeth tried it out on the young David Scott and as she suggests in her Preface for a Bath Classics edition of this phenomenally popular story, it went down well. Some years before Elizabeth's birth Harriet Beecher Stowe had in fact visited the church where the Robins family worshipped in Putnam, across the road from the Old Stone House. Her brother was its pastor and as a young woman Elizabeth heard Henry Ward Beecher preach at his Brooklyn church.

The book's success can be explained by locating it as part of the popular domestic genre of nineteenth-century books so widely read by women. It elevated motherhood, regardless of race, with its message of salvation through maternal love. In Jane Tompkins's words, 'it rewrites the Bible as the story of a Negro slave'.[24] Yet critics have pointed out (since Elizabeth's time) that Stowe's attack on the inhumanity of slavery involved substituting an alternative racist stereotype of blacks as passive victims. As Clare Midgley puts it, Stowe became a symbol of white woman's philanthropy and missionary power to liberate and Christianise grateful black slaves so that ultimately the book offered most to white mid-nineteenth-century abolitionists, giving them a role in combating slavery.[25]

Elizabeth was inspired by neither Christianity nor domesticity. She did, however, have some residual identification with Kentucky and her links with Florida made her increasingly interested in the 'black & white question'. She had just met in New York the black educator Booker T. Washington, principal of the Tuskegee Institute, Alabama. A few months after writing her Preface she discussed with William Archer his rather reactionary essay on race written after touring the southern states. Her 1908 Preface suggests the naïveté of white Americans giving their former slaves manumission papers and simultaneously waving them off the premises, washing their hands of responsibility. Only by 'victories in the mind and heart of man' would true emancipation come. Elizabeth viewed current race relations as America's most serious problem. Her Preface referred to the 'lingering poison' of recent lynchings and race riots.

In some respects Elizabeth can be viewed as progressive for her time. She had refused to read out the word 'nigger' in Henley's Prologue to *Admiral Guinea* in 1897.[26] When the Lyceum Club's sponsorship of the black academic turned propagandist W.E.B. Du Bois was opposed by Madame Thayer, Elizabeth intervened and in June 1911 introduced him with a speech (which unfortunately has not survived) at the club's dinner. Proud of the Wilberforce connection, though she does not seem to have known of William Wilberforce's opposition to Ladies Associations and women's involvement in the politics of anti-slavery, she invited Du Bois to Sussex to meet Octavia.[27] In 1894–6 he had been a classics professor at Wilberforce University, a college for blacks in Ohio.

In a letter to Raymond in the early 1900s Elizabeth explained how she wanted to write a book set in the American south which dealt with race and in which 'I would try to do thoroughly the negro question. I would have a great lynching scene & a study of the obscure & horrible passions of the mob.' In some of her writings she makes analogies between women's dependence on men and conditions of slavery.[28] Yet whereas she was wary of male attempts to speak on behalf of women she seemed to feel that she could speak for black people. Similarly she wondered about doing a book on Jewishness, discussing this with her German Jewish friend Lady Lewis with whom she spent a holiday in Switzerland whilst the Dreyfus trial was taking place in France.[29]

Her papers include a wide range of material about black America ranging from the offensive, reactionary *Southern Symposium* with its advocacy of Caucasianism and warnings about miscegenation to articles in the *International Socialist* and *The Crisis*, the journal edited by Du Bois for the National Association for the Advancement of Colored People.[30] Elizabeth also possessed a number of Booker T. Washington's pamphlets and a copy of his famous 1895 address to the Cotton States and International Exposition at Atlanta, Georgia which has been interpreted both as a consummate exercise in racial diplomacy and as an abysmal surrender of black civil and political rights to the forces of racism. The more she read, however, and the more she talked to people such as the psychologist William James (Henry's brother) who had addressed black students in the south, so she began to appreciate the complexities and to change her mind about writing a book on race.[31] In her eighties she interviewed in her New York hotel 'possibly our ablest negro-educator', Mordecai Wyatt Johnson, president of Howard University DC. They discussed integrationist policies. A few years later, after a trip to India, Johnson lectured in Philadelphia. Martin Luther King Jnr heard him and so became interested in the teachings of Gandhi.

Elizabeth did not write the book she had outlined to Raymond but her last novel *The Secret That Was Kept* (1926) incorporated some of her views. It was whilst staying with Vita Sackville-West and Harold Nicolson that she decided on its plot. Originally conceived as a fast-moving story which could be written quickly, serialised and become a play, it was initially entitled 'The Millionaire Father'. For the first time her friend Tom Wells, editor of Harper and Brothers, gave his wholehearted approval. He was more enthusiastic about the subject and sales than its author: 'I am not very happy about this book—it isn't my kind' she wrote in 1924. Her doubts were justified when it appeared in the spring of 1926 to little critical acclaim.

Set in Florida, its subtitle is 'A Study in Fear'. On one level it is a fast-moving thriller with blackmail, embezzlement, a feigned death, revenge, mistaken identity and murder. June Purdey's fear of her husband finding her helps sustain the suspense but underlying this are other kinds of fears. And it was these fears which really concerned

Elizabeth rather than the story-line. There is the white woman's fear of rape by one of the 'darkies'. It is also pointed out that white men who don't even notice black servant girls by day have no fear of taking advantage of them by night. This was the time of a revived Ku Klux Klan—claiming four million members by 1924—and of reactions to the spread of lynching and to proposals to legislate against it. Elizabeth was well aware of 'the corroding fear of the negro', a belief which she argues (elsewhere) is groundless; 'danger if danger there be, is the danger we white folk bring there.' She believed that the very existence of white prosperity in such places was dependent 'on those negroes we despise & to whom we so successfully teach our lesson of Fear that they are deserting (i.e. leaving us)'. The horror which so disturbs June at the beautiful Asseola, a sort of Chinsegut, is entirely of white people's making.

Yet all this is tempered by Elizabeth's habit of representing the black servants' speech in 'broken English'. Such a device infantalises and reduces (it is also used in the dialogue of the inhabitants of the Upper Yukon in her 'Go to Sleep' tales for children). The effect is exacerbated since those presented as the dominant English or white Americans do not have their particular forms of pronunciation thus transcribed. In *Camilla* (1918) the eponymous heroine loves the 'kindly, smiling coloured folk'[32] here unfortunately rendered picturesque and also, through their speech 'comical'—the Fielder Harris character Uncle Pax utters words such as 'I disremember'. Yet in *The Secret That Was Kept* Elizabeth suggests that the generation of late nineteenth-century black servants (the book is set in the 1890s) hold very different views from those of their predecessors. They denounce as 'old trash' the Plantation songs and stereotypes which whites persist in associating with them. Elizabeth feels that the educated negro holds some hope for the future but the poor whites, the Crackers, represent the 'depressing' side of civilisation.

A significant portion of the introduction to *Ancilla's Share* is devoted to 'the gathering smoke of the dark races' discontent'.[33] Elizabeth criticises the French practice of using black conscripts to fight white men's battles, refers to the humiliation and exploitation of black South Africans and discusses the Jamaican-born Marcus Garvey's plan for redeeming Africa from white colonial rule. She also points out that if a man of mixed blood shows impressive qualities they are ascribed to his white blood whereas if he is deemed evil or weak 'the darker strain is held responsible'. She was conscious of the sinister influence of eugenics which, through the 'production of fine offspring by improvement of inherited qualities', sought to further the 'science of the race' and she had attended a lecture on the subject in 1922. At the end of the book she declares 'what childishness is this about race-purity'.

Yet underlying this writing there remains an essential belief in white supremacy. In her critique of the determination to deny black people a share in conditions which make for civilised education, not only is her benchmark of civilisation that of the white western world but the impact of British imperialism upon her reasoning is also revealed: 'We can still lead all the peoples of the globe … we can still instruct, administer and reap reward by divine right of a high order of intelligence applied through goodwill.' What matters is not just repudiating the wrong form of leadership bred by competing in violence but also learning how best to lead and enlighten because only by this will pre-eminence be maintained and white nations avoid being overrun by 'coloured hordes'.[34] In her Alaskan diary Elizabeth had recorded talking to an Episcopalian clergyman who told her he preferred working among the natives to working with the whites. She added:

> Doesn't that stamp a man? To be content to spend his life in a work in which satisfaction came to him not from people of intelligence, inheritors of the future—but from the Indians! *They* give him his only reward.

Such breathtaking assumptions about him, them and the future were quite possible for someone who had come to see the 'Other' through the complacent lens of late Victorian imperial Britain.

Edward Said has shown how allusions to the fact and meanings of empire saturate the British novel of the nineteenth and early twentieth centuries.[35] British imperialism is central to the structure and understanding of *Time Is Whispering* yet ostensibly the story is about post First World War southern England. The experience of colonialism is, however, what has shaped and embittered Henry. He who has not only exercised authority during his years in India but also condoned atrocity by others, now learns to listen to another voice. India, so far away, is made omnipresent. It is something that Henry and Judith share since she too has a past in India. The implicit relationship between the world of Ellerton's estate and India was something Elizabeth had absorbed by osmosis from so many years of living in England. The novel applauds the notion of service and the imperial ideal but, whilst still accepting leadership, suggests the need for the 'increasingly greater part which others must be allowed, encouraged to play'.[36] Aided by Judith, Henry seeks to redeem some of his difficult past via a study of Indian economics.

Although her accounts of life in India in the novel are retrospective, during the time that Elizabeth was writing her book India witnessed constitutional reforms, riots and the emergence of Gandhi as the leader of a new all-India mass nationalism. At the time of its publication he was in prison. Elizabeth explains in the novel that Henry's fictional work had come 'too late to smooth the transit from the old order to the new in the East' but the philosophy of government it advocated could, it is argued, help 'the younger world in Europe'.

For her background information Elizabeth had consulted William Archer's brother Colonel Charles Archer who had spent thirty years in India as the chief resident British official in mountainous Baluchistan. Interestingly, in the same year as Elizabeth began her book, William Archer wrote his play *The Green Goddess* set in the Himalayas, a melodrama in which 'British decency outwits foreign cunning'.[37] It became a smash hit in America and Britain, was made into a silent film then remade as a talkie (the first Elizabeth saw). Archer, like the fictional Henry Ellerton, believed that he knew what was best for India. In 1917 he wrote *India and the Future*. Despite its title, it was an anachronistic, patronising study based on only five months in India.

Elizabeth wrote various scenarios for stories centred around racial conflict. One concerned a man of mixed parentage who erects a monument to his black mother. It is in the form of an angel supposed to symbolise her white soul. His daughter is taken to see this but town ruffians have painted it black. In attempting to consider the difficulties facing such families, one of whom she had known in Zanesville many years earlier, Elizabeth fails to escape from connoting white with true goodness, purity, etc., and black as something destructive.

Her first sustained attempt at fiction had been a novella based on her experience as a North American visiting Central America escorted by a South American. Originally entitled 'The Peruvian Bark' but renamed *Under the Southern Cross*, this novella draws upon her diary accounts of the relaxing journey she made in 1888 on the SS *José* from California to New York via Panama, after a punishing theatrical tour. The carefully written diary is punctuated with descriptions of luxuriant scenery, tortilla-making and a well-connected Peruvian who attempted to make 'fast & furious love'. In her story, which is written in the present tense and is chiefly in dialogue, the young woman is called Blanche, her whiteness and sense of a superior race and culture constantly and uncritically emphasised even to the point of describing 'evil looking natives' in Acapulco and comparing one old woman to a chimpanzee. She is reading the classic account of the sixteenth-century Spanish conquistadores (written by an American), Prescott's *History of the Conquest of Mexico*. The Peruvian, as he is described for most of the journey though he is of European descent and called Baron de Bach, is ridiculed via his poor command of English and malapropisms. He is made to utter at every conceivable opportunity, 'I loaf you'. There is a scene on shore where Blanche struggles against his unwanted advances in a dark street at night but the way that he has been set up as a comic figure makes the one attempt to become serious and turn the story into a cautionary tale fall somewhat flat. What tends to linger for the modern reader is less the attempted seduction than the crude characterisation with its depiction of 'them' and 'us'.

Although written in 1889 in London, it was not until 1907, the year of the publication of the markedly different novel *The Convert*, that *Under the Southern Cross* appeared in print. It was published in book form only in the States where it was illustrated and packaged as a romance. In Britain it appeared in *Cassell's Magazine* the following year.

An early unpublished story 'Pengarnack's Necklace' also presents the 'foreigner' as threatening. Phil Pengarnack, a 'very un-English-looking creature', Cornish but of Egyptian descent, makes the English heroine feel that 'he was a being not only of another race, but of another order from myself'. She opts for Norman with his 'thorough Englishness' but Pengarnack gets his revenge through his Egyptian necklace and supernatural powers.

Elizabeth occupied an ambivalent position as a long-term American resident in England. Although never naturalised she tended to identify herself with the English. She not infrequently wrote 'England' when 'Britain' would have been more accurate and sometimes conflated the diverse cultural experiences of the British Isles. She adopted standard English spelling in her diary (though a long spell in the States in the early 1940s saw a reversion to American spelling) and she saw herself as part of the English intelligentsia. She claimed that her friends had forgotten she was not English and that she felt a stranger at parties at the American Embassy. She lived in England for longer than many people's entire lifetime.

Sometimes her disparate worlds came together. In the mid-1920s her childhood friend Julia Blandy visited and together they attended the Women Citizens' International Luncheon, hearing Ramsay MacDonald, Lady Astor and Mrs Fawcett speak. Elizabeth became one of eight women in Britain on the International Advisory Council of the (American) National Woman's Party.

She remained interested in politics, attending a number of Commons debates in the inter-war years. Despite her friendship with the colliery owner Sir Hugh Bell, during the General Strike it was Maude Royden who most impressed her with her plea for understanding the miners' position and defending them as brothers. Elizabeth believed that the strike terms 'most cruelly depress the men who ran that great risk out of class sympathy & pride'. Her political friends had become Labour MPs and Cabinet ministers, figures such as Frederick Pethick-Lawrence, Margaret Bondfield, Ellen Wilkinson and Dr Thomas (Tom) Jones. The first chapter of Thomas Jones's *Rhymney Memories* is deliberately called 'The Magnetic South'.[38]

On the day that Elizabeth heard the King's abdication speech in 1936 she attended a 'Peace or Barbarism' talk by George Lansbury at the Dome in Brighton, sitting on the platform behind him. Her diary became punctuated with fears of the savagery of Hitler's actions. She had many Jewish friends. Elizabeth and Octavia subscribed to Baldwin's fund for Jewish refugees and in 1938 requested that instead of giving them Christmas presents their friends subscribe instead to this fund.

The 1930s were sad years for Elizabeth both publicly and privately. Increasingly rheumatic and suffering old and new pains she was in poor health for much of the time. By the end of 1939 she weighed only just over 6 stone (38 kg). She had to do exercises to try to correct her increasingly humped back. Weeks were spent in hospitals or nursing homes consulting doctors and dentists and recuperating from surgery, all of which was a drain on finances particularly since there were no more novels (bar the book form of the children's story *Prudence and Peter*) to pay the bills after 1926. Temporary relief came in cures in Switzerland. A sense of racing against time made her anxious not to lose any opportunity to work: '*must not play with time while I am fit for writing.*' Her idea of taking things easy was to sort out her massive notes and correspondence. Back in 1919 she had written, 'To be a successful old woman—that's the great achievement.'

Her independence was fiercely guarded. When, in 1927, wearing her doctor's hat, Octavia had tried to persuade Elizabeth to live permanently at Montpelier Crescent, Brighton, she had rebelled. She couldn't live under such bondage and wouldn't have decisions made for her. Although she actually now spent most of her time in Brighton, she would not relinquish London completely. In 1937 the Montpelier Crescent house was sold to Brighton Corporation and Octavia then rented it from them. Elizabeth insisted on paying her when she was in residence.

In the 1930s she wrote an unpublished study of Annie Besant the socialist, theosophist, president of the Indian National Congress[39] and orator *par excellence*. It is not difficult to see the appeal. Both women lived long lives with a range of catholic interests. Both were successful in very different kinds of undertakings, were internationalists, performers, thinkers, committed to women's rights and indefatigable in their addiction to work. They had friends in common such as W.T. Stead and both women had spoken at the same vast WSPU gathering at the Albert Hall. Recoiling against European dictatorships Elizabeth used Annie Besant's dedication to liberty to demonstrate the horrors of curbing freedom. She even included a passage on Ataturk's reforms. In her 1936 diary she wrote:

If the world had had after the war an Annie Besant 30 years
younger & not involved in the clouds of mysticism what she & all
those other war-forged woman-weapons might have done. There
were armies waiting for leadership to Peace.

Elizabeth also began thinking and writing once more about her early
years. She tried reworking her Rocky Mountain story helped by the
prolific writer and Labour politician Mary Agnes Hamilton but this
came to nothing. With some difficulty she got her correspondence
with Henry James published then turned to the first twelve years of
her life in England. She divided this into two, rather unequal, parts
focusing on the first volume which took her up to 1890. She managed to interest Virginia Woolf in this project. The Woolfs' Sussex
home Monk's House at Rodmell was not far away and Elizabeth and
Octavia, who was distantly related to Virginia, had got to know them
socially. Virginia's half-brother Gerald Duckworth had been treasurer
of the New Century Theatre in the 1890s and Elizabeth had also
known her mother with the 'Madonna face' and habit of uttering
totally unexpected comments.[40] She told Virginia this on their first
meeting in 1928 when Virginia won the Femina Vie Heureuse Prize
for *To the Lighthouse*. Virginia loathed the occasion but felt it was at
least made bearable by conversation with 'little Miss Robins, like a
red-breast'.[41]

The Woolfs published *Ibsen & The Actress* and, not long before her
death, Virginia confessed to Octavia that she felt Elizabeth to be so
great a writer that she was surprised that her own opinions mattered
to her.[42] Since Elizabeth viewed Virginia as the greatest living writer
of prose she was thrilled when Virginia responded positively to her
work. Virginia appears to have enjoyed reading Elizabeth's manuscript
of her reminiscences and suggested a number of titles including the
one finally adopted, *Both Sides of the Curtain*.[43] Although it was never
mentioned, this title had actually already been used in the memoirs
of Elizabeth's erstwhile actress friend, Genevieve Ward. Neither was
the title of its unpublished sequel 'Whither & How?' totally original.
Charles Webster Leadbeater and Annie Besant had edited a theosophical study in 1913 entitled *Man: Whence, How and Whither*. When
publishers began rejecting *Both Sides*, Virginia declared them 'stone
blind'[44] though the Hogarth Press never took it on. Virginia confessed

to Ethel Smyth that reading Elizabeth's memoirs 'on a scale of one year to 500 pages' was like following an insect across an Ordnance Survey map but 'very fascinating'.[45] Publishers were concerned about its narrow focus and concentration on events and people no longer in vogue. But it was eventually and fittingly published by Heinemann in 1940.

Elizabeth was a remarkable mixture of ancient and modern. In 1925 she had had her hair bobbed and five years later had it cut short. In her late seventies she decided to try air travel. Marjorie Hubert who was a mere forty-four was nervous of accompanying her but Elizabeth tried to laugh her out of her fears. She flew to Switzerland from Croydon aerodrome having found a less anxious travelling companion and enjoyed a perfect flight.

She continued going to the theatre, enjoying modern plays by J.B. Priestley and Noël Coward as well as the classics. On the centenary of Ibsen's birth she attended a dinner held by the Norwegian Ambassador. The guests included Forbes-Robertson, Mrs Patrick Campbell, Shaw ('Shaw talked Shaw'), Gosse and Lilian Bayliss. Mrs Pat was still acting and Elizabeth saw her and John Gielgud in *Ghosts*. Her favourite Mrs Alving was, however, Sybil Thorndike, Florence Bell's protégée. Elizabeth and Florence never willingly missed a play starring Sybil Thorndike.

Elizabeth had some reservations about the cinema. The ex-actress was critical of 'the failure with the human voice' when she attended 'talkies', feeling that actors' voices jarred. She was, however, involved in various plans to make films out of her novels. There were protracted negotiations over screen rights for *The Magnetic North*, *The Messenger* and *My Little Sister* (see Chapter 8). Florence and Elizabeth also worked on cinema synopses of *The Secret That Was Kept*. She received $5,000 for the film rights for *A Dark Lantern*. The Realart Picture Corporation's film of 1920 made the story contemporary, the heroine having a breakdown after the war.[46]

Elizabeth recognised the potential of radio. In 1922 the BBC had begun broadcasting on a regular basis on the Home Service. Five years later and a year after Gertrude Bell's death they contacted Sir Ernest Benn (who published Gertrude's letters) for suggestions for a speaker for a fifteen-minute talk about her life.[47] Benn mentioned five possibilities, one of whom was Elizabeth. He felt that, if available, she could do an excellent job. Elizabeth had written a lengthy review of Gertrude's travel books and as a close friend, writer and proven public speaker, was an ideal choice. Elizabeth panicked slightly, worrying that 'I've nothing to cast as yet' just four days before her September 1927 broadcast. In fact Hilda Matheson assistant director for talks declared it to be one of the best talks she ever heard on the radio. Elizabeth told Florence that this new experience was very alarming ... an awful inevitability about it ... as if one were writing a draft on brass'.

Hilda Matheson was a key figure in shaping the BBC programmes policy in these pioneer days, an advocate of freedom of expression and former secretary to Lady Astor's Consultative Committee on Women's Organisations. The following year she arranged for Elizabeth to give a wireless talk on Ibsen. 'Poor as [the] stuff is, it's speakable & the authorities are pleased. A ton's weight is lifted' wrote Elizabeth.

A more ambitious broadcasting plan was conceived after the outbreak of war. At the invitation of the BBC Elizabeth visited Langham Place in 1940 to discuss how she might appeal to Americans via the wireless. She was persuaded to produce something which could be published in the *New York Times* then broadcast. Air raid warnings in Brighton necessitated some of her notes being written in the basement by candlelight. In 'To the Home-Keepers in America from the Home-Keepers in England' Elizabeth pointed out that it was the ordinary person who was going to count most in this war. She painted a picture of a dramatically changed country, 'sandbags smothering some of that beauty'. She emphasised the spirit of fearlessness and the degree of preparedness in Britain in the face of 'a threat of slavery more abject than ever darkened Africa'. This Nazi-Fascist war was not only being waged against the great armies but also involved women and children. She challenged Americans on the threat of invasion: 'You think you know: you are not on the threshold of realisation.' What did they propose doing to keep decency alive in the world?

Events, however, overtook Elizabeth's broadcasting plans. The American Embassy began urging those Americans remaining in Britain to return home whilst it was still possible. Although Elizabeth's definition of home was different she still refused to become naturalised.

She became persuaded that she might be of greater use to Britain by becoming something of a publicist in America. So, in July 1940 a month before her seventy-eighth birthday, she left Britain. She insisted on taking with her the second volume of her reminiscences. No printed or even manuscript material was allowed out of the country but fortunately Tom Jones got clearance for this. She flew to neutral Portugal. David Scott was unable to meet her on landing as planned, it was oppressively hot in Lisbon which was crammed with refugees and she had little cash. After a few nights in a hotel she was moved by a doctor to the British hospital. Shortly afterwards she travelled on by Clipper to New York City where she stayed at the Cosmopolitan Club. Her letters tell how she was 'consumed with homesickness'.

Exactly a year after Britain declared war, Elizabeth wrote 'The Spirit of the People', incorporating much of the material from her BBC project.[48] She stressed that until 'the days of enlightenment' people believed in peace. She refered to pacifist friends who found themselves changing since 'There was a quality in this war that was new in the world'. She ended with the plea that 'America must defend herself—from being too late to defend herself from being part of the graveyard of good intentions'.[49] It was, of course, not until December 1941 that the United States entered the war.

Feeling ill and a stranger in her homeland, Elizabeth's identification was with her adopted home. Intellectually she was well aware of the 'epidemic obsession with the idea of nationality' but the pamphlet she wrote in February 1941 just three days after hearing of Dolly Yates Thompson's death, presented this 'free soul' of 'oak-like Englishness' as a symbol of her nation and time. Published by the Hogarth Press, it was entitled *Portrait of a Lady or The English Spirit Old and New*.

When Raymond saw Elizabeth he was shocked at her appearance. Her loss of weight had made her fear that she had cancer but tests proved otherwise. In 1941 the vertebral fracture caused by skeletal decalcification resulted in a surgical brace being made for her back. A brief visit to Chinsegut early in 1942 did nothing to lift her spirits. Margaret had had a stroke and serious heart attack and the invalid Raymond devoted all his remaining energy to either his wife or his typewriter. Elizabeth declared that she had never before felt such a stranger there.

She divided the next few years between staying in academic environments and in Maine where she spent a couple of summers close to Mary Dreier's home. In the spring of 1942 she became the resident guest at the Alumnae House at Vassar. It was an appropriate venue. Founded by an English brewer Matthew Vassar, the college had opened in 1865 at Poughkeepsie on the Hudson, devoted to giving women as good a Liberal Arts education as men. Here Elizabeth managed to do some writing and even lectured to the students on Ibsen. In June, however, she fell and cracked a pelvic bone facing what she called the worst days of her life since George had died. She had a blood transfusion in a New York hospital. Her plans to return to Vassar were thwarted by the government requisitioning her residence.

Her next move was to the Princeton Inn where she made a number of friends attached to the prestigious university. In 1940 she had lunched with the New Yorker Alice Duer Miller whose emotive epic poem *The White Cliffs*, about an American woman who marries an Englishman and has to face the losses and horrors of war, appeared in Britain in 1941 and within three years was in its twenty-third edition having sold over 200,000 copies. Miller died in August 1942 and, spurred on by Octavia's postal encouragement, Elizabeth now decided to write about her. She did research in Princeton University Library and was scheduled to give an Address on Alice Duer Miller at the university in the spring of 1943 but illness intervened.

Although aged eighty, she still felt that she must take herself in hand. Despite further illnesses necessitating a special diet, injections and drugs which made her drowsy, she pushed herself to work whenever at all feasible. A couple of years later she admitted that she had overdone things and been merciless to herself at this time. Letters from Octavia (some cut by the censor) were amongst her few comforts but often the news they contained was disturbing. The previous year she had learned from Octavia about the circumstances surrounding Virginia Woolf's death.[50] Desperate about her mental state, Leonard had asked Octavia to see Virginia professionally (she was not her official doctor). Suffering from influenza Octavia did so but within twenty-four hours of consulting her, Virginia had disappeared. Octavia was devastated by her suicide. Elizabeth was badly shaken. Now the bombing raids on the southern coast of England gave Elizabeth further cause for anxiety.

In October 1944 whilst staying at a Manhattan hotel, Elizabeth discovered that if she returned immediately to New Jersey she could be in time to register to vote in Princeton. The woman who had fought all those years ago for suffrage in Britain, lost no time in boarding a train. She stood for over an hour on the steps of the town hall and finally, for the first time, was placed on the electoral roll. Sadly, when it came to the Presidential elections the following month, Elizabeth was too ill to vote.

As soon as war ended she arranged for her eleven trunks and two suitcases to be shipped home. Her luggage was rifled at Liverpool docks and the Alice Duer Miller manuscript which she had recently broadened into a study of the new and alien America she had found on her return (entitled 'The Returned Native') went missing. Meanwhile, once she had secured a passport and visa, Elizabeth had left, travelling in pitch dark in a cramped aeroplane. Octavia was at Croydon to greet her on 17 June 1945.

At first, simply being back and having Octavia near, gave Elizabeth a 'kind of suspended happiness'. The previous year she had written that Octavia was the best she had met 'on the long road'. Octavia returned the compliment, 'day in, day out I always refer my thoughts to you. ... You've been the beacon, the searchlight, the inspiration over all the years. ... And you must feel this always—distance makes no difference.' On the envelope Elizabeth added later 're-read in sadness 24 March 1946 but kept in hope'.

Returning home was disorientating. Distance, or, rather, the lack of it, did make a difference. Frequently in pain, Elizabeth was increasingly intolerant and unprepared to make allowances for the changes war and time had brought. Although he admired her talents Leonard Woolf believed Elizabeth to be 'a dedicated egoist' with a 'vampire nature' which drained the strength and vitality of the young and made her increasingly 'invincible, indefatigable, imperishable'.[51] In fact Elizabeth felt far from invincible—her acute consciousness of incipient mortality accounted for much of her irascibility—but she was determined to put up a good fight and, twenty years older than Leonard, could still exhaust him. In his autobiography he describes his state after three hours of conversation at the bedside of this frail old woman in the last years: 'I have often staggered out of the house shaky, drained and debilitated.'[52]

Octavia was now in her late fifties and in constant demand at Backsettown, where she was used to staying most nights. Elizabeth felt herself to be the forgotten owner there. When Octavia casually suggested that she might soon give up General Practice and concentrate on working at Backsettown, Elizabeth felt as though all the support she had given Octavia over the years was being negated. In her autobiography Octavia ascribes Elizabeth's disillusionment to the loss of her manuscript.[53] Certainly her inability to write (for this and other reasons) when work had always been so central to her very being, was devastating but her sense of personal displacement was also profound. She had long dreamed of coming home, feeling that she no longer belonged in America. Her dependence on Octavia was increased by her less intense relationship with Raymond in these years. In 1949 shortly before a spell in Guy's Hospital she wrote: 'If only O. had been able to see any possible work-power in the woman who came "home" after the war.' 'O' was, however, used to dealing with elderly patients and treated Elizabeth accordingly. The situation was not helped by Elizabeth harbouring little discontents (as she had in the past against Margaret), failing to articulate them at the outset then torturing herself when she could contain her anger no longer. The last years of the diary are poignant and melodramatic. In 1948 she wrote, 'God what I need is a friend.' Now that she could no longer be a creative writer she dramatised her daily life and in the process hurt herself and those closest to her.

Occasionally there were stirrings of the old spirit. She saw Sybil Thorndike once more on the stage. Molly Trevelyan became her confidante. She reminded Elizabeth of Florence and lived too far away to upset her. Elizabeth stayed with the Trevelyans at Wallington in Northumberland and a few weeks before her eighty-fifth birthday expressed a desire to attend the Miners' Gala in Morpeth. She sat on the speakers' platform with the Trevelyans, enjoying most of all the speech by Aneurin Bevan. The Labour victory had been one of the few changes in recent years which had not dismayed her.

In August 1950, needing a new brace, she flew to the States with Dr Martindale (who was going to a conference). Thanks to cousins in Pittsburgh they attended one of the early sessions of the United Nations. In Florida she saw Raymond for what proved to be the last time and was with him on his birthday. Yet although he was now widowed (Margaret had died in 1945), it was not an easy visit. Mary Dreier wrote afterwards to Raymond, 'perhaps the kindest thing is to write that she is very old and has lost her sense of proportion and is also somewhat confused'.[54]

Elizabeth's diary now became more cryptic and sporadic. There were no entries for 1946 or 1950 and the handwriting was increasingly shaky. As with many elderly people, in her last years she became obsessive about 'tidying' her life, rereading and cataloguing as much as possible of the vast accumulation of papers gathered for so long. She had always been a hoarder. She left 102 packing cases and Molly found twenty-five black hats, all in perfect condition.[55] Leonard Woolf who sorted through her possessions was convinced that she never destroyed any letters, documents or scraps of paper.[56] In the autumn of 1951 Elizabeth fell downstairs. No bones were broken but she was confined to her room and never really recovered. On 8 May 1952, the year when another E.R. succeeded to the throne, Bessie Robins, child of the American Civil War, died in Brighton in her ninetieth year.

APPENDIX 1

Plays in which Elizabeth Robins acted in Great Britain, 1888–1902

DATE (day, month, year)	PLAY	PART	VENUE	OTHER INFO
20/10/88	*Cheiromancy* by William Poel	Mrs Horton	St George's Hall matinée, London	semi-private comedietta
Dec. 1888	*The Merchant of Venice* by Shakespeare	Portia	Exeter, Devon	Frank Benson production
17/1/89	*Little Lord Fauntleroy* by F. Hodgson Burnett	Mrs Errol (replacing Mary Rorke)	Opéra Comique Sat. matinées	London debut Beringer, Kendal prod.
April– 8/10/89	*The Profligate* by Pinero	Irene (understudy, played 29 June), Janet (understudy)	Garrick	Hare

8/5/89– end July	*Forget-Me-Not* by Merival and Grove	Alice Verney	Opéra Comique matinées	Beringer, Kendal prod.
5/7/89	*Forgotten* by F. Moore	Grace Hargrove	Grand, Islington	trial matinée
17/7/89	*The Pillars of Society* by Ibsen	Martha Bernick	Opéra Comique	benefit for Vera Beringer
Oct. 1889	*Forgotten*	Grace (understudy for Mrs Tree)	Peterborough	Tree
3/11/89	*A Man's Shadow* by Buchanan	Henriette (understudy for Mrs Tree), Julie (understudy for Julia Neilson), Played 4 perfs.	Haymarket	Tree
6/11/89	*Her Own Witness* by Dr Dabbs	Pauline	Criterion	Wyndham
Dec. 89	*Little Lord Fauntleroy*	Mrs Errol		revival
30/1/90	*Adelaide*	Adelaide	Streatham Hill	drawing-room prod.
1/2/90–Aug.	*Dr Bill* by Hamilton Aide	Louisa (also understudy for Fanny Brough)	Royal Avenue	Alexander
19/5/90	*Cheiromancy*	Mrs Horton	Lord Magheramorre	private revival

1890	*Quicksands* by Miss Morland	Rose Laroque	Haymarket	Tree
24/6/90	*Punchinello* by Dr Dabbs	Nina	Adelphi	one-act play written for E. Robins
1890	*The Will and the Way* by Justin McCarthy	Sybil	Avenue	curtain-raiser for Dr Bill
8/10/90	*The Sixth Commandment* by Buchanan (adapt. Dostoievsky's *Crime and Punishment*)	Liza	Shaftesbury	Miss Wallis prod.
27/1/91	*A Doll's House* by Ibsen	Mrs Linden	Terry's matinée	Marie Fraser as Nora
13/3/91	*A Joint Household* by Florence Bell		Steinway Hall matinée	comedietta
20/4/91– 1/6/91	*Hedda Gabler* by Ibsen	Hedda Gabler	Vaudeville. 2 wks matinées, 1 wk eves	Robins–Lea Management
17/6/91	scene from *Hedda Gabler*		Portman Rooms for Mary Eliza Haweis	soirée
from 7/8/91	*The Trumpet Call* by Sims and Buchanan	Constance	Adelphi	Gatti brothers

26/9/91– Dec. 91	*The American* by Henry James	Claire, Comtesse de Cintré	Opéra Comique	Compton

(rehearsed *The Fringe of Society* at the Criterion in 1892 but Lily Langtry replaced her in the actual production)

(2,3,4/11/91 *Denise* by Dumas Fils, adapted Clement Scott, produced by Robins–Lea Management at Criterion, matinées)

22/2/92	*Deborah* by Langdon Mitchell	read Prologue		
10,12/5/92	*Karin* by Florence Bell (trans. from Alfhild Agrell)	Karin	Vaudeville	Robins–Lea Management
5–11/10/92	*A Doll's House* and *Hedda Gabler*	Mrs Linden and Hedda Gabler	Theatre Royal, Brighton	Charringtons, Robins
7/12/92	*Bygmeiser Solness* (Ibsen's *The Master Builder*)	Hilda Wangel	Theatre Royal, Haymarket	copyright perf.
from 20/2/93 for 2 weeks	*The Master Builder*	Hilda Wangel	Trafalgar Square (mats)	Robins, Waring
3 weeks ending 25/3/93	*The Master Builder*	Hilda Wangel	Vaudeville (eves)	Robins, Waring
30/3/93	*The Master Builder*	Hilda Wangel	Theatre Royal, Brighton	Robins, Waring

28/8/93	*Alan's Wife* by Anon. (ER and FB), from Elin Ameen story	Jean Creyke	Terry's	Grein's Independent Theatre Society
29/5/– 10/6/93	*Rosmersholm, The Master Builder, Hedda Gabler, Brand* (4th Act), all by Ibsen	Rebecca West, Hilda, Hedda, Agnes	All at Opéra Comique, 6 mats, then 6 eves	Ibsen Series Committee under ER's direction
12/6/93	*A Woman's Revenge* by Henry Pettitt	Mary Lonsdale	Adelphi	Gatti brothers
Sept.– 16/12/93	Diplomacy, adapted by C. Scott and Stevenson from a Sardou play	Countess Zicka (replaced Olga Nethersole)	Liverpool, Manchester, Birmingham, Edinburgh, (Lyceum), Glasgow, (Royalty), Aberdeen	Hare

(26 October 1893—performed before Queen Victoria at Balmoral)

7/4/94	*Mrs Lessingham* by George Fleming (Constance Fletcher)	Gladys	Garrick	Hare
27/11, 30/11, 1/12/94	*Hedda Gabler* and *The Master Builder*	Hedda, Hilda	Gentlemen's Concert Hall, Manchester	Manchester Independent Theatre Committee

7/12/94	*Lille Eyolf* [*Little Eyolf*] by Ibsen also (same programme) *The First Step* by W. Heinemann	Rita — Lizzie	Theatre Royal, Haymarket	copyright perf.
23/11– 19/12/96	*Little Eyolf*	Asta	Avenue mats then 3 wks eves	Ibsen– Echegaray Series ER
Dec. 1896	*John Gabriel Borkman* by Ibsen	Ella Rentheim		copyright perf. under direction of Eliz. Robins
22–26/2/97	*Mariana* by José Echegaray (trans. James Graham)	Mariana	Court	George Foss, producer Ibsen– Echegaray Series
3–7/5/97	*John Gabriel Borkman*	Ella Rentheim	Strand	New Century Theatre
29/11/97	*Admiral Guinea* by Robert Louis Stevenson and W.E. Henley	read Prologue (first night only)	Avenue	
Feb.–6/3/99	*Coriolanus* by Shakespeare	Volumnia (replaced G. Ward)	Edinburgh, Glasgow	Benson prod.
16/12/99	*Nar vi Dode Vagner* [*When We Dead Awaken*] by Ibsen		Theatre Royal, Haymarket	copyright perf., a.m. reading

6/3/–14/6/1902	*Paolo and Francesca* by Stephen Phillips	Lucrezia	St James	Alexander
30/10–15/11/1902	*Eleanor* by Mrs Humphrey Ward	Alice Manisty	Court	final prof. role

APPENDIX 2

Elizabeth Robins' major publications (excluding material on women's suffrage, letters to the press, book reviews, obituaries, brief observations, etc).

1890   'Across America with Junius Brutus Booth', *Universal Review*, vol. vii, no. 27, July.

1893   *Alan's Wife*, London, Henry and Co. (Anonymous, with Florence Bell).

1894   *George Mandeville's Husband*,★ London, Heinemann; New York, D. Appleton and Co. (C.E. Raimond).

　　　　'A Lucky Sixpence', *New Review*, vol. x, no. 56, January.

　　　　'Dedicated to John Huntley', *New Review*, vol. x, no. 61, June.

1895   *The New Moon*,★ London, Heinemann; New York, D. Appleton and Co. (C.E. Raimond).

　　　　''Gustus Frederick', *New Review*, vol. xii, no. 70, March.

　　　　'Confessions of a Cruel Mistress', *Chapman's Magazine of Fiction*, vol. 1, no. 4, August.

　　　　'Miss de Maupassant', *New Review*, vol. xiii, no. 76, September; *Eclectic Magazine*, no. 125.

1896   *Below the Salt and Other Stories*, London, Heinemann; in the United States published as *The Fatal Gift of Beauty*, Chicago, H.S. Stone and Co. (C.E. Raimond).

　　　　'Below the Salt', *New Review*, vol. xv, no. 86, July.

1898   *The Open Question. A Tale of Two Temperaments*,★¨ London, Heinemann (C.E. Raimond); New York, Harper and Brothers, 1899, 1913; Nelson, 1915.

Offene Frage, serialised in *Die Frankfurter Zeitung*, Leipzig, B. Tauchnitz, 1899; Heinemann's Sixpenny Novels edition, 1907.

'The Threlkeld Ear', *Cornhill Magazine*, New Series, vol. iv, January, and in *Littell's Living Age*, no. 216, March.

'La Bellerieuse', *Pall Mall Magazine*, vol. xv, no. 61, May.

1899   'Among My Books', *Literature*, 4 February.

'A Modern Woman', *Anglo-Saxon Review*, vol. 1, no. 1.

1900   'The Very Latest Goldfield in the Arctic Circle', *Review of Reviews*, October.

'A Masterpiece the World Never Saw or Aphrodite of the West', *Universal Magazine*, vol. 11, no. 8, December.

'On Seeing Madame Bernhardt's *Hamlet*', *North American Review*, no. 171, December.

'Living under Martial Law' and 'The Court Arrives', *Post-Intelligencer* (Seattle), August.

1901   'Geen Baceler' in *The May Book*, compiled by Mrs Aria, London, Macmillan.

'Embryo Americans', *Harper's Magazine*, September.

'A Visit to Cape Nome', *Pall Mall Magazine*, vol. 23, January.

1902   'Pleasure Mining', *Fortnightly Review*, New Series, vol. 71, March.

1903   'The Alaska Boundary', *Fortnightly Review*, New Series, vol. 74, November.

1904   *The Magnetic North*, London, Heinemann, 1906, 1919; New York, Frederick A. Stokes; synopsis in Harmsworth Educational Publications, 1910; Nelson edition, 1915, Louisville, Kentucky, Lost Cause Press, 1963; Upper Saddle River, New Jersey, Gregg Press, 1969.

'Mrs Bassett's Fall', *New England Magazine*, New Series, 30, May.

'The Need of the London Stage', *Review of Reviews*, vol. xxix, March.

1905   *A Dark Lantern*, London, Heinemann.

'Monica's Village', *Century Magazine*, May.

'Lady Quassia', *Century Magazine*, 48, September.

'The Caribou Stand', *Pall Mall Magazine*, 36; *Argosy*, September 1929.

1907   *Under the Southern Cross*, New York, Frederick A. Stokes; *Cassell's Magazine* edition, 1908.

1907–8 *Come And Find Me*, London, Heinemann; serialised *Century Magazine*, April 1907–March 1908, London, Heinemann, 1908; New York, Century Co., 1908; Nelson edition, 1914.

1908   'The Mills of the Gods', *Fortnightly Review*, vols 83–4, June, July; New York, Moffat, Yard and Co.

1909   *The Florentine Frame*, London, John Murray; New York, Moffat, Yard and Co.; Leipzig, B. Tauchnitz, 1909; New York, Everleigh, Nash and Grayson, 1929

Preface to Bath Classics edition of Harriet Beecher Stowe's *Uncle Tom's Cabin*, Cedric Chivers (proofs though possibly not published in book form); *The Author*, vol. 20, no. 1, October.

Selections from her writings in *The Library of Southern Literature*, vol. for 1909.

1910   'Miss Cal', *English Review*, December; *McClure's Magazine*, 36, December 1911.

1911   'The Derrington Ghost', *Harper's Magazine*, 123, August.

1913   *Where Are You Going To … ?*, London, Heinemann; Toronto, William Briggs; in the United States published as *My Little Sister*, first serialised in *McClure's Magazine* from December 1912; New York, Dodd, Mead and Co.

1914   *What Can I Do?*, pamphlet on the Lady Chichester Hospital for Women and Children, *c.* 1914.

'War Service at Home', *The Nineteenth Century*, no. 77, November.

1915   'Lost and Found', *Harper's Magazine*, September.

1916   'A Changed England', *New York Times*, 11 March.

1917   'Conscription for Women', *Contemporary Review*, vol. cxi, April.

1918   *Camilla*, London, Hodder and Stoughton; serialised in *Cosmopolitan Magazine*, September; New York, Dodd, Mead and Co.

1919   *The Messenger*, London, Hodder and Stoughton; *Century Magazine*, November 1918–July 1919, no. 85, New York, Century Co.

'Bolt Seventeen', *Fortnightly Review*, vol. 107, January.

'Soldiers Two', *Reveille*, February.

'A New View of Country Life', *The Nineteenth Century*, vol. lxxxv, March.

1920   *The Mills of the Gods and Other Stories*, London, Thornton Butterworth.

'Prudence and Peter' serialised in *Time and Tide* from 27 May, reprinted in book form as *Prudence and Peter. A Story for Children about Cooking Out-of-Doors and Indoors*, London, Ernest Benn, 1928 (with Octavia Wilberforce); New York, W. Morrow and Co., 1928.

'Paternalism', *Daily Express*, 29 May.

'The Frog Baby', *Woman's Leader*, February.

1923   *Time Is Whispering*, London, Hutchinson; New York, Harper and Bros.

1924   *Ancilla's Share. An Indictment of Sex Antagonism*, London, Hutchinson (Anonymous); New York, Transatlantic Arts; reprinted Westport, Connecticut, Hyperion Press, 1976.

1926   *The Secret That Was Kept*, London, Hutchinson; New York, Harper and Bros.

1928   *Ibsen & the Actress*, London, Hogarth Press; New York, Putnam's.
        'Henrik Ibsen', *Time and Tide*, 16 March.

1929   'Some Personal Opinions on the National Theatre', *Drama*, December.

1932   *Theatre and Friendship. Some Henry James Letters*, London, Jonathan Cape; New York, Putnam's; Books For Libraries Press, Freeport, New York, 1969.

1940   *Both Sides of the Curtain*, London, Heinemann; New York, Transatlantic Arts.

1941   *Portrait of a Lady or The English Spirit Old and New*, London, Hogarth Press.

1956   *Raymond and I*, London, Hogarth Press (posthumous); New York, Macmillan.

★Also in Wright American Fiction microcard edition. See Joanne E. Gates, '"Sometimes Suppressed and Sometimes Embroidered". The Life and Writing of Elizabeth Robins 1862–1952', Ph.D., University of Massachussetts, 1987, pp. 557–8.

See also Susan Thomas's *Elizabeth Robins* (1862–1952): *A Bibliography*, St Lucia, Department of English, University of Queensland, Australia. 1994, Victorian Fiction Research Guide Series 22 and Idem, in George M. Johnson (ed.), *Dictionary of Literary Biography: British Novelists, 1890–1918*, Detroit, Gale, 1998.

APPENDIX 3

Elizabeth Robins' writings on women's suffrage

1906   Letter in *The Times*, 6 November.

1907   *Votes For Women!*, Chicago, Sergels Acting Drama, Dramatic Publishing
       Company; London, Mills and Boon, 1909; in C. Hayman and D.
       Spender (eds.), *How The Vote Was Won and Other Suffragette Plays*, London,
       Methuen, 1985.

       'Woman's Secret', Garden City Press for WSPU.

       The Convert, London, Methuen, Women's Press, 1980; New York, Grosset and
       Dunlap, Macmillan's Standard Library, 1907, reprinted; New York, Feminist
       Press, 1980.

       'The Feministe Movement in England', *Collier's Weekly* (June).

1908   Message of encouragement in *Votes For Women*, 20 February. 'The Meaning
       of It', *Daily Mail*, June; also in *Woman's Journal*, Boston, July.

       'The Newcastle By-Election', Votes For Women, 17 September.

1909   'The Signs of the Times', *Votes for Women*, 19, 26 March.

       Votes For Women!, London, Mills and Boon, Methuen, 1985; Fort Worth,
       Harcourt Brace, Anthology of Modern Drama, forthcoming; K.E. Kelley,
       (ed.) Modern Drama by Women 1880s–1930s, London, Routledge, 1996.

       'The Hunger Strike', *Westminster Review*, 21 July, also in *Votes For Women*,
       30 July.

       'Why?', *Everybody's Magazine*, December; in *Votes For Women* in 9 parts from
       3 December; WWSL Pamphlet, Woman's Press.

       'Shall Women Work?', *Metropolitan Magazine*; *Fortnightly Review*, May, 1910.

1910   'Mrs Partington's Mop', *Votes For Women*, 12 August.

1911   'Come and See', *Westminster Gazette*, 16 June.

        Message in *Votes For Women*, 21 July.

        WWSL Speech in *Votes For Women*, 30 June.

1912   Letter in *The Times*, 7 March; in WSPU Pamphlet as *In Defence of the Militants*.

        Letters in *The Times*, 14 March, 27 July.

        'Under His Roof', WWSL Pamphlet; in *Good Housekeeping*, May 1913; in Elizabeth Robins, *The Mills of the Gods*, London, Thornton Butterworth, 1920; in Dale Spender and Janet Todd (eds), *An Anthology of British Women Writers*, London, Pandora Press, 1989.

        'Perfidy', *Votes For Women*, 22 March.

        'Sermons in Stones', *Contemporary Review*, April.

1913   'Woman's War. A Defence of Militant Suffrage', *McClure's Magazine*, March. *Way Stations*, London, Hodder and Stoughton, 1913; New York, Dodd, Mead; Leipzig, B. Tauchnitz.

        'Must Be Repealed', *The Suffragette*, 1 July.

        'Why Suffragettes Go to Jail', *Hearst's*, September.

        'Christabel', *Harper's Weekly*, December.

1915   Preface to Evelyn Sharp's *Rebel Women*, 2nd edition, London United Suffragists.

1916   'Solidarity of Sex', *New York Times*, 17 June (name misprinted as Elizabeth Tobin).

        Signatory to letter in *The Times*, 24 November.

1917   'Women at Home and Beyond the Seas. An Anomaly', *The Nineteenth Century*, vol. lxxxi, March.

1921   Letter in *The Times*, 4 May.

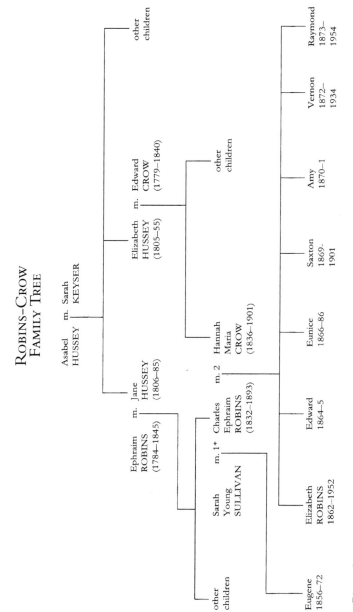

ROBINS–CROW
FAMILY TREE

Asabel HUSSEY   m.   Sarah KEYSER

Jane HUSSEY (1806–85)   m.   Ephraim ROBINS (1784–1845)

Elizabeth HUSSEY (1805–55)   m.   Edward CROW (1779–1840)

other children

Charles Ephraim ROBINS (1832–1893)

Sarah Young SULLIVAN   m. 1*

Hannah Maria CROW (1836–1901)   m. 2

other children

other children

Eugene 1856–72

Elizabeth ROBINS 1862–1952

Edward 1864–5

Eunice 1866–86

Saxton 1869–1901

Amy 1870–1

Vernon 1872–1934

Raymond 1873–1954

* Divorced

NOTES

The major source is the Elizabeth Robins Papers in the Fales Library at the Elmer Holmes Bobst Library of New York University. Unless mentioned below, material and quotes are from there. For those wishing to examine the Robins Papers, in addition to the excellent Finding Aid which gives details of how and where material is catalogued, the author has deposited with the Fales a list detailing sources from the Elizabeth Robins Papers in each chapter of this book.

Other major sources/archives are as follows: Harry Ransom Humanities Research Center, University of Texas at Austin; Women's Library, London Metropolitan University; Margaret Dreier Robins Collection, University of Florida, Gainesville; W.T. Stead Papers, Churchill College, Cambridge; C.P. Trevelyan Papers, Gertrude Bell Collection, Robinson Library, University of Newcastle upon Tyne; George Bernard Shaw Correspondence, British Library; John Masefield Letters, Berg Collection, New York Public Library.

The following abbreviations are used in the notes:

Berg John Masefield Letters, Berg Collection, New York Public Library
CP Christabel Pankhurst
CPT C.P. Trevelyan Papers, Gertrude Bell Collection, Robinson Library, University of Newcastle upon Tyne
EP Emmeline Pankhurst
ER Elizabeth Robins; the full references to Elizabeth's published works are given in Appendix 2 (major publications) and Appendix 3 (works on women's suffrage)
WL Women's Library, London Metropolitan University

GB   Gertrude Bell; see above, CPT
HRHRC   Harry Ransom Humanities Research Center, University of Texas at
            Austin
MDR   Margaret Dreier Robins Collection, University of Florida, Gainesville
OW   Octavia Wilberforce
Shaw, BL   George Bernard Shaw Correspondence, British Library
WA   William Archer
WTS   W.T. Stead Papers, Churchill College, Cambridge

Introduction

1 Information from May Morey (née Powell), interviewed 28 March 1992 and the
   Guardian, 28 November 1960.
2 C.S. Nicholls (ed.), *Dictionary of National Biography 'Missing Persons'*, Oxford,
   Oxford University Press, 1993, pp. 560–1.
3 *The Times*, 9 May 1952. Her literary fortunes fluctuated. By 1918 she was commanding advances of £500, a very respectable figure but half the size of her 1907
   advance. When the BBC wanted to use *Votes For Women!* in 1937 for its 'Scrapbook
   for 1907' programme, they were unable to find a copy until Elizabeth supplied one;
   Leslie Bailie, BBC Written Archives Centre, Caversham, R 19/1110, Letters, 9 and
   12 July 1937. Samuel Hynes in *The Edwardian Turn of Mind*, Princeton, Princeton
   University Press, 1968, p. 201 called Elizabeth 'an interesting but forgotten woman'.
   In *Women of Ideas and What Men Have Done to Them*, London, Ark, 1982, pp. 620–3
   Dale Spender draws attention to Elizabeth.
4 I am grateful to Mabel Smith for this information. Students at RADA performed
   Votes For Women! in 1987 and at Manchester University in 1992.
5 Jane Connor Marcus, 'Elizabeth Robins', Ph.D., Northwestern University 1973;
   Mary Gay Gibson Cima, 'Elizabeth Robins. Ibsen Actress Manageress', Ph.D.,
   Cornell University, 1978 and Joanne E. Gates, '"Sometimes Suppressed and
   Sometimes Embroidered". The Life and Writing of Elizabeth Robins 1862–
   1952', Ph.D., University of Massachussetts, 1987. Gates's book published by the
   University of Alabama Press is called *Elizabeth Robins, 1862–1952. Actress, Novelist,
   Feminist*, 1984.
6 See Appendix 2.
7 Nellie L. Buckingham, Diaries 1 and 2, 17 and 26 February 1877, Pioneer and
   Historical Society of Muskingum County, Ohio. The Buckinghams were prominent merchants in Putnam.

8   Lady Bell, *Landmarks*, London, Ernest Benn, 1929, p. 107.

9   *Criterion Illustrated Weekly Journal* (New York), 12 March 1898.

10 *The Listener*, 17 July 1952; Virginia Woolf claimed that Elizabeth had eyes 'like pale cinders'; Nigel Nicolson and Joanne Trautmann (eds), *The Letters of Virginia Woolf 1936–41*, vol. vi, *Leave the Letters Till We're Dead*, London, Chatto and Windus, 1980, p. 335.

11 Communication with Mrs Susannah Richmond, 1989.

12 Max Beerbohm to Ada Leverson in Rupert Hart-Davis (ed.), *Letters of Max Beerbohm 1892–1956*, London, John Murray, 1988, p. 56. Beerbohm was Tree's half-brother (see below).

13 Morey, op. cit.

14 Paul Fussell, *The Great War and Modern Memory*. Oxford, Oxford University Press, 1975, p. 157.

15 Backsettown. *Elizabeth Robins and Octavia Wilberforce*, privately printed, Brighton, 1952, p. 23.

16 Eric Homberger and John Charmley (eds), *The Troubled Face of Biography*, London, Macmillan, 1988; Ira Bruce Nadel, *Biography. Fiction, Fact and Form*, London, Macmillan, 1986 edition. For discussion of feminist biography see Sara Alpern et al. (eds.), *The Challenge of Feminist Biography*, Urbana and Chicago, University of Illinois Press, 1992; Bell Gale Chevigny, 'Daughters Writing. Towards a Theory of Women's Biography', *Feminist Studies*, Spring 1983, vol. 9, no. 1; Carolyn Heilbrun, *Writing a Woman's Life*, New York, Ballantine Books, 1988; Teresa Iles, *All Sides of the Question. Women and Biography*, New York, Teachers' College Press, 1992; Liz Stanley, *The Auto/biographical I. The Theory and Practice of Feminist Auto/biography*, Manchester, Manchester University Press, 1992 and Carolyn Steedman, *Past Tenses. Essays on Writing, Autobiography and History*, London, Rivers Oram Press, 1992, and the special issues of *Gender & History*, Spring 1990, vol. 2, no. 1 and *Sociology*, February 1993, vol. 27, no. 1. I am grateful to Kathryn Kish Sklar for letting me read her paper 'Biography in the Writing of Women's History'.

17 Nina Auerbach, *Ellen Terry. Player in Her Time*, New York, W.W. Norton, 1987; Carolyn Steedman, *The Radical Soldier's Tale*, London, Routledge, 1988 and Idem, *Childhood, Culture and Class in Britain. Margaret McMillan 1860–1931*, London, Virago Press, 1990 which shows how Margaret McMillan purported to write her sister's story in the *Life of Rachel McMillan* but actually wrote her own life. Compare this with Elizabeth in *Both Sides of the Curtain* (see below). Rachel M. Brownstein, *Tragic Muse. Rachel of the Comédie-française*, New York, Alfred A. Knopf, 1993. See also Kali A.K. Israel, 'Drawing from Life. Art, Work

and Feminism in the Life of Emilia Dilke (1840–1904)', Ph.D., Rutgers University, 1992 which reclaims biography as a historical genre; Eunice Lipton, *Alias Olympia*, New York, Charles Scribner's Sons, 1992; Revel Guest and Angela V. John, *Lady Charlotte. A Biography of the Nineteenth Century*, London, Weidenfeld and Nicolson, 1989; and Norma Clarke, *Ambitious Heights. Writing, Friendship, Love. The Jewsbury Sisters, Felicia Hemans and Jane Carlyle*, London, Routledge, 1990.

18 Israel, op. cit., p. 2.

19 See Chapter 8. For the fictive quality of diary-writing see Judy Simons, *Diaries and Journals of Literary Women from Fanny Burney to Virginia Woolf*, London, Macmillan, 1990. I am grateful to Joanne Gates for letting me read her MLA Paper, 'Elizabeth Robins: Diary as Source in Fiction and Autobiography'.

20 ER, *Both Sides of the Curtain* (1940), p. viii. Elizabeth told Virginia Woolf how people kept intruding into her writing and diverted her against her will from her original intention of writing about herself; Monk's House Papers, University of Sussex Archives, ER to Virginia Woolf, 11 December 1936.

21 Carolyn Heilbrun, 'Non-Autobiographies of "Privileged" Women: England and America' in Bella Brodzki and Celeste Schenck (eds), *Life/Lines: Theorizing Women's Autobiography*, Ithaca, Cornell University Press, 1988, pp. 70–7.

22 Tricia Davis et al., '"The Public Face of Feminism". Early Twentieth-Century Writings on Women's Suffrage' in Richard Johnson et al. (eds), *Making Histories*, Centre for Contemporary Cultural Studies, Birmingham, Hutchinson, 1982, p. 308.

23 Jane Marcus, 'Invincible Mediocrity: The Private Selves of Public Women' in Shari Benstock (ed.), *The Private Self: Theory and Practice of Women's Autobiographical Writings*, London, Routledge, 1988, especially pp. 137–8. Marcus stresses how Elizabeth and other women involve the collaboration of readers in their writing.

24 Brownstein, op. cit., p. 4. See too Elaine Aston, *Sarah Bernhardt*, Oxford, Berg, 1989 and William Weaver, *Duse. A Biography*, London, Thames and Hudson, 1984, p. 362.

25 Despite several broadcasts, no recording of Elizabeth's voice seems to be extant. When first acting in Boston she was accused of having a southern twang and Mrs Kendal thought she broadened her vowels when in London. Soon, however, contemporaries such as Pinero were commenting that she spoke 'pure English'.

26 *Sunday Times*, 26 April 1891.

27 Richard Le Gallienne, *The Romantic '90s*, London, Robin Clark, 1993 edition, p. 47.

28 *Manchester Guardian*, 10 May 1952.

29 When an artist sought to paint the portrait of the American anarchist Emma
Goldman to capture 'the real Emma Goldman', Goldman asked which was the
real one, adding, 'I have never been able to unearth her.' Alice Wexler, 'Emma
Goldman and the Anxiety of Biography' in Alpern, op. cit., p. 39.

1 Whither & How?

1 An outline of the Robins–Crow family tree is given on p. 335,

2 The one-page dedication did not appear in the first edition since it was initially
published pseudonymously. See WL, OW, 'The Eighth Child' Ms., vol. 2, p. 270.

3 *Zanesville Signal*, 8 February 1899.

4 The house has now reverted to its original name of the Stone Academy and has
been renovated by the Pioneer and Historical Society of Muskingum County to
which it was bequeathed.

5 Nellie L. Buckingham, Diary 4, Pioneer and Historical Society of
Muskingum County.

6 Joanne E. Gates, 'The Herstory of a Button 1875', *American Voice*, Summer 1990.

7 *Zanesville Signal*, 8 February 1899.

8 Claudia D. Johnson, *American Actress. Perspective on the Nineteenth Century*, Chicago,
Nelson-Hall, 1984, p. 4. Clara Morris (1848–1925) was Canadian-born but acted
on the American stage.

9 Nina Auerbach, *Woman and the Demon: The Life of a Victorian Myth*, Cambridge,
Mass., Harvard University Press, 1982, p. 205.

10 ER, *Both Sides of the Curtain* (1940), pp. 60–1. See also Lady Bell, 'Elizabeth Robins'
in Idem, *Landmarks*, London, Ernest Benn, 1929, pp. 108–9.

11 Judy Simons, *Diaries and Journals of Literary Women from Fanny Burney to Virginia
Woolf*, London, Macmillan, 1990, pp. 108–15.

12 Johnson, op. cit., Chapter 6.

13 For O'Neill see Myron Matlaw, 'Robins Hits the Road: Trouping with O'Neill
in the 1880s', *Theatre Survey*, 1988, vol. xxix, no. 2, pp. 175–92.

14 See Eugene O'Neill, *Long Day's Journey into Night*, London, Nick Hern Books
and Royal National Theatre edition, 1991.

15 ER, *Way Stations* (1913), p. 190.

16 Though on 27 October she had written to her grandmother, 'I feel awfully
homesick today. I depend on your advice & help, don't stop writing to me,
don't *please*.'

17 Peter Bailey, 'Parasexuality and Glamour: the Victorian Barmaid as Cultural Stereotype', *Gender & History*, 1990, vol. 2, no. 2, pp. 148–72.

18 Reproduced (on Bernard Shaw's advice) as the Frontispiece to *Both Sides* (1940).

19 Mary Gay Gibson Cima, 'Elizabeth Robins. Ibsen Actress Manageress', Ph.D., Cornell University, 1978, p. 82.

20 An earlier letter from Field had rejected her request, stating that she lacked experience despite unusual promise. Lloyd Tevis was described (on his death in 1898) as 'one of the wealthiest men of the Pacific slope'.

2 The Open Question

1   For the Boston Museum Company see Kate Ryan, *Old Boston Museum Days*, Boston, Little, Brown and Co., 1915.

2   ER, *Ibsen & The Actress*, p. 12. Lady Bell, *Landmarks*, London, Ernest Benn, 1929, p. 109, claimed she played 380 parts.

3   e.g. *Boston Daily Herald*, 13 June 1889.

4   ER, *Both Sides of the Curtain* (1940), p. 55.

5   WL, OW, 'The Eighth Child' Ms., vol. 2, p. 270.

6   For press reports see *Boston Daily Globe*, 6 and 9 June 1887, *Boston Daily Advertiser*, 7 and 13 June 1887, *Boston Daily Herald*, 13 June 1887, *Medford Mercury*, 17 June 1887.

7   ER [C. E Raimond], *The Open Question* (1898), p. 193.

8   See Jane Connor Marcus, 'Elizabeth Robins', Ph.D., Northwestern University, 1973, Chapter 1.

9   ER's close friend Florence Bell wrote in *Landmarks*, op. cit., p. 107, 'In *The Open Question*, part of which may no doubt be looked upon as autobiographical …' For suicide and the 1890s see John Stokes, *In the Nineties*, Hemel Hempstead, Harvester, 1989, Chapter 5.

10 Michael Meyer, *Ibsen. Plays: One*, London, Methuen, 1980 edition, p. 21.

11 ER, *Ibsen & The Actress* (1928), p. 30.

12 ER, *The Open Question* (1898), p. 184.

13 Ibid., p. 172.

14 For her stage interpretation of Hedda's suicide see Tracy C. Davis, 'Acting in Ibsen', *Theatre Notebook*, 1985, vol. 39, no. 3, p. 121.

15 WTS Papers, 1/61, ER to W.T. Stead, 31 December 1898.

16 *The Poetical Works of Elizabeth Barrett Browning*, London, W.P. Nimmo, Hall and Mitchell, 1850 edition, p. 570.

17 *The Journal of Marie Bashkirtseff*, London, Cassell and Co., 1890, Introduction, p. vii. George Bernard Shaw, *The Quintessence of Ibsen*, London, Walter Scott, 1891, p. 32.

18 *The Universal Review*, July 1890, vol. vii, no. 27, pp. 375–92. When it appeared she was disappointed to find 'so many errors in my article—it no longer seems very bright or even very interesting'.

19 Michael Meyer, *Ibsen*, Harmondsworth, Penguin, 1985 edition, p. 17.

20 Information supplied by Bull's great-granddaughter, Olea Karland.

3 Ibsen & The Actress

1 Although Wilde's advice against her appearing in *A Fair Bigamist* was sound in that the play was a flop, Kerry Powell points out that the experience would have familiarised Elizabeth both with working in the Royalty Theatre managed by a woman, Kate Santley, and with the kind of play for which she was to become famous. Kerry Powell, *Women and Victorian Theatre*, Cambridge, Cambridge University Press, 1997, Chapter 7. See also Richard Ellmann, *Oscar Wilde*, London, Hamish Hamilton, 1978, p. 179.

2 Here she stressed that 'his fall was shattering not to him alone'.

3 ER, *Both Sides of the Curtain* (1940), p. 242.

4 See especially Tracy C. Davis, *Actresses as Working Women. Their Social Identity in Victorian Culture*, London, Routledge, 1992; Sandra Richards, *The Rise of the Victorian Actress*, London, Macmillan, 1993; Michael Baker, *The Rise of the Victorian Actor*, London, Croom Helm, 1978.

5 ER, *Both Sides* (1940), p. 178.

6 Ibid., Chapter 25. At a later date Ellen Terry wrote to tell Elizabeth how she had dreamt of their acting together, though insisted that it was only a dream! Quoted in Nina Auerbach, *Ellen Terry. Player in Her Time*, New York, W.W. Norton, 1987, p. 423.

7 Shaw's 'Aside' in Lady Keeble (Lillah McCarthy), *Myself and Friends*, London, Thornton Butterworth, 1933, p. 1.

8 ER, *Ibsen & the Actress* (1928), p. 11.

9 Ibid., p. 13.

10 Elaine Showalter, *Sexual Anarchy, Gender and Culture at the Fin de Siècle*, Harmondsworth, Penguin, 1991, p. 39; Lucy Bland, 'Sexual Politics of the 1890s'

in Jane Rendall (ed.), *Equal or Different. Women's Politics 1800–1914*, Oxford, Basil Blackwell, 1987, p. 146.

11 Judith Walkowitz, 'Science, Feminism and Romance: the Men and Women's Club 1885–1889', *History Workshop Journal*, Spring 1986, no. 21, p. 54.

12 ER, 'Some Aspects of Henrik Ibsen', Lecture at the Philosophical Institute, Edinburgh, 27 October 1908. See also Jane Marcus, 'Nostalgia is Not Enough' in Idem, *Art and Anger. Reading Like a Woman*, Columbus, Ohio State University Press, 1988, pp. 56–63.

13 Angela Holdsworth, *Out of the Doll's House*, London, BBC Publications, 1988.

14 Julie Holledge, *Innocent Flowers. Women in the Edwardian Theatre*, London, Virago Press, 1981, pp. 35–6. See too Tracy C. Davis, '*A Doll's House* and the Evolving Feminist Agenda' in P. Tancred-Sheriff (ed.), *Feminist Research. Prospect and Retrospect*, Kingston and Montreal, McGill-Queens University Press, 1988.

15 Peter Whitebrook, *William Archer. A Biography,* London, Methuen, 1993, p. 99.

16 Clement Scott, quoted in Michael Egan (ed.), *Ibsen. The Critical Heritage*, London, Routledge and Kegan Paul, 1972, p. 114.

17 Egan, ibid., p. 10.

18 *Sunday Times*, 29 January 1989.

19 Joanne E. Gates, 'Elizabeth Robins and the 1891 Production of *Hedda Gabler*', *Modern Drama*, 1985, vol. xxviii, no. 4.

20 Ibid; Thomas Postlewait, *Prophet of the New Drama. William Archer and the Ibsen Campaign*, Westport, Ct, Greenwood Press, 1986, Chapter 3; John St John, *William Heinemann. A Century of Publishing 1890–1990*, London, Heinemann, 1990, Chapter 5; Ann Thwaite, *Edmund Gosse*, London, Secker and Warburg, 1984, pp. 341–2. Initially Archer was keen for Elizabeth to play Lona in *Pillars*.

21 Gosse also praised Elizabeth's acting: 'She elucidated to an extraordinary degree, the poet's intention.' Gates points out that the changes in Elizabeth's prompt book aren't actually in Gosse's printed version. Accepting this, it doesn't, however, necessarily follow that the latter was not actually the product of Gosse plus Archer with Elizabeth and Marion's input.

22 Postlewait, op. cit., pp. 72–4. Justin McCarthy (*The Gentleman's Magazine*, June 1891) argued that Elizabeth defied Ibsen's stage directions and supplemented the text, adapting the performance too much to herself and playing for success. In *Black & White*, 25 April 1891, he described her as too obviously melodramatic and machiavellian.

23 Michael Meyer, *Ibsen*, Harmondsworth, Penguin, 1985 edition, pp. 516, 862.

24 Mary Gay Gibson Cima, 'Discovering Signs; The Emergence of the Critical Actor in Ibsen', *Theatre Journal*, 1983, vol. 35, p. 22; Mary T. Heath, 'A Crisis in

the Life of the Actress: Ibsen in England', Ph.D., University of Massachusetts, 1986, p. 152.

25 Mrs Patrick Campbell, *My Life and Some Letters*, London, Hutchinson, 1922, p. 65.

26 ER, *Ibsen & the Actress* (1928), pp. 52–4. See Jane Conner Marcus, 'Elizabeth Robins', Ph.D., Northwestern University, 1973, Introduction.

27 Meyer, op. cit., Chapters 5 and 6.

28 See ER, *Ibsen & the Actress* (1928), pp. 52–4.

29 *The Times*, 17 March 1928.

30 *Lady's Pictorial*, 25 April 1891.

31 Yvonne Kapp, *Eleanor Marx. The Crowded Years 1884–1898*, vol. 1, London, Virago Press, 1976, p. 476. Ibsen sent signed photographs to Elizabeth and Marion.

32 Egan, op. cit., p. 230; *Saturday Review*, 23 April 1891; Theatre Museum, Covent Garden, London, William Archer Collection, Box 6, *Pictorial World*, 9 May 1891.

33 *The Stage*, 25 April 1891. Alongside the description of her being 'possessed' (*Weekly Despatch*, 26 April 1891), Elizabeth has added that it made a refreshing change from being sweet at £12 a week.

34 Quoted in Egan, op. cit., p. 227 (*Illustrated London News*, 25 April 1891).

35 ER, *Ibsen & the Actress* (1928), p. 18.

36 *The World*, 29 April 1891.

37 ER, *Ibsen & the Actress* (1928), p. 18.

38 George Bernard Shaw, *Collected Letters. 1874–1897*, New York, Dodd, Mead, 1965, p. 292.

39 Meyer, op. cit., p. 692.

40 *The World*, 29 April 1891.

41 *The Theatre*, 1 May 1897.

42 Campbell, op. cit., p. 65.

43 Tracy Cecile Davis, 'Critical and Popular Reaction to Ibsen in England 1872–1906', Ph.D., University of Warwick, 1984, p. 270.

44 Elizabeth had also seen Florence Farr's *Rosmersholm*, a production of *The Lady from the Sea* and Rose Norrey's revival of *A Doll's House*.

45 ER, *Theatre and Friendship* (1952), p. 59.

46 Leon Edel (ed.), *The Diary of Alice James*, New York, Dodd, Mead, 1964, p. 211, entry for 16 June 1891.

47 Ibid., p. 224, 30 December 1892; C.C. Hoyer Millar, *George du Maurier and Others*, London, Cassell, 1937, p. 94.

48 Leon Edel, *Henry James. The Middle Years 1884–94*, London, Rupert Hart-Davis, 1963, pp. 231–2. See also my Chapter 4.

49 Wyndham negotiated with Elizabeth for an adaptation of a Dumas play, *The Fringe of Society*. Elizabeth began rehearsals but was not keen to act in it in America as Wyndham wanted. When she sought temporary release to join Janet Achurch in a revival of *A Doll's House*, Wyndham replaced her with Lily Langtry. She also lost the Mrs Linden role to Marion.

50 Mary Gay Gibson Cima, 'Elizabeth Robins. The Genesis of an Independent Manageress', *Theatre Survey*, 1980, vol. 21, p. 163.

51 ER, *Ibsen & the Actress* (1928), p. 42. She also used the term in relation to Hedda Gabler.

52 Postlewait, op. cit., p. 106.

53 *Pall Mall Gazette*, 17 February 1893 in Egan, op. cit., pp. 266–9.

54 Heath, op. cit., p. 229.

55 Florence wrote a skit called *Jerry-Builder Solness* which was performed by the Independent Theatre Society at St George's Hall, 10 July 1893.

56 Campbell, op. cit., p. 65.

57 Michael Billington in the *Guardian*, 28 September 1989.

58 ER, *Ibsen & the Actress* (1928), p. 38.

59 Compare this statement with Shaw's of 30 March 1895: 'Whether Miss Robins would know Hilda if she met her in the street, any more than Mr Waring would know Solness, I doubt; but Miss Robins *was* Hilda', in George Bernard Shaw, *Our Theatre in the Nineties*, London, Constable and Co., 1954 edition, vol. 1, p. 78. The world premiere was held simultaneously in Germany and Norway.

60 Campbell, op. cit., p. 65 which also reproduces Elizabeth's letter to her. See also Alan Dent, *Mrs Patrick Campbell*, London, Museum Press, 1961, p. 57. Privately Stella Campbell was far less enamoured of Elizabeth, believing that Archer had 'lied so terribly about her art as an actress'. She told her friend Edwin Balfour Lyttelton that both 'buzzed so on the wheel of Ibsen's genius & thought themselves so fine'. Quoted in Margot Peters, *Mrs Pat. The Life of Mrs Patrick Campbell*, London, Bodley Head, 1984, p. 226.

61 See Mary Gay Gibson Cima, 'Elizabeth Robins. Ibsen Actress Manageress', Ph.D., Cornell University, 1978, Chapter 3; Heath, op. cit., Chapter V; Marcus thesis, op. cit., Chapter VI; Leon Edel, *Henry James. The Treacherous Years, 1895–1900*, London, Rupert Hart-Davis, 1969, pp. 6–7, 42.

62 Scott's words, quoted in Heath, op. cit., p. 253.

63 Quoted in Postlewait, op. cit., p. 112. See also Gretchen P. Ackerman, *Ibsen and the English Stage 1889–1903*, New York, Garland Publishing, 1987, p. 115.

64 William Weaver, *Duse. A Biography*, London, Thames and Hudson, 1984, p. 7.

65 Playbill for Opéra Comique in Theatre Museum, Covent Garden, London.

66 ER, 'Some Aspects of Henrik Ibsen', op. cit., p. 8.

67 ER, *Theatre and Friendship* (1932), pp. 157–67

68 Playbill in William Archer Collection, Box 7, op. cit.

69 See Margot Peters, *Bernard Shaw and the Actresses*, New York, Doubleday, 1980, pp. 173–203 and Cima thesis, op. cit., Chapter 5; Meyer, op. cit., p. 780; also an unpublished play, 'Ibsenites', by Francine Volker of Toronto.

70 Tracy Davis has rightly warned us to use the labels 'Ibsenite' and 'anti-Ibsenite' carefully. She provides a useful diagram of the network of Ibsenite support in 1891 with Ibsen at the centre, Archer on the inner circle and Elizabeth on the outer circle, Davis thesis, op. cit., p. 121.

71 See James Woodfield, *English Theatre in Transition 1881–1914*, London, Croom Helm, 1978, Chapter 3. The Independent Theatre was dissolved in 1898. An amalgamation between the Stage Society and NCT was mooted in January 1901 but came to nothing.

72 ER, *Theatre and Friendship* (1932), p. 201.

73 Shaw, *Our Theatre*, op. cit., vol. 1, p. 19.

74 Davis thesis, op. cit., pp. 366–8.

75 ER, *Theatre and Friendship* (1932), pp. 197–9.

76 Francis West, *Gilbert Murray. A Life*, London, Croom Helm, 1984, pp. 78–9. 77 Woodfield, op. cit., p. 127.

78 See John Stokes, *Resistible Theatres. Enterprise and Experiment in the late Nineteenth Century*, London, Paul Elek, 1972, p. 8; Whitebrook, op. cit. and Postlewait, op. cit.

79 *Review of Reviews*, 1904, vol. xxix, pp. 292–3. See also 1904, vol. xx, pp. 488–9 where Stead quotes ER on the impact of Antoine's productions on Parisian theatregoers, 'art having opened the door of their sympathies, the meaning came home'.

80 Elaine Aston, 'The New Woman at Manchester's Gaiety Theatre' in Viv Gardner and Susan Rutherford (eds), *The New Woman and Her Sisters, Feminism and Theatre 1850–1914*, Hemel Hempstead, Harvester Wheatsheaf, 1992, pp. 205–20.

81 Michael Jamieson, 'An American Actress at Balmoral', *Theatre Research International*, February 1977, New Series, vol. 11, no. 2.

82 CPT Papers, Molly Trevelyan's Diary, 30 October 1902, vol. vii.

83 Archer suggested to Barker in 1906 that Elizabeth revive her Hedda for the Court Theatre. He replied that she might have become rather stale. It would be better to find a 'live' actress. When Archer pressed further he protested that Elizabeth could not assume moral proprietorship because she had first played the part. British Library, Add. Mss. 45290, William Archer Papers, Granville

Elizabeth Robins: Staging a Life

Barker to William Archer, 27 June and 31 August 1906. Stella Campbell eventually played Hedda in 1907. Elizabeth's diaries for this period do not suggest personal interest in acting again. I am grateful to Peter Whitebrook for this reference.

84 ER, 'Some Aspects of Henrik Ibsen', op. cit., pp. 7–9, 20. Elizabeth later considered her former performances more critically. Rereading McCarthy's review (*Gentleman's Magazine*, op. cit.), in July 1938, where he referred to her 'very clever but over-coloured, over-emphasized performance', she added, 'Justin wasn't so wrong.'

85 ER, *Ibsen & the Actress* (1928), p. 55. See also her review of Georg Brandes's *Henrik Ibsen* in the *Academy*, 22 July 1899.

86 Quoted in Edwin Clark, 'Henry James and the Actress', *Pacific Spectator*, 1949, vol. 3, pt 1, p. 86.

87 *The Listener*, 17 July 1952.

4 Theatre and Friendship

1 James is quoted in Judith R. Walkowitz, *City of Dreadful Delight. Narratives of Sexual Danger in Late-Victorian London*, London, Virago Press, 1992, p. 15.

2 See, for example, reporting on the affair that became known as 'David Mellor and the Actress' in 1992. When writing about Ms Sanchez and Mellor, a government minister, even the reputable newspaper *The Independent* (5 July 1992) claimed that she told her side of the story 'in the mannered style and tones of a professional actress'.

3 See Stead's account of his 'first wanderings in Theatreland' with Elizabeth in his *Review of Reviews*, 1904, vol. xx, pp. 488–9 where he describes plays they saw together and his realisation that the play 'takes you by the throat and will not let you go until you answer its imperious interrogations'.

4 Peter Whitebrook, *William Archer. A Biography*, London, Methuen, 1993, p. 56. See too Lieutenant-Colonel Charles Archer, *William Archer, Life, Work and Friendships*, London, Allen and Unwin, 1931 (which Elizabeth felt gave only a faint recollection of 'the one I knew'); Thomas Postlewait, *Prophet of the New Drama. William Archer and the Ibsen Campaign*, Westport, Ct, Greenwood Press, 1986.

5 Elaine Showalter, *Sexual Anarchy, Gender and Culture at the Fin de Siècle*, Harmondsworth, Penguin, 1991, p. 150.

6 *Morning Leader*, 21 February 1901.

7   Quoted in Postlewait, op. cit., p. xviii.

8   Claire Tomalin, *The Invisible Woman. The Story of Nelly Ternan and Charles Dickens*, Harmondsworth, Viking Penguin, 1990, Chapter 11.

9   Whitebrook, op. cit., p. 201.

10 Postlewait, op. cit., p. xvii.

11 Ibid.

12 Elizabeth and Marion devised the symbol WA for Archer.

13 Postlewait, op. cit., pp. 79–81. George Moore's article about the influence of pretty actresses and theatre managers on critics had provoked a denial from Archer and increased Shaw's provocation. ER, *Both Sides of the Curtain* (1940), p. 169.

14 Michael Holroyd, *Bernard Shaw*, vol. 1, *The Search for Love 1856–1898*, Harmondsworth, Penguin, 1990 edition, p. 311.

15 Ibid., p. 312; *Margot Peters, Bernard Shaw and the Actresses*, New York, Doubleday, 1980, p. 86; Idem, 'As Lonely as God' in Michael Holroyd (ed.), *The Genius of Shaw: A Symposium*, New York, Holt, Rinehart and Winston, 1979, pp. 198–9.

16 Leon Edel, *Henry James. The Middle Years 1884–94*, London, Rupert Hart-Davis, 1963, p. 30.

17 See, for example, the letters at the beginning of ER, *Both Sides* (1940) and Shaw, BL, Add. Mss. 50527, Folio 212, ER to Shaw, n.d.

18 Edel, *The Middle Years*, op. cit., p. 29.

19 Idem, *Henry James. Letters*, vol. iii, London, Macmillan, 1986, p. 239.

20 Idem, *The Middle Years*, op. cit., p. 29. James wrote to ER in 1893: 'You have advantages over almost *every one* else in having an *author* at your complete disposal'; quoted by Edel, p. xv, Introduction to Henry James, *The Other House*, London, Rupert Hart-Davis, 1948 edition. James would have liked his Ibsenesque 'Bad Heroine' Rosa Armiger to have been played by Elizabeth but by the time he finished his (unperformed) play, Elizabeth was no longer on the stage. The novel appeared in 1896.

21 Susan Lowndes (ed.), *Diaries and Letters of Marie Belloc Lowndes 1911–1947*, London, Chatto and Windus, p. 18.

22 HRHRC, Henry James to ER, 30 January 1914.

23 John St John, *William Heinemann. A Century of Publishing 1890–1990*, London, Heinemann, 1990, p. 76.

24 Ibid., p. 86.

25 HRHRC, WA to ER, 5 August 1908.

26 Whitebrook, op. cit., pp. 392–3; ER [C.E. Raimond], *The Open Question* (1898), p. 378. Elizabeth contributed to a bronze memorial bust in honour of W.A.

27　For Florence Bell's life see my Introduction to Lady Bell, *At the Works* (1907), London, Virago edition, 1985. I am grateful to Dr Kirsten Wang for letting me read the draft manuscript of her biography, 'Dame Florence Bell DBE: her times, her people, her work'.

28　ER, *Theatre and Friendship* (1932), Introduction.

29　Ibid.

30　CPT Papers, Molly Trevelyan's Diary, 20 May 1892, vol. i.

31　Elsa Richmond (ed.), *The Earlier Years of Gertrude Bell*, London, Ernest Benn, 1937, p. 237.

32　Shaw, BL, Add Mss. 50512, Folio 284, ER to Shaw, 12 May 1892.

33　[Anon], *Alan's Wife* (1893).

34　Linda Fitzsimmons and Viv Gardner (eds), *New Woman Plays*, London, Methuen, 1991. Elin Diamond, 'Realism and Hysteria: Toward a Feminist Mimesis', *Discourse*, 1990–1, vol. 12, no. 1; Catherine Wiley, 'Staging Infanticide: The Refusal of Representation in Elizabeth Robins's *Alan's Wife*', *Theatre Journal*, 1990, vol. 42.

35　ER [Anon.], *Alan's Wife* (1893), p. 25.

36　Ibid., p. 23.

37　For the treatment of infanticide in England in the 1980s see *New Statesman and Society*, 23 March 1989.

38　See C. Damme, 'Infanticide: the Worth of an Infant under Law', *Medical History*, 1978, vol. 22, pp. 14–15. In 1912, urging the vote for women, Elizabeth wrote of 'those grossly misunderstood cases of infant murder' and how 'the effect upon the victim of social justice and puerperal mania may be imagined by women, if not by men'. ER, *Way Stations* (1913), p. 306. In 1922 the Infanticide Act removed the charge of murder for a woman found guilty of killing her child where she was shown to be suffering from the effects of childbirth.

39　*The Speaker*, 6 May 1893.

40　Archer in ER [Anon.], *Alan's Wife* (1893), pp. xvi–xxix. Elizabeth does not seem to have let Florence know that Archer was aware of the authorship. She told the former that Archer felt that his fulsome Preface was putting his friendship with Walkley to the test.

41　William Archer, *The Theatrical World for 1893*, London, Walter Scott, 1894, pp. 114–15. For Shaw's response see HRHRC, George Bernard Shaw to ER, 28 August 1899.

42　Lady Bell, *Landmarks*, London, Ernest Benn, 1929.

43　Shaw, BL, Add. Mss. 50513, Folio 206, ER to Shaw, 23 August 1899.

44 In an undated letter to Molly (which probably refers to the early stages of writing *Angela*), Florence describes how she spends her mornings writing in the school-room whilst Lisa works in her room. 'In two more days I think we shall have got the plot quite straight and then we shall begin to write it.' CPT Papers, Letter.

45 For details of Elizabeth Robins's books see Chapter 5 and Appendix 2.

46 MDR Collection; Folder 1906(2), ER to MDR, 22 November 1906.

47 Interview with Patricia Jennings (née Trevelyan), Newcastle, 10 June 1993. Correspondence with Mrs Valentine Vester and Mrs Susannah Richmond, 1989. Interview with Lady Plowden, London, 28 November 1989.

48 Frances Bell, interviewed aged ninety at Arncliffe Hall, 7 July 1985.

49 For Gertrude see GB Collection, Letters 5 and 6 August 1898; HRHRC, GB to ER, 31 August 1907; GB, *The Desert and the Sown* (1907), London, Virago edition, 1985, Introduction, p. lx. See also H.V.F. Winstone, *Gertrude Bell*, New York, Quartet Books, 1978 and Idem, 'A New Art of Travel', *Fortnightly Review*, March 1911, vol. 89, p. 492. On 17 May 1934 Elizabeth wrote in her diary of the sense of pain and frustration behind her brilliance.

50 HRHRC, FB to ER, 22 January; n.d. but 1907. It is interesting to note that Florence, Elizabeth and Gertrude all published key works in 1907.

51 Bell, *Landmarks* op. cit., p. 201. 'That each one should stick to his own part. It's more advantageous. And the world will only find it better.'

52 MDR Collection, Folder 1908(3), ER to MDR, 1 August 1908. For fuller involvement in women's suffrage see Chapter 7.

53 Ibid.

54 *Newcastle Daily Chronicle*, 15 September 1908. One of the guests at Rounton had given her a newspaper which criticised the 'wild women' suffragists in Newcastle. This was probably the *Newcastle Daily Journal* which on 18 September referred to the suffragists 'capering so hysterically'.

55 HRHRC, FB to ER, 10 March 1912.

56 Ibid., 12 March 1912.

57 Fitzsimmons and Gardner, op. cit., p. 3.

58 In Bell, *Landmarks*, op. cit. See below Chapter 9.

59 *The Times*, 17 May 1930.

60 Leon Edel, *Henry James. The Treacherous Years 1895–1900*, London, Rupert Hart-Davis, 1969, p. 29.

61 In Idem (ed.), *The Complete Tales of Henry James 1891–2*, vol. 8, London, Rupert Hart-Davis, 1963. 'Nona Vincent' first appeared in the *English Illustrated Magazine* in two parts.

5 Come and Find Me

1   Tracy C. Davis, '"Does the Theatre Make for Good?"': Actresses' Purity and Temptation in the Victorian Era', *Queens Quarterly*, Spring 1986, vol. 93, no. 1, p. 42.

2   Sandra Richards, *The Rise of the English Actress*, London, Macmillan, 1993, p. 110.

3   ER, *Both Sides of the Curtain* (1940), chapters 32, 33.

4   Elizabeth and W.A. discussed a number of possible scenarios for plays including one about Shakespeare's son—she favoured focusing on his twin daughter Judith.

5   ER [Anon.], *Ancilla's Share* (1924), p. 83.

6   Reviews could be quite entertaining. *The Spectator* saw Mr Raimond as an artist of great power who understood 'women's distinctive graciousness and ungraciousness as few women appear to understand it'. Quoted in Frontispiece to ER [C.E. Raimond], *The Open Question* (1898).

7   In ER, *Way Stations* (1913), p. 5.

8   John St John, *William Heinemann. A Century of Publishing 1890–1990*, London, Heinemann, 1990, p. 76.

9   *Green Room Book*, London, T. Seaky Clark, 1907, p. 300.

10 Unfortunately no manuscript or typescript exists for this novel or for *The New Moon*.

11 ER [C.E. Raimond], *George Mandeville's Husband* (1894), p. 195.

12 Ibid., p. 158.

13 Ibid., p. 219.

14 John Sutherland, *The Stanford Companion to Victorian Fiction*, Stanford, Stanford University Press, 1989, p. 541; Elaine Showalter, *A Literature of Their Own. British Women Novelists from Brontë to Lessing*, London, Virago Press, 1978, p. 109; Idem, *Sexual Anarchy. Gender and Culture at the Fin de Siècle*, Harmondsworth, Penguin, 1991, pp. 59, 61.

15 ER [C.E. Raimond], *George Mandeville's Husband* (1894), p. 7.

16 ER [C.E. Raimond], *The New Moon* (1895), p. 80.

17 Ibid., p. 76.

18 Geoffrey Trevelyan's correspondence with the author, 12 September 1993.

19 For this society and spiritualism generally see Janet Oppenheimer, *The Other World. Spiritualism and Psychical Research in England 1850–1914*, Cambridge, Cambridge University Press, 1985; Alex Owen, *The Darkened Room. Women, Power and Spiritualism in Late Victorian England*, London, Virago Press, 1989; and Judith R. Walkowitz, *City of Dreadful Delight. Narratives of Sexual Danger in Late-Victorian London*, London, Virago Press, 1992, Chapter 6.

20 Elizabeth relied heavily on her diary for Chapter 13 of *Both Sides* on occult powers.

21 'BAC' edited the letters of Diana, Lady Chesterfield. David Rubinstein, *Before the Suffragettes. Women's Emancipation in the 1890s*, Brighton, Harvester Press, 1986, pp. 12–14.

22 The story was originally sent to Frank Harris for the *Fortnightly Review* but withdrawn after an offer of under £10 for publication. *New Review*, 1894, vol x, no. 56, Editorial.

23 Elaine Showalter (ed.), *Daughters of Decadence. Women Writers of the Fin de Siècle*, London, Virago Press, 1993. See too Patricia Stubbs, *Women and Fiction. Feminism and the Novel 1880–1920*, London, Methuen, 1981 edition, pp. 104–8.

24 For example, in 'The Descent of Man' (1904) she has a professor who has written a skit on the popular scientific book. This fools the publisher who then deliberately deceives the public. In Edith Wharton, *The Muse's Tragedy and Other Stories*, Harmondsworth, Penguin, 1990.

25 See Sue Thomas's 'Elizabeth Robins and the *New Review*', *Victorian Periodicals Review*, 1995, no.28, which links this story to her editor's treatment of 'A Lucky Sixpence'. The journal's assistant editor had published an article on what he saw as excessive frankness in New Woman writers, something he connected with woman's nature.

26 For example, Stead's daughter Estelle pointed out that a character in the story 'Miss Cal' (see Chapter 6) was worryingly similar in interests and appearance to the politician Balfour.

27 ER, *A Dark Lantern* (1905), p. 10; ibid., p. 9 for following quote.

28 Revel Guest and Angela V. John, *Lady Charlotte. A Biography of the Nineteenth Century*, London, Weidenfeld and Nicolson, 1989, p. 27.

29 *Time and Tide*, 21 May 1920. This and ''Gustus Frederick' were dropped from the American edition.

30 Charlotte Perkins Gilman, *The Yellow Wallpaper and Other Writings*, New York, Bantam, 1989, pp. 29–40.

31 Quoted in the *Bookman*, January 1913, p. 564. The Bennett quote is from *The Journals of Arnold Bennett 1896–1910*, London, Cassell, 1932, p. 92. The Walpole quote is from the Robins Papers.

32 See Gail Cunningham, *The New Woman and the Victorian Novel*, London, Macmillan, 1978; Lucy Bland, 'The Married Woman, "the New Woman" and the Feminist: Sexual Politics and the 1890s', in Jane Rendall (ed.), *Equal or Different. Women's Politics 1800–1914*, Oxford, Basil Blackwell, 1987; Jenni Calder,

Women and Marriage in Victorian Fiction, London, Macmillan, 1976; Ann Ardis, *New Women, New Novels. Feminism and Early Modernism*, New Brunswick, Rutgers University Press, 1990; Rubinstein, op. cit.; and *Studio International*, 1993, vol. 201, nos. 1021/1023.

33 See John Stokes, *In the Nineties*, Hemel Hempstead, Harvester, 1989, Chapter 5.

34 Showalter, *A Literature of Their Own*, op. cit., p. 61.

6 The Magnetic North

1 ER, *Raymond and I* (1956), p. 15.

2 Neil V. Salzman, *Reform and Revolution. The Life and Times of Raymond Robins*, Kent, Ohio, Kent State University Press, 1991, pp. 387–8.

3 Ibid., p. 22.

4 Leonard Woolf, *An Autobiography of the years 1911–1969*, vol 2, *The Journey Not the Arrival Matters*, Oxford, Oxford University Press, 1980 edition, p. 426; ER, *Raymond and I*, (1956), pp. 211–12.

5 GB Collection, GB to Hugh Bell, 8 July 1903.

6 Salzman, op. cit., p. 33. See too Terence Cole, 'Raymond Robins in Alaska. The Conversion of a Progressive', *Pacific Northwest Quarterly*, vol. 72, no. 2.

7 CPT Papers, GB Collection, GB to Elsa Bell, 14 February 1898.

8 ER, *Raymond and I* (1956), p. 31.

9 CPT Papers, Molly Trevelyan's Diary, 9 December 1897, vol. ii.

10 WTS Papers, 1/61, ER to W. T. Stead, 24 January 1891.

11 For discussion of Stead's part see ER, *Raymond and I*, (1956), pp. 48–50.

12 Her reading included a US geological survey and the Alaska Commercial Company's book on the Klondike and Alaskan gold-fields which described how to stake a claim. She also spoke to people such as Flora Shaw, *The Times* correspondent to the Klondike.

13 Transcribed and introduced by Joan Moessner and Joanne E. Gates, *The Alaskan-Klondike Diary of Elizabeth Robins 1900*, forthcoming., Fairbanks, University of Alaska Press, 1999.

14 Ibid., Introduction, pp. 53, 61. Betty John (ed.), Libby. *The Alaskan Diaries of Libby Beaman 1879–1880*, Boston, Houghton Mifflin, 1989.

15 For details of this and other articles and fiction about Alaska see Appendix 2.

16 ER, *Both Sides of the Curtain* (1940), p. 65. It was believed that Saxton was killed by Indians—see, for example, *Zanesville News*, 2 February 1941.

17 ER, 'Miss Cal' in Idem, *The Mills of the Gods* (1920), p. 19.

18 ER, 'Monica's Village' in Ibid., p. 133. *The Century* published the story in 1905 and it was also reprinted *c*. 1910. Margaret Dreier Robins thanked Elizabeth for permission to reprint it. See chapter 10 for a discussion of race.

19 ER, 'Monica's Village' in ibid., p. 150.

20 Ibid., p. 165.

21 *Review of Reviews*, 1903, vol. xxix. Stead's journal provided a glowing review of the novel, complete with an eight-page summary, pp. 496–503.

22 For an account of how Euro-Americans have perceived and presented Eskimos historically, see Ann Fienup-Riordan, *Eskimo Essays, Yup'ik Lives and How We See Them*, New Brunswick, Rutgers University Press, 1990, Introduction. She explains here that although the term Inuit has replaced Eskimo in Canada and parts of Greenland, it has not taken root in western Alaska where the Eskimos are members of the Yup'ik-speaking (not Inuit/Inupiaq-speaking) branch of the large family of Eskimo cultures.

23 See Patrick Brantlinger, *Rule of Darkness. British Literature and Imperialism 1830–1914*, Ithaca, Cornell University Press, 1988, p. 39.

24 Pat Jalland (ed.), *Octavia Wilberforce. The Autobiography of a Pioneer Woman Doctor*, London, Cassell, 1989, p. 14. Edith Wharton admired it (Elizabeth later 'puffed' her Pulitzer-prize book, *The Age of Innocence*, 1920).

25 W.L. Courtney, *The Feminine Note in Fiction*, London, Chapman and Hall, 1904, p. 193, see also Introduction and pp. 188–95.

26 In her Foucauldian analysis of women's travel-writing and colonialism, Sara Mills has pointed to the discursive pressures on production and reception negotiated by women writers and the conflicting demands of the discourses of feminism and the literature of colonialism: Sara Mills, *Discourses of Difference. An Analysis of Women's Travel Writing and Colonialism*, London, Routledge, 1993 edition, pp. 6, 22.

27 Frontispiece to 1908 edition. There is a dispute as to whether Cook or the American commander, Robert E. Peary (who reached the Pole in 1909), should be credited. In 1993 an American, Ann Bancroft, became the first woman to reach both Poles across the ice. E.R.'s story was serialised in America from April 1907.

28 ER, *Come and Find Me* (1907–8), p. 361.

29 Idem, *Way Stations* (1913), pp. 1–2.

30 ER, *Come and Find Me* (1907–8), op. cit., p. 354. The Cook quote is in the Frontispiece. See also Elaine Showalter, *Sexual Anarchy, Gender and Culture at the Fin de Siècle*, Harmondsworth, Penguin, 1991, p. 81.

31 ER, *Come and Find Me* (1907–8), p. 242.

32 HRHRC, Marie Adelaide Belloc Lowndes, 7 October 1933. Apart from the personal references, the book recounts (with the name only thinly disguised) the corrupt exploits of the Reverend Wirt, Raymond's superior in Alaska.

33 Salzman, op. cit., p. 81.

7 The Convert

1   David J. Scott, born on 29 August 1898 and educated at Repton, first features in Elizabeth's diaries in her Blythe years. He was not her son. In March 1913 she and Zoe (an old friend of Flora's) became his joint guardians. Flora moved to Sweden. During the First World War Elizabeth was one of his sponsors for a War Office job. After serving in the army he went up to Oxford, eventually becoming a journalist. He was a correspondent for *The Times* in Paris, later working for Reuters. Elizabeth kept in touch with him (see Chapter 10). He wrote several books. Flora may have been his mother. One of her close male friends was the art critic Sir Walter Armstrong, director of the National Gallery in Ireland, who could possibly have been his father.

2   ER, 'Under His Roof. A Story of Militant Suffrage', in Idem, *The Mills of the Gods* (1920), p. 112.

3   MDR Papers, Folder 1909 (2), ER to MDR, 11 April 1909.

4   The members of the WSPU became known as suffragettes, a term coined by the *Daily Mail*. They tended to call themselves militant suffragists. Today the term suffragist is often used to describe only the constitutionalists, Mrs Fawcett's NUWSS members.

5   *The Times*, 6 November 1906.

6   'The Feministe Movement in England' reprinted in ER, *Way Stations* (1913), p. 38.

7   Compare this with ER, *The Convert* (1907), pp. 138–9.

8   See Jane Marcus's comment on Dangerfield's work in her Introduction to Idem, *Suffrage and the Pankhursts*, London, Routledge and Kegan Paul, 1987.

9   Sheridan Morley, *Sybil Thorndike. A Life in the Theatre*, London, Weidenfeld and Nicolson, 1977, p. 37.

10 Joanne E. Gates has edited Barker's prompt book of the Court Theatre production of 1907 (unpublished, 1989). I am grateful for a copy of this.

11 Clara Collet wrote: 'There is no hardship in women working for a living, the hardship lies in not getting a living when they work for it.' Clara Collet, *Educated Working Women. Essays on the Economic Position of Women in the Middle Classes*, London, P.S. King and Son, 1902, p. 23.

12 FL, ER to Lady Strachey, 14 February 1907.

13 CPT Papers, Molly Trevelyan's Diary, 4 November 1906, vol. ix.

14 Hannah Mitchell, *The Hard Way Up*, London, Virago Press, 1977 edition, p. 163.

15 The reports are typed and some of them seem unlike Elizabeth's own style. At the top of the eight reports it says that the typescript is from K.B.'s shorthand notes. K. Bompas was a secretary. Possibly she attended some of the meetings for/with Elizabeth. Certainly the author was present at some of them.

16 HRHRC, EP to ER, 19 November 1906. See HRHRC, CP's letter to ER, 26 April 1907.

17 E. Sylvia Pankhurst, *The Suffragettes*, London, Gay and Hancock, 1911. For discussion of *The Convert* see Joanne E. Gates, 'Elizabeth Robins: *From A Dark Lantern* to *The Convert*. A Study of Her Fictional Style and Feminist Viewpoint', *Massachusetts Studies in English*, 1978, vol. vi, nos. 3, 4, pp. 25–40; Jane Marcus's Introduction to the Women's Press edition, op. cit.; Susan M. Squier, 'The Modern City and the Construction of Female Desire: Wells's *In the Days of the Comet* and Robins's *The Convert*', *Tulsa Studies in Women's Literature*, Spring 1989, no. 8, pp. 63–75; Wendy Mulford, 'Socialist-Feminist Criticism: A Case Study, Women's Suffrage and Literature 1906–14', in P. Widdowson (ed.) *Re-Reading English*, London, Methuen, 1982 pp. 179–92; P. Brooker and P. Widdowson, 'Literature for England', in R. Colls and P. Dodd (eds.), *Englishness. Politics and Culture 1880–1920*, London, Croom Helm, 1986, pp. 151–2; and Eileen Sypher, *Wisps of Violence: Producing Public and Private Politics in the Turn-of-the-Century British Novel*, London, Verso, 1993, pp. 144–8, criticising its 'fascination with the romantic'.

18 ER, *Way Stations* (1913), p. 38.

19 National Union of Women Workers Annual Conference, Minutes, Tunbridge Wells, 25 October 1906, pp. 95, 98. Talks and discussion on women's suffrage chaired by Mrs Fawcett. E. Sylvia Pankhurst, *The Suffragette Movement* (1931), London, Virago Press edition, 1977, p. 237. Sylvia does not seem to have appreciated that Mrs Raymond Robins was Elizabeth's sister-in-law.

20 Manchester Central Reference Library, Millicent Fawcett Collection, M50/2/1/232, ER to Mrs Fawcett, 27 October 1906. Mrs Fawcett wrote to *The Times* (26 October) praising Elizabeth's intervention. See also David Rubinstein, *A Different World for Women. The Life of Millicent Garrett Fawcett*, Hemel Hempstead, Harvester Wheatsheaf 1991, p. 152.

21 *The Times*, 6 November 1906.

22 MDR Papers, Folder 1906 (2), MDR to Mary Dreier, 20 November 1906.

23 Wl, ER to Lady Strachey, 14 February 1907.

24 Ibid.

25 WL, ER to Mrs Fawcett, 1 November 1906.

26 Gates, op. cit., Appendix, pp. 220–1.

27 Sheila Stowell, *A Stage of Their Own*, Manchester, Manchester University Press, 1992, p. 2.

28 *The Sketch*, 15 May 1907. See too Dennis Kennedy, *Granville Barker and the Dream of Theatre*, Cambridge, Cambridge University Press, 1985, pp. 57–61.

29 HRHRC, WA to ER, n.d. 1907 (?).

30 James Woodfield, *English Theatre in Transition 1881–1914*, London, Croom Helm, 1984, p. 122 and Andrew Davies, *Other Theatres. The Development of Alternative and Experimental Theatre in Britain*, London, Macmillan, 1987, pp. 17–18.

31 Stowell, op. cit., p. 15.

32 *Morning Post* quoted in Elaine Showalter, *A Literature of Their Own. British Women Novelists from Brontë to Lessing*, London, Virago Press, 1978, p. 222. See also Samuel Hynes, *The Edwardian Turn of Mind*, Princeton, Princeton University Press, 1968, pp. 202–4.

33 MDR Papers, Folder 1907 (2), Katherine Dreier to MDR, 1 May 1907.

34 For suffrage theatre see Stowell, op. cit.; Julie Holledge, *Innocent Flowers. Women in the Edwardian Theatre*, London, Virago Press, 1981 and Claire Hirshfield, 'The Suffragist as Playwright in Edwardian England', *Frontiers*, 1987, vol. ix, no. 2, pp. 1–6. The play also helped inspire Cicely Hamilton's *Marriage as a Trade*. Hamilton told Elizabeth that the book represented what the play meant to her—'the refusal to be judged only by the standard of "attractiveness"'. HRHRC, Cicely Hamilton to ER, 1 August 1909. Hamilton's book was reprinted by Virago Press in 1981 with an Introduction by Jane Lewis.

35 HRHRC, Gertrude Forbes-Robertson to ER, 13 January and 18 January 1909.

36 Ibid., John E. Vedrenne to ER, 23 March 1907. In 1912 a benefit matinée of *Votes for Women!* was performed for the Women Writers' Suffrage League.

37 Tierl Thompson (ed), *Dear Girl. The Diaries and Letters of Two Working Women 1897–1917*, London, Women's Press, 1987, p. 174.

38 HRHRC, EP to ER, 17 September 1907.

39 Ibid., Evelyn Sharp to ER, 5 July 1907. For information on this game see Diane Atkinson, *The Purple, White and Green*, London, Museum of London, 1992, Catalogue, p. 43. The others on the Committee were Mrs Pankhurst and Mrs Tuke, Hon. Secs, Christabel Pankhurst, Organising Sec., Mrs Pethick-Lawrence, Treasurer, Mary Neal, Elizabeth Wollstoneholme-Elmy, Annie Kenney, Mary Gawthorpe and Mrs Martel.

40 MDR Papers, Folder 1907(1), ER to MDR, 19 January 1907.

41 Ibid.

42 ER, 'Some Aspects of Henrik Ibsen', Lecture at the Philosophical Institute, Edinburgh, 27 October 1908, p. 18.

43 H.W. Nevinson, *More Changes. More Chances*, London, Nisbet and Co.; 1925, p. 320.

44 Gerald Cumberland, *Set down in Malice. A Book of Reminiscences*, London, Grant Richards, 1919, p. 179.

45 HRHRC, EP to ER, 23 October 1908.

46 Evelyn Sharp, *Unfinished Adventure*, London, John Lane at the Bodley Head, 1933, p. 130. Elizabeth's Introduction to the second edition of Sharp's *Rebel Women* was published by the United Suffragists, 1915.

47 MDR Papers, Folder 1909(3), Katherine Dreier to MDR, 30 September 1909.

48 Marcus, *Suffrage and the Pankhursts*, op. cit., p. 10. Constance Gore-Booth wrote, 'Silence is an evil that might easily be remedied and the sooner we begin to make a row the better'; quoted in Gifford Lewis, *Eva Gore Booth and Esther Roper: A Biography*, London, Pandora, 1988, p. 61. Elizabeth's consideration of women's silence also encompassed its subtle uses.

49 ER, *Way Stations* (1913), p. 20.

50 See Chapter 18 in ER, *Both Sides of the Curtain* (1940).

51 G.M. Trevelyan, *A Shortened History of England*, Harmondsworth, Pelican edition, 1965, p. 528; HRHRC, Sir Edward Grey to ER, 3 November 1907.

52 WTS Papers, 1/61, ER to W.T. Stead, 4 November, n.y.

53 ER, *Way Stations* (1913), p. 70.

54 HRHRC, Sir Edward Grey to ER, 8 October 1908; ibid., the following quote.

55 Andrew Rosen, *Rise Up, Women!*, London, Routledge and Kegan Paul, 1974, p.95.

56 HRHRC, CP to ER, 7 September 1908.

57 *Newcastle Daily Chronicle*, 15 September 1908.

58 Martha Vicinus, *Independent Women*, London, Virago Press, 1985, p. 264.

59 Pankhurst, *The Suffragettes*, op. cit., p. 243. The *Daily News* of 4 July 1908 seems to have been the first to state this. For information about the suffrage demonstrations see Lisa Tickner, *The Spectacle of Women. Imagery of the Suffrage Campaign 1907–14*, London, Chatto and Windus, 1987.

60 For suffrage and fashion see Ibid and Katrina Rolley, 'Fashion, Femininity and the Fight for the Vote', *Art History*, March 1990, vol. 13, no. 1, also Jane Marcus's comments about political freedom, femininity and desire in 'The Asylums of Anteus. Women, War and Madness: Is there a Feminist Fetishism?', in Elizabeth Meese and Alice Parker (eds), *The Difference Within: Feminism and Critical Theory*, Philadelphia, John Benjamins' Publishing Co., 1988, p. 73.

61 CP to ER, 29 April 1910, 21 October 1911. Christabel suggested that Elizabeth make known to Cabinet ministers an article on Ireland in *Votes For Women*.

62 HRHRC, EP to ER, 23 October 1908.

63 Ibid., CP to ER, 4 January 1907, 19 October 1908.

64 Ibid., 4 August 1910.

65 Ibid., ER to CP, 23 November 1912.

66 *Votes For Women*, November 1907, p. 19 and ER, *The Convert* (1907), p. 171.

67 Pankhurst, *The Suffragette Movement* op. cit., p. 221 states that 'Elizabeth Robins the novelist, fell in love with her [Christabel], and with the movement'.

68 MDR Papers, Folder 1909(1), ER to MDR, 12 March 1909.

69 Martin Pugh, *Women's Suffrage in Britain 1867–1928*, Historical Association pamphlet, G97, 1980, pp. 26, 28.

70 HRHRC, Sir Edward Grey to ER, 9 November 1911.

71 Elizabeth did use some of the material from this letter in her *Way Stations* 'Time Table' (1913).

72 A manuscript exists for a play and a transcript for a short story. Harper's expressed some interest but felt it too esoteric for an American audience.

73 The story includes symbols personal to Archer and Elizabeth; for example, September as a significant anniversary, a description of the moon and a woman's loosened hair.

74 *The Times*, 11 March 1912.

75 ER, *Way Stations* (1913), p. 305. Mrs Pankhurst's division of *My Own Story*, London, Everleigh Nash, 1914 into 'Four Years of Peaceful Militancy' followed by 'The Women's Revolution' underlines this shift.

76 *McClure's Magazine*, 1913, vol. xl, no. 5.

77 Letter in Millicent Fawcett Collection, Manchester, op. cit.,

78 HRHRC, Mrs Pethick-Lawrence to ER, n.d. In the spring of 1912 Elizabeth did consider naturalisation.

79 HRHRC, EP to ER, 14 April 1912.

80 Brian Harrison, *Peaceable Kingdom. Stability and Change in Modern Britain*, Oxford, Clarendon Press, 1982, pp. 26–81. See also Rosalind Billington, 'Ideology and Feminism: Why the Suffragettes Were "Wild Women"', *Women's Studies International Forum*, 1982, vol. 5, no. 6, pp. 663–74; Antonia Raeburn, *The Militant Suffragettes*, London, Michael Joseph, 1973; Les Garner, *Stepping Stones to Women's Liberty*, London, Heinemann, 1984; and Sandra Stanley Holton, 'In Sorrowful Wrath: Suffrage Militancy and the Romantic Feminism of Emmeline Pankhurst' in Harold L. Smith (ed.), *British Feminism in the Twentieth Century*, Aldershot, Edward Elgar, 1990.

81 HRHRC, CP to ER, 12 December 1912.

82 Tickner, op. cit., p. 200.

83 According to Gates, op. cit., p. 217, 'Woman's Secret' was originally intended as a Preface to *The Convert*.

84 Though Claire Tylee did discuss it as a political autobiography in a panel at the Women's Lives/Women's Times Conference at the University of York, 26 January 1991 and Kate Flint's *The Woman Reader 1837–1914*, Oxford, Oxford University Press, 1993, pp. 313–14 acknowledges the 1909 lecture to the WWSL in *Way Stations* as 'an important piece of feminist criticism', looking backwards and to the future.

85 ER, *The Convert* (1907), p. 200. Sandra Holton has argued that 'The most striking aspect of British suffragism … is that it did not present feminist goals in terms of equivalence with men but in terms of an autonomously created system of values derived from women's particular experience'; Sandra Stanley Holton, *Feminism and Democracy*, Cambridge, Cambridge University Press, 1986, p. 18.

86 Stowell, op. cit., p. 33.

87 ER, *Way Stations* (1913), p. 291. Elizabeth's writings were frequently reported in the *Woman's Journal* which had been founded in Boston by Lucy Stone. Some of her information for *Way Stations* came from this source. See also Jane Marcus, 'Translatlantic Sisterhood. Labor and Suffrage Links in the Letters of Elizabeth Robins and Christabel Pankhurst', *Signs*, Spring 1978, vol. 3, pp. 744–55.

88 See Meta Zimmeck, 'Jobs for the Girls: the Expansion of Clerical Work for Women, 1850–1914' in Angela V. John (ed.), *Unequal Opportunities. Women's Employment in England 1800–1918*, Oxford, Basil Blackwell, 1986.

89 BR, *Way Stations* (1913), p. 99.

90 HRHRC, (Lady) Mary Murray to ER, 11 September 1909.

91 Ibid., Evelyn Sharp to ER, 14 October 1912.

92 See Les Garner, *A Brave and Beautiful Spirit. Dora Marsden 1852–1960*, Aldershot, Avebury, 1990, pp. 36, 45.

93 *The Times*, 4 May 1921.

94 ER [Anonymous], *Ancilla's Share* (1924), p. 244.

95 Pankhurst, *The Suffragette Movement*, op. cit., p. 41.

96 ER [Anonymous], *Ancilla's Share*, (1924), p. 244. In 1937 Elizabeth supported a petition to obtain a place in the Honours List for Mrs Pethick-Lawrence. WL, ER to Miss Newsome, 1 November 1937. See Frederick Pethick-Lawrence, *Fate Has Been Kind*, London, Hutchinson, 1942, p. 83 and Emmeline Pethick-Lawrence, *My Part in a Changing World*, London, Victor Gollancz, 1938, p. 281.

97 MDR Papers, Folder 1911(1), ER to MDR, 30 May 1911.

98 HRHRC, ER to CP, written 23 November, posted 30 November 1912; CP to

ER, 2 and 5 December 1912.

99 WL, OW, 'The Eighth Child' Ms., vol. 2, p. 197.

100 HRHRC, EP to ER, 23 October 1908.

8 Where are You Going to … ?

1   ER, *The Convert* (1907), p. 108.

2   Susan M. Squier, 'The Modern City and the Construction of Female Desire:
    Wells's *In the Days of the Comet* and Robins's *The Convert*', *Tulsa Studies in Women's
    Literature*, Spring 1989, no. 8, p. 73.

3   For this and the following quotes relating to Wells see HRHRC, ER to H.G. Wells,
    11 June 1910, draft scraps, n.d.; ER to Bessie Hatton, 8 January 1910 (copy); H.G.
    Wells to ER, 26 May 1904, 7 August 1909, 12 January 1910; Blanco White, Mrs
    Amber Reeves to ER, 1909–12, Maud Pember Reeves to ER, 1909–10.

4   ER [Anonymous], *Ancilla's Share* (1924), p. 84. See below, Chapter 9.

5   *Time and Tide*, 19 September 1924.

6   Gerald Cumberland, *Set Down in Malice. A Book of Reminiscences*, London, Grant
    Richards, 1919, p. 75.

7   Incomplete manuscripts of this and of Masefield's first novel, *Captain Margaret*,
    were found amongst Elizabeth's possessions after her death. University of Sussex
    Archives, Leonard Woolf Papers, 11F1b, correspondence with Hamill and Barker
    of Chicago, 1944.

8   For Masefield see C. Babington Smith, *John Masefield. A Life*, New York,
    Macmillan, 1978.

9   J. Masefield, *So Long to Learn*, New York, Macmillan, 1952, p. 67.

10 Cumberland, op. cit., p. 178.

11 These letters are in 53 folders in the Berg Collection at New York Public Library.
    Unless otherwise indicated the quotations from letters in this chapter are from
    this source. Elizabeth's correspondence from 25 January 1910 is also in this collec-
    tion.

12 Masefield later conducted further voluminous correspondence with women. For
    example, he exchanged over 2,000 letters with the wealthy American Frances
    Lamont.

13 For a discussion of such issues in relation to the Pattison-Dilke case see Kali A.K.
    Israel, 'Drawing from Life: Art, Work and Feminism in the Life of Emilia Dilke
    (1840–1904)', Ph.D., Rutgers University, 1992.

14 See J. Masefield, *Collected Poems*, London, Heinemann, 1984, p. 77.

15 In Berg Collection, op. cit.

16 See Derek Hudson, Munby, *Man of Two Worlds*, London, John Murray, 1972 and Angela V. John, *By the Sweat of Their Brow. Women Workers at Victorian Coal Mines*, London, Routledge, 1984 edition, Chapter 4.

17 Masefield, *So Long to Learn*, op. cit., p. 67.

18 HRHRC, Mrs Pethick-Lawrence to ER 16 February 1910, CP to ER, 5 December 1910.

19 ER, *Both Sides of the Curtain*, (1940), p. 54.

20 When the actress Lena Ashwell adopted a child, the reaction was 'Without a doubt the child was mine and I was ashamed to own her'; Lena Ashwell, *Myself A Player*, London, Michael Joseph, 1936, p. 133.

21 Babington Smith, op. cit., p. 103.

22 Elizabeth told Octavia Wilberforce a simplified version of the story. A young poet used to visit her frequently and read her his poems. 'She, on her side, would discuss with him the work she was doing at the time. It was helpful and stimulating to them both.' When he explained that he could not tell his wife of their friendship as she would not understand, 'Miss Robins had blazed out that nobody could *misunderstand* and if he was not entirely frank with his wife he must give up his visits. There was a scene and he never came again. Even at the memory her eyes flamed blue lightning.' WL, OW, 'The Eighth Child' Ms., vol. 1, p. 82.

23 Babington Smith, op. cit., p. 105.

24 Masefield, *Collected Poems*, op. cit., pp. 135–40.

25 J. Masefield, *The Street of To-Day*, London, J.M. Dent, 1911. June Dwyer identifies Mary Drummond with Elizabeth; see June Dwyer, *John Masefield*, New York, Ungar, 1987, p. 49.

26 Berg Collection, holograph in Masefield's hand, n.d.

27 *McClure's Magazine*, 1912, vol. xl, no. 42.

28 For his contribution see, for example, ER in Berg Collection, op. cit., holograph, Masefield letter of 2 February 1910 and 'Animula' Notebook.

29 Judith R. Walkowitz, 'Patrolling the Borders', *Radical History Review*, 1989, no. 43; Idem, 'The Politics of Prostitution', *History Workshop Journal, 1982*, no. 13; Idem, *City of Dreadful Delight. Narratives of Sexual Danger in Late-Victorian London*, London, Virago Press, 1992; Carol Smart, 'Disruptive Bodies and Unruly Sex. The Regulation of Reproduction and Sexuality in the Nineteenth Century' in Idem (ed.), *Regulating Womanhood*, London, Routledge, 1992, p. 26. See also Lucy Bland, 'Feminist Vigilantes of Late-Victorian England' in ibid.; Idem, 'Sex and Morality' in *The Edwardian Era*, London, Phaidon Press

and Barbican Art Gallery, 1987; and Sheila Jeffreys, *The Spinster and Her Enemies, Feminism and Sexuality 1880–1930*, London, Pandora Press, 1985.

30 ER, *Way Stations* (1913), pp. 327–8. See also her claims here and on pp. 318–29 (where she quotes *The Times*) of a pact between the government and the Women's Liberal Federation on this issue.

31 ER, *Where Are You Going To … ?* (1913), p. 258.

32 Joanne E. Gates, '"Sometimes Suppressed and Sometimes Embroidered". The Life and Writing of Elizabeth Robins 1862–1952', Ph.D., University of Massachusetts, 1987, Chapter vii.

33 See Jill Davis, 'The New Woman and the New Life' in Viv Gardner and Susan Rutherford (eds), *The New Woman and Her Sisters. Feminism and Theatre 1850–1914*, Hemel Hempstead, Harvester Wheatsheaf, 1992, pp. 22–5 for a critical discussion of Shaw's play; Walkowitz, *City of Dreadful Delight*, op. cit., Chapter 3.

34 Olive Malvery (Mrs Archibald Mackirdy), *The White Slave Trade*, London, Stanley, Paul and Co., 1912. The essays were written in conjunction with an Australian MP. Elizabeth used incidents recalled by Mary Higgs in her *Three Nights in Women's Lodging Houses* (1905 and 1906) to form part of the experience Vida narrated in *Votes for Women!* See Sheila Stowell, *A Stage of Their Own*, Manchester, Manchester University Press, 1992, p. 26.

35 Julie Holledge, *Innocent Flowers. Women in the Edwardian Theatre*, London, Virago Press, 1981, p. 132.

36 Elizabeth Anne Payne, *Reform, Labor and Feminism. Margaret Dreier Robins and the Women's Trade Union League*, Urbana and Chicago, University of Illinois Press, 1988, pp. 23–6.

37 In an essay on Christabel and white slavery.

38 WL, OW, 'The Eighth Child' Ms., vol. 1, p. 148.

39 Tierl Thompson (ed.), *Dear Girl. The Diaries and Letters of Two Working Women 1897–1917*, London, Women's Press, 1987, 26 June 1914, p. 226.

40 HRHRC, CP to Lady Sybil Smith, 5 April 1913.

41 *The Suffragette*, 18 and 25 April 1913. It also appeared as a pamphlet and in *The Great Scourge and How to End It*. Susan Kingsley Kent, *Sex and Suffrage in Britain 1860–1914*, London, Routledge, 1990 edition, p. 7 points out that Christabel's figures were consistent with those accepted by the medical profession at the time.

42 ER, *Where Are You Going To … ?* (1913) pp. 266–7.

43 See the correspondence in the WL, Josephine Butler Collection, Old Box Files, Army Matters, vol. 1, 1917–20, from ER, 7 March 1918, and from Neilans, 8 March 1918.

44 See Sheila Fletcher, *Maude Royden. A Life*, Oxford, Basil Blackwell, 1989, pp. 101–7

and David Rubinstein, *A Different World for Women. The Life of Millicent Garrett Fawcett*, Hemel Hempstead, Harvester Wheatsheaf, 1991, Chapter 8 and pp. 204–6, 235 for Mrs Fawcett's work with the National Vigilance Association, with women in India, and for her opposition to a reimposition of a double standard in morals via punitive measures in 1918 for women infecting soldiers with VD.

45 Michael Holroyd, *Bernard Shaw*, vol. 1, *The Search for Love 1856–1898*, Harmondsworth, Penguin, 1990 edition, p. 296.

46 For Hamilton see Lis Whitelaw, *The Life and Rebellious Times of Cicely Hamilton*, London, Women's Press, 1990 and HRHRC, Cicely Hamilton to ER, 1 August 1909.

47 British Library, Ms. LCP CORR. LR 1914 310/14; Unlicenced LCP List 1, vol. 4.

48 In July 1944 Elizabeth wrote to the London literary agent Curtis Brown about movie rights in *My Little Sister*. This suggests that she was unaware that her book had been made into a film. In 1919, however, the Fox Film Corporation had made *My Little Sister*. I am grateful to Sue Thomas for this information. See Chapter 10, note 46.

9 Ancilla's Share

1 See WL, OW, 'The Eighth Child' Ms., for all the remarks by Octavia unless otherwise identified. See also Pat Jalland (ed.), *Octavia Wilberforce. The Autobiography of a Pioneer Woman Doctor,* London, Cassell, 1989.

2 See also ER, *Where Are You Going To … ?* (1913), pp. 146–7.

3 ER, *A Dark Lantern* (1905), p. 128. Perhaps she had in mind Samuel Butler's words, 'There's a dark lantern of the spirit which none see but those who bear it.' See also Joanne E. Gates, 'Elizabeth Robins: From *A Dark Lantern* to *The Convert*. A Study of her Fictional Style and Feminist Viewpoint', *Massachusetts Studies in English*, 1978, vol. vi, nos. 3, 4, pp. 25–40.

4 For rest cures see Janet Oppenheim, '*Shattered Nerves*'. *Doctors, Patients and Depression in Victorian England*, Oxford, Oxford University Press, 1991; Elaine Showalter, *The Female Malady. Women, Madness and English Culture. 1830–1890*, London, Virago Press, 1987, Chapter 5; Ann J. Lane, *To Herland and Beyond. The Life and Work of Charlotte Perkins Gilman*, New York, Pantheon Books, 1991.

5 Nigel Nicholson and Joanne Trautmann (eds), *The Letters of Virginia Woolf*

1888–1912, vol. 1, *The Flight of The Mind*, London, Chatto and Windus, 1975, p. 190 (to Violet Dickinson).

6   See Lilian Faderman, *Surpassing the Love of Men*, London, Women's Press, 1985, p. 190; *Feminist Studies*, Fall 1992, vol. 18, no. 3, especially Martha Vicinus, "'They Wonder to Which Sex I Belong': The Historical Roots of the Modern Lesbian Identity' and Lisa Moore, "'Something More Tender Still Than Friendship": Romantic Friendship in Early-Nineteenth-Century England'. The latter questions whether the romantic friendships which predated the writings of the sexologists were as socially acceptable as has been suggested by recent historians. See too Liz Stanley, *The Auto/biographical I. The Theory and Practice of Feminist Auto/biography*, Manchester, Manchester University Press, 1992, pp. 225–33.

7   Quoted in Jalland, op. cit., p. xxii.

8   *Sunday Times*, 15 March 1922.

9   *The Times*, 20 March 1919. This was reprinted by the Women's Consultative Council.

10 ER, *What Can I Do? The Lady Chichester Hospital for Women and Children*, n.d. (*c.* 1914).

11 Daily Mail, 18 August 1915. Elizabeth also wrote an article for *Reveille*, February 1919, no. 3 which was edited by her friend Galsworthy and devoted to discharged sailors and soldiers. In part a disquisition on Englishness, it included a sketch of one of the wounded patients at Endell Street.

12 ER [Anonymous], *Ancilla's Share* (1924), p. 254.

13 In ER, *The Mills of the Gods* (1920).

14 ER, 'Lost and Found' (1915).

15 ER, 'The Frog Baby' (1920).

16 Jill Liddington, *The Long Road to Greenham. Feminists and Anti-Militarism in Britain since 1820*, London, Virago Press, 1989, Chapter 5.

17 On 4 October 1918 John Masefield wrote a formal letter from the Ministry of Information's Department of Hospitality to American Forces asking Elizabeth if she would be prepared to speak occasionally to the forces in the rest camps and stations of southern England. She declined, giving the excuse of food lecturing.

18 Interview with May Morey (née Powell), 18 March 1992.

19 ER, 'A New View of Country Life' (1919), pp. 584–96.

20 Idem, 'Conscription for Women' (1917), pp. 478–85.

21 ER [Anonymous], *Ancilla's Share* (1924), p. 222.

22 ER, 'Women at Home and Beyond the Seas' (1917) pp. 640–50.

23 ER [Anonymous], *Ancilla's Share* (1924), p. 304.

24 *The Times*, 12 May 1920.

25 ER, 'Bolt Seventeen' (1920). See also Martin Pugh, *Women and the Women's Movement in Britain 1914–1959*, London, Macmillan, 1992.

26 See Susan Kingsley Kent, 'The Politics of Sexual Difference: World War I and the Demise of British Feminism', *Journal of British Studies*, July 1988, 27, pp. 232–53; and Harold L. Smith (ed.), *British Feminism in the Twentieth Century*, Aldershot, Edward Elgar, 1990.

27 See Shirley M. Eoff, *Viscountess Rhondda. Equalitarian Feminist*, Columbus, Ohio State University Press, 1991; Muriel Mellown, 'Lady Rhondda and the Changing Face of British Feminism', *Frontiers*, vol. ix, no. 2, p. 9.

28 She also had given a talk to the Pioneer Club, Brighton in 1919 on getting as many women as possible into public service.

29 *Daily Express*, 28 May 1920.

30 Dale Spender, *Time and Tide Wait for No Man*, London, Pandora, 1984. *Time and Tide*, 14 May 1920. The first editor was Helen Archdale. It had a readership of at least 12,000–15,000 in the early 1920s. Eoff describes it as 'strongly feminist and slightly left-wing' at this time; Eoff, op. cit., p. 120.

31 ER and OW, *Prudence and Peter* (1928). For reviews see, for example, *The Daily Express*, 20 April 1928 and *Punch*, 30 May 1928. Much of the story is set 'below stairs' and the kindly cook is probably based on Octavia's family's cook Mrs Rodgers with whom she sought refuge from her brothers when she was young. See too Elizabeth's fragment of a children's story set in Surrey with children building a den in a tree and making cherry wine. The name Paddock was plucked from *The Times* marriage column, which Elizabeth frequently raided for fictional names.

32 *Time and Tide*, 18 July 1924 (Scharlieb), 21 January 1927, (criticising a review), 30 September 1933 (urging readers to boycott Austin Motors after Sir Herbert Austin advocated displacing women by men as a solution to unemployment) and 9 June 1934 (praising a story by E.M. Forster in the paper which had denounced war).

33 Ibid, 19 January 1923, Eoff op. cit., Chapter 5.

34 HRHRC, Sir Charles Trevelyan to ER, 21 November 1922.

35 ER [Anonymous], *Ancilla's Share* (1924), Introductory.

36 See Sheila Fletcher, *Maude Royden. A Life*, Oxford, Basil Blackwell, 1989.

37 See Frances Kellor's article in *Time and Tide*, 19 April 1924 and ER [Anonymous], *Ancilla's Share* (1924), pp. 295–9.

38 Liddington, op. cit., p. 132; Pugh, op. cit., p. 106.

39 HRHRC, ER to Lord Robert Cecil, 15 September n.y.

40 See Claire Tylee, *The Great War and Women's Consciousness*, London, Macmillan,

1990, p. 103. For her book Elizabeth consulted an official at the Admiralty Intelligence Department, read accounts of German submarines in *The Times* and read Bertrand Russell's work. Lady Rhondda survived the torpedoing of the *Lusitania*.

41 Elizabeth's friend Zoe told Elizabeth that Colonel Repington's diary made her more 'Bolshevik than ever … will nothing make the so-called ruling class serious?'

42 Jane Marcus, 'Art and Anger', *Feminist Studies*, February 1978, vol. 4, no. 1, p. 76.

43 *Times Literary Supplement*, 17 June 1920.

44 ER [Anonymous], *Ancilla's Share* (1924), p. 300.

45 In the *New York Times*, 17 June 1916 in response to an article on the Democratic Convention and a denial of sex solidarity amongst women, Elizabeth argued that woman's inclination is to work with, not against, man. But when man as a sex acts against woman as a sex, then it may become the duty of woman as a sex to prove that she can act in concert first and then to work on a broader human ground. Originally her book was called 'The Short Cut'—the short cut to real union lying in the temporary abandonment of insistence on union. In an article on 'Girls Who Make Up' (*Daily Mail*, 4 April 1919) she criticised the false beauty cult among women which she took up again in Chapter 4 of *Ancilla's Share* (1924).

46 H. G. Wells, *A Year of Prophesying*, London, T. Fisher Unwin, 1924, pp. 255–8.

47 Kent, op. cit., p. 244.

48 *Time and Tide*, 27 June 1924. A good review appeared in Sweden but the *Times Literary Supplement* (29 May 1924) was very critical. See also Johanna Alberti, *Beyond Suffrage. Feminists in War and Peace 1914–18*, London, Macmillan, 1989, p. 107. For *Ancilla's Share* and race see Chapter 10.

10 Time is Whispering

1 Due to the success of this book, Hutchinson wanted exclusive rights to publish her next three novels. Although most of Elizabeth's novels were not set in southern England, a few short stories were specifically located in Sussex. In 'The Derrington Ghost' in ER, *The Mills of the Gods* (1920), the centrepiece is a fifteenth-century Sussex house falling into disrepair. Here Elizabeth describes how Sussex folk value continuity. As in *Camilla* (see below), she introduces a wealthy American who breaks the stereotype. He buys up the old house but, against the odds, possesses staying-power (literally) and so proves his match for Sussex.

2 *Time and Tide*, 1 June 1923.

3 The information about Backsettown is provided in the two volumes of Minutes now in the possession of the author.

4 Financial losses and the need for repairs led to the closure of the house on 30 September 1988. The Royal United Kingdom Beneficent Association took over the Trust. Backsettown was sold and reverted to a private home.

5 ER, *Camilla* (1918), p. 185. This was the novel which Octavia most identified with.

6 Dedicatory Note to Florence Bell in ER, *Come and Find Me*.

7 ER, *Come and Find Me* (1907–8), p. ix.

8 Blurb for Mary E. Dreier, *Margaret Dreier Robins. Her Life, Letters and Work*, New York, Island Press, 1950.

9 Elizabeth Anne Payne, *Reform, Labor and Feminism. Margaret Dreier Robins and the Women's Trade Union League*, Urbana and Chicago, University of Illinois Press, 1988, p. 7.

10 Ibid., p. 124. See the character in Elizabeth's unpublished play, 'Evangeline', an American woman who devotes herself to anyone who needs mothering.

11 WL, OW, 'The Eighth Child' Ms. vol. 2, p. 309. Margaret's letters to Elizabeth were quite affectionate and in the year before she died she wrote to tell her 'how great a woman I think you are'.

12 CPT Papers, GB Collection, GB to FB, 23 June 1926.

13 Originally a Democrat, Raymond had stood (unsuccessfully) in Illinois as the Progressive Party candidate for the US Senate in 1914 but during the administrations of Harding, Coolidge and Hoover became a political adviser and campaigner as a 'progressive Republican'; Neil V. Salzman, *Reform and Revolution. The Life and Times of Raymond Robins*, Kent, Ohio, Kent State University Press, 1991, p. 309.

14 Interview at Chinsegut with Lisa von Borowsky, 15 April 1992. Raymond called Lisa 'the little daughter of Chinsegut'. See also Salzman, op. cit., p. 334 and *Daily Mail*, 10 October 1932.

15 Interview with Theodore Dreier, Orlando, Florida, 15 April 1992.

16 OW, 'The Eighth Child', op. cit., vol. 2, p. 320.

17 The first half of her story 'The Centaur' concerns a Sussex man living in Florida whose only companions are his black servant Uncle Ben and his horse Dixie. His stable is set on fire.

18 Gary Felumlee, 'Oratory and Religion. A Recipe for Riot. Theodore Weld and the Abolitionists in Putnam', Zanesville, Pamphlet for the Pioneer and Historical Society of Muskingum County, May 1992. See too Norris F. Schneider,

Y Bridge City. The Story of Zanesville and Muskingum County, Cleveland, Ohio, World Publishing Co., 1951.

19 ER, *Way Stations* (1913), p. 60.

20 ER [C.E. Raimond], *The Open Question* (1898), pp. 23–32.

21 ER, *The Florentine Frame* (1909), p. 97.

22 ER [C.E. Raimond], *The Open Question* (1898), p. 24.

23 Galley proofs exist for this but it may have appeared only in *The Author*, October 1909, vol. 20, no. 1.

24 Jane Tompkins, *Sensational Designs. The Cultural Work of American Fiction 1760–1860*, Oxford, Oxford University Press, 1985, p. 134.

25 Clare Midgley, *Women Against Slavery. The British Campaigns 1780–1870*, London, Routledge, 1992, p. 148.

26 See Henry James's thoughts in ER, *Theatre and Friendship. Some Henry James Letters* (1932), p. 199.

27 She had read his renowned book *The Souls of Black Folk*. Du Bois did not, in the end, have time to visit Sussex.

28 e.g. ER, *Way Stations* (1913), p. 61.

29 On her travels with Lady Lewis in 1899 Elizabeth observed crowds of people leaving Leipzig station. In her diary she marvelled that this 'swearing & ignorant cattle-like crowd' could fashion potentates and princes. See her article 'Embryo Americans' (1901).

30 For the Atlanta Compromise Address, John White, *Black Leadership in America from Booker T. Washington to Jesse Jackson*, London, Longman, 1992 edition.

31 ER, *Theatre and Friendship* (1932), pp. 270–1.

32 ER, *Camilla* (1918), p. 185.

33 ER [Anonymous], *Ancilla's Share* (1924), p. xix. See also p. xxvii and p. 310 for the following quotes.

34 Ibid., pp. xxxiii–iv.

35 Edward Said, *Culture and Imperialism*, New York, Alfred A. Knopf, 1993, p. 62.

36 ER, *Time Is Whispering* (1923), p. 226; and p. 304 for the following quote.

37 Peter Whitebrook, *William Archer. A Biography*, London, Methuen, 1993, pp. 295–8, 361.

38 Thomas Jones, Cabinet minister and founder of Coleg Harlech, Wales (to which Dolly Yates Thompson gave her books) sent Elizabeth a copy of his book (published in 1938).

39 In about 1929 Elizabeth contributed to a pamphlet advocating the Bengal League of Social Services for Women which sought to create trained, salaried health and welfare workers. She stressed the importance of helping those far

away: 'neither the mountains nor the great seas can divide us—and in that fact is the hope of the world.' Oriental and India Office Collection, British Library; Sorabji MSS, F165/163.

40 Leonard Woolf (ed.), *Virginia Woolf. A Writer's Diary*, London, Triad Grafton, 1985 edition, p. 128.

41 Leonard Woolf, *An Autobiography of the Years 1911–1969*, vol 2. *The Journey Not the Arrival Matters*, Oxford, Oxford University Press, 1980, p. 427.

42 OW, 'The Eighth Child', op. cit., vol. 1, p. 164.

43 Monk's House Papers, University of Sussex Archive, Virginia Woolf to ER, 29 July 1939. Genevieve Ward and Richard Whiteing, *Both Sides of the Curtain*, London, Cassell and Co., 1918.

44 Monk's House Papers, op. cit, Virginia Woolf to ER, 8 November 1939.

45 Nigel Nicolson and Joanne Trautmann (eds), *The Letters of Virginia Woolf 1936–41*, vol. vi, *Leave the Letters Till We're Dead*, London, Chatto and Windus, 1980, p. 352.

46 Patricia King-Hanson and Alan Gerinson (eds), The American Film Institute *Catalog of Motion Pictures Produced in the United States, Feature Films 1911–20*, Berkeley, University of California, 1988, pp 189, 645, includes cast lists, synopses and lists of reviews. Both films are acknowledged as based on Elizabeth's novels. *A Dark Lantern* was made in Chicago. The review in *Variety* (13 August 1920) also mentioned Elizabeth's story.

47 BBC Written Archives Centre, Caversham, R. Cont, 1 Sir Ernest Benn, 26 August 1929.

48 It seems that she did broadcast on American radio since in December 1941 Octavia received her 'radio record' called 'Freedom Front' and listened to Elizabeth on a borrowed gramophone.

49 In ER, *Portrait of a Lady or The English Spirit Old and New* (1941), p. 23. The title was presumably prompted by her renewed acquaintance with Henry James's nephew of the same name who was now living on Long Island.

50 Virginia wrote to Elizabeth two weeks before her death, the letter arriving only after she had died. Criticism of Octavia (for example, in Jane Dunn, *A Very Close Conspiracy*, London, Pimlico, 1991 edition, p. 298) seems unwarranted since contemporary evidence suggests that it was too late for a GP to step in and save Virginia at the point that Leonard appealed to her.

51 Woolf, *The Journey Not the Arrival*, op. cit., p. 429.

52 Ibid., p. 430.

53 OW, 'The Eighth Child', op. cit., author's version, p. 359.

54 I am grateful to Neil Salzman for this reference dated 25 September 1950 from the

Raymond Robins Papers in the State Historical Society, Madison, Wisconsin.

55 CPT Papers, CPT 260, Molly Trevelyan to Elsa Richmond, 18 March 1953. Octavia and Leonard Woolf were also executors. Elizabeth was cremated in Brighton.

56 Woolf, *The Journey Not the Arrival*, op. cit., p. 430. When Octavia died at the end of 1963 seventeen tea-chests and two large trunks belonging to Elizabeth came to light in storage in Brighton. Elizabeth's Papers came to the New York University Library in 1964 from the Chicago firm of rare book dealers Hamill and Barker. At one stage Leon Edel, biographer of Henry James and a professor at New York University, had been engaged in correspondence with Octavia about a projected biography of Elizabeth but despite some work on this, it did not happen. Elizabeth left Backsettown to Octavia who bought land and built a house near the home. Her Brighton home is now the local Red Cross Headquarters. Backsettown continued as a convalescent home for many years, bolstered by £8,000 from Elizabeth's executors. When Octavia died it was left to the Trust. Elizabeth left £9,284 in her Will.

INDEX

If you are interested in purchasing other books published by Tempus,
or in case you have difficulty finding any Tempus books in your local bookshop,
you can also place orders directly through our website

www.tempus-publishing.com